Don't Believe the Hype!

The Incredible History of Communist Subversion in America's Black Community

FIRST REVISION

Dedication

*I want to dedicate this book to my family, to my children to my Mother, **Rosalyn** (1937-1995), my Father **Melvin** (1938-2005), my God Parents, the **William** (1903-1977), his wife **"Momma" Jeanette** (1908- 1985). Lastly, I want to dedicate this book my **"Baby Sis"**, **Ms. Dawn "Dolly" Graham** (1971-2015).*

Table of Contents

~ 4 ~

ACKNOWLEDGMENTS

I want to give thanks & acknowledgement to a teacher & mentor who have created openings of my mind, to research historical facts and truths; "Mr. Trivia", Mr. David Strauss.

"When you control a man's thinking, you do not have to worry about his actions."

Carter G. Woodson

Woodson's quotation highlighted above reflects an accurate descriptive picture of the United States of America in 2017; especially when it comes to the Black Community in-particular. When Woodson pinned his book, **The Mis-Education of the Negro** [1] [2] in 1933, he was describing the geo-political conditions of the era.

However, despite the differences in time, Woodson's quote cab be easily applied to all generations of Americans, regardless of skin color or culture. What his quotation really means, is that once you have a selected group of people and/or entities, whose main purpose is to push their agenda, down the throats of their targeted population mentally, using lies and disinformation, that same targeted population will believe what is told to them and take such information as being fact. Even though, such information is blatant lies, what the targeted population of people are told, they will say or will do whatever they believe is true, without any type of rationale. Therefore, it is highly important for the reader to understand, that this is exactly what's going on this very minute inside the United States.

One must wonder, how could this be; there is no way in the world, that just a few people in power, can control the thought processes and actions of millions of people. There is no way such people can control the actions of people and their very existence; impossible! Well, unfortunately, it is **_possible_**! However, for some, despite the huge historical precedence in achievements in this country, regarding the advancement of her race relations, there have been a selected group of individuals, living in the America in the present-day, that want you to believe that such racial achievements are not enough.

Why?

Because we in the Black Community, have allowed ourselves to be psychologically conditioned to accept such lies and falsehoods for decades. The very lies that we have been led to believe that *"racial relations have not improved"*, and *"Jim Crow"* is still alive and well, even in 2017. To make things worse, there is even a book written by somebody, titled **The New Jim Crow**, that tote the very lies and deception I have previously mentioned. The publication was written by someone who has not one clue, about the true history of Black America. However, such propaganda has become popular lately, because of the lies and deception being pumped into the soft heads of African American youth today, is being sold as a normal course of history. It is not!

Of course, by using every aspect of the American Media, Public Education System, Religious Organizations and so-called *"Black Leaders"*, we've been constantly told that regardless of advancement in racial relations, our economic standards, while simultaneously electing the First Black President of the United States, the Black Community itself, will still never amount to anything successful, because the color of our skin.

This is NONSENSE!! It is an absolute lie!!

The sad part of this non-sense is this; the consistent re-enforcement of these lies being done daily, via the aforementioned media, education and religious sectors of American society subliminally plant the lies, that Blacks will always be inferior to Whites in here in America, no matter what! An even sadder part of these lies that exist is that such messages are all being perpetrated by those who call themselves members of *"Black Leadership"* or *"Community Organizers"* within the inner-cities of America.

Organizations such as the National Association for the Advancement of Colored People (NAACP), Nation of Islam (NOI), National Action Network (NAN), Black Lives Matter Movement (BLM), the New Black Panther Party (NBPP) and many others, ratchet up the lies via emotions, using terms like *"Systematic Racism"* or *"White Privilege"*, to further stoke the hate and discontent within the American and African American community intentionally. When doing this, groups such as these, will almost certainly cause peoples' emotions to be driven to the point, where they themselves, cannot make any sensible conclusions to any situation, which has become one of the many reasons, why people start to act out their anger and/or frustrations based on such falsehoods. By causing others to act out irrationally, the affected section of the Black Community, will resort to any and everything, including violence and outright anarchy, to portray their anger and discontent to look legitimate. The after-mentioned groups and many others like them, intentionally initiate such emotional lies, under false pretenses, both for monetary gain and media stardom, while simultaneously assisting the real White Racists of Marxists, in keeping the Black Community segregated, from the rest of society.

When you hinder a community from advancing as a collective bunch, they will by human nature, began to fight back and resist. In other words, what these so-called Black Leaders do, is to keep their own people ***controlled***.

It is a known fact, that the so-called "Black Leaders" lay in the same bed with corrupt and crooked Politicians, rich elite Marxists within the Entertainment, Banking and Investment Industries, Ideological College Professors, and those holding various positions of power throughout government in America. Yes, this list of characters also includes the 44th President of the United States, Barack Hussein Obama, and others within his inner circle, who are just as ideological like himself. The race and gender of these persons don't matter. It's all rooted in Marxism, which only sees two colors; ***Red and Green***. Red for their allegiance to Communism and Green for-the-amount of money or capital they invest into fundamentally, transforming the United States of America into a Stalinist-type Russia.

Each one of us can see it plain and clear with your own eyes, only if you take the blinders off and think rationally for yourself without any outside influences, such as the news media. The idea that is driving behind this nonsense, sparking what is known as ***"The Victim Mentality Syndrome"*** or professionally termed ***"Narcissism"*** within the Black Community, is to use the population emotionally, in-order for them to act a certain way (***because their mind has been controlled***), to drive a specific agenda.

By in-planting such lies and deception of truth, historical facts and manipulating the social skills and rationality processing of young, Millennial-aged Blacks, the end goal of that specific agenda, called ***"Global Communism"***, will usher in a ***"New Society"***. In other words, by controlling their minds, as Carter G. Woodson said, you don't have to worry about their actions. Doing such deeds will put enormous political and social power in the hands of a certain few bureaucrats to rule over the many, with the end solution of self-genocidal "revolution", that will finally destroy The Black Community, slowly and for sure. Both from outside controlling forces and within the community itself.

So, one of the many questions that may come to mind, as to why would they do such a thing? Why would the people who represent the Black Community, the persons who put them into many positions of power, along with their trust and faith in them, to have a voice in everyday society, lie and deceive the very people who they identify themselves with? The answer may shock you, however, but it will be easy for this author to explain. Why? Because the people re-enforcing the stereotype subliminally, that Whites will always be superior to Blacks, no matter how much progress in race relationships have been made over the past 50-plus years, really think, that at the end of this new transformation of this country, The United States, that they will have a "special place" and power in this new society.

The people, such as the Reverend Al Sharpton and others, whom they use to trick them emotionally to help these pathetic "leaders", who falsely represent them, to advance society to this latter point, they need a select section of the Black Community to both emotionally and physically support their fake cause of "equality". Unfortunately, true written history has taught us, that such actions only end with deadly and fatal results.

Chapter 1 TRUTH VERSUS DECEPTION: AN OVERVIEW OF
KARL MARX, FRIEDRICH ENGELS, AND COMMUNISM

"For you shall know the truth and the truth will set you free."
Anonymous

For many people, this statement represents a powerful meaning in which all Human Beings, regardless of Race, Sex, Culture or Color of Skin, take personally. Everybody would like the truth to be told to them so that they themselves can rationalize an appropriate plan of action to take to either solve a problem, sets of problems or come to a sensible conclusion as to what follow-on action that needs to be taken now or near future.

However, if lies are inserted in place of true, information, the probability of some type of backlash or ramification could occur, therefore changing the original intended outcome, which may detrimental for all parties involved at the end. In many political events, historically, if a lie is told often enough, repeatedly, the parties receiving such misinformation may or may not rationalize for themselves, thus concluding that such lies are true.

When lies are intentionally told, by people who know for themselves, that the information that is being presented is absolute lies, in-order to control the outcome of a certain situation or control a selective set of people, on purpose, this is called **deceit**. [1] The act or practice of deceit is called **deception**. [2] When one looks at blatant deception practices, aimed at a specific population of people, based on race or economic class, the key factor of the motivation behind the lie is to advance a specific agenda, using them as pawns in a deadly game of control of power over the masses by a collective few individuals. It is in this case, Marxism plays a major role in fundamentally transforming whole societies into a false, and often oppressive, self-destructive entities.

An example of this fact can be seen historically in the country of Germany before and during World War II.

Germany's Chancellor, Adolf Hitler, along with other men in the Nationalist Socialist Worker's Party (NAZI), used the same type of lies and deceptive practices to persuade whole populations that they, the government, will guarantee their safety and protect them from outside influences. As a charismatic speaker, Hitler used his power, influence and the media to play among the masses to support him and the radical change in Germany to show the world that they were one of the mightiest countries on Earth.

In the meantime, the Nazis further promised safety of Jewish, Gypsies, Jehovah's Witnesses, Catholics and other denominational Christians, that the community psychologically believed that the walls being built around their neighborhoods were being done for their safety. Even though, deep behind closed doors, the opposite was true. [3]

Hitler and the Nazis used the population to further their agenda, to create a separate race of people, shaped in their image, by psychologically conditioning them that the threat being faced by the country itself, was on the brink of being done. However, as time went on, the threat was becoming more and more "credible" as the German officials portrayed, the population in the "ghettos" needed additional protections to ensure their safety even more. Believing that their political, social and economic leaders were telling the truth, many people who were inside the walled neighborhoods, were rounded up and boarded box cars of trains and head off to these so-called "safe places" for their protection.

In reality, the people were headed off to one of the 15,000-plus Concentration Camps located throughout Germany, built for such purpose, to kill who they, the NAZI were deemed "unfit" and too "feeble minded" to be a part of the new society being created. In one of the most tragic stories of the 20th Century, well over 11-14 million Jews, Poles, Communists, Homosexuals, Trade Unionists, Gypsies, and Christians were killed via lies and deception of government officials that they were going to protect them. At the end, Hitler and his henchmen were planning a systematic "**Eugenic System**" in-order to create a pure Aryan Race. What Hitler and his totalitarian regime created was a special version of Marxism, termed "*Fascism*". However, both terms are used interchangeably, but have the same meaning; a political, social and economic system based on a centralized, autocratic government, using military-style enforcement.

The dictionary definition of *Marxism* is the political, economic and social principles and policies advocated by Karl Marx, the founder of this ideology. [4,5,6] This system of thought, which is based on the non-reality of the founder, when it's been tried in Human History, in situations like the example above, that the result was extremely deadly and has resulted in the murder of over 140-150 million people around the world! In the following subchapters, the reader will explore and understand who Karl Marx was as a person, his ideology and why he created such series of often deadly and non-reality political/social system, which has changed the world for the worse. Marx, with the help of another person who financially backed him, Friedrich Engels, is two of the founders of Marxist Ideology, which is now being played out as of this writing inside America's Black Community.

Karl Marx: Founder of Marxist Ideology

Photo of the Founder of Marxist Ideology, Karl Marx took in 1878.
(Courtesy of Wikimedia)

Karl Marx was born on May 5, 1818, in Treves, Germany to Heinrich Marx and Henrietta (Pressburg) Marx. Karl was the third child out of a total of nine children. His Father was a Jewish Rabbi, who later became a Lawyer and a Protestant Minister, while Karl's Mother Henrietta, was an illiterate Housewife. As Karl grew up, he began to reject his family outright, instigating numerous quarrels between his Father and his Siblings; most of them became outright physical confrontations.

Biographers considered that the hostility between Karl and his family stemmed from the lack of compassion and empathy that he showed for them and from Karl's ever demanding of money from them, along with his egotistic self-absorption. Despite his torment upbringing, Karl Marx attended the University of Bonin in 1835 to study Law. Even though many of his academic professors considered him brilliant in the mind, his tenure as a student there went nowhere. Because of his hot-headed temper, Marx's grades and demeanor was so poor, that the university labeled him as a drunkard and trouble-maker. [7,8]

The school's assessment of Karl Marx was spot on and true, when in 1836, during a duel challenge between him and another student, Karl suffered a wound to his right eye. The University had enough of him and transferred him to the University of Berlin, now majoring in Philosophy. It was here, that Karl Marx made his introduction to the world, with an ideology named after him and is still being practiced or implemented in various countries, including The United States of America 180 years later! While attending the University of Berlin, Karl Marx began to associate himself with hardcore Leftists, who were Anti-Semitic, hated Christianity and any teachings of the Holy Bible. When Karl Marx's introduction to the German Philosopher Georg Wilhelm Hegel's teachings, this lit a spark that started the fire which consumed the rest of Marx's adult life.

Georg Wilhelm Friedrich Hegel (1770-1831), was an absolute mad man in his own right. Hegel's philosophy regarding societal norms and religion was based on the same conclusions of the Greek Philosopher Plato and Immanuel Kant. Hegel hated religion, particularly Christianity, where he constantly wrote that the gospels in the Holy Bible were myths, concocted by the imagination of early Christians. [9,10,11]

One of Karl Marx's associates at the University of Berlin, was one Bruno Bauer. Bauer wrote a thesis in 1840, based on both Hegel and Kant's assessment and teachings of religion, named "**Historical Criticism of Synoptic Gospels**", Bauer claimed that Jesus Christ never existed and that the passages written in the Bible were lies. [12,13,14]

The following year, Marx and Bauer co-authored a series of pamphlets (magazines), called "**A Journal of Atheism**", which was to be distributed throughout Berlin. However, the magazine project failed because of the lack of public interest in the publication. Of course, the failure of the Journal did not deter both men to stop publicizing their beliefs. As Bauer and Marx continued to study the philosophical writings of Hegel, Kant, K. L. Reinhold (1757-1823), Voltaire (1694-1778) and Plato (427-347 B.C.E) plus many others, Bauer transferred to Bonin while Marx stayed at Berlin, both men enlisted the help of another one their contemporaries, Ludwig Feuerbach (1804-1872).[15]

Bauer, Feuerbach, and Marx wrote "**Essence of Christianity**", a publication based off Feuerbach's many theses, where the men charged that the religion of Christianity was a farce and Man is the center of the Universe. The men further wrote, that Man was also the highest form of intelligence in the Universe and that God never existed! The power and sheer jaw-dropping writing caught the public attention, which included high Government Officials.

Of course, the Prussian Government did not take this Anti-Religion Crusade propaganda well and they took immediate action towards the men.

Bruno Bauer was immediately kicked out of the University of Bonin, Marx was banned forever to teach or publicly speak anywhere in Germany and Feuerbach was fined heavily for his "counter-revolutionary activities".

The governmental actions against Marx and the other men still did not stop the men Anti-Religious beliefs. As a matter of fact, Karl saw the action as a step forward and embolden his fiery rhetoric, as he began to ramp up his act to find a wife that would support his work. It didn't take long to find one. Enter one Jenny von Westphalen, the Daughter of a very wealthy, very influential German Baron from Marx's hometown of Treves, Germany. After months of courtship between the two, Karl and Jenny were married in June 1843. Jenny's family paid for the wedding, in which she will soon find out for herself, she and her husband will be broke the rest of their lives. Karl was unemployed by the time he and Jenny were married, but his consistent unemployment, on purpose, would later have a detrimental effect on the family that they were going to raise. Regardless, Karl Marx's wife Jenny would be by his side, despite her husband's constant failures in creating a worldwide revolution and his ambition to change the world as he saw fit.

At this point, enter the only true friend and co-sponsor with Karl to create and institute "*Marxism*" or "*Communism*", interchangeable labels used to describe the same ideology.

Karl Marx meets Friedrich Engels

Drawing of Friedrich Engels, Co-Author of *"The Communist Manifesto"* and Author of *"Das Kapital"*.
(Courtesy of Marxist.org)

It is informative for the reader to not only understand the historical text of Marxism but as it applies to today's 21st Century American society, you will gain intimate knowledge as to the answers as to how this ideology formulates the cultural destruction of our society today. As for Karl Marx, another contemporary and probably the only friend that Marx ever had, who co-wrote "*The Communist Manifesto*" and "*Das Kapital*", was Friedrich Engels Junior. [16,17,18]

Friedrich Engels Junior, or simply Friedrich Engels, was the total opposite of Karl Marx growing up, but they both followed similar paths in their lives, which had allowed them to become compatible with each other as adults. Born November 28, 1820, in Bremen, Germany, Engels was the eldest Son of Friedrich Engels Senior and his wife Elizabeth.

The Senior Engels was a wealthy businessman, who operated huge textile manufacturing plants in both Germany and in Manchester, England. Unlike Karl Marx, the younger Engels was raised as a Protestant, did not attend prestigious Universities of Bonin or Berlin, what he lacked academically, he was smart individually. The younger Friedrich Engels hated the Senior Engel's factories and everything they represented. It was the junior Engels that coined the term "*Bourgeois*" and "*Proletariat*" in Marxist/Communist Ideology.

What the younger Engels did to make up such shortfalls in education, he learned two additional languages, English and French and served in the Prussian Army as an Artilleryman in 1841. It was here, while serving in the Army, in Berlin, that Engels began to form his Atheistic view of the World.

He read Georg Wilhelm Hegel's teachings, attended young, Hegelian meetings and events and absorbed as much knowledge as he can during his off time in the Army. Also during this off time, Friedrich Engels began to anonymously write and publish books describing in detail, the horrible conditions of his Father's factory workers. The Prussian Army high command never knew Engels himself wrote such publications and by 1842, he was discharged from the Army under honorable conditions.

At the age of 22, free from government service, Engels hoped that he would continue his work in Berlin as a part of young crowd

Atheists, but his father had other plans for the 22-year-old. The elder Engels knew that his son was beginning to become actively involved in the Atheist movement in Berlin, so what he hoped that by moving him away from that city, or away from Germany period, and send him to work as an agent in Manchester England, the junior Engels would return to his Christian values. It didn't work.

The move from Berlin to Manchester only inflamed the younger Engels hatred of his father's businesses even more and intensified his passion of his Atheist beliefs. While working in England, Friedrich Engels began to write editorials about the horrors, dangerous and unsanitary working conditions inside his father's textile plant there. Engels also wrote about the use of Child Labor inside these oppressive working conditions that included other manufacturing businesses as well as his own father's facility.

In 1845, Friedrich Engels pinned and published a book named *"The Condition of the Working Class in England"*, where he made the case for the *"Grim Future of Capitalism and the Industrial Age"*, where he accused the rich business owners of making "*huge profits off the backs of the workers*". {Sounds familiar?}

As Engels continued to publish his articles and published his book in three different languages, English, French, and German, Karl Marx took the interest of his writings. Engels himself had already known about Marx even when he was stationed in the Prussian Army in Berlin, but the two never met each other in person. However, this was about to change. Both men met up with each other in Paris France in the summer of 1844, which lasted for 10 days, as the men began to become acquainted with each other, which went off perfectly. Historians consider that this meeting in Paris is where the ideology of Karl Marx fundamentally transformed Friedrich Engels, from a witness of the so-called *"evils of the Industrial Revolution"* of the 1840's, to a raving, Narcissistic Marxist lunatic, like himself!

At the end of the 10-day visit, both men formed a partnership and called for an **International Communist League**, based on the need to agitate and start a violent worldwide Communist Revolution. It is here, where the "*Marxist Theory*" comes into play and forms the basis to explain the social-economic conditions inside the United States of America at the present.

"My objective in life is to dethrone God and destroy Capitalism!"[1]

Karl Marx

Karl Marx was right in the above quote. The essence of Marxist ideology **PERIOD** is to dethrone God as a supreme being of all humans throughout the world and fundamentally destroy **ALL** Free-Market Principals and Capitalism Economics. By replacing it with a Socialist/Communistic economic system, society can rebuild itself into an image where everybody produces in accordance with everyone needs, equally. How would Karl Marx and Friedrich Engels plan on doing these very things without any serious pushback, is beyond comprehension?

Once the alliance between Marx and Engels was solidified, both began their work to assemble an **International Communist League**, to kick off this violent revolution immediately. For this league to materialize, a set of rules must first be created. After all, The International Communist League should operate in some type of orderly direction and specific set of rules, to plan and execute a worldwide revolution of such size and scope.

First, they needed the support of lower-wage workers from different countries to form the core of the Communist Revolution Movement. To do this, they must psychologically subvert (corrupting the minds, morals, and faith of a populous) these workers to accept that their social condition isn't their fault. By doing this, the workers themselves will be taught to blame their living conditions the feet of those in positions of power and money, Bourgeois, to make money and profits off the backs of the low-wage workers. This mental subversion, in turn, will make the low-wage earners be filled with emotional rage, hate and discontent of their bosses, thereby setting up the environment for a violent revolution.[2,3,4]

In November 1847, Marx and Engels commissioned themselves the lead agents during the Federation of Just (later, The Communist League) meeting in London England, to write a set of principles to establish the basis of a worldwide Communist Revolution. The "Principles" the men created, cumulated into print as to what is known today as "**The Communist Manifesto**". Inside this publication, Marx and Engels set the tone of what the International Communist Movement stood for;

1. *To overthrow Capitalism*

2. *The abolition of private property*

3. *The elimination of the family as a social unit*

4. *The abolition of all Economic and Social Classes*

5. *The overthrow of <u>ALL</u> governments*

6. *The establishment of a Communist Order with Communal ownership of property in a classless, stateless society.*

Marx and Engels stated in the Communist Manifesto;

"In short, the Communists everywhere support every revolutionary movement against existing social conditions. Let the ruling classes tremble at a Communist Revolution. The Proletarians have nothing to lose but their chains. They have a world to win. Working men of all countries, unite!"

So, what is the Marxist Theory?

Besides the Six Principles of Communism listed above, the reason behind creating this ideology, is two-fold; 1) the need of universal peace and 2) the need of universal prosperity. What Marx and Engels really created, however, is a form of Communist Order, which is not only self-destructive but self-genocidal for whole populations at best. Some Historians, Writers, Politicians, and people in Academia say that Communism looks good on paper, or it will sound better to people if only they become so-called "open-minded" to accept an overall universal "prosperity" argument.

Yet, what this author will explain in detail in the following chapters and sub-chapters, Communism does not work and it doesn't look good on paper! Historical records have also proven, that such ideology is dangerous and for short, it's a pipe dream of a universal Utopia that can never exist in a world where every human being is different in culture, gender, and way of life among many other things. Unlike Marx and Engels, even Plato ended his novel **Plato's Republic** to conclude the same thing, that a genuine Utopian society will never materialize because of "man's inherent differences".

The Marxist Theory or Communist Order, both terms are used synonymously, operate from three basic thoughts; **The Law of Opposites**, **The Law of Negation** and **The Law of Transformation.** Let's take a brief look at all three.

The Law of Opposites [5,6]

The Marxist Theory insists that everything in existence are opposites of each other. However, the way Marx and Engels explain this theory, ***The Law of Opposites is that Man is himself.***

The men state that each human has qualities of attraction and repulsion, to include opposites in character and qualities. Here, Marx and Engels say, opposites in Nature, in which they concluded that Man is a part of, (since in Marxism, God doesn't exist) is auto-dynamic which needs constant motivation to move Men in a specific direction and force them to change. In their minds, *anything* or *anyone* who goes **against** the Opposite of Nature, conflict with Nature itself and should be destroyed.

A perfect example of a geopolitical issue today that is a hot topic being discussed is the false notion of ***"Climate Change"***. Marxists have been programmed to think that Man is responsible for the functions of Planet Earth and is always in constant motion to destroy it, with high-carbon pollution, Carbon-Dioxide, etc. Those people who say that "Climate Change" is a farce, are going against the Opposite of Nature and thus need to be destroyed! This answer many questions on why people who are so-called compassionate about the lie of Climate Change, want those people who are against it to be severely punished or even put to death!

The Law of Negation [7,8]

In the Marxist Theory, the tendency of Nature to increase in number (reproduce), negates itself (nullifies or doesn't exist) to reproduce in quantity; this doesn't make any sense. However, what Marx and Engels theorized is that Nature reproduces itself on its own, without any assistance from outside sources.

Engels outlines that a Barley seed is put into the ground, the seed would grow into a fully-grown Barley Plant. Once the Barley Plant has fully grown, it creates seedlings that can be spread, planted into the ground and grow, thereby reproducing. What Engels fail to mention, is that a plant does not grow on its own without **some** type of outside assistance for it *to* grow! For example, it takes some type of labor or machine to plant those Barley seeds into the ground, and water, food/fertilizer, pest control and optimal growing seasons, are all needed for that Barley plant to grow and reproduce.

However, that outside influence that is really needed for that Barley seed to grown into a plant and reproduce goes against The Law of Negation, since Marx and Engels theorized that Nature negates itself totally repeatedly to reproduce.

The Law of Transformation [9,10]

In Marxism, The Law of Transformation describes that a continuous quantitative development by a particular-class of people, who can adapt and empower themselves in Nature and can transform themselves into a new form or entity. In his outstanding book, ***"The Naked Communist"*** written by the late-great author and former FBI Agent during the Cold War, W. Cleon Skousen (1913-2006), explains this law as such;

> *"Chemistry testifies to the fact that Methane is composed of one atom of Carbon and four atoms of Hydrogen. Now, if we add to Methane, another atom of Carbon and two more atoms of Hydrogen, we get an entirely new chemical substance called Ethane. If we add another atom of Carbon and two more atoms*

~ 21 ~

*of Hydrogen to Ethane, we get Propane…. **Add another addition
of a Carbon atom and two atoms of Hydrogen results in a fourth
chemical substance, Butane. And still another quantitative
addition of an atom of Carbon and two more atoms of Hydrogen
results in a fifth chemical substance, Pentane."***

Marxist philosophers consider the example above a
"Transformation" using Nature's creative power, by matter being auto-
dynamic and inclined to increase itself in numbers by adaptation and
empowerment to "***leap***" to new forms of reality. In other words, like
energy, Marx and Engels claim that since Man is the highest living being
and most intelligent being in the universe, Man along within its
environment in nature, can fundamentally transform itself by adopting
(by being forced) to such natural changes as required, will enable Man
to "leap" into a new form of reality.

A better way to understand their Law of Transformation is that
Marx and Engels by destroying the current economic system of Free-
Market competition and traditional institutes of family, marriage,
property ownership and others, so Man ***will*** adapt automatically and
accept a new form of society, based on the natural order of things.

When it comes to everyday life, The Marxist Theory is simple in
this following way. In Marxism, Man was accidentally created by Nature
without any outside influences, who possess the highest intelligence in
the Universe. Here, Karl Marx and Friedrich Engels uses Ludwig
Feuerbach's thinking of life as illustrated in his book ***"Essence of
Christianity"***, "…the only God of Man is Man himself." Which is why, in
Marxism, religion must be destroyed. So, you, the reader, are probably
asking the following question. Why is it important to understand this
dangerous ideology, especially when it comes to the 21st Century
regarding the destruction of the Black Community?

The answer is simple.

Marxist ideology has some in the Black Community (and The
United States of America itself) believe, that God doesn't exist as the
Supreme Being. There are some within the Black Community that
believe that the scriptures in the Holy Bible are lies, fabricated by
delusional people during the Middle Ages, Morals (the difference
between good and bad) goes against the natural order of things,

therefore good morals need to be destroyed in its entirety. The same people who follow Marxist Ideology, whether they admit it or not, that Immorality does exist within nature, external judgment, the spirit and sanctity of human life are just the natural order of things, or "**matter**", just because. People who believe in Marxism tend to be very materialistic people, who only worship themselves and anybody who doesn't think like them, are against them, thus need to be destroyed.

The next chapter, further explains Marxism, as it relates to Modes and Means of Production, Class Distinction and the Marxist Plan of Action, which is a very important aspect of this ideology.

---

3 Marxism's Means of Production, Class Distinction, and Plan-of Action

---

"Society as a whole is more and more splitting up into two great hostile camps, into two great classes, directly facing each other: Bourgeoisie and Proletariat."[1]
Friedrich Engels

As stated in the quotation above, both Marx and Engels wrote that the mode of production and the means of distribution, in history, have always created two separates, but unequal classes of people.

Engels used the term ***Bourgeois***, French for a middle-class person, to describe people who they considered as rich and wealthy individuals. The ***Bourgeoisie*** is described as a social order of middle-classed people, who owned all the businesses, factories and business entities of manufacturing production. Engels claimed that the Bourgeois exploited the low-wage worker, termed the ***Proletariat***, by using their backbreaking, often abusive human labor to earn profits, while in return, the worker receives nothing for their work. This is described in the "***Communist Manifesto***" as the Bourgeoisie making large sums of money off the back of the workers, thereby creating different levels of achievement.

However, human history as it has been written, tells the story opposite of what Marx and Engels only theorized, then put down on paper. Societies have always worked together creating a dynamic force, that propelled the selected societies to develop and grow into an independent and free-market system. Their perception of Capitalism was that those benefiting as they described "fruits of labor" of others, the Bourgeoisie, were selfish, greedy, arrogant, imperialistic people who never rightly shared their ill-gotten wealth with the low-wage workers.

The low-wage workers, who made the Bourgeoisie wealthy from the get go, resulted in the Proletariat to be poor and stay poor in horrible, unsanitary, inhabitable living conditions for the rest of their lives. Marx and Engels considered this as wrong, and since it is the Proletariat that does all the work and production of societies goods, the Bourgeoisie should share their wealth, ("redistribution of wealth") to the Proletariat. Since the Bourgeoisie owned property, the land, and the factories, the main instruments of production, places where such items are created and built, the rich created their own system called *"Law and Order"*. This, as Marx explained, consisted of laws, rules, and regulations to protect the Bourgeoisie's ownership of land from the exploited classes (the Proletariat), to keep themselves rich and wealthy. Marx and Engels wrote that a selective section of the Bourgeoisie Class, which they termed as *"The State"*, or *"Government"*, was tasked with the power to make and enforce the aforementioned "Law and Order", as they put it;

> *"...is...simply a product of society at a certain stage of evolution. It [the creation of any kind of government] is the confession that this society has become hopelessly divided against itself in irreconcilable contradictions which are powerless to banish."*

Both men wanted to do away with the ownership of private property and "The State", because they felt, that by eliminating these conditions in society, the class struggle, the Bourgeois versus the Proletariat, would automatically wither away.

As for religion, the previous chapters have mentioned that Karl Marx, Friedrich Engels, and their supporters were all a bunch of raving lunatic Atheists, who totally discredited God and his teachings altogether. They felt, that in addition to the almighty State, the religion practiced by the Bourgeoisie, was a device used to sequester the Proletariat, who were considered the "Exploited Class", to prevent them from rising up in a rebellion. Karl Marx in the Manifesto has written that religion was **"the opiate for the oppressed."** This is one of the main reasons why, that in 21st Century America, especially in the younger generations of people in the Black Community, the Institution of Religion have-to be rejected, which is further re-enforced by various media avenues and the public education system. Younger generations such as the Millennials (persons born between 1980-2000), were psychologically taught. that they are the exploited class, and any faith in religion is considered a "moral crutch" to the poor.[3,4,5,6]

Marx further explained, that the **"moral crutch"** of God, Morality, and Religion is only used by the Bourgeois to protect their wealth, ownership of land and capital from the Proletariat.

Marxists, ideological people who practice and support The Theory of Marxism, have been taught that such passages of the Gospels like **"The 10 Commandments"**, that such phrases as "Thou Shall Not Steal" are used to protect upper classes of people, they consider the exploiters of the Proletariat. What the Marxist Theory does explain, that Communism/Marxism does away with ___**all**___ Judaic-Christian morals and principles, which they, the Marxists, will replace it with a society, where ___**no**___ morals or principles exist! In other words, a "fair" and "equal" society that is rich in anarchy!

When the reader hears words by people who either are outright Marxists or duped supporters of the ideology mentions, "___*the end justifies the means*___", understand that such persons have been conditioned to believe that whether their tactics to destroy Capitalism or Religion, are either "legal" or "moral", does not concern them. The idea behind Marxism is "the lack of a moral compass". This will, in their minds, will ensure that any heinous act or actions that they do to bring down the Bourgeoisie Class by the Proletariat, by any means necessary, will be effective. ___*Even it if cost innocent lives, in the process!*___

Marx and Engels further concluded, to bring down the Bourgeoisie Class, is to create a violent revolution to overthrow the current society, who they felt, was a result of the political system originated during the Medieval Times, which they consider as *Feudalism*. [7,8,9] By rendering their services to the Lord, people during that era of human history, in turn, received protection and land because of their faithful services to God. Here, Marx contends that Capitalism came into being. Both men explained that prior to Capitalism and Feudalism, Man did his own work and reaped the benefits from it, because he was entitled to it. Both men contended that when the Industrial Revolution came along in the 1840's and 1850's, they wrote that the Industrial Revolution was an appendage of a Capitalistic Society, where Man's private business ventures were destroyed by the implementation of the factories.

Once the factories came along and began to mass produce products, the factory itself became a social production rather than a private entity. Marx and Engels felt that it was wrong that such manufacturing of goods and products was controlled by a selected few (i.e. Executive Management, Middle Management) because they would reap the benefits from products that many other people made.

The Marxist Theory goes on to say, that the wages that the factory Employees were receiving were inadequate for the labor produced. Marx and Engels concluded that workers should receive all profits made on the sale of the commodity since it was the **Employees** and not the **Employers** that created the product in the first place. When asked whether the management of the factories, labor cost, material cost and overhead costs that the manufacturer considers in creating the product, Marx and Engels concluded that these entities were only "clerical in nature".

Again, they contended, that the Employees should rise and take over the manufacturing entity to operate on their own, thereby reaping the profits of such commodities for themselves. When asked about the outside investment and money in which Investors provide to the manufacturing companies, for the manufacturing process to flow to make such work and materials profitable, while simultaneously paying workers in such businesses.

Both men said that **all** wealth is created by the worker. To them, capital (money) means **nothing**! Such capital is only accumulated by the Bourgeoisie and should be confiscated from them and **redistributed** to the Employees of the factories, who are considered as the exploited class or the Proletariat. The Marxist Theory goes on to explain that as technology improves in a Capitalistic Society, the number of rich, wealthy factory owners will increase, while the number of poor, property-less people doing the actual work in these places, will increase as well. As these technological advances take place, both classes of people will cause, between themselves, a violent clash of social anarchy, which will be the overall end of civilization period. [10,11]

At this point of The Marxist Theory, Marxists and Socialists differ in opinion, as to how these two classes of people will, in the future, somehow overthrow Capitalism. Socialists are people who believe in the same principles of Marxists, that the Bourgeois harbor all their wealth away from the Proletariat. However, Socialists believe that the "**Almighty State**", be the centralized control entity in a society of **all** land and **all** industries of production can be achieved by a "peaceful" (forced) legislation. [12,13]

Karl Marx adamantly rejected the Socialistic notion, of the "***State***", in which he concluded, as earlier, that the state protected the Bourgeois' wealth via the means of "law and order". Even though Marx seen the kind of argument that Socialists made that they control all means of production and all ownership of land and capital, he was still convinced that even this would lead to an all-out violent and bloody revolution between the rich and the poor.

Despite their differences in opinion as to how the class struggle will eventually lead to a violent revolution at the end, Marx voiced that the only way a Socialistic society will transform or "leap" into full Communism, can only be achieved if the all mighty central government, would voluntarily, turn over the means of production, wealth, and land to the Proletariat without a fight. Other than that, Marx mentioned that the Socialists voluntarily turn over the aforementioned is a "pipe dream" and will never happen, so regardless a violent revolution against Capitalism is ***unavoidable***!

A Classless, Stateless, Society

Every hardcore psychologically-subverted Marxist and their duped followers, dreams of one day, that the system of Capitalism and Free-Market Principals, will once and for all, soon, will be destroyed. The so-called rationality behind this dream is that Full-Communism will one day radically change human nature away from the old system of free-market competition, which provides an opportunity to succeed and create a better life for the individual and their families. [14,15]

If Full-Communism is installed, that social-economic system will, usher in a new society that is not designated by class, separated by state or by differences. Using the Marxist Theory, followers hope that all of the society around the world, will not be considered as a part of an Economic Class of people.

People who are either rich (Upper Class), Small Business Owners (Middle Class) and those who are on the Low-Income scale, will be equal across the board. For Full Communism to exist, the premise that Marx and Engels wrote that "each will produce according to his ability and each will receive according to his need..." will be the standard life of all human beings. Marxism teaches that everybody must give up the way the Old Society allowed them to, that they make money for themselves and/or create a higher standard of living for them and their loved ones.

This ideology will force people to change their behavior, so they can be turned into a socially-minded people so that he or she can work just as hard as they used to under the old system of Capitalism, but this time, work hard for the whole of society instead.

In the new society, people will be satisfied and content to receive compensation for their work in the amount, based on their needs in consumption. [16,17]

Marx and Engels figured that if everybody in this new society will work hard for the benefit of everyone, instead of themselves, the output of production of goods and services will be so great, that the supply of such commodities would be stockpiled in such an abundance, that everyone could help themselves based on their needs. Vladimir Lenin, the first Russian Communist Dictator, that rose to power following the abdication (forcefully resign) of Russian Tsar Nicholas II in 1917, stated shortly after coming to power;

"...that after the Capitalistic Society is gone and Full Communism is implemented after the Socialist Government has

withered away, then society will finally become a true classless, stateless world, then it becomes possible to speak of freedom!"

However, this is pure fantasy and is one of the many reasons why Marxism when forced on a whole society, has never worked since 1848! It's an inefficient system, which in the long term, destroy ***any and all incentives*** for anybody to produce unless they are forced by violence to do so. Let's take the following hypothetical scenario below as it applies to the part of The Marxist Theory where "each will produce according to his ability and each will receive according to his need."

Let's put this Marxist Theory in practice, by using a hypothetical example below.

Inside a large manufacturing facility, located in _____ City, this company employs about 1,000 workers to produce a certain product that every one of us buys and uses daily.

Say that the 1,000 workers at that manufacturing plant are geographically made up of people from all cultures, all races and different sexual orientations. Each employee is paid $15.00 per hour, Full-Time Equivalent, working 8-hour days (8:00 am-4:00 pm), 6 days a week. Each worker will make a total of $120.00 per day, $720.00 per a week, $1,400.00 every two weeks, $2,800.00 per month or $34, 500.00 per year, before taxes.

Let say, that half of the 1,000-man workforce in that manufacturing plant or 500 people, will only show up for work, clock-in their timecard and ***for the rest of the day, sit around and do nothing!*** Remember, in this scenario, nobody can or will get fired because everybody produces for the whole of society, not for themselves.

Say, the same 500 people continue to do the same thing, day-after-day, week-after-week, month-after-month not doing a thing, no work, no help, no assistance to their other co-workers, but they still get paid the same amount of money that the other 500 people who are working (probably even harder) receives.

If this scenario continues, what do you think will happen to 500-people who **are** producing?

The same 500-employees who are consistently working and doing their jobs, even harder to make up the slack of work that the other 500-people won't do, will eventually get angry, mad and frustrated as to why the other half of the workforce are not being **pushed** to help them.

What do you think, would happen to the 500-workers who are working all the time? ***They will quit doing their job!***

Human nature will take over and any incentives for producing any of the company's products will come to a halt!

Tempers will flare between those 500 who are ***producing*** work and the other 500 ***not producing*** any work. The result will lead-to a sharp decrease in the workforce's morale of the company to an all-time low, to the point where **production will stop**. Hostility between those producing and those not producing will commence, which will lead to a **violent confrontation between both sets of workers.**

In a Socialist/Communist society, the company's "**authority**", who are all bureaucrats working for "**The State**", will have no choice but to implement their own form of "**justice**" to get production going again.

Here, all 1,000-workers will be **forced to work, for less or no pay and if any of those workers who chose not to work or voice displeasure with their working conditions, severe punishments will be meted out as dictated by the company's authority.**

At the end, the 500 people who chose not to work in the first place, the ***non-producers***, will not comprehend or even understand what just happened to them!

Marx and Engels failed to understand for themselves, that you cannot simply force human beings to produce according to their ability and according to their needs; because ***Communism reduces, and destroys all incentives for workers to produce! PERIOD!***

Since human beings are different and require different needs, what would be the standard as to who needs what? Without these incentives, to include ownership of land, rewards for increased quality and quantity of work produced, production will come to a screeching halt. Then means goods produced by forced labor, will not be as 'plentiful' as Marx and Engels envisioned, but ***products will be substandard and scarce at best.***

It is here, where a "***Black Market System***" will commence and those goods being produced, substandard or not, will be sold by individuals at a higher price than what they would pay for in a store or such goods being rationed by the State. The countries of Cuba and Venezuela at this very moment does this. They are economic disasters as we speak.

The Marxist Theory on Religion [18]

As explained earlier, the Marxist Theory absolutely rejects, discredits and denounces all religion, period! Communism alleges that religion is not of a divine origin, but a man-made myth or fallacy used as a tool by the Bourgeoisie (the Dominant Class), to suppress the Proletariat (the Exploited Class).

Marx and Engels considered religion as lessons which are taught to the Exploited Classes to respect property rights. Secondly, both men concluded that religion teaches the poor their duties towards the property and prerogatives of the ruling class. Third, they viewed religion, as a force that brainwashes the poor to destroy any revolutionary spirit.

Marx and Engels' allegations in regard to the Judeo-Christian Religion teachings are false and baseless! The Biblical teachings of respect for property applies to both the rich and poor alike.

The Bible admonishes the rich to give to the Laborer his proper wages and to share their riches with the needy. Even during the Middle

Ages, whenever the Christmas holiday was celebrated, have been a time of the year in the Pagan sect of Christianity, where the Rich would come to the poor and downtrodden and exchange gifts or a certain amount of wealth as a loving gesture among Men. Even **Matthew 19:24 states:**[19]

> *"It is easier for a camel to go through the eye of a needle, than for a rich man to enter into the kingdom of God."*

However, the very basis where Communism and Judeo-Christianity, and the fact any religion, comes in conflict with each other, is that ___religion doesn't teach one to lie, steal or command another being into submission.___ He shall not shed innocent blood.

Vice, Communism has been proven, time-and-time again that it has been tried, that the "**Almighty State**" systematically exterminate entire nations and classes of people, by persons who have been mentally conditioned to lie, cheat, command and shed innocent blood without remorse.

Another example where the Marxist Theory on Religion has been displayed can be found in the tragic, but a historical incident of The People's Temple under the leadership of the Reverend Jim Jones, in the 1970's.[20]

Horror of Jonestown Touches Lives of Two Long Beach Police Officers

BY ROBERT J. GORE
Times Staff Writer

The incredible horror of Jonestown has come from Guyana to touch the lives of two Long Beach police officers.

Robbery Det. Michael Woodward went on a dangerous South American odyssey to find his 84-year-old grandfather, who became the first Jonestown survivor to reach the United States. Woodward's grandmother did not survive.

And Deputy Chief William Stovall has spent the last three days making funeral arrangements for his cousin and her three daughters, who died under the lethal influence of Jim Jones.

Woodward slipped quietly back to work Wednesday.

But the date his grandparents left for Guyana is etched in his mind.

"Aug. 3, 1977," he said. "They didn't tell anyone, but my mother got a letter from them and she caught them just as they were leaving."

Woodward's story unfolded like there being told by the relatives of other People's Temple members. But his journey, in the company of a re-

porter for a local newspaper, makes the tale as unusual as Jonestown itself.

At first, everything apparently went well. Letters from his grandfather, Miguel De Pina, and his grandmother, Levie, said everything was fine and asked for small items.

The packages, Woodward found out, were never delivered to his grandparents. Someone at Jonestown would sign for them and keep the contents.

Woodward, who returned to Long Beach on Monday, was still tired. He was telling his story in a soft voice. He leaned forward.

"Until seven or eight years ago, we were a real poor family. Then I became a police officer and my brothers started graduating from college," he said.

"We couldn't do anything for our grandparents like most families. Now we were in a position to do something," Woodward explained.

His mother began saving money to go to Guyana.

"She could never get permission from Jim Jones. She would write him and he would have my grandma write back to tell her it wasn't possible," Woodward said.

When his mother became ill, Woodward decided he would go. However, he didn't see any way he could get to see his grandparents.

Then the news from Jonestown. A congressional fact-finding party was dead. Rumors of mass suicide.

Woodward's family was sick with worry. The suicides were confirmed. He decided to fly to Guyana.

"I got my passport and my shots in one day. I was really running," he said.

Woodward picked up a small suitcase his wife had packed, tried to explain to his uncertain mission of mercy. He was accompanied by a reporter from the Long Beach Independent, Press-Telegram newspapers.

"I wasn't scared until the minute the plane touched the runway in Georgetown," Woodward said. "I could see police and soldiers all over the place."

The morning after his arrival, Woodward went to the U.S. consul, where an official reluctantly told him that his grandfather was one of the few survivors and was under police guard at a hospital.

"The U.S. officials couldn't violate *Please Turn to Page 8, Col. 1*

Los Angeles Times article reporting loved ones lost during the Guyana Tragicty of People's Temple Members November 1978.

(Courtesy of Newspapers.com)

Prior to him being ultimately responsible for the poisoning and the death of 908 members of his own church, in Jonestown Guyana, in

November 1978, began to teach his church members to reject the Judeo-Christian principles.

During one of his sermons recorded in 1974, Jim Jones told his majority African-American congregation, numbering in the thousands, that the Holy Bible has been holding the Black Community down for the past, in his words, 200-years. Jones held up the Bible stated;

"Do you see this Black Book, I'm going to show you that this has no power".

Here he took the Bible, reached way back like he was going to throw a football and launched the Bible towards the congregation. As the audience got quiet and showed the emotion of shock, the Bible hit the floor. Jones began to look around him, showing no emotion, then stated to his followers;

"Now, did you see lightning come out the sky and strike me down?"

Most of his followers went wild and cheered their pastor. A very small number left the service, prematurely voicing their displeasure as to what they just witnessed. Jones then followed this cheering by stating;

"This is only one hope of glory...that's within you! Nobody's gonna come out the sky! There is no Heaven up there...We'll have to make Heaven down here [on Earth]!"

During the PBS Documentary in 2006, talking out the Guyana Tragic, that interviewed former members and former survivors of the People's Temple. One of them, Hue Folston, a longtime temple member, goes further to solidify the Marxist Theory on Religion, that Jim Jones stated;

"What you need to believe-in is what you see, he said, if you see me as your Friend, I'll be your Friend, he said if you see me as your Father, I'll be your Father for those who don't have Fathers, he said if you see me as your Savior, I'll be your Savior, he said even so, if you see me as your God, I'll be your God!" [21]

The Marxist Theory on Morals [22,23,24]

Since Karl Marx and Friedrich Engels believe that ownership of property is the cause of class warfare and class antagonisms, they added religion, where the Dominant Class suppresses the Exploited Class of people to protect their property. Now both men began to define morals in a similar fashion. Such commandments, such as "Thou Shall Not Steal", Marxist Men are taught that such phrases are examples where the Bourgeoisie, protect their property from the Proletariats, who in their lives, one-day, will have their own wealth and property just like the Bourgeoisie.

However, Marx and Engels reject human morality, because they theorized that all human conduct should be motivated exclusively by the needs of society and not for your individual self. Of course, this is an abject lie, because human nature, in general, can only benefit society collectively if they benefit for themselves initially, then expand their wealth by creating products where people will buy, hiring people and providing them wealth in the form of capital (money), so they can eventually can become successful and so-on and so forth.

Unfortunately, such morals are taboo to a Marxist. Communism is a system, which will replace Judaic-Christian values and Morals, by rejecting such principles, and installing a system that has absolutely no morals or self-value! That is why Marxist Men and their dupes, are taught that no matter what they do, or how they do any action, whether or not it is both morally corrupt or abject criminal in nature, the end justifies the means.

Such persons are mentally conditioned, that what is legal or moral does not apply to them, for as long as their actions are effective to control a certain outcome, it is okay for them to do it. Understand, that anything that pertains to a Marxist, such terms like "legality", "Fairness", "Rights", does not apply to them nor their actions. Because they are doing such actions for the betterment of society as a whole and not for a certain class of people.

Karl Marx and American Slavery Assessment [25,26]

After the failed and disastrous Proletariat Revolution in France in 1848, Karl Marx for the next few years, went seeking money to finance his next revolution against the Bourgeoisie. By the year 1851, still broke and destitute, Marx turned to other countries around the world seeking to communicate his ideology of Marxism/Communism to a wider audience. He didn't have to wait long, because one American Journalist reached out to Marx that year, which lead to some subscribers of his newspaper, reading Marx's outlandish, gibberish began to ask the question "who is this man?".

A better question should be asked is, who was this Journalist that gave Marx an expanded audience for him to spread the ideology of Marxism? His name was a Mr. Horace Greeley, former high-ranking member of the U.S. Whig Party, former 1860 Presidential Candidate, and owner of the ***New York Daily Tribune***.

Dubbed "The Daily Tribune", both Marx and Greeley had some goals in common. For example, in-order to spread the ideology of Communism, Karl Marx needed a wider audience of readers, to psychologically subvert them into accepting it.

Horace Greeley needed a bigger audience of readers of his publication, so he could expand The Daily Tribune's distribution network overseas. For this to be accomplish, Greeley sought out the most widely popular people from different countries, such as Karl Marx to provide their editorials on current events around the world. So, in 1851, Karl Marx became The Daily Tribune's Foreign Correspondent in London England, where he resided with his wife and children, after being booted from France in 1848.

Both men harbored similar views of the world of the day, such as Marx's criticisms of manufacturing presidents in England, France, and Prussia, exploiting the low-wage earner to sell goods on the open market to make huge profits. Likewise, Greeley spoke out in opposition against the American Railroad Companies, who were creating their own territorial monopolies, brought on by the westward expansion of the United States, making them plenty of profits in return.

However, only minor similarities between the men existed. When Greeley called for the centralization of The Bank of the United States via privatization, Marx called for all capital to be placed in the hands of the Proletariat, the low-wage earner. Besides, the latter man had the tendency to be very vocal and straight to the point in his editorials, which cause some of the Tribune's readers to voice their complaint against Marx's unhinged, psychotic irrational views, while still advocating a worldwide revolution as a solution to the world's ills.

As the complaints increased in numbers, Managing Editor for The Daily Tribune, Charles Dana, who by the way, was not a fan of Karl Marx, pushed Greeley to write the following in one of his 1852 editions of the newspaper;

"Mr. Marx has very decided opinions of his own, with some of which we are far from agreeing, but those who do not read his letters are negating one of the most instructive sources of information on the great questions of current European politics."

This comment about Marx's editorials was meant to put some of Tribune's readers at ease about the author writing style and heavily opinionated pieces of information. What this comment also showed the readers of the paper, was that whatever Marx's opinions were, they did not reflect the opinion of the Tribune's staff. In other words, Greeley wrote a disclaimer!

One of the many things that people who have allowed themselves to be drawn up emotionally into believing the ideology of Karl Marx and Friedrich Engels, especially those who are of African-descent, are never taught how the men viewed Slavery in the United States. After all, the Institute of American Slavery in the South, after the Northern States abolished the practice early in the 1800's, was well-known throughout the world before the outbreak of the Civil War.

It is also interesting to note, that since both men were working on their next set of worldwide revolutions in England, that country was one of the largest consumers of America's importation of raw Southern-grown cotton, harvested from plantations throughout the South. Yet, Marx and to the lesser extent Engels did have an opinion about Black Slavery in the United States at the time and both men wrote about it in numerous articles. Whether these opinions were taught to those who accepted Marxism, is anybody's guess. However, there may be a strong possibility that their opinions were not taught, either intentionally or unintentionally to hide the true-identity of both men. If African-Americans found out about the **_real_** Karl Marx, it can be a safe bet that many Blacks in America would not support anything pertaining to Marxism. It is here, where we uncover the true opinion of Karl Marx and American Slavery.

Recall that one of the basis of The Marxist Theory states, that the Bourgeoisie society must be overthrown in a bloody and violent revolution, by an uprising by the Proletariat. The latter who have been exploited by the former to make huge profits off the backs of the low-wage worker. When it comes to American Slavery, however, Karl Marx saw, what was called "Direct Slavery" in the World as a part of the Bourgeoisie society, that included machinery, credits and other means of production, a part of the economic system of Capitalism. Marx wrote;

"Without Slavery, there would be no Cotton; without Cotton, you have no modern industry. It is Slavery that have given the colonies their value; it is the colonies that have created world trade, and it is world trade that is the pre-condition of large-scale industry. Thus, Slavery is an economic category of the greatest importance."

The aforementioned is what Marx theorized about Human Chattel, period. However, he is what he wrote about American Slavery;

"Without Slavery in North America, the most progressive of countries would be transformed into a patriarchal country. Wipe out North America from the map of the world, and you will have anarchy-the complete decay of modern commerce and civilization. Cause Slavery to disappear and you would have wiped America off the map of nations."

He continues;

"Thus Slavery, because it is an economic category, has always existed among institutions of the peoples. Modern nations have been

able only to disguise Slavery in their own countries, but they have imposed it without disguise upon the New World."

Karl Marx's understanding of American Slavery was very different from reality, probably because he had never been to the United States of America to witness the practice itself and he only understood the practice of Human Chattel based on ancient times to the formation of the Industrial Revolution. Marx further assessed that Slavery, no matter in what form, was two-separate social systems;

Ancient Slavery

Capitalist Slavery

Ancient Slavery, in what Marx called "Pre-Capitalist Slavery", dates back to Roman times, vice **Capitalist Slavery**, accompanied the emergence of Capitalism, in his assessment, started around the 16th Century. However, for the sake of simplicity, clarity, time and space, we will only discuss the latter.

Even though both forms of Slavery is characterized by the exploitation of Human Chattel, which still exists today, Marx considered Slavery in America in 1857 as;

"A country where the Bourgeoisie society did not develop on the foundation of the feudal system, but developed rather from itself, where this society appears not as the surviving result of centuries-old movement, but rather as a starting point of a new movement, where the State in contrast to all earlier national formations, formed the beginning subordinate to the bourgeoisie society, to its production and never could make pretense of being an end-in-itself, where, finally, Bourgeoisie society itself, linking up the productive forces of an old world with the enormous natural terrain of a new one..."

Marx continues;

"...has developed to hitherto unheard-of dimensions and unheard-of freedom movement has far outstripped all previous work

in the conquest of forces of nature, and where, finally, even the antitheses of Bourgeois society itself appears only as vanishing moments."

In translation, Marx concluded the American Slavery wasn't a part of the old society, called Ancient Slavery/Pre-Capitalist Slavery, and not of the current Capitalist Slavery, as he concluded existed in Europe and East Asia at the time. What Marx described, was that American Slavery was not old but a rather a new movement within itself of "unheard-of dimensions", completely-separate in nature.

Friedrich Engels supported Marx's assessment of the Institute of American Slavery by writing;

"Slavery in the United States of America was based far less on force than on the English Cotton industry; in those districts where no Cotton was grown, or which, unlike the border states, did not breed Slaves for Cotton-growing states, it died out itself without any force being used, simply because it did not pay."

Interesting, isn't it?

Both men in agreement further concluded that Capitalism in Agriculture, which was the mainstay industry in the Slave-owning South and stated matter-of-factly, that Agricultural profit is only determined by Industrial Profit and "not the other way around."

There is more.

Value of A Slave in America [27,28]

Karl Marx clearly stated, that in the United States of America, the price paid for the purchase of a Slave of African-descent was **_nothing_**, but the anticipated and capitalized surplus-value for profit, would be grounded out of them by their labor, sometimes for life in certain cases.

In **_Das Kapital_**, Volume one, Marx wrote that the capital (money) paid for the purchase of a slave does not belong to the capital by which profit, surplus labor, is extracted from him. In other words, Southern Plantation Owners purchased Slaves from money that they already have on-hand, not by the money which was accumulated from any profits the Planter made of the products he sold.

It gets better.

Marx concluded also, that both Slavery and Wage-Labor are exploitative forms of a Commercial Capitalistic System. However, American Slaves had ***exchange value***, where the low-wage factory worker had ***no value***.

The Black Slave in America was only replacing the value of his own means of existence, which the Slave works for him or herself; it is rather his power of disposing of his labor that affects the Black Slave Value. On the other hand, Marx stated that the low-wage factory worker, who had no value, is not compensated by the manufacturer owner's profits, made by the selling of the products which the low-wage worker produced.

In layman's terms, Karl Marx and Friedrich Engels simply considered, that African-descent Slavery in America was an acceptable means of production inside Capitalism, where the value of their work, does not contribute to the overall profit production of the Bourgeoisie society.

It is the low-wage Manufacturer Worker, who has no value inside Capitalism because their work is a part of the production of the factory. Since their work is produced in the factory, the factory owner takes these goods made by them, sells them on the open market, make large sums of money in return and pays the Manufacture worker nothing out of those returns.

American Slavery was acceptable in value, where the low-wage worker in the factory, wasn't acceptable in value because they never profit from the goods sold.

"The immediate aim of the Communist is the same as that of all other Proletarian parties; formation of the Proletariat into a class, overthrow of the Bourgeois supremacy, conquest of political power by the Proletariat."[1]

Friedrich Engels

Photo collage of Marxist Men that has advocated for a "Globalist World" of Communism.

(Author's collection)

Karl Marx and Friedrich Engels knew, that for their plan of Full Communism to take shape, a new breed of Human Beings must be psychologically conditioned to carry out the Marxist mission, for worldwide domination.

Well-known Author, the late W. Cleon Skousen (1913-2006), in his best-selling book "***The Naked Communist***", highlighted in detail as to how this psychological conditioning of people have taken shape, and to what actions they have been programmed to enforce to fulfill their goal. Skousen named these persons "***Marxist Man***", in which this author will use that term as a guideline, to describe such persons who have and continue to be produced in superior numbers in every cultural community in the United States.

__The objective of Marxist Man, at the end, is to force society into Socialism first, then Full Communism last. Whether society like it or not.__[2]

To explain who and what Marxist Man is, and expose their plan to achieve world domination, the reader must objectively understand from the get-go, that the mindset of such persons is dangerous. This selected group of people have been chosen by other Marxist Men and Women, to further carry out The Marxist Theory, in accordance with Marx and Engels writings.

However, Marxism has since been modified, one way or another by other former followers of Marxism, who ended up being domineering dictators of their respective countries, like Vladimir Lenin and Joseph Stalin (Soviet Union/Russia), Mao Tse Tung (China), Patrice Lumumba (Congo), Maurice Bishop (Granada), Idi Amin (Uganda) and many others, which are too numerous to list in this publication.

__*Marxist Man is a conditioned criminal*__. They are persons who have been mentally subverted to only react, to specific verbal stimuli from their masters who control them.

For this psychological change to occur, some retooling of their reasoning must be accomplished at first, to keep them focused in-order to react to their master's every beck and call. Marxist Men are programmed to outright reject all dependency on free will, ethics, morals, to include their inability to think to rationalize for themselves, regardless whether-or-not, true information is right in front of their face. This Marxist Man concept isn't new to human history.

Many power-hungry people in the past, have had this kind of dream that one day, they would be the ones, who can dominate the World and create their own version of a societal Utopia. Such historical figures include Nimrod, the Son of Cush and Great-Grandson of Noah was the first person to invent the idea of Marxist Man to exist. Greek Philosopher Plato (428 B.C.-347 B.C.) wrote about such a utopic world in his book "__*Republic*__", while Saint-Simon the Zealot advocated for it. Karl Marx and Friedrich Engels, succeeded by materializing Marxist Man into physical existence.[3]

To make it clear, let's explore **_how_** Marxist Man is conditioned to be a psychopathic-conditioned criminal.

On the outside, Marxist Man seems to appear irrational in thought and behavior, to those who either work with him or see them in the public. However, this a deceptive tactic, because those who have mentally subverted to become Marxist Men, have reduced his or her thinking to the lowest common denominator; **_Negative One Zillion!!_** In-actuality, Marxist Men are slick, cunning and conniving creatures, who are snobbish, selfish individuals who decisions are highly predictable for those who can see right through their think-skinned deception. They are devoid soul and repudiates their capacity for immortality.

They believe that there is no universal Creator and have accepted the notion, they were "**_accidents_**" of Nature. Marxist Man has absolutely do have morals, which they don't whatsoever, and approaches all issues directly, and will flat out deny that such radical behavior is not his or her own doing. They blame others for their actions, calling them "**_stupid_**", "**_ignorant_**" and accuse such distractors of harboring "**_self-motives_**" against them. Marxist Men have a constant thirst for power and they have a serious appetite for control over larger and larger populations. Remember, their mission is to dominate the World.

They perceive themselves as being "**_special_**" and have been placed into society to conquer Nature, the Universe and all senses of reality. The latter part, they have been taught to control all senses of reality, to the point where they themselves write the narrative and sell it as something real, which is not.

The idea behind this deed, is to formulate a paranoia-type atmosphere, to project superiority over everyone else, with the criminal intent of creating mass chaos. Marxist Men feels that they are superior to everyone, regardless who close or how distant of the relationship others have who associates with them; and even claim that they themselves are 'Kings and Queens of the Jungle"!

These conditioned criminals are not shy or even care about who they really are, or what others think about them or how they portray themselves to the outside world. The only thing they understand is destroy Capitalism, destroy the family, divide people by race, culture, and sexual orientation or their own nation's sovereignty. They will believe this objective regardless or not they personally benefit from the very same economic system that they are trying to destroy!

It is a hate mentality.

Marxist Man venomously despises the Military and its members of Active Duty Servicemen, Women and Veterans, because they perceived such people as a threat, who has the capability in foiling their plan of worldwide domination. He or she envisions a small body of people who have been criminally-conditioned like themselves who has the power to legislate, adjudicate and operate via **The United Nations** as "**The State**" to take charge of the World prior to implementation of Full Communism.[5,6]

Once Marxist Men are created in sufficient quantity, they are driven by their creators to teach others, who they feel are weak-minded individuals, to think like they do. You might ask as to what type of people who they considered being weak-minded folks?

Easy, Marxist Men specifically target people who sometimes don't live in-reality by themselves, who are very susceptible to accept what is told to them as being factual, without verifying whether such information is true or not.

They target these people who occupy areas of society that have low self-esteem issues, the downtrodden poor and the demoralized younger generations, because Marxist Men understand, that this section of the country's population are easy targets for manipulation.[7,8,9]

By doing this, the people become "***useful idiots***", to be used as verbal tools and support Marxist Man's agenda to implement Socialism and full Communism worldwide. [10]

The type of people specifically targeted to conversion to become a psychologically-conditioned criminal, includes people who occupy the institutions of Education, Media, Science, Economics,

Business, and those who are leaders of Religious organizations. This targeting is extended even further to encompasses social communities as well, like the low-income sections of Black, Hispanic and White Communities, found mostly within the inner-cities of America.

Marxist Man's psychological subversion have also extended to even those who are members of some of the most innovative generations in the United States to date, such as the last portion of the "X" Generation (persons born from 1977-1980) and "Millennial"-Generation (people born between 1981-2000).[11,12,13] However, unlike the rest of the aforementioned institutions, generational subversion is only taught a selective portion of Marxism, subliminally, to control their actions, emotions and responses coming in the near future. Called "Demoralization", or what is popularity known today as "***The Victim Mentality Syndrome***".

Using these labels interchangeably, both require criminally-conditioned Marxists to create a slow, 20-plus year process to tear down any, and all rational thinking of the population, and make them feel emotionally bad, that they are victims of their own circumstances. Marxist Men will blatantly lie and deceive the weak-minded people, that their conditions and/or environment will never change, because of some "outside forces" that are against them, in which cannot be controlled. Examples of such outside forces, who Marxist Man uses to make this argument, are a person's skin color, the inherited traits that they received from their parents, which they will pump into the soft brains of weak-minded people, that these forces will never make them "***productive citizens***".

Marxist Men consistently tell these people, that they are the ones who understand their "plight" and they will be the ones who will lead the weak-minded people, who they called "victims of oppression" to revolt against any or all opposition to the Communist Order.[14]

Marxist Men will be the people who will fight and defend the poor, the downtrodden, the drug dealer, the Elderly, the Felons and those who haven't "**had a fair shake in life**", when they won't. As a matter of fact, once Marxist Men have successfully conditioned these the aforementioned people to do their bidding, they are taught to manipulate the same people doing the dirty work for "***The Cause***" of "***Freedom***" and "***Equality***".

Code words that tends to keep such mentally-subverted people, subjected to the conditions which they have been reduced to. Also, such weak-minded persons, in Marxist Man's world view, must stay subjected to them and only ***them***, even if it means paying the manipulated money and benefits in the form called "***government entitlements***" to keep them subjected and controlled.

Thus, creating a "***Victim Mentality Syndrome***" attitude in such persons that Marxist Man has subverted.

Marxist Man despises and look down on such easily manipulated people, to the point where they will use other specific words or phrases to make it clear, without hesitation, that they are using these people they have absolute contempt towards.

Such phrases like ***"Persons of Color"***, when referencing Minorities, or "***White Privilege***" is just one out of many examples, which Marxist Man uses to keep such persons subjected to them, while simultaneously demeaning those who they have absolute control over.

In the next section, we will explore the Victim Mentality Syndrome, where the author will simply outline and highlight what the syndrome is and who are the intended target audience that Marxist Men have been using to further their plan to destroy Capitalism and usher in Full Communism.

The reader should be very alarmed about people who have been conditioned like Marxist Man. Because a criminally-conditioned mind set does not respond the same way, as a person who does not have such ill intentions or mentality. This evil affliction of this mental disorder, make Marxist Men, just as dangerous to society as a serial murderer causing mayhem in a small-populated community.

"Self-pity is easily the most destructive of the non-pharmaceutical narcotics; it is addictive, gives momentary pleasure and separates the victim from reality"[1]

John Gardner

Many of you readers have heard the term "***The Victim Mentality Syndrome***", either in person, through mainstream media or via social media platforms, such as Facebook, Instagram, Twitter or Snapchat. However, the term is often used interchangeably to describe a real mental health illness called "***Narcissistic Personality Disorder***", "***Narcissistic Psychopathic Disorder***" or NPD for short.[2,3]

Regardless of which term is used, persons who are inflicted with the illness are dangerous and do not lives in reality. Which is why people who have been mentally converted into Marxist Man mentioned in the previous chapter, love using these people that have NPD because they can serve as, what Vladimir Lenin termed "***useful idiots***". Because, they can be easily "duped" or suckered into believing whatever Marxism Men tells them to be true, regardless whether the information is true or not, persons afflicted with NPD will follow willingly **without question**.

Persons with NPD are used by Marxism Men to form the core of Communism because they are the ones who will be labeled as the Proletariat, if or when the Communist Revolution starts. These hoodwinked people, not only are found in America's Inner-City Black Communities but also in Inner-City Hispanic and poor White Communities as well.

Unfortunately, in recent times, Inner-city Black Communities have fallen prey to becoming the biggest and most numerous pawns in the game of "equality" that Marxism falsely portrays. Since Marxist Man sees such people as weak-minded individuals, such persons can be found in abundance in places of higher learning, such as Public Schools, Community Colleges and even inside major Universities across America. Many of the institutions of higher learning are operated and administrated by academic faculties, who have been criminally-conditioned as Marxist Men themselves.

Inside this chapter, the reader will have a better understanding as to what the Victim Mentality Syndrome/NPD illness is and how Marxists take these duped persons and convert them into being the useful idiots, to do the dirty work.

People afflicted with Narcissistic Personality/ Psychopathic Disorder (NPD), are categorized with a long-standing sense of Grandiose, either in fantasy or in real, everyday behavior.[5] Commonly called "**_Narcissists_**", they are inflicted with an overwhelming need for admiration and have a complete lack of compassion or empathy for others.

Persons who have this condition truly believe that **_they_** are the primary importance in everybody's life and whoever they meet. Narcissists are often displayed a snobbish, self-loathing attitude. They exaggerate their achievements, talents and often claims to be superior in intellect or "logic" about real-life subjects or things that they don't even have any knowledge or experience with.

A person with this disorder, often speak badly behind the backs of their family members and friends, by putting them down in conversations that they themselves are 'clearer thinkers' than say, their significant others, siblings or even distant relatives or friends, they haven't seen in many years. Anybody who Narcissists feel superior to, when it comes to public opinion or during a discussion of something substantive, such as politics or social issues, must explain to **_them_**, the

Narcissists, as to why you think the way you think at the time, without offering any explanation of their views, to counter-balance their opposition's view or opinion of things whatsoever!

People with NPD claim that they don't have to explain themselves because they are considered "***the smartest people in the world***" and despite what you say, you are always going to be wrong to them in their eyes. Narcissists are often preoccupied with fantasies of unlimited success, power, beauty or ideal love about themselves.

Just like Marxist Man, they consider themselves "special", "the chosen ones" and the only type of people who can understand them, are those who are just like them, mentally. In all actuality, Narcissistic people have very low Self-Esteem about themselves, which is why they always seek out admiration from others. They always need others to praise them for their made-up 'superiority' regardless if their actions prove otherwise.

This makes them perfect targets for Marxist Men to use because the latter will constantly coddle the former by constantly giving praise and admiration to persons afflicted with NPD.

Persons with the disorder, have a strong sense of entitlement and expect favorable treatment and/or automatic compliance with their demands for everyone, regardless whether their expectations are unrealistic or difficult to attain. As for empathy for other people's feelings, Narcissists could care less about that! They are exploitive of others, take advantage of everyone else's work or success and claim it as their own. People with NPD are jealous and envious of others, even though on the surface, they will discredit such accusations against them, then twist the accusation around to make it appear like you are jealous of them.[6,7,8]

Narcissists are ***arrogant people***, and if anybody questions their fake sense of grandiose and mental superiority, they will be called nasty names, such as '**stupid**', '**evil**', '**mean**' and '**too dumb**' to recognize their '**brilliance**'. Remember, they could care less if such words demean the people who they target with such insults because by doing so, they receive personal satisfaction because of such uppity actions and feeling of superiority.

They are sick mentally and are physical wrecks, who act differently in public than in a private setting, which is why Narcissistic people have-to put up their false façade. They feel that they deserve more than they have already accumulated, as they dream of winning big cash prizes, who perceive themselves as absolute perfect Human Beings, who are flawless in Nature and they blatantly deny that they are the ones who can never do anything wrong; even though their actions prove otherwise.

When such Narcissistic people are exposed that they were wrong in their decisions, discussions, or in their actions by others, all they will do is deny it.

When denials don't work, persons stricken with NPD will start lying and when lying fails, they began to blame others.

If blaming others doesn't work, then they will launch themselves into a tyrannical rage, consisting of jumbled words, phrases, and vulgar language, which doesn't make sense and accusatory in nature.

To those who are not Narcissistic, these actions further show how mentally unstable that NPD sufferers really are and some of them afflicted with the disorder may react to take physical or criminal actions to prove to those doubting them, who they say they are; superior, unblemished figures.

Here is an example of such Narcissistic persons using such tyrannical rage, hate-fill language, sense of grandiose and more, which one may see or experience when dealing with those afflicted with NPD;

"You can talk that shit all day and night. Or you can just prove it. I own my words and my politics haven't changed in the past 20 years. The shit you claim to be revealing about the Democrats and the left (and all the other bullshit) are conversations i was having when I was in my 20's dawg. So, you will never find anything that would give you any indication that I support the fucking Democrats. You choose not to listen because you think you are smarter than everyone else (i hope you realize that you are not). My main disagreement with your whole presentation is your lack of understanding of crowd you want to rep. That's it. Where you see the Dems as a problem (and they have pimped ignorant blacks forever), i see both sides as the same fucking problem. Why? They are controlled by the same Devils. Left or Right; Liberal or Conservative - same Devil. This is my politic dawg."

Using lies, deception, and manipulation to achieve their goals, they will exploit others in such fashion to gain the upper advantage of those who they feel superior to. NPD-afflicted people regularly provoke others to fight, then end up losing the fight and blaming the provocation of the fight on others! Narcissistic people are not grateful to those who they seek help from and will take all the credit for the idea at the end, claiming as such *'it was my idea in the first place'* when it wasn't.

As for criticism, Narcissists hate it!! Any criticism, whether constructive or not, will send these people into a rage and will respond with foul-mouth words meant to critically demean the criticizers, to the point where they will short-fuse themselves and appear psychotic. One must clearly understand, that people afflicted with NPD, cannot fend for themselves because they think the world revolves around them. Because of everything previously mentioned, Marxist Men want Narcissistic people who act and are mentally inept just like them, because they can easily be duped to help do their dirty work, to destroy the current society.

So, what is the difference between Marxist Men and people that have Narcissistic Personality/Psychopathic Disorder (NPD)? Marxist Men were born, raised and taught throughout their lives, from day one as Marxist Men, from other Marxist Men who, for the most part, are either parent, grandparents or even In-laws of close family members.

As an illustration, let use former-President Barack Hussein Obama's known past for him being a Marxist Man.[11,12,13]

Obama was mentored by a close family friend, Frank Marshall Davis, an outright Marxist and Communist Party of the United States of America (CPUSA) member, Journalist and Editor of the ***Chicago "Red" Star***, ***Atlanta Daily World*** and ***The Honolulu Record***.

On Obama's Maternal side of his family, his Mother, Stanley Anne Dunham, his Grandparents Stanley and Madelyn Dunham, who ended up raising him from the age of 10, were outright hardcore Marxist-Leninists Communists, who themselves were born and raised to believe such dangerous ideology. Vice, people with NPD have Socially conditioned via lies, deception and demoralization techniques, which in turn changed their understandability and rationality of things surrounding them. In the next chapter, the latter will be explained in detail as to how this is and continued to be accomplished.

6: The Psychological Subversion of the United States of America

"...Subversion in Soviet terminology is always an aid and to destroy the country, nation or geographical area of your enemy."[1]

Yuri Bezmenov (A.K.A. Thomas Schuman)

Photo of Soviet KGB Propagandist Agent, Defector, and Journalist, Yuri Bezmenov a.k.a. Thomas/Tomas Schuman.

(Courtesy of Wikimedia)

In 1970, while working as a high-ranking Soviet Union KGB Agent, Translator and Public Relations Officer in India, Yuri Bezmenov defected his post there and sought asylum in the West. He did so at great risk to his life, because of his personal discuss of the Soviet System of Socialism.

After debriefing by U.S. Intelligence Agents in Athens, Greece, he was granted asylum to live in Canada. He is best known for his numerous publications for his Anti-Communist lectures, books and television interviews during the 1980's until his death in 1993.

Why is it important to know who Yuri Bezmenov was and why is it important for the reader to know who he was? Simple.

Mr. Benzmenov worked as a Journalist for the Pro-Marxist publication by the Russian International Agency's **Novosti** magazine, in which him and other KGB agents co-opted, edited and wrote propaganda materials to foreign media outlets throughout the world. Some of their materials were featured in highly-publicized newspapers in the United States, such as the New York Times, Washington Post, Los Angeles Times and many others, to aid, abet and to fundamentally transform countries of their enemies, (America being one of them) to accept Socialism/Communism.[2]

Mr. Bezmenov job was to also psychologically subvert other countries Intellectuals, Business people, Hollywood Actors and Actresses and others to mentally change their own country's perception, from reality into lies. Again, by changing their perception of reality, the hoodwinked persons of high society, will believe such lies & obvious deception to the point where, when they return to their home countries, they will become Marxist Men and spread the ideology of Marxism to their peers, to destroy the basic-fundamentals of their country's Free-Market Capitalism.

Just as Marx and Engels planned to do.

However, decades prior to Yuri Bezmenov's job to spread such propaganda of Socialism/Communism, underneath the 30-year reign of Russian Dictator Joseph Stalin (1922-1952), such weak-minded individuals of high society and wealth, were duped just like the people who Mr. Bezmenov did, during the latter-half of the 1950 until his defection in 1970.

The difference between the two were under Stalin, such Intellectuals, Actors, Entertainers and the such were duped more tangible during the 1920's and 1930's. The Russians created what was known as **Potemkin Villages**. These fake town and villages were constructed and located throughout Soviet Russia, that were used for exactly one purpose; create a false reality, by seeing for themselves of how good and great Socialism/Communism was supposed to be, which was operated by Stalin's inner circle of men, called the Bolsheviks.

Usually, the westerners that traveled to Russia to see for themselves "this great new way of life" were Progressives, who heard about the actual horrors that Stalin and his men decimated the population there. These visitors were reassured by these Soviet officials, that what they heard were "lies", as they escorted and watched these visitors every single hour they were in the country. [3,4]

During their visit, the Western Progressives were shown fake schools, attended by *real* children, all happy and content inside their classrooms learning their A-B-C's, their Reading, Writing, and Arithmetic being taught by happy Teachers. The visitors were also shown playground full of younger aged children, all playing outside on the playground, chasing each other as having fun. The children were, in reality, were playing outside of such places that were a Juvenile Gulag (Prison), whose parents were serving time in Adult Gulags as political prisoners throughout Russia.

Of course, such tours were done very quickly and timely, so that the visitor's hosts do not expose their guests to what was really going on behind closed doors in these institutions. In these Potemkin Villages, there were fake Hospitals, all manned by Doctors, Nurses, Specialists and Patients, all who were really actors playing such parts, telling how wonderful and free access that the Soviet Healthcare System was.

They were told how great advancements were being achieved in conducting research and finding medicine and cures for diseases or illnesses. They were shown false Obstetrics Wards and institutions, that showing births of newborn babies, who were treated with special care in super-clean medical facilities. Such places that these Western Progressives visitors toured, also painted a false picture of women health issues, such as Abortion, under the guise of "*Family Planning*" and "*Birth Control*".

Russian's Progressive visitors were even shown fake factories and business centers, where all means of production were going along fine, as dictated by the Russian Government. They were shown large amounts of goods being stored in warehouses, in which they were told that the items were going to be distributed to the population.

The KGB even conducted fake Wedding Ceremonies for their foreign guests! Such events were deliberately staged by other KGB Agents or actors, to show how happy their citizens were and that everyday society in Russia under Socialism/Communism wasn't much different than any other society around the world. However, the truth of the matter was that everything that was shown to these high members of society-Progressives, was all an illusion.[5,6]

During their tours, KGB agents were ordered by their superiors to keep such visitors to consume much alcohol as possible, from the time they arrived at Moscow Airport, until the time they left the country. In between, the Russians rolled out the red carpet for their Western guests. Yuri Bezmenov wrote that visitors were served numerous glasses of Vodka, when they were attending gala banquets, cheering and toasting during lunch and dinner times while there. The KGB Agents conducting these fabulous luncheons and dinners for their guests were either drinking water, dressed up as Vodka or they would sip their vodka drink while shyly consuming pills which would ward off the effects of the alcohol.[7]

Guests were treated to Ballets, nights at the theaters and if their visitors were African-American or from various countries located on the African Continent, their KGB tour guides also convinced them that racism and bigotry were abolished, and all cultures in the Soviet Union were treated as equals among their fellow citizens, despite skin color.

Famous Blacks men of the time visited these Potemkin Villages and were treated the same as their White constituents while visiting the same places. Famous Black men such as Singer/Athlete **Paul Robeson**, Head of the American Negro Labor Congress (ANLC) **Lovett Fort-Whiteman**, Author and Poet **Langston Hughes**, **W.E.B. DuBois**, Head of the American League of Writers **John Reed** and many others.

Those who went to Russia and visited these fake villages were labeled "***Potemkin Progressives***", a name that described for those so-called "smart and Intellectual" person, were duped big time by their Russian hosts and they never ever knew it.[8,9]

During a 1984 television interview, hosted by Author, Historian, Political Commentator and the creator of the movie ***The Creature from Jekyll Island***, G. Edward Griffin, Yuri Bezmenov explained in clear detail, the methods used by the KGB for gradual subversion of the political system of the United States. Under the disguise called *"**Globalism**"*, *"**The World-Wide Communist Conspiracy**"* or *"**The Illuminati**"*, Mr. Bezmenov this describes such brainwashing used to change the perception of reality of Americans into *four basic stages*.

He stated that the idea behind these mental subversion techniques was to destroy the United States of America from within, to usher in the economic system of Socialism, first, ending with Full Communism second. He further mentions that any obstruction of this subversion, in what he calls *"**Americanism**"*, would rise-up and challenge Marxists who have been brainwashed into accepting the Marxist Theory. The four basic stages of this psychological subversion are;

Demoralization

Destabilization

Crisis

Normalization

Demoralization

Demoralization is the process where individuals in society no longer believe in themselves, in their families, in their communities, or in their country.

You can see this happening right now with your own eyes, as of this writing. Demoralization of American citizens originally taught to the "Baby Boomer" Generation of people (1946-1966), the last half of America's X- Generation (1977-1980) * and Millennial Generations (1981-2000).

If you noticed, these generations of Americans, no longer care for anything that goes on in society period inside the United States. The Demoralization process is conducted through multimedia avenues, such as the Video Game Industry, (makers of X-Box 360, X-Box One, Play Station 4), Hollywood Movies and Television Shows (Twelve Years a Slave, Real Housewives of Atlanta) Social Media, and Public Media, such as ABC, NBC, CBS, PBS, MSNBC, Head Line News, Fox News, TV One, BET, Univision. Other avenues of demoralization occur via the Internet, Public Education System, Books, Magazines and the like.

Demoralization of a major population center such as the United States takes form when at least two or three generations of American people have been brainwashed to accept Marxist-Leninism.[10,11,12]

Yuri Bezmenov stated that such process typically takes 15-20 years to complete, when he was interviewed back in 1985. Directly afterward, he further stated that *"**the process of Demoralization in America is complete. There is nothing you can do about them, you're stuck with them**."*

The first generation, the *"**Baby Boomers**"*, where the first mass generational psychological subversion that took place by Soviet Propagandists, America's own Communist Party of the United States of America (CPUSA), via the Potemkin Progressives and the media/education complex.

Once the process of Demoralization is complete by one generation, duped Americans will continue to instill Marxism into younger populations repeatedly. Here, Yuri Bezmenov stated that those who were influenced by events back in the 1960's, (the "Baby Boomers") are *"**contaminated**"* and they cannot be reprogrammed back into reality. This generation of Americans, have been programmed by their Marxist Men Masters, to think and react to a certain stimuli or words, in a specific pattern. Since this first generation has been completed, other generations that followed them, as previously mentioned, are Demoralized as well. Once the second generation has completed the process, a third generation will be trained.

However, this last generation's process has gotten to the point where *"**The Victim Mentality Syndrome" or Narcissistic*** in personality traits are vividly shown in public. To illustrate this, such useful idiots doing the brainwashing (Marxist Men) will explain to those who they consider weak-minded people (particularly African-Americans and Hispanics) that their social-economic conditions that they live in are *"**not their fault**"* and that *"**the deck has always been stacked against you**"*.

Other words and phrases are used to assist in demoralizing these selected generations of people, such as *"since you will never have justice or equality because of your skin, you will never amount to anything in life."* These psychologically-conditioned criminals will also go on and say something like *"since you will never be about nothing, you might as well die for something."*

The abject racist term *"**People of Color**"*, are used by Marxist Men to keep the demoralized population, into always thinking that their skin color has always been and always will be a negative condemnation.

In other words, belittling publicly that a certain group of populations will never succeed or amount to anything constructive in their lives, demoralize them to keep such persons subjected to the conditions that they have been reduced to.

The purpose of these lies are used to incite and agitate anger, hate, and discontent within themselves; in other words, rebel against those who have kept them in their current conditions in the first place. A Demoralized society will believe in such lies, will allow them to feel emotional, regardless if it is true or not, that everybody and everything around them, including those people who carry themselves in positions of authority, like Parents or Law Enforcement Officers, are *"out to get them"*.

When a person who has been Demoralized in this way, it's become a part of their human nature to rebel and act out their frustrations. This is exactly what Marxist Men want!

Once they rebel against those who they feel that are against them, such persons will not give a damn about how they dress, or what other people think when they walk around the streets wearing their pants down around their knees, what type of vulgar language they use, what color hair they wear, how much junk food they eat, how much illicit drugs they use. ***Facts and perception outside of their mentality means absolutely nothing to them***.[13,14,15]

Because they have been psychologically subverted to accept their fate at face value. These demoralized souls can only comprehend such obviously open lies, that since nobody gives a damn about them, they won't give a damn about anything or anybody else whom they deal with daily. It is at this point where a person's belief in morality declines. Marx and Engels wanted a society where individual morals don't exist because they understood that morals, which means between what's good or what's worse were an appendage the Bourgeois society.[16]

There have been other things that have enhance the systematic brainwashing of the American people, to further demoralize them. For example, the act of Meditation is where one's state of consciousness will transport themselves into an alternate state of mind, to come up with solutions to personal or societal problems they currently face. By creating a "bubble-like" setting, Meditation has been believed to provide solutions to all the world's ills.

However, this type of alternate state of mind or reality, assist in the process of Demoralization of the American people. Because Marxist Men see an opportunity where those who meditate, can be manipulated easier, so *they themselves* can have control over one's thoughts and opinions of real issues right in front of them. Remember from the previous chapters, Marx and Engels wrote that Man can "leap" or be forced, even if subconsciously, into a new reality or a new society.

Meditation is just one of much accepted cultural relaxing and spirituality techniques that Marxist Men find the opportunity to exploit the weak.

Another aspect of the Demoralization process in America is when the Federal Government in Washington D.C. becomes expanded and massive. The majority number of these bureaucratic agencies become a part of the Executive Branch of government. Entities such as the Central Intelligence Agency (CIA), The Department of Justice (DOJ), The Department of Health and Human Services (DHHS), The Department of Commerce (DOC) and many others, began this expansion be creating and increasing individual departments from within them.

By doing so, each of these departments will require more bureaucratic policy and enforcement divisions, which also requires more taxpayer money to sustain and operate. The idea of placing a big blob of government in Washington D.C., is to purposely and massively regulate every aspect of the country's population.

By creating these new departments within the Federal Government, Marxist Men can begin to fill these vacancies of bureaucrats, who have been psychologically-conditioned criminal converts like them. This is done in order to drive and shape governmental policies, to destabilize the United States of American from within. This bloating of the Federal Government is done, while simultaneously hiding their real intentions from the American people under the guise of *"protection"*, *"civil rights"* and *"safety"* of the country's citizens.

The newest Federal Government agency created in recent times that reflect this issue, is The Department of Homeland Security (DHS), which was established under the George W. Bush Administration directly after the tragic Islamic Radical Terrorist Attack on America on September 11, 2001.

Of course, this massive expansion of government has an alternate purpose, sinister in nature, that very few people understand or willing to talk about it publicly. That purpose is to assist in destroying sacred institutions, in America.

The same institutions in which Karl Marx argued that were appendages of the Bourgeois society, like Marriage, Religion, Law and Order, Military Systems, Economy and the marginalization of America's allies, such as Israel, are just a few of such moral institutions that Communism wants to destroy.

Since the 1960's and even more since the election of President Barack Hussein Obama in 2008, we have large voracity of and ideological subversion destruction of the aforementioned institutions.[19,20,21]

Regarding the Institute of Marriage, for example, almost since mankind has been on this Earth, by tradition, and by religion, that Marriage, has always been perceived and accepted, to be between a Man and a Women. This belief was further backed up with the passage of a Bill in the 104th Congress named *"**The Defense of Marriage Act of 1996**"*[22,23] (DOMA), passed both houses of Congress and signed into Law by then-President William Jefferson "Bill" Clinton, on September 21, 1996.

However, Marxist Men, along with their ideological belief, that Morality is another appendage of the Bourgeois society and needed to be destroyed, have placed a full-frontal assault on this institution of Marriage for more than 50 years in the United States. Despite the consistent backlash politically, Marxists have been continuing to convince the public and their useful idiot dupes, that such families, specifically Parents of children within the family, have had a so-called "negative Influence" on them.

This type of deception reverts-back to the Communist Manifesto as well, when Marx and Engels created seven specific purposes of what the International Communist Movement stood for; ***The Elimination of the Family as a Unit***.[24,25,26]

The Demoralized process took effect at the Institute of Marriage, when the Supreme Court of the United States (SCOTUS) struck down Section 3, of the Defense of Marriage Act of 1996, (DOMA) on June 26, 2013. The Supreme Court ruled that Section 3 of D.O.MA was unconstitutional under the ***Due Process Clause*** of the 5th Amendment of the U.S. Constitution. Of course, they were not done with the destruction of Marriage.

Exactly two years later, June 26, 2015, in the case ***Obergefell vs. Hodges***, The Supreme Court ruled that Section II of DOMA was unenforceable, citing the 14th Amendment of the U.S. Constitution, which they interpreted that all U.S. State Laws was supposed to recognize Same-Sex Marriages.

Another addition of the Demoralization process of United States, where the bloated government had seriously hampered, via the Department of Justice and the Department of Homeland Security, is the severe limitations put on the Law Enforcement Agencies nationwide. Stringent rules of engagement and law enforcement operations to enforce Law and Order, inside their respective jurisdictions, became almost non-existence. This occurred during the last eight years, under the Barack Hussein Obama Administration, because of lies and deception campaigns waged by the media against Law enforcement communities, in which Black-on-White Police Officer shooting deaths claimed the lives of;

Michael Brown

Freddie Gray

Alton Sterling

Michael Brown, Freddie Gray, Alton Sterling, in Ferguson, Missouri, such as the Border Patrol, Immigration, Customs and Enforcement (ICE), State, County and even Local-level Law Enforcement Officers are now hesitant to do their jobs, because of the threat of severe backlashes of anarchist protests or riots, from groups like **Occupy Wall Street (OWS)** and **Black Lives Matter (BLM), La Rasa (The Race), Democrat Socialists of America (DSA)** and other Marxist-Communist Front Groups, financed by a multitude Marxist Men such as Multi-Billionaire George Soros and Warren Buffett. The idea behind such Marxist Men is to create a Race War, between the economic classes of lower-income inner-city minorities and Police to bring the country into crisis.[27,28]

By planting the false lie and distortion of facts, with the help of the media, political appointees have for the longest portrayed Law Enforcement Officers as ignorant, stupid and weak racists. By painting the picture that Law Enforcement personnel, are individuals who hate the low-income minority communities because they want to insert their "dominance" over them. This is ***pure fiction*** and needs to be exposed, literally for what it is. However, Karl Marx and Friedrich Engels did label the term "Law and Order" as another appendage of the Bourgeois society, created to protect their riches from the Proletariat, in this case, low-income, inner-city dwellers.

Other expanded Federal Agencies are filled with Marxist Men converts include the Federal Bureau of Investigations (FBI), the Federal Election Commission (FEC), the Internal Revenue Service (IRS) and much more. These agencies handle high-profile cases, service and regulatory bodies, which are enforced as they are laws passed by the U.S. Congress, that have been charged with Voter Intimidation and Fraud, targeting opposition groups for their Federal Tax Exemption Status, illegal Assault Weapon purchase and running to the Mexican Drug Cartels to name a few.

As for Military Systems of the United States, the repeal of **"Don't Ask, Don't Tell"** Law governing the disclosure of homosexuality in the military ranks, the erosion of military tradition and loyalty oaths throughout the services, Demoralization of the ranks have suffered over the decades, resulting from Psychological Subversion of Communism This has allowed Marxist Bureaucrats to occupy positions of power and command.

This system even extends to massive defense spending cuts, slicing military personnel benefits and strength to the lowest level since World War II, while using Active Duty Service Members as social experiments, heavily affecting the American Military to maintain comradery, Esprit De Corps, battle readiness and trust throughout the ranks. Other issues that the Demoralizing process has affected the U.S. Military, includes degrading military equipment and hardware to further weaken planning, operation, and the execution of military forces.

As for the Economy, Demoralization has a direct effect on the American Economic System, especially today, where Marxism has become prevalent within the past ten years. Using Keynesian Economics,[31] where changes in monetary policy in the hands of the Federal Reserve, Banking giants, such as J.P. Morgan-Chase, Wells Fargo, and others, with the Federal Government backing, has caused the U.S. to have a stagnant economy.

When you have such an economic condition within a nation, a domino effect is created that can be detrimental to all who's day-to-day living conditions rely on it. A country, that has an economic condition, that produces less growth, (less than 1% between 2009-2016) has an after-effect, where the cost of living becomes bad for a lot of people and their families.

This can range from large increases in food prices, housing, and rental property costs, increases in prices for consumable items, high unemployment, high business regulation and taxation and many other things, which can cause the American people to have a sense of uncertainty about their future.

Such an economic uncertainty within a population of over 322 million-plus people, can essentially stoke frustrations, hate and even discontent with the country and the Federal Government at large. Whether such Demoralization of America's Economy is deliberate, evidence shows that the answer is **_yes_**.

When Marx and Engels mentioned in the **Communist Manifesto** and their second book, **_Das Kapital_**, both agree, that that money and profits only benefit only those at the top classes of society, the Bourgeoisie society. Both men also agree that to destroy society as it stands in the present, Man must undo all accomplishments brought forth to the present day, using Capitalism as a vehicle to have such a social-economic success, that undoing such a system, will make a just society, in accordance with them.

However, history has shown that Keynesian Economics have spelled disaster for a country, thereby, destabilizing the economic system, bring the country into a crisis, where Socialism, then full Communism can replace it.

Destabilization

After demoralizing a large population in a country like the United States, another psychological brainwashing process occurs at the same time, called "**Destabilization**". Yuri Bezmenov describes these phenomena, where Marxist Men and their Liberal dupes in the population start to radicalize three main areas that drive the Free-Market Competition and the stability of the society-as-a whole. These areas include;

Economy

Law and Order

Media

When it comes to the Economy, the objective of Marxist Men and their dupes is to completely-destroy the compromise in labor relations, between Employer and Employee. Where people use to settle their differences peacefully and legitimately, on a one-on-one or Employee-Management basis, has now become irrelevant in the present day.

Here, fake labor movements form, such as the Lesbian, Bisexual, Gay, Transvestite, and Queer (LGBTQ) Organizations, when it comes to Gender and Sexual orientation in the workplace, the Council on American-Islamic Relations (CAIR), Coalition Against Religion Discrimination (CARD) and many other groups, who have gain political power and finances to drive their agenda in the destruction between Employer and Employee relations, using either "*gender identity*" or "*Religious Equality*" as an excuse.

Other more influential organizations, such as the American Federation of Labor and Congress of Industrial Relations (AFL-CIO), which controls well over 69-plus affiliate public labor unions, are contributing to the destabilization of the American social-political system, in phenomenal ways. Most of these unions are headed and led by a multitude of Marxist Men and their duped Liberal minions because such entities wield major political power to stir public opinion and by their lobbying efforts to shape federal government policy.

It's been known for some time, but usually denied by these unions, that tactics of "getting what they want" from Employers who operate with them includes, blackmailing, intimidation, false media attention and other tactics that are far worse in definition and scope, while maintaining that they operate under the mask of fighting for "*worker's rights*".

As for Law and Order, when the Destabilizing process has commenced, an, even more, change in perception on the American public is being deceived as something that has been artificially created. For example, Law Enforcement Officers in the past were portrayed as individuals who were deemed heroic by their image, which requires them to patrol the streets to fight against crime and criminals who conduct them and create an environment to make the streets of this country safe and quiet again.

They were also seen by younger kids, as heroes in uniform and inside the community (next to Firefighters, Paramedics, and Military Personnel). In today's-society, under the process of Destabilization of the United States, the opposite becomes true. This time, criminals will be held as heroes of society, no matter whether-or-not they have been influenced by psychological disorders or illicit drugs, such as Marijuana, Heroin, Methamphetamines or Cocaine.

The false deception put out by Marxist Men and their duped media and/or supporters, blame such actions as "society's fault". Policemen and women have now been painted as dumb, ignorant, weak on the inside and have a superiority complex, in which their tactics and actions against the so-called loving criminal lie, are abused by their power and force, especially on Minorities.

Here, groups such as the LBGTQ communities, communist front groups like Black Lives Matters (BLM), La Raza (the Race) will rise to the surface and make themselves politically relevant and expedient under the cloak of "*civil rights*". At this point, these and other groups who have been duped or paid criminally will have violent clashes between Law Enforcement Officers, sometimes using deadly force as necessary. We have seen these types of actions transpired many times, over the past several years, ending in riots, looting of personal property and burning of businesses in wake of the deaths of Trayvon Martin, Michael Brown, Philandro Castile, Alton Sterling, Freddie Gray, Seville Smith, Eric Gardner and Keith Lamont Scott between 2012 and now (2016).

Some incidents, between American society that included clashes of Law Enforcement Officials, causing similar damages to private and public property occurred between the years 2010 and 2011, courtesy of the Marxist front group called Occupy Wall Street (OWS). In each case, the unelected and ideological media, via the major television networks like ABC, CBS, NBC, and CNN have been there to not just cover these incidents of anarchical violence between these groups and police, but to stoke the flame of aggression towards Law Enforcement Officials to drive public opinion in the way, they themselves want to drive it.

These issues are instrumental in the fundamental transformation of the United States of America, into a Socialist/Communist based society, envisioned by many as the savior of mankind's ills in the world.

Crisis

Directly after the destabilization of the country, the process of "**Crisis**" is developed. At this point in America, the legitimate bodies of the governmental power structure, law and order, defense systems and relationships with our allies overseas, completely collapse. During this process, ***the United States of America ceases to function as a nation***. There are two ways that a crisis of this magnitude could completely, annihilate this country in its entirety;

A Civil War

Foreign Invasion

During the crisis, a civil war will commence where bloody riots, clashes, and all-out anarchy will begin when one set of citizens, fight another set of citizens within the same country. Unlike the U.S. Civil War fought between 1861-1866, this new civil war will not be organized as military armies fighting each other.

In this crisis, it will be every man, woman, and child for themselves, because the power structure of the country will no longer be effective any form or shape to restore law and order anymore. As for Foreign Invasion, this can take place in many ways. Some portions of this, we are witnessing now seeing with our own eyes, at the southern border with Mexico of the United States.

Such "invaders" will come through the borders of the United States, in so large of numbers, that it will be almost impossible to stem the flow of illegitimate foreign personnel, who harbor the ideological intent, on destroying the country from within.

As of this writing, there is an ongoing debate as to the 550% increase of illegal immigrants from middle eastern countries like war-torn Syria, by Marxist Men inside the Democrat Party. There have been numerous reports that have proved, that their true intentions are to harm the citizens of the United States and replace its power structure under what is called "***Sharia Law***". With this influx of people, a lot of them are able-bodied males between the ages of 18-30, that law and order will no longer be possible to maintain.[32,33,34]

Written history has shown these two crisis conditions have happened, like when the Soviet Union invaded Eastern European countries like Czechoslovakia and Poland shortly after the ending of World War II and lasting throughout the 1950's and '60's. Other countries in recent history, had the same kind of foreign invasion, like in June 1950, when the Asian country of South Korea, as invaded by North Korea with the Red Chinese Army, with the help of the Soviet Union in 1950. The same can be said about the invasion of South Vietnam by the North, resulting in over a 10-year war provided by the United States and her allies, causing the deaths of 55,000-plus U.S. personnel and over 5 million Vietnamese. We have seen it in places like Lebanon, Grenada, Afghanistan in 1979.

We are seeing it right now in countries like Germany, France, and England.

If this country was to fall into a crisis mode, if we the American people allow it to happen to us, as Yuri Bezmenov and other former KGB Agents defectors from the old Soviet Union, there will be no other place where we, the people, will be able to run to. It is at this point, where the self-appointed rulers of society, who were instrumental into demoralizing the population, begin to claim power in the form of *"Committees"*, *"Czars"* or *"Revolutionary Committees"*.

During the crisis process, if such political power entities are denied, either by the ineffective government or by the people of the United States, such committees will take their power by force, usually resulting in the loss of many innocent lives in the process. Here, these committees will wield such enormous power and enforcement, that they will transform into a "quasi-type" government, which will have the power over judgment, the power of execution, power over legislation and judiciary proceedings.

These situations can be clearly seen currently in the South American country of Venezuela, under their current President and Marxist Dictator, Nicholas Maduro. Maduro, who was Hugo Chavez's Vice-President, assumed power of the country, when Chavez, died from Cancer on March 5, 2013.[35]

Since taking over power, Maduro has continued to instill Full-Communism principles throughout its society, in accordance with Marx and Engels's **Communist Manifesto** and **Das Kapital**, modernized along the lines of Vladimir Lenin, Joseph Stalin and the Castro Brothers in Cuba. This has resulted in some sort of Police State, where the country's military, and **_not_** law enforcement personnel, have assumed the role of societal law enforcement, where the citizens have no rights to peaceful protest and assembly, free speech or freedom to own personal property

Food and fuel have been rationed, accordance with governmental policy, causing said government of Venezuela to set price-controls of commodities and take-over of privately-owned industries, resulting in a severe economic meltdown. The country has a very high unemployment rate of over 8.0%, causing a staggering 82% poverty-rate throughout the country.[36,37,38] The situation has become so grim, that people have not only resulted in a large Black Market economic system, but reports have even shown that in certain parts of the country, Venezuelan citizens, have resorted to primitive hunting of birds, stray cats and dogs to use as food for their families.[39,40,41]

Most of these so-called committees will be headed by one person, who has not played a part in the Demoralization or Destabilization processes. Prior to the ending of crisis-mode in a country, such as the United States, because of all the anarchical violence and power structure breakdown, the population will be looking for some type of a "savior" and some form of a centralized government to help solve problems.

This savior will take the quasi-type government, build off them and make such committees and czars become a part of the almighty new American Federal Government, in which all positions may be filled with Marxist Men, in which afterwards, the last and final psychological subversion process will begin, which will last indefinitely, called "**_Normalization_**".

Normalization

Normalization is considered a cynical expression that was coined by the Soviet Union propaganda machine when the Russians invaded Czechoslovakia in 1968. What normalization **_does mean_**, is that all crisis actions inside the country like the United States have been controlled.

Here, the self-appointed rulers of society are no longer needed anymore; their job is completed.

The country needs to be stabilized, with the use of force, for Socialism to take place prior to the installation of Full Communism later-on.

All entities, such as self-created committees, czars, and communist front groups will have no purpose to be used anymore. The new Socialist Government of what would no longer be the United States of America must go; meaning they will be marked for *"Liquidation"* or *"Purged"* from the new society altogether.

The following groups of people, whose job was to Demoralize and Destabilize the country and bring it into crisis mode, are the people who will be marked for extermination during this period of normalization;

All self-appointed committees, czars or movements

All Civil Rights Leaders

All Communist Front Groups like Black Lives Matter (BLM), La Rasa, Democrat Socialists of America (DSA)

All leaders of Public Service Labor Unions

Leaders and members of the LGBTQ Community

Marxist-Leninists

Marxist-Leninist Professors and Education Teachers

Business Leaders and major Chief Executive Officers (CEO's) of large Corporations

Hollywood Actors/Actresses/Entertainers

Any-and-all opposition groups not mentioned

The groups above will all have to be eliminated, or murdered by forces who will be loyal to the new Socialist Government. Some of the people who are members of these groups and organizations, maybe publicly executed by firing squads, hangings, or secretly become "*missing*" without a word or mention as to what happened to them or why.

Many countries have conducted such purges to key members of their populations in this way and in some countries, like in Syria at this very moment, along with the Islamic State of Iraq and Syria (ISIS) are doing this very thing. Other examples include the country of Iraq, under the Dictatorship of Saddam Hussein, who solved dissents within his country after he took power, by committing mass murder of men, women, and children, mutilating them by decapitation and burying the bodies in unmarked mass graves throughout the country.

During the Vietnam War, when the Battle for Hue City commenced in February 1968, as a part of the TET Offensive, 74,000 North Vietnamese Army (NVA) and Communist-led Vietcong, with help of the Soviet Union's KGB, sent infiltrators into that city, months before the invasion, collecting names and locations of those who allied themselves with the United States. Within 24 hours of the NVA and Vietcong invasion and holding of that city for only two days, over 2,800 residents from Hue City were rounded up by the Vietcong, Men, Women, and Children, taken to the outskirts of the city and mass-murdered with machine guns into opened-pit, mass graves.

After the North Vietnamese forces invaded the South in April 1975, after the American pullout of her military forces and the fall of Saigon, during the NVA and Viet Cong's "*Spring Offensive*". Those persons who were not evacuated by the Americans, how for so long aligned themselves with us, ended up murdered, tortured or went "missing", never to be heard again.

Don't think this could happen here in the United States of America? It can and we are well on the way to the crisis point, if we, the people of this country, stop this process by Marxist Men and their Liberal dupes from trying to destabilize the country.

American soldiers during the Tet Offensive

(Courtesy of Marines.mil)

"The more you can increase fear of drugs and crime, welfare mothers, immigrants, and aliens, the more you control all the people."[1]

Noam Chomsky

Meme creation of The United Socialist States of America (USSA).

(Author's Collection)

There is one problem with the quotation above, that the so-called Intellectual and Marxist dupe Noam Chomsky failed to point out. Who is responsible for increasing the fear of drugs, crimes, welfare dependency, open borders and the like to control "all the people"?

It isn't the Conservative Movement who are doing such things in the United States, but those who are Marxist Men like him and many others, who instill such fear on the public psyche with the explicit intention to control the population, destroy the system of Capitalism and Free-Market Principles of the country and usher in worldwide domination. By destroying the culture and sacred institutions of American society, you must have such a plan in place, to demoralize, destabilize and bring the country into crisis mode to replace the "old society" with one where everything "is better for the whole of society" and not rugged individualism.

In the Communist Manifesto, Marx and Engels not only just outlined the six principles of the Communist Revolution but the basic blueprint in which all so-called "advanced countries" must follow to change society into a new form. Called the "***Ten Planks of Communism***", this blueprint is structured like the Ten Commandments found in the Judaic-Christian Religion. However, the idea behind the Ten Planks is to provide the basis of economic transformation of countries from Free-Market Principles to Socialism, where the almighty state dictates and operate means of production in a Socialist-Communist society (in order of precedence);[2,3,4]

Abolition of property in land and application of all rents of land to public purposes

A heavy progressive or graduated income tax

Abolition of all rights of inheritance

Confiscation of the property of all emigrants and rebels

Centralization of credit in the banks of the state, by means of a national bank with state capital and exclusive monopoly

Centralization of the means of communication and transportation in the hands of the state

Extension of factories and instruments of production owned by the state; the bringing into cultivation of waste lands, and the improvement of the soil generally in accordance with a common plan

Equal obligation of all to work. Establishment of industrial armies, especially for agriculture

Combination of agriculture with manufacturing industries; gradual abolition of all the distinction between town and country by a more equable distribution of the populace over the country

Free education for all children in public schools. Abolition of children's factory labor in its present form. Combination of education with industrial production, etc.

Once the Ten Planks of Communism has been implemented, Marx and Engels further concluded that *"class distinction will have disappeared and all production has been concentrated in the hands of a vast association of the whole nation, the public power [structure] will lose its political character."*

What the Ten Planks really did do, unfortunately, especially in the United States, was to massively increase the size and political power inside the Federal Government. The Ten Planks gave such power and control of America, to the point where almost everything in our lives has been regulated by bureaucrats in Washington D.C. and other places.

For example, *"Abolition of Private Property and the application of all rents of land to public purposes"* have created such laws and actions such as Zoning Ordinances, Personal Property Taxes, Acquisition of land via the Bureau of Land Management (BLM), and *"Eminent Domain"*.[5,6,7,8,9]

The latter law is where Federal, State, and Local governments may seize private property for public usage, following payment of just compensation to the owner of said property.

Under the Second Plank of Communism, Marx and Engels advocated for "**A heavy progressive or graduated income tax**", where the rich or Bourgeois are taxed at a rate where profits made by them are taken away gradually and given to the state.

An example of this began with the passage of the 16th Amendment of the U.S. Constitution, passed by the U.S. Congress on July 2, 1909. The Constitutional Amendment was ratified by the states on February 3, 1913, which authorized Congress the power to lay and collect taxes on *incomes*, from whatever sources derived. The 16th Amendment also says that Congress can collect said taxes, without apportionment among several states, and without regard to any census or enumeration.[10,11,12,13]

This allowed the Federal, States, and Local Governments to legislate and set percentages of business, corporate and personal income tax rates to be paid to such governments to operate; "**paying your fair share**" in other words.

The Third Plank of Communism, "**Abolition of all rights of inheritance",** as Marx and Engels way to forbid any personal property and monies or anything of value, from passing such wealth down from individuals to their heirs upon their death, without the State taxing such products. Inheritance, in their minds, would prolong or extend the Bourgeoisie society, which needed to be destroyed to rebuild society, and led by the Proletariat class of people.

Laws like the Federal and State Estate Tax Act of 1916, was the first of such rules and regulations that addressed this plank of Communism. However, such taxes became very unpopular with the public and by 2016, only eight states impose an Inheritance Tax, ranging from as low as 1 percent to as high as 20 percent on the value of the property or asset that you inherit.[14,15]

The eight states that have these tax laws that govern Inheritance are Tennessee, Iowa, Indiana, Kentucky, Maryland, Nebraska, New Jersey and Pennsylvania. The Fourth Plank of Communism, "**Confiscation of the property of all emigrants and rebels**" is done in the United States when the Federal Government Issues Tax Liens, or seizures of private property, using Asset Forfeiture Laws, or when the Internal Revenue Service (IRS) confiscate capital assets without due process.

The Fifth Plank of Communism, "**Centralization of credit in the banks of the state, by means of a national bank with state capital**

and exclusive monopoly", is simply called *"The Federal Reserve Act of 1913"*. Under the Liberal Democrat President Woodrow Wilson, members of the 63rd Congress, passed the act on December 23, 1913, establishing the U.S. Federal Reserve System. Commonly called *"The FED"*, they are the Central Bank of the United States of America, which manages the country's monetary policy. They also manage the following aspects of the U.S. Economic System;

1. *Influencing money and credit conditions in the economy*

2. *Provide stabilization of prices and full employment*

3. *Supervising banks and financial institutions*

4. *Maintaining the stability of the nation's financial system*

5. *Operating the nation's payment system*.

The Fed is a private entity, whose Board of Directors are appointed by the President of the United States, confirmed by the U.S. Senate to serve for one non-renewable 14-year term. This also means that the FED cannot be audited by Congress of its operation because the act prohibits such accountability on purpose.[16]

The Sixth Plank of Communism, "Centralization **of the means of communication and transportation in the hands of the state**", is the United States of America, these entities are called The Federal Communications Commission (FCC), Department of Transportation (DOT), Department of Homeland Security (DHS) and the following;

1. *Executive Orders 10990, Reestablishing the Federal Safety Council*

2. *Executive Order 10995, Assigning Telecommunication Management Functions*

3. *Executive Order 10997, Assigning Emergency Preparedness Functions to the Secretary of the Interior*

4. *Executive Order 11003, Assigning Emergency Preparedness Functions to the Administrator of the*

Federal Aviation Agency

5. *Executive Order 11005, Assigning Emergency Preparedness Functions to the Interstate Commerce Commission*

The purpose of these agencies and Executive Orders is to control all communication and transportation assets of the country in case of a national emergency, as designated by the President of the United States, the state will control all communication and transportation assets of the country.

This includes all Radio Broadcasts, Television Broadcasts, Internet and Phone Services to include Cell Phone operations.[16,17,18,19] The Seventh Plank of Communism, "**Extension of factories and instruments of production owned by the state; the bringing into cultivation of waste lands, and the improvement of the soil generally in accordance with a common plan**".

One can find such activities where a multitude of governmental entities within the Executive Branch of the Federal Government, with help from private foundations, are reclaiming land, including land that has been abandoned in the inner cities like St. Louis and Detroit.

Instead of improving the economic development consisting of building new houses and increasing business investment in such communities, to bring up the quality of life in these areas in the effort to eradicate poverty, such after-mentioned cities and others, are allowing the Seventh Plank of Communism to take root. {no pun indented} Cities like St. Louis, Detroit, San Francisco and other major cities are creating what is called "*Community Gardening Programs*" (CGP).

Such programs are operated mainly by the *American Community Gardening Association (ACGA)*, where these gardening programs are in-acted in eleven states, inside low-income, economically-depressed areas, that cultivate agricultural plants, fruits and vegetables, using non-repayable Grants, from both Executive Branch governmental agencies and private foundations. Leading the charge of this program, Federal Agencies such as the U.S. Department of Agriculture (USDA), Department of Health and Human Services (DHHS), Department of Commerce, and the Environment Protection Agency (EPA), are administering taxpayer money to fund these community gardens.

Foundations such as the St. Louis-based Monsanto Foundation, Wisconsin Medical Society, the National Youth Rights Association (NYRA), and Students for a Democratic Society (SDS), plus others, directly or indirectly fund these activities. All the previously mentioned private foundations, also have known ties to funding "social justice", "equality" and "civil rights" causes, headed by the Communist Party![20,21,22,23,24,25,26,27]

The mission statement of the American Community Gardening Association (ACGA) to what Marx and Engels have stated in the Communist Manifesto, which also takes us to visit the Eighth and Ninth Planks of Communism;

"Promote community food and ornamental gardening, preservation, and management of open space, urban forestry and integrating planning and management of developing urban and rural lands."

Such organizations have advocated to continue to regulate and control more manufacturing industries than ever before, and mirror them up with all forms of agriculture. Both Eighth and Ninth Planks of Communism states;

"Equal obligation of all to work. Establishment of industrial armies, especially for agriculture"

and

"Combination of agriculture with manufacturing industries; gradual abolition of all the distinction between town and country by a more equable distribution of the populace over the country"

Next to the Community Gardening Programs, the equal obligation for all, including the mentally ill and the avocation for foreign-born workers to enter the United States illegally and establish so-called industrial armies, for agriculture, since the late-1960's, such actions have been put into place, starting with the Lyndon Johnson Administration. Plus, as the inner-cities become no longer major population centers as they once were, the city limits of Chicago, St. Louis, and Detroit, have been gradually losing large populations of residents, to the suburbs, because of high taxation, uncontrollable crime and drug-trafficking/usage, and gang violence. It is here, where Marx and Engels proclaimed that the "**gradual abolition of all distinction between town and country**" has been taken place as well.

Another perfect example to illustrate the Eighth Plank of Communism is *Executive Order 11000, Assigning Emergency Preparedness Functions to the Secretary of Labor*, signed by the President John F. Kennedy on February 16, 1962.

This order establishes that the Secretary of Labor develops plans and contingencies to mobilize American Citizens to provide manpower in the case of a declared national emergency. However, this Order was revoked under President Ronald Reagan by Executive Order 126046, signed November 18, 1988. However, the story just doesn't end here.

There is more.

Executive Order 11647 "Federal Regional Councils" was signed by President Richard M. Nixon on February 12, 1972, consolidated all 50 states in America and divided them into 10 regions as shown below, backed up by the passage of Public Law 89-136.

The latter law was signed by President Lyndon B. Johnson, which created 10 "*Super Regions*" that will function like a separate country within the United States in case of a national emergency. These 10 super regions would set the stage for the abolishment of every level of government in the United States, to include the county and local levels. These same regions will also be governed in accordance with *Executive Order 11921* titled, *"Adjusting Emergency Preparedness Assignments to Organizational and Functional Changes in Federal Department and Agencies"*, signed by former President Gerald Ford on June 11, 1976, allowed the Federal Emergency Management Agency (FEMA) to establish control over the mechanisms of production and distribution of energy sources, wages, salaries, credit and the flow of money in U.S. Financial Institutions in ***any undefined*** National Emergency inside these 10 Super Regions!

Today, these same super regions are popularly known as *"FEMA Regions"*, which will control every aspect of the population inside the Super Regions, under their control. There is even more. Executive Order 11921 further states that if a national emergency is declared by the President, the U.S. Congress ***cannot review the action for six months!***

In other words, FEMA would have unelected regulatory powers which will control every aspect of the United States, in which their actions cannot be investigated or reviewed for a period of six months. E.O. 11921, therefore, strengthens E.O. 11647 and Public Law 89-136. Lastly, both Executive Orders 11647 and 11921 were consolidated into another **Executive Order 13603** titled *"National Defense Resources Preparedness"*, signed by President Barack Obama on March 16, 2012.

Executive Order 13603 reassigned responsibility of the 10 super regions from FEMA to the Department of Homeland Security (DHS). However, FEMA has become a separate department under DHS, therefore retains its original control of the 10 regions as designated under the other Executive Orders previously mentioned. Another change in Barack Obama's order, which is not contained in any previous Executive Order that any other President signed, authorizes the President to conduct the following;

1. *Requisition (take) private property,*

2. *Force industries to expand production and the supply of basic resources,*

3. *Impose wages and price controls,*

4. *Settle labor disputes (probably by the barrel of a gun),*

5. *Control consumer and real estate credit,*

6. *Establish contractual priorities and allocate raw materials towards national defense.*

In other words, Executive Order 13603 is a massive power grab of tyrannical proportions, that coincides that Eighth and Ninth Planks of Communism. As for the equitable distribution of the population over the country, people will either be forced to relocate, just like the Five Civilized Tribes of the Cherokee Native Indian Nation did, under Democrat President Andrew Jackson, in the 1830's, during the **"Trail of Tears March"**, or people will be 'assigned' to work via population controlled entities or "centers", such as Planned Parenthood, or through the Department of Labor, will be based on the number of persons needed to work in each of the 10 regions.

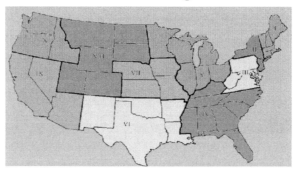

The 10 "Super Regions" of the United States Established in 1972 (above)

The Current 10 FEMA Regions (below)

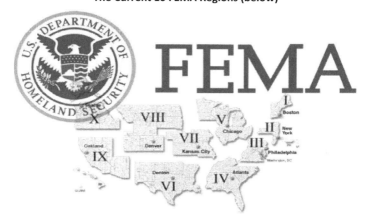

As for the Tenth and final Plank of Communism, **"Free education for all children in public schools. Abolition of children's factory labor in its present form. Combination of education with industrial production, etc."** can easily be seen during the past Presidential Primaries for both political parties of the United States.

Democrat/Independent and Marxist Man Senator Bernard "Bernie" Sanders from Vermont, advocated when he was running against Hillary Clinton for the Democrat nomination for President, advocated for "Free College" for all students.[28,29,30] This mantra caught on quickly by the duped, younger generation of Millennials, because of the notion that free college would mean free opportunity for them to get higher-paying jobs.

However, free opportunity doesn't mean that you will get any high-paying job whatsoever when there aren't any ***paying jobs*** out there, to begin with!

On top of that, nothing is free, when it comes to economics and social issues because somebody pays somewhere. Which means, more working Americans will be taxed for their pay, that they truly work for, to take care of their families for the younger generation to do nothing for their achievements, which in turn, ***will make them subjected to the State***.

These young people will fulfill the Tenth Plank of Communism, in which their Public Education Degree would be worthless, ending in becoming Slaves with industrial production just as it mentions above. Slaves to the almighty State, which will not provide a better life for themselves, but eternal misery because of lies and deception by evil Marxist Men such as Sanders and others who have been conditioned to lie in your face and take it as cheap value.

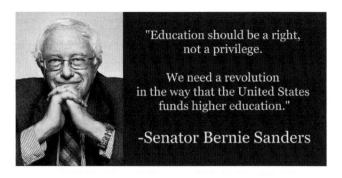

"Education should be a right, not a privilege.

We need a revolution in the way that the United States funds higher education."

-Senator Bernie Sanders

The 45 Goals of Communism

Best-selling author of the ***Naked Communist***, W. Cleon Skousen, stated this in his book in regards to how certain sections of the population in the U.S. have been subverted to accept the premise of Communism;

"The biggest mistake of the West has been allowing itself to drift into a state of mental stagnation, apathy, and inaction."[31]

Skousen's statement is spot-on, considering that the pathetic state of what is called "***Political Correctness***" have taken over everyday speech and life. Marxist Men have been teaching our younger generation not to offend anybody, which firmly took hold and became more prevalent in society during the 1990's.

It was also at-this-time, where a significant decrease in patriotism, loyalty, rugged individualism and suppression of the incentive to succeed on your own, through hard work and opportunities provided for you, lost traction in the mainstream public. Political Correctness (PC), has essentially paralyzed the aforementioned, of love for country, the spirit of freedom and democracy and replaced it with a state of mind of weakness and vulnerability.

Some of you may ask, how did all this start in such a short period-of-time?

The answer is simple.

We as American citizens have allowed the Communists to take over our original way of thinking and rationality of the world around us, and reshape our thinking in a way which suits them.

Again, the goal of these Communists is to destroy the last beacon of freedom throughout the world, the United States of America and the Capitalistic Society. Marxist Men along with their sociopathic 'useful idiots' dupes, afflicted with NPD, have created a major campaign of Psychological Warfare on their own brethren's, to soften up the United States for the final takeover.

This type of Psychological Warfare is an undeclared war of attrition, that doesn't consist of uniformed armies, weapons or materials to dupe people to believe in what Marxist Men want you to believe in. It requires that a chosen amount of people, who can be loud, angry, vocal and demonstrate hate and discontent in front of the Leftist Media, to stoke the flames of this so-called pretend oppression, to get you to believe that they are the-majority-of the population, in which they are not!

In Skousen's book, he outlined a set of goals called "***The 45 Goals of Communism***"[32], which he lists specifically the Marxist Men '***Plan of Action*'** to wage such a psychological war against us, the American People. These goals prove the above-mentioned points that we have allowed the Communists to take over our way of thinking.

Consider the timing of Mr. Skousen's Marxist Plan of Action, that's pretty much is still taking place in America, even more, that during the 1960's. During that time in history, when he pinned these goals in his book, just like in the present-day, the 1960's were filled with Leftist anarchy, Segregationists in the Democrat Party, the rapid spread of Marxist-Leninism from during the American Civil Rights Movement, to Cuba, to the Congo under Marxist Patrice Lumumba, Uganda under Communist Idi Amin, Vietnam, the China and many other places.

Many officials in the U.S. Federal Government have had concerns about incidents like these, which caused some of them to pay really-close attention as to why the spreading of Communism was taken place, even after Senator Joseph McCarthy's outcry about Communist infiltration in the U.S. Government. One of these officials who seriously took note of these incidents was House of Representative Albert S. Herlong Jr. (1909-1995).[33]

Sometime in late 1962, Congressman Herlong was approached by a concerned citizen in his district named Patricia Nordman, who also was one of the editors of the De Land Florida Courier, when she talked to him about the uncontrollable spread of Communism.

Ms. Nordman used her argument based on Skousen's book and asked if Herlong would address these fear and concerns during the next session of Congress. Herlong agreed and on January 10, 1963, Herlong addressed the House Chamber to the 88th Congress and entered into the Congressional Record, as follows;[34,35]

Communist Goals (1963)
Congressional Record--Appendix, pp. A34-A35
January 10, 1963
Current Communist Goals
EXTENSION OF REMARKS OF HON. A. S. HERLONG, JR. OF FLORIDA
IN THE HOUSE OF REPRESENTATIVES
Thursday, January 10, 1963

Mr. HERLONG. Mr. Speaker, Mrs. Patricia Nordman of De Land, Fla., is an ardent and articulate opponent of communism, and until recently published the De Land Courier, which she dedicated to the purpose of alerting the public to the dangers of communism in America.
At Mrs. Nordman's request, I include in the RECORD, under unanimous consent, the following "Current Communist Goals," which she identifies as an excerpt from "The Naked Communist," by Cleon Skousen:

[From "The Naked Communist," by Cleon Skousen]

CURRENT COMMUNIST GOALS

1. U.S. acceptance of coexistence as the only alternative to atomic war.

2. U.S. willingness to capitulate in preference to engaging in atomic war.

3. Develop the illusion that total disarmament [by] the United States would be a demonstration of moral strength.

4. Permit free trade between all nations regardless of Communist affiliation and regardless of whether or not items could be used for war.

5. Extension of long-term loans to Russia and Soviet satellites.

6. Provide American aid to all nations regardless of Communist domination.

7. Grant recognition of Red China. Admission of Red China to the U.N.

8. Set up East and West Germany as separate states in-spite of Khrushchev's promise in 1955 to settle the German question by free elections under supervision of the U.N.

9. Prolong the conferences to ban atomic tests because the United States has agreed to suspend tests as long as negotiations are in progress.

10. Allow all Soviet satellites individual representation in the U.N.

11. Promote the U.N. as the only hope for mankind. If its charter is rewritten, demand that it be set up as a one-world government with its own independent armed forces. (Some Communist leaders believe the world can be taken over as easily by the U.N. as by Moscow. Sometimes these two centers compete with each other as they are now doing in the Congo.)

12. Resist any attempt to outlaw the Communist Party.

13. Do away with all loyalty oaths.

14. Continue giving Russia access to the U.S. Patent Office.

15. Capture one or both of the political parties in the United States.

16. Use technical decisions of the courts to weaken basic American institutions by claiming their activities violate civil rights.

17. Get control of the schools. Use them as transmission belts for socialism and current Communist propaganda. Soften the curriculum. Get control of teachers' associations. Put the party line in textbooks.

18. Gain control of all student newspapers.

19. Use student riots to foment public protests against programs or organizations which are under Communist attack.

20. Infiltrate the press. Get control of book-review assignments, editorial writing, policymaking positions.

21. Gain control of key positions in radio, TV, and motion pictures.

22. Continue discrediting American culture by degrading all forms of artistic expression. An American Communist cell was told to "eliminate all good sculpture from parks and buildings, substitute shapeless, awkward and meaningless forms."

23. Control art critics and directors of art museums. "Our plan is to promote ugliness, repulsive, meaningless art."

24. Eliminate all laws governing obscenity by calling them "censorship" and a violation of free speech and free press.

25. Break down cultural standards of morality by promoting pornography and obscenity in books, magazines, motion pictures, radio, and TV.

26. Present homosexuality, degeneracy and promiscuity as "normal, natural, healthy."

27. Infiltrate the churches and replace revealed religion with "social" religion. Discredit the Bible and emphasize the need for intellectual maturity which does not need a "religious crutch."

28. Eliminate prayer or any phase of religious expression in the schools on the ground that it violates the principle of "separation of church and state."

29. Discredit the American Constitution by calling it inadequate, old-fashioned, out of step with modern needs, a hindrance to cooperation between nations on a worldwide basis.

30. Discredit the American Founding Fathers. Present them as selfish aristocrats who had no concern for the "common man."

31. Belittle all forms of American culture and discourage the teaching of American history on the ground that it was only a minor part of the "big picture." Give more emphasis to Russian history since the Communists took over.

32. Support any socialist movement to give centralized control over any part of the culture--education, social agencies, welfare programs, mental health clinics, etc.

33. Eliminate all laws or procedures which interfere with the operation of the Communist apparatus.

34. Eliminate the House Committee on Un-American Activities.

35. Discredit and eventually dismantle the FBI.

36. Infiltrate and gain control of more unions.

37. Infiltrate and gain control of big business.

38. Transfer some of the powers of arrest from the police to social agencies. Treat all behavioral problems as psychiatric disorders which no one but psychiatrists can understand [or treat].
39. Dominate the psychiatric profession and use mental health laws as a means of gaining coercive control over those who oppose Communist goals.

40. Discredit the family as an institution. Encourage promiscuity and easy divorce.

41. Emphasize the need to raise children away from the negative influence of parents. Attribute prejudices, mental blocks and retarding of children to suppressive influence of parents.

42. Create the impression that violence and insurrection are legitimate aspects of the American tradition; that students and special-interest groups should rise up and use ["]united force["] to solve economic, political or social problems.

43. Overthrow all colonial governments before native populations are ready for self-government.

44. Internationalize the Panama Canal.

45. Repeal the Connally reservation so the United States cannot prevent the World Court from seizing jurisdiction [over domestic problems. Give the World Court jurisdiction] over nations and individuals alike.

As you can see, clearly the 45 Goals of Communism has extended in such areas throughout the United States and its territories that these goals mentioned should seriously alarm everyone reading this book!

To put things in perspective, however, one individual addressed these goals of Communism with so much skill and poise, that his outstanding contribution to society and to the United States of America allowed him to one of the most revered and outstanding radio personality of the modern era; his name was Paul Harvey.

If I were the Devil Broadcast

Paul Harvey receiving the Presidential Medal of Freedom in 2004
(Courtesy of Wikimedia)

The late-great Radio personality, Paul Harvey Aurandt, known as Paul Harvey, was born in Tulsa, Oklahoma on September 4, 1918, and passed away on February 28, 2009, at the age of 90.

During a span of over 70 years in talk radio, Paul Harvey was known for his show "The Rest of the Story", which was broadcasted in ABC Radio Networks. His radio program, which included current news, events that ended with a poem which described some of the very events in the United States and the World that were taken place. His audience was estimated at 24 million people, where people listened to on 1,200-plus radio stations, 400-plus Armed Forces Networks and had written editorials that expanded to 300 newspapers publications in America.[36,37]

Of course, being a Conservative Talk Radio host during that span of time not only awarded him with many friends in high places but also gained him enemies in such high places as well. However, his close associations with big-time government officials, such as the former FBI Director J. Edgar Hoover, Senator Joseph McCarthy, Reverend Billy Graham and Minister George Vanderman, pretty much protected him from such scrutiny from the diabolical Communist Left.

His radio program was famous for opening his radio program "Standby for NEWS!" and ending with either "**Paul Harvey...Good Day**" or "**Now you heard the rest of the story**" in later years. However, in 1965, during the height of some of the fiercest geopolitical turmoil in American History, Paul Harvey poems, in which he told was the truth of the issues he spoke about, was named "*If I were the Devil*".

This same broadcast of his poem, which clearly mirrors accurately most of author Cleon Skousen's 45 Goals of Communism, has gain popularity today, as Communism and Marxist Men rear their ugly heads again in the public psyche in their effort to destroy America. Below is the transcript of this poem;

"If I were the Devil,
If I was the Prince of Darkness,
I'd want to engulf the whole world in darkness,
And I would have a third of its real estate and four-fifths of its population
But I wouldn't be happy
Until I had seized the ripest apple on the tree
T'is thee

So I'd set about, however, necessary to take over the United States
I'd subvert the Churches first
I'd begin with a campaign of whispers
With the wisdom of a serpent,
I would whisper to you as I whispered to Eve
'Do as you please'

To the young, I would whisper
That the Bible is a myth
I would convince them that Man created God
Instead of the other way around
I would confide that what is bad is good
And what is good is 'square'
And to the Old, I would teach to pray after me;
'Our Father, which art in Washington'

And then I would get organized

I'd educate authors in how to make lurid literature exciting
So that anything else would appear dull and uninteresting
I'd threaten TV with dirtier movies and vice-versa
I'd peddle Narcotics to whom I could
I'd sell alcohol to Ladies and Gentlemen of Distinction

I'd tranquilized the rest with pills

If I were the Devil,
I'd soon have families at war with themselves
Churches at war with themselves
And nations at war with themselves
Until each in its turn was consumed
And with promises of higher ratings
I'd have mesmerizing media fanning the flames

If I were the Devil,
I would encourage Schools to refine young intellects
But neglect to discipline emotions
Just let those run wild
Until before you knew it
You'd have to have drug-sniffing Dogs and Metal Detectors
At every schoolhouse door

Within a decade, I'd have Prisons overflowing
I'd have Judges promoting Pornography
Soon I would evict God from the Courthouse
And then from the Schoolhouse
And then from the Houses of Congress
And in his own Churches
I would substitute Psychology for Religion
And Deify Science
I would lure Priests and Pastors
Into misusing boys and girls
And Church money

If I were the Devil,
I'd make the symbol of Easter an Egg
And the symbol of Christmas a bottle

If I were the Devil,
I would take from those who have
And I would give to those who wanted
Until I had killed the incentive of the ambitious
And what will you bet
I could get whole states to promote gambling
As-a-way to get rich
I would caution against extremes
In hard work

~ 91 ~

In patriotism
In moral conduct

I would convince the young that Marriage is old-fashioned
That swinging is more fun
That what you see on TV
Is the way to be

And I can undress you in public
And can lure you in bed
With diseases for which there is no cure
In other words,
If I was the Devil
I'd just keep right on doing what he's doing...

Paul Harvey...Good Day.

https://youtu.be/ZKgHeNTajDU

"The punishment which the wise suffer who refuse to take part in the government is to live under the government of worse men."[1]

Plato

To make the complicated easier to understand, one must look at the above paradigm shift in the United States of America using Layman's terms. In other words, how do they apply in today's geopolitical world of the 21st Century?

Let's take a portion of the 45 Goals of Communism, break them down in accordance with the past and current events and sum them up into one final-conclusion. This would allow you, the reader come to terms with yourself to understand that each of these goals is being completed as we speak.

However, there is still time for much of the American Population, Black, White and indifferent, to wake up and stop these actions before they become out of control to the point where no matter what we do, the United States of America as we know it, has been destroyed where nothing can be done to save her.

4./6.   *"Permit free trade between all nations regardless of Communist affiliation and regardless of whether or not items could be used for war."/ "Provide American aid to all nations regardless of Communist domination."*

The term "**Free Trade**" is a monomer term, that doesn't equate to anything close to "Free Trade" because somebody pays the costs of Importation and Exportation of goods, Taxes or Duties of goods and transportation of items between countries.

However, there are times where Free Trade Agreements with other countries whose government supports and control their societies as Communistic Economies, will result in addition prices for the American Consumer, but will put the American Worker and Businesses at a disadvantage, by lowering the quality of the goods being bought and lowering the standards for workers in said Communist countries. This is exactly what happened with the North American Free Trade Agreement (NAFTA) in 1996.[2,3]

Now, The Trans-Pacific Partnership (TPP) is a new "Free Trade" Agreement that has been advocated by the Obama Administration will finally complete this goal of Communism. Per a recent poll conducted by Politico-Harvard, shows that 65% of Americans oppose TPP, because of the fear that such a trade policy will allow U.S. Manufacturing jobs will be relocated overseas, causing high unemployment, stagnant wages and increasing cost of living.[4,5,6] Such Communist countries who will benefit handsomely from TPP are China, Vietnam, Laos, Myanmar and many Socialists countries in South America, like Columbia and Peru, by creating cheap labor to produce sub par goods, that are shipped to America that will cost the consumer to pay double or triple the price for these items, which will not last long.

11. *"Promote the U.N. as the only hope for mankind. If its charter is rewritten, demand that it be set up as a one-world government with its own independent armed forces. (Some Communist leaders believe the world can be taken over as easily by the U.N. as by Moscow. Sometimes these two centers compete with each other as they are now doing in the Congo.)"*

This Communist goal is real, and it has moved steadily towards completion, since the United Nations' founding in 1945. Affectionally known to many as "***The U.N.***", the original idea behind this organization was to address and solve three of Man's greatest issues throughout the world; poverty, war, and terrorism. Therefore the U.N.'s mantra has been stated as *"**Mankind's last and Best Hope for Peace**"*.

In other words, The U.N. was to bring all the world's countries together and solve the problems, to include ending wars.[7,8]

Unfortunately, this lie of solving Man's issues via The U.N. may sound good to many, but it is what it is; a big lie! Ever since 1945, Man has been in a constant state of conflict of civil war, poverty, terroristic warfare and injustice since then! It's been estimated by many that over 35,000,000 people have been killed and murdered by their own governments; the same governments that provide representatives to The U.N. Security Council.

Historically, Communist countries such as China, Rwanda, and Zimbabwe have used famine to destroy their own people, vice Communist countries like Bosnia, Herzegovina, Rwanda, Somalia and Sierra Leone have used civil wars which killed tens of thousands of innocent people.

The U.N.'s Charter, is written as an open-ended document, unlike the U.S. Constitution, it is based on Lenin and Stalin's Soviet Union Constitution, where they authorize limitations on rights, if those limits are prescribed by law.[9]

In other words, the U.N. Charter ***does not recognize any other higher power other than themselves!***

The U.N. answers ***to no one***, not even to their respective population of people whom they claim they represent! Each member of the U.N., consisting of 193 countries, is currently advocating and planning for an overwhelming expansion of becoming a one-world government, that will control every aspect of human activity, to include the United States of America!

The UN currently has a *"**Sustainable Development Agenda**"*, launched by the organization at its **Sustainable Development Summit**, held in New York City in September 2015. The goal of this summit of course, is not to provide a rich, free society, where everyone will dictate their own way of life, by providing the opportunity to succeed, but to forcefully destroy Capitalism and Free-Market Enterprise, then replace such system it with a one-world government, which will dictate how everyone should live!

How do you do that? Easy.

You create lies and deceptions, in-order for the rest of the global countries, within the United Nations, to allow themselves to be slowly and methodically, brainwashed to their liking. Subverted by Marxist Men to steadfastly give up their entire system of government, to the will of the U.N. While this is being done, a mantra is put in place, to make it appear, that such noble deeds/goals of the U.N. are being put into practice, for the "*good of humanity everywhere*". But, in-reality, this is a front by the Worldwide Communist organizations throughout the globe, to instill Marxist-Leninist Principles, to form a one-world government.

A *New World Order* so to speak.

For example, UNESCO, the United Nations Educational, Scientific and Cultural Organization focuses on everything being taught in the Public-School System throughout the world, including the United States, from teacher training, "*protecting*" important historical and cultural sites for future generations.

Accordingly, UNESCO is one of the many lead agencies within The U.N. that is pushing the 17-step strategic plan called "*Sustainable Development Goals*" (SDG), which will drive whole nations to submit all their power and regulatory processes to the *United Nations by 2030!*[10,11,12]

Yes, this includes the United States of America as well!

However, the caveat of below-listed goals may seem great idea-wise when one looks on the surface of each of the **17 Sustainable Goals**. However, beneath each goal, lays a much sinister, ideological purpose that shows, why *#11 of the Goals of Communism* is well on its way of being true;

1. *No Poverty*
2. *Zero Hunger*
3. *Good Health and Well Being*
4. *Quality Education*
5. *Gender Equality*

6. *Clean Water and Sanitation*
7. *Affordable and Clean Energy*
8. *Decent Work and Economic Growth*
9. *Industry, Innovation, and Infrastructure*
10. *Reduced Inequalities*
11. *Sustainable Cities and Communities*
12. *Responsible Consumption and Production*
13. *Climate Action*
14. *Life Below Water*
15. *Life on Land*
16. *Peace, Justice and Strong Institutions*
17. *Partnerships for the Goals*

Remember, every one of the 17 "*Sustainable Developmental Goals*" will be headed and ran by the ***United Nations and every listed organizations operated by them***; soon to be the true One-World Government or the "**Almighty State**" that Marx and Engels have envisioned.

The following is a list of United Nations Agencies tasked with the implementation of the after-mentioned Sustainable Developmental Goals. Remember, the listed agencies are bureaucratic entities of the **United Nations**;

>*UN's Intergovernmental Panel on Climate Change (UNIPCC)*
>*UN Development Programme (UNDP)*
>*UN's Children's Fund (UNICEF)*
>*UN's High Commissioner for Refugees (UNHCR)*
>*World Food Programme (WFP)*
>*UN Office on Drugs and Crime (UNODC)*
>*UN Population Fund (UNFPA)*
>*UN's Conference on Trade and Development (UNCTAD)*
>*UN Environmental Programme (UNEP)*
>*UN Relief and Works Agency for Palestine Refugees (UNRWA)*
>*UN-Women*
>*UN-Habitat*
>*World Bank*
>*World Bank Group*
>
>>*International Bank for Reconstruction and Development (IBRD)*

International Centre for Settlement of Investment Disputes (ICSID)

International Development Association (IDA)

International Finance Corporation (IFC)

Multilateral Investment Guarantee Agency (MIGA)

International Monetary Fund (IMF)
World Health Organization (WHO)
UN Educational, Scientific and Cultural Organization (UNESCO)
International Labor Organization (ILO)
Food and Agriculture Organization (FAO)
International Fund for Agricultural Development (IFAD)
International Maritime Organization (IMO)
World Meteorological Organization (WMO)
World Intellectual Property Organization (WIPO)
International Civilian Aviation Organization (ICAO)
International Telecommunication Union (ITU)
UN Industrial Development Organization (UNIDO)
Universal Postal Union (UPU)
UN World Tourism Organization (UNWTO)
Joint United Nations Programme on HIV/AIDS (UNAIDS)
UN Office for Disaster Reduction (UNISDR)
UN Office for Project Services (UNOPS)
International Atomic Energy Agency (IAEA)
World Trade Organization (WTO)
Preparatory Commission for the Comprehensive Nuclear-Test-Ban Treaty Organization (CTBTO)
Organization for the Prohibition of Chemical Weapons (OPCW)
International Organization for Migration (IOM)

15. *"Capture one or both of the political parties in the United States."*

This goal of transforming the United States into a one-world, Soviet Union-type political system, is very important for Marxist Men, especially when you can capture both the Democratic and Republican Parties and consolidate them into one.

The call to action by Marxists have been in development since the late 1920's and well into the 1930's. In 2016, as of this writing, one can find hard, tangible evidence of such actions by looking at this past Presidential Election of 2016.

The contrast between both parties is strikingly so different in views and ideologies, that one cannot miss the differences between them. For example, the Democrats want bigger government, massive regulations to govern everybody's lives daily, the lies and disinformation campaign being waged on a consistent basis. The idea behind such actions was to keep the rest of the American People in a state of emotional agitation, fear and panic, over purposely-created and/or manufactured crisis.

This issue really has taken a public stance when in April 2012, while being interviewed by Cable News Network (CNN)'s *"Situation Room"* program with Anchor Wolf Blitzer, where then Florida's Congressman and former Army Combat Brigade Commander, Colonel Allen West mentioned that he believed that between 78 to 81 members of Congress were actual members of the Communist Party of the United States (CPUSA)![13,14,15,16]

Of course, Allen West got crucified about this comment, even going so far as being called a *"McCarthyite"* by Wolf Blitzer. However, Mr. West's statement cannot be further from the truth.

As a matter of fact, most people who have not been duped by the Marxist Men lies and deception estimate that CPUSA memberships in Congress from both parties are much higher than what Colonel West stated. In Trevor Loudon's outstanding book, *"Enemies Within Communists, Socialists and Progressives in the U.S. Congress"* back up Colonel West's statement.[17]

Once you look at some of Congress member's fleeting association with various Marxist Front Groups, such as the Democratic Socialists of America (DSA), La Raza (The Race), Council for a Livable World (CLW), and many others, some of the members of Congress below, have been proven to be card-carrying CPUSA members, have the same objectives in-mind;

Black Congresswomen:

Barbara Lee (Democrat-California)

Maxine Waters (Democrat-California)

Eleanor Holmes Norton (Democrat Delegate, Wash. D.C.)

Corrine Brown (Democrat-Florida)

Sheila Jackson-Lee (Democrat-Texas)

Fredericka Wilson (Democrat-Florida)

Black Congressmen:

John Lewis (Democrat-Georgia)

John Conyers (Democrat-Michigan)

Keith "X" Ellison (Democrat-Minnesota)

Bobby Rush (Democrat-Illinois)

Donna Edwards (Democrat-Maryland)

William Lacy Clay Jr. (Democrat-Missouri)

Jim Clyburn (Democrat-South Carolina)

To destroy the USA in its entirety and transform it into something else; a false utopian dream that will never exist! All the above-mentioned politicians listed, and more, are also members of the **Congressional Progressive Caucus (CPC)**, and the **Congressional Black Caucus (CBC)**.

16. *"Use technical decisions of the courts to weaken basic American institutions by claiming their activities violate civil rights."*

Roe vs. Wade Supreme Court of the United States (SCOTUS) decision in 1973 was one of such many court decisions used to weaken our basic institutional traditions, in this case, the right for a woman to kill her unborn baby, via Abortion.[18,19,20,21]

Other cases that SCOTUS have ruled with the intent, are the **Defense of Marriage Act (DOMA) of 1996**. This piece of legislation was passed by an overwhelmingly Republican Congress on July 12, 1996, and signed into law by Democrat William J. "Bill" Clinton on

September 21, 1996. DOMA was challenged repeatedly by front groups aligned with LBGTQ community and activists.

DOMA was finally by SCOTUS in a 5-4 decision overruled DOMA on June 26, 2013, in the landmark case **United States vs. Windsor**, by stating that Marriage between a man and a woman is unconstitutional. The Justices determined that the act was "a deprivation of the liberty of the person protected by the Fifth Amendment." making the way for them to approve Same-Sex Marriage shortly thereafter.[22,23]

17. *"Get control of the schools. Use them as transmission belts for socialism and current Communist propaganda. Soften the curriculum. Get control of teachers' associations. Put the party line in textbooks."*

Photo of New Oxford High School (Pennsylvania) Band in their Pro-Soviet costumes in 2012.
(Courtesy of The New America)

No one can ignore or provide an excuse as to what number 17 of the 45 Goals of Communism is doing to our public education system, nationwide.

Marxist Men and their Progressive Dupes called 'Educators' are heavily influencing the teaching of Marxism in classrooms every day. Soviet Propagandist Defector Yuri Bezmenov has consistently stated that to change a country's population perception of reality, you must educate at least one generation of students in Marxist-Leninism before being challenged by Americanism. He wasn't wrong when he stated this.[24]

For example, The Public Education System's "***Common Core Curriculum***", was supposed to be an equal standard of classroom learning from Pre-K to 12th Grade, which supposed to get students advantage to compete academically with other countries in the world.[25] However, what the Common Core Curriculum does is put the power of educating children in Public Schools into the hands of the Federal Government, using monetary incentives for states, teacher unions, and local education administrators to teach the curriculum, instead of teaching the basics of English, Math, Science and History.

By doing these actions, it further softens the curriculum and comprehension of the student's learning ability, thereby providing the opportunity of "dumbing down" our kids for monetary gain[26,27].

There is more.

Besides dumbing down our kids in the public education system for them not comprehend, or even rationalize as to what they are supposed to learn, to compete in the Global Economy, tag along with the problem with the First Lady of The United States (FLOTUS) Michelle Obama's horrible National School Lunch Program. Implemented in 2012, the **National School Lunch Program (NSLP)** have been challenged to adverse cut back on both a number of lunch meals served to the nation's students, but dramatically reduce portion sizes of lunches. The effect has caused a large subpar quality of nutritional food, which is needed for younger students to learn effectively.[28,29,30,31,32]

FLOTUS's National School Lunch Program has been such a dismal failure, that the National School Nutrition Association (NSNA) estimates that 1 million fewer students are participating in the school lunch program since its conception and a number of kids who are participating in the program, seriously hate the food being served. When food is not liked by the people who are supposed to consume it, ends up being wasted. The NSNA estimates that such food waste in school is up 81.2% nationwide.[33]

For example, in the Los Angeles School Public School District, one of the nation's largest with a total enrollment in 2015 of 1,567,782 students, are wasting over $100,000.00 worth of food per student per day![34] The result, often confusing school curriculum, along with students not having enough calorie intake to learn the curriculum, not only waste money and food but also heavily "dumbing down" our students so they ***cannot learn***.

Twitter photo of one of Michelle Obama's Public-School lunches.

(Courtesy of Twitter via Public Domain)

Another aspect of Marxist Men and their duped Progressive Liberals actions are when they "***modernize***" (by the way of "expulsion") classroom textbooks involving true written and evidential facts regarding American History, World History, Geography, and Economics. By removing historical facts as it has been written, Marxist Men, such as the late-Communist Howard Zinn, have changed the way the curriculum is being taught in the classroom.[35]

By spreading lies, disinformation, and propaganda, through textbooks, such Potemkin Progressives are teaching the younger generation that murderers and killers of whole populations of people, such as Joseph Stalin, Vladimir Lenin, Mao Zedong and many others, our kids are being heavily re-indoctrinated right in front of our eyes. They are also being taught, that such persons in power, who were responsible for the abject slaughter and murder of over 140 million people worldwide, that they were not "***all bad***", and that criminals and terrorists roaming the planet are people who have been "misunderstood" about their actions, and blame such hatred as the fault of the United States.[36,37]

Yes, believe it or not, such garbage is being taught right now, this very instant by duped Progressive-Liberal Teachers and Professors in Academia, using such lies, distortion of written historical facts, replaced with fictional stories of these men.

For example, in one of the many high school textbooks being used inside public schools, one of these books titled "***Americans Who Tell the Truth***" by Robert Shetterly teaches about how Marxists and

Liberal Activists are so-called "telling the truth" about how our social-economic society in the recent past, like War and Famine, is caused by Capitalism and those supporting such economic system.[38]

However, people like Iraqi War Protestor Cindy Sheenan, Communist Professor/Marxist Man Noam Chomsky and Marxist Singer Peter Seeger, Obama Administration's former "Green Czar", Van Jones are hailed as heroes, because those who support the Military and Free-Market Principles are considered frauds and liars! Preposterous and hypocritical indeed![39]

On Community College and University campuses nationwide, you have both Marxist Men and duped Liberals getting paid large sums of money to speak to students about how wonderful Socialism and Communism is and why it is important, from their perspective, that Capitalism and the current form of the United States of America needed to be changed.

One of them, Jarvis Tyner, the Executive Vice Chairman CPUSA, even spoke to students at the University of Missouri, on November 12, 2009, where he has stated;

"[Obama] He's only the beginning...I think he's a transitional president. I think somebody else is going to come in and take it even further [to the Left]."[40,41,42]

CPUSA Executive Vice-Chairman and former Communist Party Vice-President Nominee in 1974 & 1976 Jarvis Tyner.

(Photo Courtesy of Wikimedia/Communist Party USA)

As the quotation above suggest, Marxist Men and their march into world domination has reached vast areas of the United States that even when public display of subversion of high school students are daily exposed by their Communist Educators, has become so blatantly apparent that # 17 of the 45 Communist Goals are still moving forward in accordance with Marx and Engels dreams.

Of course, the outcome of the 2016 Presidential Election _**did not yield a follow-on President, which would have taken this country further to the Left**_, as Tyner mentioned. Instead, the American people, Black, White and Indifferent elected Donald J. Trump as the 45th President of the United States; not former Secretary of State under Barack Obama and First Lady under Bill Clinton, Hillary Clinton.

She was supposed to be the next President of the United States, which would have taken this country deeper into Socialism/Communism. Which is why, since the election, Marxist Men and their brainwashed dupes continue to undermine both the American people and the duly elected President of the United States, Donald Trump for the past year of this writing.

But, the Marxist Elites in the American Communist Party and the Socialists/Communists in power, will continue their march into pushing their agenda, into making the United States of America into another Communist Satellite country of Russia, headed by the United Nations!

Digressing back into the year 2012, New Oxford High School, located near historic Gettysburg, Pennsylvania, during a half-time break during a football game, trotted out its marching band, wearing something that caught many people's eye.

The band comes out dressed like old Russian Revolutionaries, carrying huge displays of the Hammer and Sickle; the symbol of Communism. The band's theme was to celebrate "**_St. Petersburg: 1917_**", the Russian Revolution where Vladimir Lenin came into power as the first Russian Dictator.

Of course, many of the parents who were witnessed this game did not like this scene! Per Fox News Radio Host Todd Stearns, ironically, New Oxford High School Mascot was named Colonials and their school colors were Red, White, and Blue.[43,44]

After many of the parents complained to the school district superintendent and took their displeasure with the marching band's act to the local media and social media, the superintendent justified the act as *"not promoting communism"*! However, the band members come out in public, during a community event, dressed as Bolsheviks, headed by then-Vladimir Lenin!

However, since this 2012 incident, there have been many conflicts between Marxist Men inside the public education system and the general public in-regards to promoting Marxism vice Patriotism in the classrooms. One can cite many examples, from schools banning the wearing of T-shirts bearing the American Flag, to banning any mentioning of God **[Allah is permitted, however]**, or even now, standing up during the singing of the National Anthem.

Former NFL Quarterback Colin Kaepernick and his team, the San Francisco 49'ers take a knee during the playing of the National Anthem to protest so-called racial injustice between White Law Enforcement Officers and African-American Men. (Courtesy of NY Daily News and Fox News)

19. *"Use student riots to foment public protests against programs or organizations which are under Communist attack."*

Marx said that the most revolutionary class of people are the Proletariats, who should rise-up, kill the Bourgeoisie class and destroy Capitalism. Using this illogic, when applying the 1848 concept of Marx and transcribing it into a modern day 2016 society, who would be the first ones considered as the Proletariat class of people? Our younger Millennials and Post-9/11 generation of students, as well as Minorities. Now think about this; where would you find a large portion of these students located at? Besides at home or at work, for those who have jobs, where would you find such huge population of youngsters? In school.

With the basic understanding that you the reader has learned thus far in this book since the American youth is constantly being bombarded with lies, distortions of facts by Marxist Men and their dupes, why would number 19 of the 45 Communist Goals be important to know?

The answer is quite easy.

In **Mein Kampf**, written by Adolf Hitler prior to him taking over as Chancellor of Germany in the 1930's, expressed this;

"The great masses of the people will more easily fall victim to a big lie than a small one."

In other words, Marxist Men will use student riots, protests and actual civil unrest on college campuses nationwide, to push back any opposition to the Communist organ of world domination. Even if they, must invent a lie and conduct a disinformation campaign for these protests to materialize.

For example, between 2010 and 2016, the University of Missouri, located in Columbia Missouri, became a scene of many student protests about fake racial discrimination, anti-gay sentiment, racial graffiti, a hunger strike and a boycott by the University's Football team. Of these incidents, as usual, were stoked by Marxist Men and their dupes in the media, causing a public attention distraction as to what was really going on around the country; high unemployment, zero to 1% economic growth, massive political corruption by Democrats and many other incidents too numerous to describe here.[46,47,48,49,50]

Other Universities around the countries conducted similar outcry and protests of their own. At the University of California at Irvine (UC-Irvine), members affiliated with the Communist Front Group Black Lives Matter (BLM) staged campus protests in October 2016, while at the same time, group members were holding up signs stating,

"Blue Lives Don't Matter" (Blue representing Law Enforcement Officers).[51,52]

There were many other protests on other college campuses, such as those conducted at the University of Chicago, University of Maryland. The idea behind this goal of Communism is to utilize students on college campuses everywhere, to ferment trouble who Marxist Men consider what or which Communist Organization is being supposedly "threatened" by outside influences.

20. *"Infiltrate the press. Get control of book-review assignments, editorial writing, policymaking positions."*

When one of the 45 Goals of Communism mentions "Infiltrate the press", these actions have already been done and completed to an extent, where not many of the nation's newspapers and book reviews are now all controlled by Marxist Men.

Major national syndicated newspapers/new sites publications, such as the **New York Times**, **Washington Post**, **Los Angeles Times**, **New York Daily News**, **USA Today** and others have become the voice of an active organ of the Communist agenda.

That includes magazine publications such as **Ebony**, **Jet**, **People's Magazine**, **Time Magazine**, **The National Enquirer** and **Rolling Stone Magazine** are all in the tank of the Communists and their dupes in the United States. This includes African-American publications, such as **Jet Magazine, Ebony, GQ, Essence, Vibe,** and many others.

As Yuri Bezmenov previously mentioned in an earlier chapter, the media are unelected persons who not only spread propaganda, to control the outcome of public opinion, but they also control the American Public's perception of reality.

21. *"Gain control of key positions in radio, TV, and motion pictures."*

Marxist Men have been at the forefront to psychologically subvert every aspect of radio, TV, Hollywood Actors, and Music/Entertainment Industries and in place good wholesome propaganda into them, to become vehicles to promote Socialism/Communism. Key positions of each industry include Radio Performers and later-on Television Performers, such as Humphrey

Bogart, Lauren McCall, Walt Disney, Kirk Douglas, Dalton Trumbo and Jane Fonda.

Such subversion also extended to the Music/Entertainment Industry, where, a very long list exists, where Marxist Propaganda have been intertwined between the lyrics of their music recordings. Persons in this category include Jazz Singer/Actress Lena Horne, Black Actor Sydney Portier, and **Paul Robeson**.

The latter person was ***the only African American to receive and accept the Soviet Union's Communist Dictator Joseph Stalin Peace Prize Award in 1952***.

When it comes to today's 21st Century United States, there continue to be a very long list of Music Entertainers who have become hardcore Marxist Men, such as Sean Penn, Alec Baldwin, Lena Dunham, Madonna, Danny Glover, Forest Whitaker, Whoopi Goldberg and Jamie Foxx.

Movie Production Executives like Jeffery Katzenberg of DreamWorks Pictures, Steven Spielberg, and several others. Entertainers include the likes of Actress Roseanne Barr, Comedian Jim Carrey, Actor/Rapper Will Smith, Cher, Barbara Streisand, Samuel L. Jackson, Oprah Winfrey and Ashley Judd.

As for Radio, then-Television News, major news networks, such as ABC, NBC, CBS, PBS, BET, HLN, CNN, MSNBC, and News One channels offer large volumes of Marxist Propaganda to the public to the point where essentially, each of the aforementioned-news reports sounds the same![56,57,58]

(Photos of three Mainstream Entertainers who are public supporters of Communism/Marxism Ideology; from top-left to right: Jane Fonda in North Vietnam, Whoopi Goldberg co-host of The View, Actress Lena Dunham)
(Author's Collection)

22. *"Continue discrediting American culture by degrading all forms of artistic expression. An American Communist cell was told to "eliminate all good sculpture from parks and buildings, substitute shapeless, awkward and meaningless forms."*

Communist Goal number 22 is pretty much self-explanatory, especially when you can obviously compare art and artistic expression within the past 20 years. For example, Artistic Expression of the 1970's and 1980's, commonly showed what is called "Neo-Expressionism" art which drew upon a variety of themes included Mythological, Cultural Pride, Music, and Erotic.[59,60]

However, by the 1990's and early 2000's, Art themes became more expressive of violence, satanic ritual, and just ugly-meaningless expression. In short, artistic expression has gone from being an avenue for the artist/artists to express themselves to those who see their work, to work that no longer have any meaning, significance or any internal logic whatsoever.

24/25. *"Eliminate all laws governing obscenity by calling them "censorship" and a violation of free speech and free press." "Break down cultural standards of morality by promoting pornography and obscenity in books, magazines, motion pictures, radio, and TV."*

It has been said somewhere that *"Sexuality sells"*. Well, this has been true and now much accepted throughout American Society since the late 1970s and early 1980's.[61]

To illustrate this, one can only look at syndicated versions of TV shows made during the 1950's and 1960's.

During that era, anything that even remotely **appeared** to be shown as sexual in nature **were not** shown on Television nor in the movies. A few episodes from the hit television show "**I Love Lucy**" starring Lucille Ball and her husband Desi Arnaz were not shown in the same bed with each other if their scenes involved any bedroom activity, but separate single beds.

Other TV Shows reflected the same theme, such as the Dick Van Dyke show and many others. However, it was during the early 1950's and the entire decade of the 1970's, sexuality between Heterosexuals and Homosexuality began to appear in many books, magazines, and movies. Starting with Playboy Magazine, founded by late-Hugh Hefner in Chicago 1953, in time, created the standard of publication for other such magazines to follow; but not without public controversy.[62,63,64]

26. *"Present homosexuality, degeneracy and promiscuity as "normal, natural, healthy.""*

Understand that in the ideology of Marxism, *__morality and the Institute of Marriage along with the concept to differentiate between Right and Wrong does not exist__*.

Of course, some may scratch their heads and wonder, Homosexuality and degeneracy goes against everything that the Bible teaches. Understand, that Marxism teaches people to rejects God in its entirety.

It must also be understood, that in some Communist circles, duped Liberals and outright Communists view Homosexuality and promiscuity as a separate aspect of the Proletariat class struggle, which Marx and Engels theorized. Though in real life, if a country such as the United States of America falls into a crisis mode, then a period of "normality", then those who are openly Homosexuals are specifically targeted by the new rules of society for *__liquidation__*.[65,66,67]

27. *"Infiltrate the churches and replace revealed religion with "social" religion. Discredit the Bible and emphasize the need for intellectual maturity which does not need a "religious crutch.""*

Vladimir Lenin once said that "***Communism must be built with Non-Communist hands***." One of the best ways to weaken a nation, by creating class warfare division, which would further lead to the division of the populace along racial lines, is to infiltrate American Social Institutions.

What is one of the largest Social Institutions in the United States? The Christian-based churches, particularly the Catholic churches. This has been done for over 100 years and it continues today, **even** in the African-American Community. More of this subject will be covered in the proceeding chapters.

28. *"Eliminate prayer or any phase of religious expression in the schools on the ground that it violates the principle of "separation of church and state.""*

Revert-back to Religion, because Marxists denounce it. However, they did not hesitate to use their mental conditioning tactics of lies, deception, and disinformation to the Liberal dupes who are a part of the Public Education System to denounce Religion and Christianity altogether.

29. *"Discredit the American Constitution by calling it inadequate, old-fashioned, out of step with modern needs, a hindrance to cooperation between nations on a worldwide basis."*

Since the beginning of the 20th Century, Marxist Men have publicly and privately discredited the United States Constitution as *"old fashion"*, that *"needed to be changed to reflect the current times"* in which we live in.

However, they love America's founding document when it benefits them, personally to provide coverage of their illegal activities, especially the *2nd, 5th, 14th, 15th and 16th Amendments*.

What's both fascinating and pathetic, is when a sitting Supreme Court Justice travels overseas and discredit the very document that they have sworn to up hold!

In February 2012, Associate Supreme Court Justice Ruth Bader Ginsberg, being interviewed by Al Hayat Television during a visit to Egypt, stated when she met with the so-called "Revolutionaries" called the Muslim Brotherhood regarding creating their own national constitution for the country of Egypt. She stated;[68,69,70]

"I would not look to the U.S. Constitution if I were drafting a Constitution in the year 2012. I might look at the Constitution of South Africa. That was a deliberate attempt to have a fundamental instrument of government that embraced basic human rights, [and] have an independent judiciary. It really is, I think, a great piece of work that was done."

30. *"Discredit the American Founding Fathers. Present them as selfish aristocrats who had no concern for the "common man."*

Marxist Men always repeat the lie, that the Founding Fathers of The United States of America were just a bunch of rich, elite men, who have owned Black Slaves and didn't give a damn about people. They preach this in church, they teach this garbage in school and even parrot this lie on Social Media. The Founding Father who they specifically pick out is Thomas Jefferson.

31. *"Belittle all forms of American culture and discourage the teaching of American history on the ground that it was only a minor part of the "big picture." Give more emphasis to Russian history since the Communists took over."*

Just as in the previous paragraph, Marxist Men have taught their Liberal dupes that anything American is considered *"Puritan"* or *"Bourgie"* or *"racist"*. As a matter of fact, Marxist Men do teach the distortion of history, by saying things like *"Abraham Lincoln was a Democrat" and not a Republican*.[71]

The idea is to teach younger generations of Americans that the Soviet Union and parts of Socialist Europe, under the European Union provides *"social equality"*, *"no racism"* and *promote freedom*.

This is laughable indeed because the younger generations are never taught the Socialist/Communist societies only kills people and ruins economic and individual freedom!

As a matter of fact, such societies are racists and are severely divided among racial, economic and gender-orientated lines, to the point that such countries will eventually collapse, right into anarchy.

32. *"Support any socialist movement to give centralized control over any part of the culture--education, social agencies, welfare programs, mental health clinics, etc."*

You can see this right now clearly. Every aspect of this new "American Culture", music, movies and the like, are owned and operated by the Marxist Men in Hollywood, California who have termed themselves as *"The Illuminati"*. Executive branches of governments that were created by Marxist Men the provides centralized control education, social agencies, welfare programs and mental health clinics are;

The Department of Education
The Department of Health and Human Services
The Department of Commerce
The Department of Agriculture

Understand that when **any groups or movements** which were produced as an apparatus of the Communist Party, when such groups are attacked by non-Communists, they are defended to the utmost ability! Even if what these agencies or movement groups, are blatantly conducting criminal and anarchical actions, publicly that are against the law, are defended by Marxist Men, who will try to explain such actions as being a part of American History, or American tradition.

33. *"Eliminate all laws or procedures which interfere with the operation of the Communist apparatus."*

In Communist Goals number 33 and number 34, it is here where *"Law and Order"* are discredited and is at times, are taken over and rendered ineffective, particularly by the U.S. Justice Department. The reasons are plentiful indeed, however, such agencies like the law enforcement community, interferes with the Communist order for worldwide domination.

What did Karl Marx say in the Communist Manifesto? He stated that the rule of Law and Order is only put there *"to protect the Bourgeoisie' wealth from the Proletariat"*. There are situations, where Law Enforcement Officers have been infiltrated by psychologically subvert persons, that will in due course, bring up false charges on the very law enforcement agency that they, themselves have sworn to protect.

A great example of such Law Enforcement infiltration and the process to render such agencies of becoming ineffective in their duties of protecting American citizens, are the police forces in Chicago Illinois, Ferguson Missouri, Baltimore Maryland and Milwaukee Wisconsin. Notice also that these cities have been locations where the false narratives of Police Brutality on African-Americans have been said to be widespread, but in real time, Black-on-Black Crime is the main indicator of such violence.

35. *"Discredit and eventually dismantle the FBI."*

As mentioned in the previous paragraph.

36. *"Infiltrate and gain control of more unions."*

The Communist infiltration of Public Services Unions, are too-numerous to detail in this book. However, such Labor Unions are inundated with Marxist Men in key positions of bargaining authority, operations and lobbying areas, all the way down to the local chapters of such service unions such as the International Brotherhood of Electrical Workers (IBEW). This action of Communist and Socialist infiltration has been going on since the late 19th Century in the United States, and continue to do so today.

37. *"Infiltrate and gain control of big business."*

Marxist Men who are working on the campuses of public colleges as "Professors" throughout the country have been teaching Socialist Economics for decades. Big businesses and corporations, via the public service unions, are used as vehicles to tote the Communist line and provide financial support for the Communist Party. Some will wonder as to why such Capitalists, Free-Market Enterprise Chief Executive Officers (CEO) and board Presidents support Marxist economics, which goes totally against what has made them successful?

One of the reasons and there are many reasons, why such entrepreneurs will support a system which will eventually destroy them at the end, is because of the lies that they are taught in business schools everywhere. They have been taught that at the end game of converting from a system of Free-Market Enterprise to a Socialist-type of economic system, that they themselves will make more money and have more control in this kind of economy in which they would profit from.

A perfect example can be applied to the ***Patient Protection and Affordable Care Act (PPACA)***, affectionally known as **Obamacare**![72,73]

Unfortunately for them, it's just another bald-faced lie, put out by Communists. What these businesses fail to grasp, is that during the end-game, they will **never** profit from their businesses. The only control that these business leaders will have will be enforcement of labor laws because the only people that will really profit off such businesses and corporations will be "***The Almighty State***".

38. *"Transfer some of the powers of arrest from the police to social agencies. Treat all behavioral problems as psychiatric disorders which no one but psychiatrists can understand [or treat]."*

39. *"Dominate the psychiatric profession and use mental health laws as a means of gaining coercive control over those who oppose Communist goals."*

Communist Goals numbers 38 and 39 can be summarized together into one explanation. Both-of-these goals have already been accomplished since the 1960's to some extent and during the 1970's up to the present-day.

In the Spring of 1970, Washington Post Journalist Robert C. Maynard reported that to combat potential criminals at an early age, the Nixon Administration wanted to provide funding to the Department of Health, Education and Welfare (now the Department of Health and Human Services) to conduct psychological testing on all children between the ages of six to eight in the country.

The objective of these tests is to find out if a number of these children being tested, may harbor or have been *"Genetically-Marked"* for any future criminal activity. Under the guidance of New York City Psychiatrist Dr. Arnold Hutschnecker, who at the time was a member of Margaret Sanger's "**Birth Control League**" and an outright Marxist-Leninist, originally proposed the plan to President Richard Nixon.

The objective of the testing is to massively provide psychological and psychiatric treatment for those children tested, who were determined to be found criminally inclined based-off the results of these tests.[74,75]

According to Dr. Hutschnecker, the justification of testing elementary-aged children to find out if they are or maybe criminally inclined to crime is to provide a short-term solution to what was then called "Urban Reconstruction". Dr. Hutschnecker told President Nixon;

"The aim is to prevent a child with a delinquent character structure from being allowed to grow into a full-fledged teen-age delinquent or adult criminal. The sooner this destructive trend is recognized and reversed, the better the chances for the prevention of crime and the cure of the individual."

Dr. Hutschnecker continues;

"...The more disturbed, the more angry, rebellious, undisciplined and disruptive boys, especially those who show criminal

tendencies, should be given aptitude tests to determine areas of interest which should be carefully encouraged. There are Pavlovian methods which I have seen effectively used in the Soviet Union. For the severely disturbed, the young hard-core criminal, there may be a need to establish camps with group activities under the guidance of counselors, under the supervision of psychologists, who have empathy (most important but also firmness and who can earn the respect of difficult adolescents."[76,77]

In 2016, the National Institute of Health's (NIH), National Genome Research Institute (NGRI) is responsible for genetic testing of Fetuses, Newborn Babies and Biological Parents (Mother and Father). They do this by using DNA to find out if your soon-to-be newborn child or, existing children have inherited diseases from their parents. There are seven different tests that can help with finding out whether your Fetus, Newborn Child or Children have genetically inherited diseases. The seven tests can help;

> *Diagnose diseases*
>
> *Identify gene changes responsible for the already diagnosed disease*
>
> *Determine the severity of the disease*
>
> *Guide Doctors in deciding on the best medicine or treatment to use for certain individuals*
>
> *Identify gene changes that may increase the risk of developing a disease*
>
> *Identify gene changes that could be passed on to Children*
>
> *Screen Newborn Babies for certain treatable conditions*

Benefits of genetic testing, NGRI states that it can eliminate some uncertainty surrounding your family's health. Such benefits can also provide an avenue for potential parents about their future, such as whether-or-not having a baby would be appropriate for them emotionally and financially in the long-term.[78,79] In Layman's terms, such government agencies encourages such testing, with mainly one thing in mind; **population control.**

40/41. *"Discredit the family as an institution. Encourage promiscuity and easy divorce."/ "Emphasize the need to raise children away from the negative influence of parents. Attribute prejudices, mental blocks and retarding of children to suppressive influence of parents."*

It should be remembered that Karl Marx himself had stated as the third goal for the International Communist Movement was "***The elimination of the family as a social unit***." Even in the Communist Manifesto, Marx wrote;

"The bourgeoisie has torn away from the family its sentimental veil, and has reduced the family relation into a mere money relation."

Marx continues;

"Abolition of the family! Even the most radical flare up at this infamous proposal of the Communists."

Marx and Engels felt that the family as a social unit should be destroyed because in their eyes and many others who are just as psychotic as they were, believe that the family is only good to protect the wealth of the Bourgeoisie.

With the elimination of the family as a social unit, Marxist Men teaches that Parents have negative influences on their children, who should be cared for by the community or in easier terms, taken care of by "The State", instead of being raised by them.

Under Socialism and eventually Full-Communism, The State will decide what child will live and enjoy all of the so-called benefits of a utopian society and decide what child or children shall live inside a utopian world. This sounds sick, but Marxist Men have been trained and conditioned to think this way![80]

In April 2013, on the cable television news channel MSNBC, Anchorette Melissa Harris-Perry was speaking inside of the channel's "infomercials". Titled "***Lean Forward***", Harris-Perry confirmed the abolition of the family concept in Marxist-Leninist ideology by stating in the "Info-mercial";

"We have never invested as much in Public Education as we should have because we have all had kind of a private notion on children that your kid is yours and totally your responsibility...We haven't had a very collective notion that these are our children...the part of it is that we have to break the private idea that kids belong to their parents or kids belong to their families and recognize that kids belong to whole communities...once it is everybody's responsibility and not just the households, then we can start making better investments."[81,82,83]

See how Marxism works? By putting a price on indoctrinating your kids, your kids if they lived under you, will become influenced by you to become better kids and better adults later on in life.

As for Mrs. Harris-Perry and her so-called investment in Public Education, let's look at the hard-numbered facts.

Just in 2014 alone, the Department of Education requested and got $71.2 Billion dollars in Discretionary Spending (Optional Spending) to invest in K-12 grade level education, in which $300 million dollars of that will be used so that four-year-old across the country will have "access" to "high-quality" pre-school education.

What has that money gotten us? Students who are falling behind other countries in Math, Science and even Reading.

42. *"Create the impression that violence and insurrection are legitimate aspects of the American tradition; that students and special-interest groups should rise up and use ["]united force["] to solve economic, political or social problems."*

Marxist Men want to create the impression that violence and insurrection are legitimate aspects of American tradition because it allows them to change and manipulate public opinion to their liking. How they get away doing this action, is they invent a false narrative of situation or incident which they control.

Doing this, also allow Marxist Men to control and manipulate the outcome of such incidents, using the slavish propagandized media to allow the created crisis to become bigger. Here, under the Communist Party's direction, front groups such as La Raza or Black Lives Matter (BLM) groups, will come out and act out or voice rage to the issue, causing massive protests. All of this is a lie, to control the reactions of people, Pavlovian style. A perfect example of this can be seen during the 2016 Presidential Election campaign season, where Leftists and their Liberal dupes are paid money to protest and agitate masses, that turned violent in places like Chicago when these front groups protest then-Republican Presidential Candidate Donald J. Trump.

43. Overthrow all colonial governments before native populations are ready for self-government.

Since the Communist Party took hold in the United States in 1919, one of the goals that they have never accomplished, was to overthrow so-called "colonial governments". These colonial governments in America are the individual states, who have their own Governors, Attorney Generals, Legislatures, and Senate, that govern their own activities in their own states.

Back in the 1920's, 30's and 1940's, the Communists have advocated for a **Negro Soviet Republic**, in the Southern States of America, which if it was successful, the idea was that the people, African-Americans living in those designated states, would rise-up, overthrow these state governments and run them, under the direction of the Soviet Union, led by then the dictator-murderous Joseph Stalin.

In present-day 2016, under the Democrat-Communist-Marxist Administration led by President Barack Hussein Obama, the same goal existed. A great example is the controversial Transgender Student Bathroom issue, where those persons in schools who identify openly as Transgenders, can use the bathroom in school based upon not their biological gender, but their self-claimed gender.

In many circles, this issue by the Federal Government is a severe overreach into state governmental authority. Therefore over 11 states have filed federal lawsuits against the Obama Administration over this overreach into state and local political operations.

44. Internationalize the Panama Canal.

Since its building and opening in August 1913, the Panama Canal, the waterway system which connects the Pacific and the Atlantic Oceans through the shortest isthmus of the Central American country of Panama, was owned and operated by the United States until the Torrijos-Carter Treaty, signed by former President James Earl "Jimmy" Carter in 1977. This the Communists have always wanted the canal to be owned and operated by Globalists to use for Marxist causes politically and allowed total control of the system under the United Nations.

45. Repeal the Connally reservation so the United States cannot prevent the World Court from seizing jurisdiction [over domestic problems. Give the World Court jurisdiction] over nations and individuals alike.

This last goal of Communism should scare you out of your skin. In 1946, Democrat Texas Senator Tom Connally, who was Chairman of the Senate Foreign Relations Committee, and who was one of the first United Nations Conference on International Organization, debated that the United Nations should not and should never their International Court to have control over every aspect of judicial laws in the United States.[84,85] The U.S. Senate created what was called the Connally Reservation.

In 1959, Minnesota Democrat Senator Hubert Humphrey proposed legislation in Congress to repeal the Connolly Amendment. This legislation was supported by future-President Bill Clinton's mentor, Arkansas Senator William J. Fulbright, and even President Dwight D. Eisenhower.

Fortunately, the people of the United States overwhelming turned any such actions down and the legislation was killed. In recent years, however, there has been a renewed effort to get the Federal Government to repeal the Connolly Amendment. Just imagine if someone has committed a crime, was arrested and had to go to court and state their case via a World Court which may or may not gives the right to an attorney, may not give you your Maranda Rights, prior to sentencing by a court of 15 Judges from around the world.

"As true as God reigns, I will be avenged for the sorry which my people have suffered."[1]

David Walker (1796-1830)

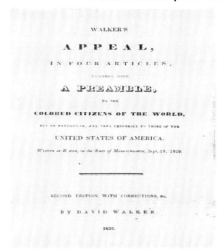

Many cultures inside this country, had never been taught or even understand the term ***Black Liberation Theology (BLT).*** Nor do they know what it stands for.

In this chapter of this book, including its subchapters, the reader shall take away full knowledge, along with a better understanding as to what this ideological entity is, its origins and how it applies into today's destruction of the Black Community. ***Black Liberation Theology (BLT)***, also is called ***Black Nationalism***, along with many other threats being formulated from within the borders of the United States, is just as dangerous to the freedom of this country now, then Radical Islam and Terrorism, being conducted by groups such as the Islamic State of Iraq and Syria or Black Lives Matters (BLM).

Black Liberation Theology is an ideology that is based on the teachings of Karl Marx and Friedrich Engels, using antisemitic rhetoric and views, mixed with a bastardization of selected verses of the Holy Bible. Those who believe in this ideology use it to promote Marxism, by interjecting racism into the mix, by implying that the light of God's revelation in Jesus Christ is equal to the Black, inner-city condition.[2,3,4] Therefore, all of America's Black Community is emancipated from those who had, in the past, victimized them unjustly.

Those persons who have done the community wrongly, are considered as oppressors of their community, and thus needed to be destroyed in their entirety. By applying that the Black Community were constantly being oppressed by "**American Slavery**", "**Evil, Rich White people**", "**Racist Police Departments**", and those who are in positions of power and authority, should be overthrown via a revolution, in the form of a Race War.

As a matter of fact, as I am writing this book, Black Nationalism continues to be taught, in numerous mainstream entities and organizations that the American Black population patronize on an often, if not, daily basis. For example, Black Liberation Theology (BLT) is being preached in many African-American Churches whose congregation follows Pentecostal, African Methodist Episcopal (AME), Protestant and even Southern Baptist sects of religious following.

BLT is also being taught in American Public Schools in the inner-cities in America, which serves an overwhelming population of Black Children and Teens, by distorting historical facts, while consistently emphasizing American Slavery, as the reason for current society's ills.

Black Liberation Theology (BLT) uses the Entertainment Industry to promote their racist and Marxist agenda to the masses, via television programming and movies. These programs and movies are constantly centered around the ever regurgitation of lies and deceptive narratives of Black men and women being exploited by persons in positions of authority, various shades of skin color and gender, along with blatant distortion of actual historical events in their broadcasted documentaries.

Organizations such as BET (Black Entertainment Television), its subsidiary station called News One, and Oprah Winfrey's television station OWN and numerous Black Hollywood Entertainers, use the above programming avenues to spread their racist views, that has been subversively taught to them too. Of course, BLT is being discussed and being spread via Social Media organizations, such as Facebook, Twitter,

Instagram, YouTube and Snapchat, whose video uploads, chat functions and Newsfeeds spread Marxist propaganda, which fills their internet threads of their hate and discontent, based on lies and falsehoods of "*White Privilege*", "*Jim Crow*" and "*Segregation*".

What the BLT ideology exploits in the Black Community, are the inner emotions of their listeners to accept that, regardless of what progress have been made in their social-economic conditions as a collective community, using the color of skin as an excuse, that their condition will never get better.

Black Liberation Theology teaches members within the Black Community, that they will never succeed or amount to anything substantial, because "*The deck has been stacked against you*" and because of the "*White Man's atrocities*" conducted during *Slavery*, Black men, women, and children will never rise to the level of greatness that other cultures. Thereby allowing such believers of the to become victims of their own circumstance.

What circumstance is that?

The answer is, *being Black*.

To put things in a better perspective, those who teach BLT mentally subverts whole sections of the American population into believing that their skin color is a curse, and no matter what happens or what they do, believers of BLT become to feel "**oppressed**" and will act out emotionally.

They will act out so emotionally, to the point, where they will feel like they themselves are being used by rich White People, so they can make "profits" off the backs of Black folks, who are working for low-wages and living in inner-city poverty.

In BLT terminology, the rich *White People* are considered the *Bourgeois* while the *African-American Community* is the *Proletariats*.

This subversion is further increased in size and magnitude, by a Marxist-ideological mass media, government officials on every level in America, to Public Service Unions to even the U.S. Healthcare System. Yes, even the U.S. Healthcare System has joined in on the fray of subverting that African-Americans have inherited diseases and mental disorders where some say, that the community will never lead a decent, productive life.

As an African American myself, I know first-hand, from birth to adulthood, there are some members, within the Black Community, that has been both psychologically and socially, subverted into accepting the **"Victim Mentality"**.

So, who or what incident started the Black Liberation Theology mess in the first place? How did this false ideology become so prevalent in such a short period, affecting the political and social landscape of today?

The term Black Liberation Theology wasn't coined in the American psyche until the late 1960's.[5] Prior to that decade, various forms of the ideology, hatred against the "White Man" via violent means, have been prevalent throughout the Black Community long before the outbreak of the Civil War, in 1861.

Most of these attitudes were advocated in the Northern states that bordered north of the Ohio River. It was during this time, between the years 1800-1860, called the Antebellum Period (before the outbreak of the American Civil War), where a man named David Walker, A Free-Black, and Slavery Abolitionist, and Public Speaker originally put the ideology of BLT into the limelight.

David Walker's "Appeal"

The Antebellum Period for the Black Community of the day contained aspirations that every person of African-descent wanted for themselves and future ones yet to be born_. **_For those who were Enslaved, most yearn to be Free, while those who were already Free, wanted to be on an equal footing with their fellow man, no matter what color of skin they wore_**.

This was the gist of the social and political environment for Black Americans living in the early-to-mid 19th Century United States. As a part of that environment, one man created a plan, aimed directly at the Enslaved masses in the Southern States, to fight to obtain that aspired freedom; even if that freedom was to be gained through violent means and the cost of their lives.

This is the story of David Walker (1785-1830) and his plan to inspire thousands of Enslaved Blacks to rise-up and gain such freedom via violence, would cause a major backlash to the social environment inside the Black Community. David Walker's actions, expressed through his emotional and fiery writings, would eventually be called, by some historians, as the *"Father of American Black Liberation Theology"*.[6]

David Walker was born on September 28, 1785, in Wilmington, North Carolina. His mother was a Free Black Woman and his father was an Enslaved man, who was born in Africa who died shortly before his birth. Since Walker's mother was a Free Black Woman, he too was considered a Free Person of Color as well.

Yet despite his status in Antebellum America of the time, David Walker grew up to witness some of the most horrendous mistreatment of Black Slaves inside the city and surrounding farmlands of Wilmington, North Carolina. As he learned to read, write and understand the environment surrounding him, David Walker himself knew that the Institute of Human Chattel or Slavery wasn't for him. As a teenager, he wrote that;

"As true as God reigns, I will be avenged for the sorrow which my people have suffered."

As an adult, David Walker left Wilmington, North Carolina in 1803 and moved to Charleston, South Carolina, where he joined an African Methodist Episcopal Church (AME). At the time, Charleston had a very large population of Free Blacks and was considered by some as a "Mecca" for them. Once he settled there and began to be involved himself in community activism and wrote fiery Anti-Slavery editorials in the area's African-American Newspapers. He once wrote;

"If I remain in this bloody land [the South], I will not live long…. I cannot remain where I must, hear Slaves chains continually and where I must encounter the insults of their hypocritical Enslavers."

Here it is interesting to note, that the Charleston South Carolina is not only had the largest Free Black Population at the time in America, but the city also had the most number of Free Blacks owning Enslaved Blacks, "their brethren" as Walker calls them, in the South.

By 1824, Walker relocated to Baltimore, Maryland for a few weeks, then to Philadelphia, Pennsylvania, and New York City, before finally settling down in Boston, Massachusetts, the following year in 1825. While residing briefly in the aforementioned cities, Walker began work as a Public Speaker and became a fiery, emotional editor in Black newspapers. He also befriended and worked with Anti-Slavery and Anti-Religious Activists, who were involved in the above cities African Methodist Episcopal Churches.

In 1826, David Walker set up his base of the Anti-Slavery base of operations on the waterfront of Boston Harbor. He bought a storefront located on one of the corners of the waterfront, opened-up a Secondhand Clothing Store and continued to write his often radical, angry, and no-holds-barred editorials, for The Freedom's Journal; a weekly Anti-Slavery publication founded by Free Black men, Reverend Peter Williams Jr., John B. Russwurm and Samuel B. Cornish.

On February 23, 1826, David Walker married Olive "Eliza" Butler, who no doubt helped Walker operate his secondhand shop, she also assisted with her husband the helping, temporary sheltering and feeding poor, needy Fugitive Slaves, who were being pursued by Fugitive Slave Hunters. These actions earned Walker a great reputation from both Boston's Black and White Communities, that were outspoken advocates of African Slavery in 1826 America. This recognition would change dramatically, when Walker pinned his most famous editions of his many writings, ***Appeal to the Coloured Citizens of the World***.

In September of 1826, Walker published the first edition out of a total of four controversial pamphlets (magazines) named Appeal to the Coloured Citizens of the World, known as the "***Appeal***" to historians. The publication, containing 76 pages in total, Walker not only condemned the Institute of Slavery in the South but made an emotional appeal for those enslaved there to revolt against their Masters and Free themselves, regardless of the risks taken.

"Had you rather not be killed, then to be a Slave to a tyrant, who takes the life of your Mother, Wife and dear little Babies?"

The Appeal was smuggled in the pockets of his secondhand clothing that he sold on the Boston Waterfront, in which Free Black Merchant Sailors would buy from him, worn at sea and traded in Southern ports, such as Charleston, South Carolina or Savannah Georgia. Some of his pamphlets also made it into the port of David Walker's hometown of Wilmington, North Carolina, Norfolk and Jamestown Virginia, Pensacola Florida, Mobile Alabama and as far west as New Orleans, Louisiana.[7,8,9,10]

Walker's plan was to have other Black Sailors, once they docked into the ports, have his pamphlets be passed on to those African Americans in the South, who were enslaved to either read them if they could or have the publication be read to them by someone else who could read, like Church Ministers, Artisans or Blacksmiths. By spreading the word in this fashion, Walker hoped that his work would cause a severe backlash against Slave Masters as Slaves would take actions to gain their freedom, no matter if it was life or death for them.

In parts of **The Appeal**, Walker not only indicts the White Slave Masters but also wrote a chilling indictment against his own race, in what he considered, aligning up with the so-called "Tyrants", who help the Slave Masters, Holders and Fugitive Slave Hunters.

"...want Slaves, and want us [Blacks] for their Slaves, but some of them will curse the day they ever saw us..."

He further wrote:

"...He may see some of my brethren in league with Tyrants, selling their own brethren into hell on Earth, not dissimilar to the exhibitions in Africa, but in a more secret, servile and abject manner."

Walker's publication also illustrated in his pamphlets, that Black men who have educated alone or those who are fine and content with the low-paying, menial jobs that some took on to feed their families, were in his words, *"May be almost ignorant, in comparison, as a Horse…".*

His rationale behind this scathing verse, Walker insists that the only way Black Americans can only beat the Tyrants (White Slave Owners), if only he becomes more educated equally as them or aspire to work jobs that are better than ANY White Man.

In layman terms, David Walker insists that the only way Blacks can beat the White Man is to become more prosperous in education and labor harder and better than any of those who he feels oppresses him. In Walker's opinion, unless they can aspire and do the latter, Black Americans enslaved in the South will never amount to anything substantial in their lifetimes, regardless of their individual progression or struggles that despite the odds, achieve in life.

In the Appeal's parts two and three, Walker condemned the American Colonization Society's solution of repatriated Freed Blacks to leave The United States of America and resettle on the African Continent, specifically in 1826, Liberia.

He proclaimed that American belonged to Black people of African-descent than the Europeans, because, as he noted, that *"We have enriched it with our blood and tears."*

Walker chastised the Christianity religion in America, by accusing White Europeans of using the religion to justify the enslavement of Blacks in the South. He uses such propagandized accusations, by further writing that Africans were brought to North American shores and enslaved, were never allowed to practice Christianity (which was false) and stated that American Christians have been contradicting the Bible, by deliberately oppressing those who had a different skin color than theirs.[11,12,13]

Walker further propagandized in his third edition of the Appeal, starting on pages 42 and 43, by making the assertion the Black men, women, and children would go to church, worship God and then afterwards, White Patrols would all at once commence to beat, assault and harass the church members just because of their skin color*. David Walker gave readers no example nor explanation, so far whether he, himself have seen such incidents or were just rumored to have happened. Further research conducted by this author and many* *historians found no truth in Walker's accusation that such incidents took place, anywhere in the South at the time.*

Also in his third edition of The Appeal, Walker accused White Christian Americans of possessing an "Innate devilishness" which prompted them to strip African Slaves of humanity on purpose. In later paragraphs in his pamphlet, Walker called for a massive Slave Revolt as an expression of manhood, even though he hoped that social change and abolition of the Institute of Slavery will not end without it.

Lastly, he called for Whites who owned Slaves to ask God for forgiveness, for their oppression against African American Slaves, who he also called them "our natural enemies". Religion Scholar Gayraud S. Wilmore, one of the most well-known persons in the world in regard to such subjects such as Christianity, wrote that **The Appeal** was;

"The most powerful piece of [anti-slavery] propaganda written by a Black."[14]

As his writings began to be found throughout the South, in the Summer of 1830, many Enslaved Blacks either ignored the pamphlets altogether, while others began plans to create uprisings against their Masters or Mistresses.

Those Slaves who started to act on Walker's recommendation, to rise and fight for their freedom, rumors began to circulate in North Carolinian cities of Fayetteville, New Bern, Elizabeth City and Wilmington of such preparations to rebel. The resulting backlash of Walker's Appeal terrified both White and Black Slave Owners in the South, where immediate laws were put in place by state legislatures restricting, even more, the teaching of Blacks to read or write than ever before.

Breaking such laws would have ended with harsh punishment, to include more whippings, lynching and even serving jail time for long periods for ANY Free Black or ANY non-Slave-owning Whites for going against these new laws.

As for the Black Sailors who were arriving at Southern Ports, whether they had Walker's pamphlets in their possession or not, they were "quarantined" in solitary confinement in the basements or buildings near the ports, to cut-off ANY contact with residential Black Communities. By doing so, the law makers argued, prevent such "implantation of rebellious actions in the minds of the port's Enslaved and Free Blacks". Manumission or the legal process of freeing enslaved Blacks were no longer in the hands of the Master or Mistress's responsibility. All Manumission documents or requests had to be presented to the state legislatures instead of the local courts, citing Walker's Appeal as the ultimate reason why the change was necessary.

Elitists Southern Whites who did own anywhere from a few dozen Slaves in number to those very few who owned hundreds of Slaves, began to offer huge bounties of cash, totaling up to $3,000 dollars ($79,500 dollars in 2015) to ANYONE, Black, White, Native American vigilante groups, to capture David Walker and murder him.[15,16]

Other Rich Southern Planters offered $10,000 dollars ($265,000 dollars in 2015) reward for anyone who could kidnap Walker and return him physically to the South alive. After receiving hundreds and thousands of threats to his person, even from Whites in Boston Massachusetts, David Walker's wife Olive, his co-workers in the A.M.E. Church, urged him to leave at once and flee to Canada. However, he refused to leave. History has written that neither the vigilante groups or individuals who were in the hunt for David Walker will never collect a dime on any of the rewards offered. David Walker's health instead got the best of him and he died of Tuberculosis at the age of 44.[17]

David Walker's Appeal, sparked a social change in attitudes between Blacks and Whites, Free or Enslaved, almost forever. ***Any talk of gradual abolition of African American Slaves was no longer considered in the South,*** as it was in the North prior to the American Revolutionary War.

Walker's fiery and militant writings were also blamed for causing the **Nat Turner Rebellion** in Virginia, which killed over 58-plus Whites and over 200-plus Free and Enslaved Blacks throughout the South after the incident.

Walker's Appeal created more hatred and discontent within the entire Black Community, Free or Enslaved, and between Slaveholders and Slave Owners. ***This attitude also extended to the point, where Whites no longer trusted Blacks, Free Blacks no longer trusted Enslaved Blacks and vice-versa, while Free Blacks trusted neither Whites or Enslaved Blacks.***

One-hundred and eighty years later, David Walker, the Father of Black Liberation Theology, words continues to resonate with people, who have no clue what his words meant in comparison to today. However, Walker wasn't the only Free Black to write about such rhetoric, blaming the White Man for Slavery. Much more such people will follow his tracks, using false or over-inflated lies and distortions, to lay down the basis of Black Liberation Theology.

**Drawing of David Walker, author of "The Appeal" in 1826.
(Courtesy of U.S. History Image)**

Martin R. Delany's "The Condition"

Photo of then-Union Army Major Martin R. Delany, taken sometime during the Civil War.

(Courtesy of Wikimedia)

Martin Robinson Delany (May 6, 1812- January 24, 1885), was another Free Black man of African-descent, who was born in Charles Town, Virginia (Now-Charles Town, West Virginia) to Samuel and Pati Delany. Since Martin's Father was an Enslaved Black man and his Mother was a Free Black woman, he was considered Free, because of his Mother's status. Growing up, Delany was taught how to read and write. Some say that Delany learned "*The New York Primer and Spelling Book*", which was given to him one day by a poor White pauper in town.[18,19]

In 1822, when he was 10 years old, his mother moved Martin and his two younger siblings to Chambersburg, Pennsylvania, then sent them all to school to further their education. Pennsylvania, a Free State, had specific educational facilities which taught Blacks to read, write and mathematics. At the age of 19, Delaney moved to Pittsburgh and Apprenticed with a city Medical Physician. Their practice did so well, that within a year, both men partnered together and opened their own medical practice.[20,21]

In 1843, Delaney began to publish his own newspaper in Pittsburgh called "*The Mystery*", where he advocated for the end of Slavery in America. His publication was successful enough, that it gave him some notoriety and recognition from both Pittsburg's Black and White Communities, especially those who were heavily involved in the Abolition Movement. One of these men was a future Great American and former Slave named Frederick Douglass. Douglass saw how passionate Delaney was expressing his views about the evils of Slavery, that he enlisted Delaney to write editorials for one of Douglass's publications "*The North Star*", in Rochester New York.

Delaney's editorials were fiery in its language and straightforward, to the point, which earned him a huge public following, which gave him more notoriety with the Abolition Movement. In 1850, Delaney and two other Black Men were accepted into the Harvard School of Medicine.[22,23]

However, the student body at Harvard wasn't as forgiving, to see three African-American Men, take the same courses and obtain grades just like them. Unfortunately, Harvard University was an Ivy League School, which trained some of the brightest and serviced the most upper-economic class of students from prominent families, some of them, parents still owned Black Slaves down in the South. Of course, this didn't sit well with the latter cadre of students, so they started a petition to have Delaney and the other two Free Black students kicked out of the medical school. As pressure mounted from the signed petitions, numerous letters, on-campus protests and assemblies, and letters from White parents of students attending there, who threatened to withdraw not only their child but all funding and donations to the school. The Dean of Students, from Harvard Medical School in Massachusetts, finally made the decision to withdraw the Black Medical Students from the program.

Angered by this action by Harvard University, a Northern School that he thought wasn't like the oppressed Southern Schools, which did not allow Black College Students at all, Delaney returned to Pittsburgh and reassumed his medical practice. Still bearing emotional scars by the Harvard Medical School event, in 1852, Martin R. Delaney wrote a scathing book, titled "The Condition, Elevation, Emigration, and Destiny of the Colored People of the United States" was published. Commonly called "*The Condition*", Delaney's book was another piece of literature describing the plight of the Black Community prior to the outbreak of the American Civil War.

In Chapter II of "*The Condition*", Delaney compares the political, religious, social and economic conditions between Europe and the enslaved Black population of the U.S. In this chapter, he opens it up by flatly stating;

"The United States, untrue to her trust and unfaithful to her professed principles of Republican equality, has also pursued a policy of political degradation to a large portion of her native-born countrymen and that class is the Colored people."

He further wrote;

"Denied an equality not only of political but of natural rights, in common with the rest of our fellow citizens, there are no species of degradation to which we are not subject."

Inside "*The Condition*", Delaney also heavily criticized and denounced the Abolition Movement, the very organization who gain him the notoriety and status to admit him to Harvard Medical School. He stated that the White Abolitionists will never accept Blacks as equals, so the only solution for America's Black Community to become equals in any right or sense, in his opinion, was to re-emigrate (return) back to Africa.

Delaney also scolded the Black Abolitionists too, concluding that they did not advocate Blacks to extend their enslaved people's elevation in society, in-order to be equal to their White counterparts, but to a secondary position to their White friends, that offered little or no advancement in race relations or economic achievement.[24,25,26]

Yet instill, inside Chapter Seven, Martin Delaney wrote that Blacks throughout America, Free or Enslaved, are not the legitimate citizens of this country, politically because they were never given a chance to have unrestricted rights in any state or given the opportunity of making great investments as part of the American Society. Couple the aforementioned with what he wrote in Chapter Nine of The Condition;

"...Our history in this country is well known, and quite sufficiently treated on in these pages already, without the necessity of repetition here...It is enough to know the most {-} cruel acts of injustice and crime, our forefathers were forced by small number and enslaved the country---the great body now to the number of three million and a half..."

He continues;

"...through shorn of their strength, disarmed of manhood, and stripped of every right, encouraged by the part performed by their brethren and fathers in the Revolutionary Struggle---with no records of their deeds in history."

Sounds like Martin R. Delaney was not mentally coherent when he wrote these words. He failed to consider the facts that he and other Free Black Men like himself, in increasing numbers, had the privilege to obtain the many opportunities afforded to him, to exploit their own potential, thereby benefiting off the same unfair and cruel system;

"that offered little or no advancement in race relations or economic achievement".

Criticism aside, in 1859, Delaney led an expedition to West Africa, to explore possible re-emigration sites for African-Americans, in his quest to create a separate Black Nation, located along the Niger River. It was Martin R. Delaney who wrote these words, who Black Nationalists and Marxist-Leninists repeat today, 157-years later;

"We are a nation within a nation, we must go from our oppressors."

In 2016-17, that same quote is still debatable in some circles of the Black Community and will come up time-after-time again, during-the-course of American History.[27]

After the outbreak of the American Civil War, which was fought by both Black and White Men on either side of the country (North and South), so that African-Americans can have the opportunity to be equal like Delaney had, returned to the United States from Africa and help the Abolitionist Movement Recruit Black Men for the war effort. In February 1865, Martin Delaney was commissioned a Major in the Union Army by President Abraham Lincoln, becoming the highest-ranking Union Army Officer during the war.

After the war, Delaney was put in command of the Freedman's Bureau sector based in Charleston, South Carolina. The Freedman's Bureau was formed by the Republican Party in Congress, as an organization to not only help rebuild the South, but help ex-Slaves to adjust to their newly given emancipation rights as American Citizens and not as property.

In 1868, Delaney openly challenged those who still held the belief that Blacks were still property instead of citizens, over 90% of them being former Plantation Owners in South Carolina's "Colleton District. He also did not hesitate to openly challenge African-Americans who were running for political office as well.

In July 1868, he opposed Black Republican Jonathan Jasper Wright, a distinguished Lawyer and John Mercer Langston, well-known Abolitionist and first Black American elected to public office, because Delaney felt that they were '*inexperienced*' when dealing with the Black Community like he was.

That same year, Delaney was appointed as a Judge in the city of Charleston, South Carolina, serving until he ran for high public office four-years later. In 1872, he became a Republican Politician, who unsuccessfully ran for Lieutenant Governor of South Carolina in 1874, losing in a tight race to another Free Black Man and Real Estate Owner, Richard Howard Gleaves. After the election, Delaney returned to his position as a Civil Courts Judge in Charleston.

In 1878, Delaney renewed his passion and interests in the now-Emancipated Blacks to leave the United States of America and resettle in Africa. That same year, he became an agent for the Liberian Exodus Steam Line, who was contracted to transport those African-Americans who wanted to leave and return to the African Continent. A year later, he pinned his second book, titled "***The Principia of Ethicology***", in-which excerpts of this publication are still being used 137-years later, to teach Black Nationalism, to college students.

In 1880, Martin R. Delaney moved to Boston, Massachusetts for two years, lecturing college student about Black Nationalism Pride and further relocated to Xenia Ohio, becoming a Professor at Wilberforce College, where he died of a Heart Attack on January 12, 1885, at the age of 73.

Martin R. Delaney, however one views his politics and rhetoric of the day, was still an outstanding individual and African-American who both early and later on in life, viewed the United States of America is not the natural land for Blacks, despite the tremendous odds that those before him and after him had to endure, to become and stay equal to their fellow man.

That was his opinion as to where he saw things in the bleachers of life. Unfortunately, it was the United States of America and its founding principles, which allowed him to speak his opinion, where very few countries on Earth, back then and now, would allow a Black Man the opportunity to succeed as he did. Regardless, to this day, Delaney is still revered as "***The Father of Black Nationalism".***

Wallace Fard Muhammad: Founder of the American Black Supremacy & Nation of Islam

Wallace Dodd Fard-Muhammad, the founder of the Nation of Islam

(Courtesy of Wikimedia)

During the era of Great Depression in the United States, between the years 1929-1941, the American Black Community suffered the most from the worst economic decline in U.S. History.[31,32] With the unemployment rate of over 50-percent, the struggle to find any meaningful work that paid enough to put food on the table, and to pay the mortgage or rent, became nearly non-existent overnight.

These factors and others, had a detrimental, psychological effect on the American Black Community, to the point where such people, could be manipulated out of rational thought. Seeing this and exploiting this vulnerability in a section of an ethnic group in the population, via brainwashing them into accepting that they are the victims of society and not the other way around, have caused them in repairable damage to their psyche for generations to come.

Who saw such weakness inside the African-American Community?

The Communist Party of the United States (CPUSA), and they were ready to take this opportunity to mentally control the community, so they can be told whatever, CPUSA required them to do, via the cause of *"equality"*, *"civil rights"* and in this case, *"superiority"* of all people.

It is here, where the story of a Mr. Wallace Dodd Fard-Muhammad enters the picture, who's rhetoric still resonates today, throughout the Black Community, as the founder of the Nation of Islam (NOI). A very well-known Black Supremacy Organization, identified by the Southern Poverty Law Center (SPLC) as a Hate Group.[33,34,35]

So, who is this Wallace Dodd Fard-Muhammad person, and why should it be important to understand the background of him. There are many reasons, which will be answered in this section of this publication. What's important is this. If you were to ask anybody, no matter what race, the color of skin and cultural background in the United States, about anything relating to the Nation of Islam, it's probably a safe bet that two names would be recalled immediately upon answering that question; Louis Farrakhan and Malcolm X.

If you were to ask the same question to those individuals who are considered or calls themselves, Black Muslims (people who associate themselves in the worship of Islam), they would probably mention a third name in the answer, Elijah Muhammad. All these answers are correct unless you ask a member of the Nation of Islam the same question, a fourth person would be revealed; W.D. Fard a.k.a "Allah".

Understand, that W.D. Fard and Wallace Dodd Fard-Muhammad is the same person, and was as well as many others, responsible for setting up the conditions within the Black Community, of establishing an organization such as the Nation of Islam.

The NOI, for the past 87-years, has been the most controversial and anti-Semitic Black Liberation Theological organizations in modern-American History.[36] However, the Nation of Islam has also produced some of the African-American Communities most-influential members in the United States of America of the past and present.

Minus those attributes, with an estimated congregation membership between 20,000 to 50,000-plus, with Mosques located in almost every major city in America, it is important for you, the reader to understand fully, how this organization was founded and who it was founded by and why it was created in the first place. As an African-American himself, this author will provide some insight, that even the Nation of Islam has publicly discredit some information about its formation of the past, which can be expected.

The main excuse such statists organization is to deny what they really were; a tool to fundamentally transform the United States of America into something like Joseph Stalin had in the old Soviet Union, devised by the Marxist Theory Plan of Action, written by Karl Marx and Friedrich Engels.

As it is, which may end up as a shock to the readers of this book, is the fact that the Nation of Islam, which preaches its own form of Black Liberation Theology (BLT) in its Mosques, *__was actually-founded by a White guy__*! This cannot be disputed, and the evidence will be presented below, in the following paragraphs.

So, again, who was Wallace D. Fard-Muhammad and why is it important for the reader to know?

Just as like many organized groups that were formed as a "voice" for Black America, like the Nation of Islam, they were originally created by Marxist and Socialists-conditioned White men and women, for a specific agenda. But, at the same time, these White Men and Women end up using citizens within the Black Community as emotional fodder to exploit them for monetary and public support to push their agenda. Wallace Fard-Muhammad did that very thing, with one exception; he taught **Black Supremacy**, instead of "equality", unlike the NAACP for example.

Wallace Dodd Fard-Muhammad, for some decades, has had some mystery surrounding his existence. However, based on FBI interviews conducted in the 1950's, under the leadership of J. Edgar Hoover and an investigative reporting by Washington Post's Karl Evanzz, who wrote an editorial piece in 1993, has put an answer to one of America's most mysterious man.[37,38,39]

Fard may have been born either on February 25th or February 26th, in either 1891, or 1893 in Auckland, New Zealand or the city of

Shinkey, Zabul Providence, Afghanistan, which is located near the Pakistan-Afghan border. Fard's Father was named Zared Fard, who some claimed he was born in Pakistan and his Mother was Beatrice Ford, a Caucasian woman born and raised in New Zealand. Fard's mother may have had contact with Wallace's father while she was working either as a Christian Missionary or working as an official for the British Government in the latter-half of the 19th Century.

At the age of 22, Fard immigrated to the United States from Auckland, New Zealand via Brisbane Australia, sailing onboard **the S.S. Maheno** in 1911, arriving at the port of Portland Oregon on February 17, 1911. On the ship's manifest, his name is listed Fard's name is listed as "W. Fard", with the birth year of 1889. However, between the years 1911 to 1934, Wallace Fard has been known to use over 56-different aliases during this twenty-three-year time frame.[40,41]

On April 14, 1914, using the name "**Fred Dodd**", Fard completed a Marriage Application in Portland, Multnomah County, Oregon to marry an 18-year-old Native American Woman named Pearl Allen/Enouf. Both bride and groom were married on May 9, 1914, by Multnomah County Circuit Judge Williams "W. N." Gatens. per the marriage license, the Witness of the event included F. D. Hennessey, a Lawyer and Mary E. Moreno, a District Court Clerk of Multnomah County. Now-Fred Dodd (a.k.a. Wallace Fard) listed his address on both Marriage Certificate and Application as Salem Oregon, with his occupation being a "**Lunch Wagon Operator**".

After residing in Portland Oregon for about three years, apparently, both Dodd and his wife separated. FBI documents stated that the couple had a bitter breakup, because Dodd (a.k.a. Fard) financially was going broke because of Pearl's alcoholism, which the former never drink, eat red meat nor smoked any tobacco products; which Fard later-on, incorporated those same principles into the fundamentals of the Nation of Islam.

After the breakup, in 1917 Fard moved to the city of Los Angeles, California and began to live under the name of "Wallie Dodd Fard/Ford" and opened his own restaurant there. During the height of World War One, Ford/Fard registered for the draft on June 5, 1917 (Appendix I). Ford/Fard listed his date of birth as being February 26, 1893, in Shinka (Misspelled on the card), Afghanistan, with his occupation being a Restaurant Owner. His address was listed as 803 West 3rd Street, Single as being his marital status and his race was listed as "Caucasian". Ford/Fard's citizenship was listed as being an "Alien" as well. However, there are no records either at the Federal Records Center, located in St. Louis Missouri or registered in the U.S. Army listing him serving in World War One.

On November 17, 1918, Los Angeles Police Department records showed that Ford/Fard was arrested for Assault with a Deadly Weapon, which we were arrested, fined and released from jail after a couple of hours. In 1919, a customer who was patronizing Ford/Fard's place of business, a Caucasian woman by the name of Hazel Barton, made acquaintance with him and the two began to date.

In January 1920, both Hazel Barton and Wallie Dodd Ford/Fard began to live with each other, at the home of another Caucasian family's home of the Bushongs, located at 347 Flower Street in LA.

According to the 1920 Federal Census of Los Angeles, California, support this claim and lists both Barton and Ford/Fard living at the Bushong's residence at the time.[44,45,46]On September 1, 1920, Hazel and Wallie had a son born, named Wallace Dodd Ford Jr., birthed at the Dr. Harley E. Mc Donald Sanitarium located at 1512 South Hope Street in Los Angeles. The Son was killed during World War Two, while serving as a U.S. Coast Guard Sailor on August 3, 1942, at Lynnhaven, Virginia.

In 1922, the couple separated from each other and Hazel and Wallie Ford/Fard's son moved to another location inside the city of Los Angeles.

During an interview with the FBI on October 17, 1957, Hazel told FBI Agents that the two never married, because Wallie had told her that he was still married to a woman in Oregon and that during the bitter breakup, they never filed for a divorce. That was proven to be a lie because investigators had found a Divorce Decree in Oregon under the name of Fred Dodd, was divorced sometime in 1916. By the time of the FBI's Interview in 1957, Hazel Barton had since remarried twice, which during the interview, she carried the last name of her then-current husband Evelsizer, after her relationship with Ford/Fard in the early 1920's.

What was interesting to note, was that during the FBI interview, Hazel described Wallie Ford/Fard as the following;

White Male

From New Zealand

About 5 foot 8 inches in height

140 pounds in weight

Slender build

Black-curly hair

Caucasian-features

Had a very dark-complexion that she describes "Like a Mexican"

Hazel admitted to FBI investigators in 1957, who by the way at the time, was investigating Fard and the entire organization of the Nation of Islam in its entirety for Communist Subversive and criminal activities, that Wallie never told her anything about his family, his date of birth, where he was born, educational background, parents or whether he had any siblings.

What Hazel did find strange about Ford/Fard, that one day when they were living together, she was putting away some of his clothes in a dresser drawer, when she saw a letter with an Oregon address written on it, sent to a "**Fred Dodd**". Wallie did tell her that he lived in Portland Oregon, before relocating to LA, however, the letter she found had a Salem Oregon Address on it. Hazel admitted to FBI Investigators that she was convinced that Wallie Ford and Fred Dodd was the same person and everywhere the couple went, Wallie Ford used the name "**Wallace Ford**".[47,48]

As the FBI Interview went on, Hazel Evelsizer recalled that a girl who worked as a waitress at Ford/Fard's restaurant, told her that she used to help Ford/Fard write letters to his parents in New Zealand, because he had very little education and had problems corresponding with them. The girl, Hazel told investigators, used to live with him in the apartment located above the restaurant prior to Wallie Ford/Fard began to date. This conversation confirmed to the women, that indeed **_Wallace Ford/Fard came from New Zealand_**.

Upon a Genealogical search, sometime after Hazel's breakup with Wallace, he began dating again in 1923 and/or 1924, which during that timeframe, he started to date a Mexican girl named Carmen Trevino. On June 5, 1924, in Santa Ana, Orange County, California, a suburb of Los Angeles, the couple were soon married.[49]

This time, the marriage application and license carried the name "**Wallie Dodd Ford**", who was born in Oregon, listed as being 26-years of age, and his bride Carmen, was 22 years of age, born in Mexico. The couple was married by Orange County Justice of the Peace, John B. Cox, and the ceremony was witnessed by a Charles C. Carrillo, another a resident and possible friend of both Wallie and Carmen.

Here are some interesting factors to note on this Marriage Certificate/License;

Wallie Dodd Ford/Fard's father is listed as Zara Dodd Ford, born in Madrid Spain

His mother's Maiden Name was Bobbie and was also born in Madrid Spain

Ford/Fard's address was listed as 803 West 3rd Street, Los Angeles California, the apartment located above the restaurant

Wallie Dodd Ford/Fard's race was listed as "Spanish"

Of course, during this entire time, Hazel Barton/Evelsizer, was still corresponding with now-Wallie Dodd Ford/Fard via telephone and letters, because they had a child together, started to tell some of the dark-side of Mr. Fard. By the mid-1920's, the 18th Amendment of the Constitution of the United States defining Prohibition, was in full-swing inside of America and the banning of alcohol was supplemented by California's own even stringent enforcement Prohibition Law named The Woolwine Act", named after former Legislature Representative from of the 63rd District, and Army Colonel Clare Woolwine who introduced the State House Bill in 1919.[50,51]

Hazel Barton/Evelsizer admitted to investigators, that during this time, Wallace Ford/Fard was operating his café business with another man, who was Half-White and Half-Chinese named Edward Donaldson. As a side business, both men were part of a LA-area syndicate, where participants were bootlegging alcohol throughout the Southern California area.

It was during one of these transactions where the men were caught smuggling liquor, on January 20, 1926. They were charged with violating that state's Woolwine Act. They were arrested and sent to jail that day, paid a $1.00 fine ($14.00 fine in 2016 dollars) and then released. According to the arrest paperwork, Wallace Ford/Fard was supposed to appear in front of a court judge on March 20, 1926, but never made it.[52,53,54,55,56]

The men also were selling wholesale Narcotics to some of their clientele as well. It was during this time of Wallace Ford/Fard's life, where he and his counterpart Donaldson got caught by law enforcement for doing their side-business of criminal activity, which sent them both to prison. While the men were selling $225.00 ($6,340.00 in 2016) worth of Heroin to undercover LAPD detectives on February 15, 1926, both men were arrested and charged with the California's Poison Control Act, which was another even more stringent law to punish those who committed crimes by selling, possessing, trafficking and distributing Narcotics to the public.

On February 26, using the name Wallie Dodd Ford, both he and Edward Donaldson was tried before a judge, by waiving their rights to a jury trial, convicted and sentenced to 6-years in prison at the notorious San Quentin State Prison in Northern California. Donaldson, after serving a year and six months, was paroled in 1927, however, Ford/Fard refused parole and decided to serve the entire sentence and be totally a free man.

During the time when Ford/Fard was incarcerated in San Quentin in the 1920's, American prisons nationwide began to instill teachings of Marxist-Leninist ideology among its population. A lot of this education were interchanged between prisoners themselves, some learning it via prison books and others by those prisoners already subverted prior to serving time. It's sensible to conclude that Wallie Dodd Ford/Fard, probably became a part of such teachings and education among his fellow inmates because of the fact, that since he was from New Zealand, he grew up in an environment which was a hot bed of installing Marxist ideology since the 1890's. This conclusion does made sense, where Ford/Fard during his time at San Quentin, was working at the prison's Jute Mill and highway road work crews, where he had access to new prisoners who not only spread the principles of Karl Marx among already incarcerated prisoners but to new prisoners who were starting their incarceration time at San Quentin as well.

On May 27, 1929, Wallie Dodd Ford/Fard was released from prison, after serving three years, three months of prison time, he immediately left California and moved to Chicago Illinois, possibly arriving there in the middle of June. According to Hazel Eversizer in 1957, Ford/Fard went to Chicago to work as a door-to-door Salesman of medical supplies. He even sent her a surgical kit to prove that he was doing such job.[57,58]

However, in the 1930 Federal Census of Chicago, Ford/Fard was living in the home of a Joseph Radwancz, using the name "**William D. Fard", with the address being 1506 Madison Street in West Chicago.**

The census, enumerated on April 22, 1930, listed now-Fard as being 32-years-old, race as being a "*Mexican*", Single Marital Status, indicating that his Father was born in Argentina and his Mother was born in Oregon. Fard's occupation in the same census, listed him as being a Clothing Salesman and a World War I veteran.[59]

Understand that during the late 1920's and early 1930's, there have been a push by the Communist Party of the United States of America (CPUSA), to send a dozen of its members down to the Southern States, in an area which was considered '*The Black Belt*' to create a series of agitation campaigns, to subvert African Americans there to accept the principles of Marxism. {Discussed in the next chapter}

This area, called "*The Black Belt*", was heavily populated with poor, rural-agricultural product producing farms, where-as the Great Depression had settled in, these African Americans were considered ripe for exploitation, not just for accepting Marxist ideology, but to create a separate country, within the country of the United States. This so-called new country in the Deep South, would be eventually led under the leadership of Soviet Dictator Joseph Stalin, located in Moscow

Russia. This separate country would have been called "The Soviet Negro Republic", where Blacks would take over all economic production and political actions of this part of the country, by overthrowing the state government systems.

All of this camouflaged intentionally by CPUSA under the orders of Moscow, which was sold to African Americans that Communism will bring 'social justice' 'equality' and 'fairness' without any racism involved to their community. However, at the same time, another movement was being conducted in the Northern states to subvert the population there, with the intent to overthrow the Federal Government to create a *Sovietized America* based on the same premise of the *Soviet Negro Republic*.

What is speculated, is the fact that Ford/Fard was undergoing subversion training at the CPUSA-famous Abraham Lincoln School, located on the Southside of Chicago, during the evenings. Many influential Marxist Men were educated there, including Frank Marshall Davis and Leon Patterson, to learn how-to subvert Blacks arriving in the Northern Cities such as Chicago and Detroit, and assist them to call for the formation these two new countries. They were taught to conduct this subversion process, by instigating a revolution, via agitation protests, demonstrations and in some cases, outright anarchy.

Another speculation concerning Ford/Fard was the theory that he went to Chicago to accept Supremacy training, sponsored by the *American Nazi Party (AmNP)*, to agitate Blacks into accepting Fascism, by stoking hatred towards the White Race and help divide the country among racial lines.[60,61,62]

None of these speculative theories are possible within the realm of training that Ford/Fard received there in Chicago, after his release from prison in 1929. Especially, when the FBI had documented evidence, that both the Nation of Islam, then-led by Elijah Muhammad, did work with the American Nazi Party (ANP), in the 1950s and 1960s on a number of issues.

Since his training was complete by June of 1930, Ford/Fard was ready to do the tasking that CPUSA and/or the ANP paid him to do; create an organization to psychologically exploit Blacks into accepting either Marxist or Fascist doctrine in the effort to create a nationwide movement to separate African Americans to form their own country within a country, called The United States and Detroit Michigan was the target.

Once Ford/Fard arrived in Detroit Michigan, he became what was told later to FBI Agents "a Turban-wearing, door-to-door Silk-stockings Salesman", carrying a Bible in one hand and a suitcase full of wears in the other hand, preaching on the corner of Detroit's Black Community.

The selected Black area of Detroit where he conducted his business was not accidental; it was incidental, and the area comprised of Blacks who migrated North from the rural South to find better financial opportunities. It is believed that this selection, would have been optimal in not just subverting Blacks coming from the South to Detroit, who were ripe for exploitation because of the Great Depression and they had other family members still residing in the South.

The goal was to double his subversion efforts to accept and advocate a separate Soviet Negro Republic.[63]

Interviews with early Nation of Islam followers have stated, that when Fard/Ford would go door-to-door selling his stockings, his customers would ask about his accept and try to inquire about where he was from. Since to them, he looked like a very light-skinned African American, with his long Black straight hair, Ford/Fard would tell them that he was from the Middle East and he will further explain to his Black customers that the Middle East was the birthplace of Blacks in America.[64]

This became intriguing to them, because up to that time, outside of American Slavery and the continent of Africa, not many Blacks at that time knew anything about the Middle East, so they were willing to invite him into their house and talk about where he was from. As Ford/Fard did more of this, and word spread throughout the Black Community of Detroit, the more people wanted to hear Ford/Fard tell them more about his travels and these places where Blacks were originated that they never knew of.

Ford/Fard continued his preaching of this lie, on the street corners of the Black Community as well, and soon, even more, people wanted to hear more from him. It was July 4, 1930, that the Nation of Islam (NOI) was officially born, as Wallace Dodd Ford/Fard, became the Prophet of Allah and is often celebrated as such within the Black Supremacy Community.[65,66,67]

By the end of 1930, Wallace Ford/Fard began to hold meetings in people homes, where they invited their family members, neighbors and those who attended Christian Sunday Church Services, to come and hear him speak. During the first couple of meetings, Ford/Fard would begin to teach selected passages from the Holy Bible, which was the only religious book readily available at the time.

As more and more people attended his meetings, the more and more he began to denounce Caucasian people and label them as *'blue-eyed Devils'*, while using the stereotypical theme that such White Devils were exploiters of the Black race and it would be up to them to destroy such persons, in the name of freedom, justice, and equality. Of course, his audience was at first shocked as to what they were hearing and some even left in protest his meetings, but slowly they returned to attending Ford/Fard's meetings and became hooked on his outlandish lies and deceptive rhetoric.

Soon, members of the community began to pool their money together to rent a community hall in Detroit, so that more people can hear him speak and gain the message that the Black Man was the original man of the Earth. By the beginning of 1931, Wallace Dodd Ford/Fard, the great con-man of con-men, started to denounce the Bible itself. It is speculated as he denounced the Holy Bible, with the help of CPUSA and/or AmNP, they sent Ford/Fard a copy of the Holy Quran, which was written in Arabic, a language which he was familiar with, via his father Zared Fard. With the Quran in hand, now he began to select even more passages from it and interpreted them as he saw fit, to dupe his Black followers that he was the Prophet of God (Allah) and that he came to;

"...the wilderness of North America to free his fellow brethren from Slavery of the White Devil, and establish and lead the Black Race out of Slavery, by establishing and independent Black Nation in the United States of America."

~ 148 ~

Ford/Fard's delivery of such outright lies and falsehoods, became so effective, that his meetings went well into the night and early mornings, as crowds of Blacks came to hear his messages and rotated attendance of people in shifts. Seeing these numbers increase rapidly, Ford/Fard began to call himself Fard Muhammad in more teaching sessions and with the help of others, began to create a formal organizational structure, named it The Nation of Islam.

The Nation of Islam, simultaneously, began to organize with its own security force, named the Fruit of Islam (FOI), which included a rank-and-file structure similar to the U.S. Military, that took orders from the Minister of Islam (MOI), which in this case was Fard-Muhammad, in the form of General Orders. The FOI's task was to also provide security at all NOI functions and meetings, guard all NOI's property, NOI Officials, police NOI members to assure compliance of Nation of Islam teachings and prepare for "***The War of Armageddon***".

The organization also created its own education system, called The University of Islam, where they were taught rudimentary education to the Nation of Islam's children, in a much-controlled environment, with strict rules and curriculum. Under Fard-Muhammad's direction, the NOI established a **Muslim Girl Training** (MGT) group, operated by the NOI women to teach the congregation's women and girls how to cook and take care of their own Fathers and Husbands. The MGT is structured the same as the Fruit of Islam (FOI) and they have the additional task to make sure that the female members of the NOI are being in-compliance with the organization's teachings.

As the group expanded, the NOI began to publish its own newspapers, which is still being sold today, called ***The Final Call***, that even operates own Editorial Staff.[69,70,71]

And what about this so-called war between the races, as Fard-Muhammad taught, The War of Armageddon? Here is how he describes such an event;

"The Negro Race does not exist and that those who were of darker-skin were Slaves of the White Race or "White Devils" in the United States and because it exploited the darker-skinned people, that

such *"White Devils"* will all be destroyed in the approaching *"War of Armageddon"*.

He had also claimed that he was ***Allah (God) in person***, and was the Supreme Being and will return to the U.S. during their lifetime to lead all true Muslim to the Promise Land. When Fard-Muhammad returns, he told his congregation, that the world will be engaged in the final conflict, the ***War of Armageddon***, which will be the war with all the White Races united fighting all the people of the darker skinned races.

He continued to state that when he returns, the White Man will be the enemy of the Muslims and that all members of the Nation of Islam will follow instructions of Fard-Muhammad, even when it comes to harming the White Man or The White Man's Government.

He continues;

"[the Nation of Islam] teach the downtrodden and defenseless Black People a thorough knowledge of God and of themselves, and put them on the road to self-independence, with a superior culture and high civilization that they had previously experienced."

The Nation of Islam considers Wallace Dodd Fard-Muhammad as the Messiah of Judaism and the Mahdi of Islam, which goes against the belief of Orthodox Islam, causing many Muslims following the latter to adamantly reject the former's version of Islam as a fraud.

Nevertheless, Fard-Muhammad never told his followers nor his successor's anything about his past and that he came from the East for the Negroes in America to come and join the Nation of Islam. He stated that he came from the Holy City of Mecca (Saudi Arabia) and that;

"... [I am] your brother. You have not yet seen me in my robes."

He also taught that Allah was a Man, in the person of W.D. Fard-Muhammad, and that no one should disclose his identity to no one. He also taught;[72]

The Devil is the White Man

The White man was a murderer, a cheater, a liar, a rapist, a thief and is always corrupt

The White man had stolen the Black Man's music and is making millions of dollars from the royalties from them

The Black Man was good, honest and untainted by evil until he was exposed to evil by the White man when he was being enslaved

<u>All of this coming from a White guy, from New Zealand!</u>

There is more.

Those who became members of the Nation of Islam or support the views of the organization are called "**Black Muslims**". Black Muslims, in general, follow a rigorous routine of eating healthy, no red meat (no cat, rat or dog), exercise intensely and publicly present themselves as cleaned-dressed and highly-educated people.

Some credit Fard-Muhammad with installing this principle early-on, because he was always cleanly dressed, eat no red meat, exercised intensely and appeared to be highly educated, during his speeches. Others have told FBI Investigators in the 1950's, that Fard-Muhammad was a great cook, but had always carried hundreds of packets of sugar in his coat pockets because he was a **Diabetic.** Sometimes, informant members have stated, Fard-Muhammad always walked around wearing gloves, because his hands were so easily injured because of his Diabetic condition.[73,74]

In 1931, when the NOI carried over 8,000 members, Fard-Muhammad, who sometimes went by *<u>W.D. Fard</u>* or *<u>W.D. Fard-Muhammad</u>*, met and converted one of the members to take the reins of the Nation of Islam; His name was **Elijah Poole**.

Elijah Poole was a short-light-skinned African American who suffered from Asthma, who had just relocated to Detroit with his family from Sandersville, Georgia, in 1917. Poole, who was married to his wife Clara and had eight-children in the household, only had a third-grade education, bounced from job-to-job, during the Great Depression, trying to keep his family fed.

In August 1931, at the urging of his wife, Poole attended a speech given by Fard-Muhammad on Islam and Black Empowerment, which not only impressed him, but he began to work full-time within the Nation of Islam to help make the commune bigger. Since the organization began to operate smoothly, the Minister of Islam did not have to attend every function that was going on, which gave time to train his replacement, in the person of Elijah Poole.

Poole changed his name to Elijah X, the latter letter was meant to the establishment of dropping the so-called "Slave surname" given by the White Devil enslaving the dark-skinned races. Elijah X eventually became Elijah Muhammad and was given the title of Messenger.[75,76,77]

One of the earliest stains that were put on the reputation of Detroit's Nation of Islam organization, was the rumor by some of its members that had beliefs to carry out and conduct human sacrifices to their God, Wallace Fard-Muhammad. During one of the FBI interviews conducted in the 1950's, one of the NOI's earliest members, have told them that;

"Fard-Muhammad was sacrificing us (Blacks) for his own personal gain. Some of his teachings had told members that in-order to commit yourself fully to Allah, one had to bring him four "Devils" heads for one coat lapel pin."[78]

There also have been rumors that it was Wallace Fard-Muhammad, who was accused into teaching and instigating such ideas of human murders of innocent Blacks and those of other races who did not like the ideas that the Nation of Islam stood for.

This, of course, did not sit well with other members of Detroit's Black Community that did not support the Nation of Islam and they petitioned the city to take-action and investigate such rumors. It didn't take long to find out the real story behind the rumors, however tragic it was.[79]

On November 20, 1932, a Nation of Islam member named Robert X Harris, a 44-year-old Black Muslim, killed another Black man who was not Muslim, as part of a human sacrifice to his God, Allah in the person of Wallace Dodd Fard-Muhammad. Harris killed 40-year-old James J. Smith also of Detroit, by crushing his skull using a rear-car axle to "quiet him" and then was stabbed numerous times in the heart with an eight-inch knife. Harris told police that;

"The ninth hour of the 20th day had come, it was predestined 1,500 years-ago that at that hour I must make a human sacrifice to my God. It must not be a member of the Order of Islam (Nation of Islam), but some stranger-the first person I met after leaving my home."

Both Robert X Harris and his wife, Bertha Harris, who witnessed the murder were arrested and jailed. However, their arrest and capture only scratched the surface of what Fard-Muhammad was teaching his followers of the Nation of Islam at its beginning.

On November 27, 1932, the front-page article in the ***Detroit Free Press*** Newspaper, titled **"List of Voodoo Plots Growing: Negro Reveals Attack Made by Harris"** tells of another incident that Robert X Harris attempted to take another Black Man's life as a human sacrifice just days earlier, before the successful attack on James J. Smith .[80]

The man, who was not named for fear at the time of retribution by other NOI members, told the Free Press, that on Thursday, November 17th, four days prior to the murder of James J. Smith, he was walking down the street near his home, when Harris accosted him and attacked by beating him over the head with an unknown object. During the attack, as the victim was trying to fight Harris off, stated that Harris stated;

"The time for crucifixions is at hand"

As the attacker tried to subdue the victim, at the same time, Harris was trying to pull the victim into his home. However, the victim managed to get away from Harris and ran off to his home a block away.

Later-on, still frightened as to what had just happened to him a few hours ago, neighbors told the victim, that he had been marked for death, via a human sacrifice by Nation of Islam members. He wasn't the only one. Two days after the Smith murder, an African American woman, who worked as a Social Worker, was sitting on her front porch of her home, when three well-dressed men accosted her on her property and threatened that if she and her employer did not stop speaking out against the Nation of Islam, that both will be marked for death by members of the organization.

With the arrest of Robert X Harris and his wife Bertha, it was revealed that several dozen African American Men and Women were listed and targeted for death by some NOI members. This prompted the Detroit Police to conduct a raid on the NOI's leader hotel room at 1 West Jefferson Avenue Saturday afternoon, November 26.

In the article, "*Wallace Farad*" provided detectives hundreds of documents and written communications, crudely written on white-bonded paper, where numerous NOI members had not only paid their "**God**" to change their "**Slave surnames**" to **Muhammad**, **Bin** or **Ali**, and other correspondence about the organization's operations, meetings, activities, sacrifices, and funding. What authorities did not catch was the one "Wallace Farad" himself, who wasn't in the room when the raid took place.

What was interesting to note about the about the newspaper article of the 27th of November, was the fact that Detroit Police had credible intelligence about the NOI's plans to conduct human sacrifices on those within the Black Community and even in the White "devil" community that spoke out against the organization. Also, the most interesting part of the article was at the end, where Detroit Police admitted that the group was not considered a group at all, but as a Nation.

A large investigation took place that surveilled the Nation of Islam by Law Enforcement officials, between December 1932 and May of 1933. By that time, they had gathered enough evidence to indict Wallace Fard-Muhammad for conspiracy for the Nation of Islam members to commit murder. On May 25, 1933, he was arrested, booked and jailed for one day. As he was interrogated by Detroit detectives, they presented voluminous evidence to him where he could be thrown in prison for the rest of his life. That, scared old Fard-Muhammad to death, going back to prison once again was not in his plans. However, in exchange for his testimony, detectives told him flat-out, that he would not go to prison if he would just leave the city and provide the names of members who were planning to conduct more homicides.[82,83,84]

This was a deal that he couldn't pass up and he chose the latter. When Detectives asked him why would lead such an organization of Blacks and be their "God", Wallace did admit that he did so, because it made him large amounts of money. It was a racket that he could not pass up doing. The rest is history.

Outside of the human sacrificial murders that were being planned by members of the Nation of Islam, Fard-Muhammad chose Elijah Muhammad as his successor as Minister of Islam. Within days of promoting Elijah and coining him as a Prophet, Wallace Dodd Fard-Muhammad told Elijah Muhammad, that he was going to return to the Holy City of Mecca Saudi Arabia and will return to the United States when the War of Armageddon commences.[85,86]

He even lied to his own Prophet Muhammad. In reality, Fard-Muhammad left Detroit to return to Chicago, where his training began three-years prior and where his debriefing began; at CPUSA and ANP Headquarters.

This wasn't the end of Fard-Muhammad.

Between June 1933 and June 1934, he traveled back and forth to Detroit, meeting numerous times with Elijah Muhammad and offering advice on problems the latter was facing in managing the Nation. Paid handsomely by both CPUSA and ANP, Fard-Muhammad returned to Los Angeles to see his Son and his former Common Law Wife Hazel Barton again.[87,88]

Hazel told FBI investigators in October 1958, that during his last visit, Fard-Muhammad had told him that he was returning-back to New Zealand. She also noticed some peculiar things about him during this last visit. For one, he was driving a 1929 Model A Ford, with California license plates, which struck her as odd. This was still during the Great Depression and buying such a car cost a lot of money. Second, he covered the seats of the car with white bed sheets for no apparent reason. She also noticed that he ate only one meal that day, and just before he left, he gave the bed sheets he used for the car to her and told her that he no longer needed them.

Hazel stated that Fard-Muhammad had always kept in contact with her, even when he was in Detroit. So, she knew what he was doing on the surface. She did not know what he did underneath that surface. Eventually, she will find out. In June 1934, that day was the last time she saw Fard-Muhammad, but however, she was corresponding with him in New Zealand for many years, addressing the letters to his Uncle's home, in Wellington, New Zealand.

Somehow, Hazel found out about Wallace Fard-Muhammad's involvement with the Nation of Islam. It is unclear as to whether he told her via a letter, telephone her or what. According to the FBI documents, she didn't like what he invented there in Detroit.

On July 1, 1940, Hazel Evelsizer petitioned the California Department of Health, to change the Birth Certificate of Fard-Muhammad's son, from Wallace Dodd Ford to Wallace Max Ford on the birth certificate.[88] It is possible, that Wallace Dodd Fard-Muhammad, did return to New Zealand and lived in the town of Wellington. It is speculated that he remarried, had children and lived another life, outside of the spotlight, until passing away between 1963 and 1978.

Black Liberation Theology and Black Nationalism in the Modern-Era

Pan-African Flag, Symbol of the Black Liberation Movement
(Author's Collection)

When you hear anything regarding Music/Entertainment or see people display a certain-colored flag that is not the American Flag (Old Glory), during protests and street riots, signifying the colors *Red*, *Black*, and *Green;* then you will now know what those colors mean to many inside the Black Community.

Those colors stand for "***Black Liberation***" and it has Marxist-Leninist roots dating back to Martin Delaney's time.

One major issue about ***Black Liberation Theology (BLT) and Black Nationalism (BN)*** Ideologies; both are just as dangerous as ***White Supremacy and Anarchy***.

This statement is very true!

Because of both use race and human supremacy, which in ***this*** case ***Black Supremacy***, as the basis of their actions. Many people of different cultures and backgrounds here in the United States are not aware of the significance of the after-mentioned ideologies, thus is one of the reasons why this book is being written.

By the end of this chapter, one will have a full-understanding of what both ideologies are and understand how extremely dangerous that they have become. We will first explore ***Black Liberation Theology***.

Black Liberation Theology (BLT) and/or Black Nationalism (BN) are ideologies that are based on the teachings of Karl Marx and Friedrich Engels, using Anti-Semitic rhetoric, mixed with a bastardization of selected verses from the Holy Bible, as stated in a previous chapter. The only difference between the two is their actions.

BLT uses psychological subversion of African-Americans to accept racist views under the guise of Marxist-Leninism, hidden beneath the surface of Christianity.[90] ***Black Nationalism*** or BN, takes Black Liberation Theology to another level in its entirety and carry out such beliefs in real-time.

In the meantime, those who firmly believe in both, promote Marxism, by implying that the light of God's revelation in Jesus Christ is equal to the Black Condition.[91,92] Therefore, all persons within the Black

Community is emancipated from those who they consider are their oppressors. Particularly other people from different races (particularly **White**), authority figures and those in positions of power. It is taught that these so-called "outside forces" are the ones who had victimized them unjustly in the past and in the present.

In both BLT and BN, people who fit such categories are Black America's oppressors, thus need to be destroyed in its entirety via **liquidation**. In simpler terms, those who the Black Community who feels and sees as their oppressors, need to die, even if they, the oppressors, die by violent action, if necessary.

This is not debatable for discussion, but it is a true unadulterated fact!

Both doctrines teach that the African Americans are still constantly being oppressed by '**Evil-rich White People'**, '**Honkies'**, '**Peckerwoods'**, '**Crackers'** and so on and so forth, are the protectors of the United States of America and need to be overthrown by a violent revolution; in a **Race War** so to speak.[93,94,95]

Black Liberation Theology continues to be taught and learned in numerous African-American Churches, Public Schools, in Black Neighborhoods, targeted specifically, to those who live in the inner-cities of America. BLT is also promoted on Television, Entertainment, Music, Social Media and even in the print media, of Books, Newspapers, and the Labor Union literature.

What BLT and BN do so well, is that the ideology exploits the inner emotions of their listeners. It uses this tactic to brainwash their listeners to accept that their social-economic condition will never get better, because of the color of their skin. By invoking this type of psychological conditioning, throughout the America's Black Community, African-Americans will feel that "**the system is stacked against them**" because their skin color is a curse. They are forced to believe falsely, that because of what they consider as an inhumane flaw, they would never rise-up to the level of greatness that other cultures have had, because of "**Slavery**". Thereby allowing their followers to become victims of their own circumstances.

In the follower's mind, they will begin to see themselves as actual victims of such circumstances, who will eventually view those like them, who live in similar situations as they are as **_Proletariats_**. In the victim's mind, they often work for low-wages, live in poverty-stricken areas, barely making ends meet, while the '**_White Man_**' or '**_Gray Boys_**' earns '**_huge profits off the backs of the workers_**' like them.

So, by going against and standing toe-to-toe with their 'oppressors', using criminal and often violent confrontations against Whites, their actions to destroy their enemies are considered justified! The madness of this doctrine is just that simple.

One last caveat of BLT is this; if another person who is African-American doesn't agree with them or their Marxist-driven ideology, they are called names to create, what Marxist Men calls "**_a bad smell_**", in-order to character assassinate such dissenters. Blacks, like this author, who can see right through this think-skinned, fake ideology of Marxism care called '**_Uncle Toms_**', '**_Uncle Ruckus_**', '**_Coons_**', '**_Sambos_**' and other derogatory names. Black Liberation Theology believers also consider those who are Black that goes against them, are protecting '**_The White Man's wealth_**' that need to be **_liquidated also_**.

So where does the term Black Liberation Theology come from, one may ask? The definition of **_Liberate_** is "to free from bondage or restraint; to raise to equal rights and status". **_Liberation_** is just the act of Liberating a selection or group of people from bondage or restraint.[96,97] The Liberation Movement started in the 1950's and '60s in South and Central America to subvert masses of people, particularly poor people, in an exploitation operation, to free themselves from the evils of Capitalism.

Sounds familiar? It should.

Those subverted who believe such nonsense considered such Socioeconomic system as 'Bondage' or 'Slavery', and that the poor need to rise-up against the social inequities of their condition, via a worldwide revolution. In other words, in the form of Marxist-Leninist Ideology. Amazingly, this Liberation Movement started in the **_Roman Catholic Church_** in Central and South America, where whole congregations of people were brainwashed to believe that God through

Jesus Christ speaks directly to the poor and hungry, and again, using selected verses from the Bible to justify their position. Most of the Marxist-Leninists who were doing the subversion, where trained Propagandists and paid-for the Soviet KGB/NKVD in Moscow Russia.[98,99]

The same holds true for Black Liberation Theology here in the United States. BLT was originally coined by Dr. James Hal Cone, who currently works as a Professor of New York City Union Theology. Some believed was Dr. Cone was psychologically subverted into Marxism by the teachings of Marxist-Man Saul Alinsky and other Marxist-Leninists while attending colleges at;

Philander Smith College in the 1950's,

Garrett-Evangelical Theological Seminary in 1961

Northwestern University between 1963-1965.[100,101]

On July 31, 1966, in Dallas, Texas, Dr. Cone, and 50 other Black Clergymen formed the **National Committee of the Negro Churchmen (NCNC)**, during the height and a new transition of the American Civil Rights Movement. According to a New York Times article dated the same day, titled *"Black Power: Statement by National Committee of Negro Churchmen"* stated in-part;

"The fundamental distortion facing us in the controversy "Black Power" is rooted in a gross imbalance of power and conscience between Negroes and White Americans. It is this distortion, mainly, which is responsible for the widespread inarticulate assumption that White people are justified in getting what they want to the use of power, but the Negro Americans must, either by nature or by circumstances, make their appeal only through conscience...."

The New Times Article continues...

"As a result, the power of White Men and the Conscience of Black Men have both been corrupted. The power of White Men is corrupted because it meets littles meaningful resistance from Negroes to temper it and keep White Men from aping [mimicking] God. The conscience of Black Men is corrupted because, having no power to implement the demands of conscience, the concerns for justices is

transmitted into a distorted form of love, which in the absence of justice is transmitted into a distorted form of love, which in the absence of justices, becomes chaotic self-surrender. Powerless breeds a race of beggars. We are faced with a situation where conscience-less power meets powerless conscience, threatening the very foundation of our nation." [102,103,104]

Time Magazine Article dated November 17, 1967, titled "*Churches: Black Power in the Pulpit*" boasted that by the time the article was written, the committee was "comprised of 300 members from twelve Protestant denominations". NCNC's purpose was to;

"*...arouse Negro Churches to a keener awareness of their own responsibilities...to form a nonprofit corporation that will solicit funds from Negro congregations and other sources to finance housing and small businesses in the ghettos...[and] to help Negroes in predominantly White Churches achieve a greater voice in policy.*"

As to where this "**other sources**" of funding is anybody's guess but can be most accurately interpreted that such funding would come from the Communist Party of the United States of America (CPUSA) and its multitude of organizations under the control of the latter.

Regardless, as anyone can tell by their rhetoric in both the New York Times and Time Magazine Articles, Dr. Cones and his minions of the Marxist Black pulpit, were more in-line with Black Supremacy Groups of The Nation of Islam Leader Elijah Muhammad, Malcolm X before conversion to orthodox Islam and Black Israelites than Dr. Martin Luther King and Booker T. Washington! As a matter of fact, Dr. James Hal Cone's radical ideology of Black Liberation Theology aligns with both Karl Marx and David Walker of the 'Appeal'. Dr. Cone in his book "*Black Liberation Theology*" written in 1969, wrote;

"*The Christian faith has been interrupted largely by those who enslaved Black People, and by the people who segregated them.*"[105]

Cone often cited in his book that the oppressed, who were Black and the Cultural Dominance Class, were White. Meaning objectively, Black Liberation Theology is considered an ideology based on racism, which encourages its followers with retribution, hate, discontent, and anger.

In all, Black Liberation Theology taught by Dr. Cone, and the Reverend Jeremiah Wright, President Obama's Church Pastor for over 20-years, plus hundreds of others throughout the nation, teaches this twisted view of Christianity. All to further the goal to align the Black Community as the Proletariats in Marxist Ideology. This conditioning of low-income Blacks by propagandists preaching hate and discontent among the masses, is ripe for exploitation by Marxist Men to stoke the flames of racial division, to create a national crisis, in the form of a Revolution.

Black Liberation Theology and Radical Islam

Black Liberation Theology and Radical Islam are both religious doctrines that have eerily similar paths and view of the world. The former is taught as a bastardization of Christianity, using carefully selected verses from the Holy Bible, as deceptive interpretations in their meanings. Radical Islam does the same, using verses in the Shura written in the Holy Quran. Both are considered philosophical entities have that have social and political goals that those who don't follow or accept their twisted views. In other words, Black Liberation Theology and Radical Islam are duality ideologies, based on one simple word; **Submission**. Submission to their own interpretation of their respective doctrines. [106,107]

Black Liberation has a God, that divides human beings based on the color of one's skin. On the other hand, Radial Islam has Allah (God) that divides human beings by beliefs. The duality between them is not a complete division between them, but a complete separation of both ideologies based on moral, ethical cultural and religious differences.

Remember, Black Liberation Theology is based on Christianity, where God's word is spoken through **Jesus Christ**, where Radical Islam is, of course, based on Islam, where Allah's will be spoken through the **Prophet Muhammad**.
     They both want and need complete submission of their targeted population bases.

~ 162 ~

For example, in Radial Islam, Allah preaches, via the Prophet Muhammad, that those who do not submit to his will are Ka firs or simply non-believers of Islam. Those who are non-believers of Islam, Muhammad preaches violence to those who do not submit to Allah's will. Vice, in Black Liberation Theology, they do not preach violence against those who they consider their oppressors, White People, but instead, advocated violence against them and excuses it via Black Supremacy.

You can see this very clearly in recent times during the month of July 2016. In that month, which is considered as one of the bloodiest days of the attack on Law Enforcement Personnel throughout the country.

When 25-year-old, former U.S. Army National Guard Soldier, Afghanistan Veteran, Micah Xavier Johnson, of Mesquite Texas, gunned down 12 Dallas Texas Police Officers in cold blood. [109,110] The tragic incident took place on July 7th, when over 800 Protestors of Black Lives Matter (BLM) Communist Front-Group, were demonstrating in response to the Police Shootings of Alton Sterling and Philando Castile, near the Dallas Police Headquarters.

The attack caught on video, Johnson killed five officers and wounding seven, including two innocent civilian bystanders. After 2-hours of intense negotiations, between Johnson and Dallas PD in nearby El Centro Community College, the latter sent in a Police Robot-armed Bomb filled with 1 pound of C-4 Explosives where Johnson was hiding out and detonated the device. Micah Johnson was killed instantly. [111,112] Prompting some members of the Black Community that the Dallas Police Department used 'excessive force' to subdue Johnson.

After the incident, investigators found that Johnson became a huge follower of Black Nationalist and Supremacy groups online, to include the Nation of Islam (NOI), New Black Panther Party (NBPP) and the Black Riders Liberation Army (BRLA); all identified as Hate Groups by the Southern Poverty Law Center (SPLC). [113,114]

Johnson was also a frequent visitor to the Facebook Social Media Page of the African American Defense League (AADL), another Marxist Front Group led by Maricelm-Lei Millere, who starting in 2014, called for the nationwide murders of Police Officers, in the wake of the fatal shooting of Laquan McDonald in Chicago. [115]

The next day, July 8th, Dallas Police raided Johnson's home early in the morning and it was searched extensively. During the raid, Law Enforcement Personnel found a plethora of Bomb-making materials, Ballistic Vests, two Semi-Automatic Rifles, a large quantity of ammunition, books on Combat Self-Defense and a handwritten journal that offered clues to his mental state of hating Whites and Law Enforcement Officers, prior to the shooting. It was determined that Johnson acted alone in his quest to kill Police Officers, which sparked another tragic incident in the next state, of Louisiana, the following week, which should be a warning to all of us, that such evil persons lurk among us in the population. This killer's name was called 'Micah X' and his crime committed was of such horror, to where some people within the African American Community were celebrating such a coward for his deadly acts, while the rest of the American Public, of all races and creeds, were shocked as to what transpired in Baton Rouge, Louisiana.

Galvin Eugene Long, A.K.A. Micah X from Kansas City, Missouri, traveled to Louisiana and methodically ambushed and killed three Baton Rouge, Louisiana Police Officers, in cold-blood. Long stated before he conducted his heinous crime, on Social Media, that he planned to conduct such an operation, in response to that city's police shooting and killing of Black Man, named Alton Sterling. Sterling resisted arrest after Law Enforcement Officers were called to the scene, after receiving reports that a suspect, matching the description of Sterling, who attempted to conduct an armed robbery on someone there on July 5th.

Long, a 29-year-old Millennial, former U.S. Marine Corps Sargent, Marxist-duped-former Nation of Islam member, began to go on a tirade about White 'Crackers', using and abusing African-Americans on U.S. soil. [116, 117] In his videos posted on both Facebook and You Tube, he discusses Black Liberation Theology (BLT) and claim that he wrote his own book, written for "For my dark-skinned brother", even though **Long himself**, was a ***light-skinned Black Man***. In some of his videos, Galvin Long looked at other Marxist Men and, Black Power Radicals of the 1960's, such as Black Panthers Huey P. Newton, Malcolm X, and Elijah Muhammad, as being his heroes. Another You Tube video that he made while visiting Dallas Texas, Galvin Long, stated this;

"If I'm peaceful protesting...I know they would try to arrest me, and I would die right there because you're not going to kidnap me. I know my rights, but I stand on my rights. That's what separates me, that's why they're afraid of me."

Long was killed by other Baton Rouge Police at the scene of his heinous crime. In one of his You Tube videos, the killer stated this; [118, 119, 120]

"I thought my own thoughts. I made my own decisions. I'm the one who's got to listen the judgment. That's it. Any my heart is pure...If anything happens with me because I'm an alpha male, I stand up, I stand firm, I stand for mine, until the end...Yeah, I also was a Nation of Islam member. Don't affiliate me with it. Don't affiliate me with anything..."

Mr. Galvin Long A.K.A. Micah X, you have been affiliated, with Marxist-Leninist principles and didn't even know it. As for judgment, many Marxists and their dupes have been judged, not by God, but by the Devil himself, which you became a member of the latter's society. Enjoy yourself down there.

Radical Islam, when looking through the lens of ethics, Kafirs can be deceived, robbed, raped, insulted, brutalized and even killed in the name of Allah, only if they don't submit to his will. Black Liberation Theology, when dealing with ethics, justifies the robbing, raping, insulting, brutalizing and yes, the killing of White people who they consider are their oppressors. Marxist Man and coiner of BLT explain this in his book "A Black Theology of Liberation" to confirm this position;

"What we need is the divine love as expressed in Black Power, which is the power of Blacks to destroy their oppressors, here and now, by all means at their disposal."[121]

Radical Islam calls for no empathy or sorrow for the killing, slaughtering or destruction of Ka firs by what the Prophet Muhammad calls in the name of "*Jihad*". Understand, that within the last 1400-plus years, Radical Islam has been responsible for the murder of over 270 million people worldwide, in the name of Jihad. Black Liberation Theology preachers, in the likes of Jeremiah Wright, Nation of Islam (NOI) leader Louis Farrakhan and many others preaches that Blacks who kill and destroy their oppressors show no remorse or empathy towards their oppressors; even those who are Black and who they consider the protectors of their oppressors, of the evil-rich White people who have enslaved Blacks for so long.[122]

Unfortunately, the duality between BLT and Radical Islam ends right there. It is at this point where they separate, in-order to achieve their end goals. The comradeships between both are ***only temporary***. At the end, since Radical Islam does not recognize the color of one's skin as "oppressors" or the "enemy", Radical Islam does recognize those who believe in Black Liberation Theology, including Farrakhan's Nation of Islam, as ka firs. In short, if Radical Islam takes a foothold and ascends into American society, ALL non-believers of Radical Islam will either convert to their version of 5th Century Islam or be killed in the name of Jihad! Yes, that will include those who believe in Black Liberation Theology, including those who follow the Nation of Islam. Understand, that the Jihadists also have a bounty on your heads too!

Micah Xavier Johnson, murderer of five Dallas Police Officers in July 2016

(Courtesy Southern Poverty Law Center)

~ 166 ~

Video Captures of Galvin Eugene Long A.K.A. Micah X, Killer of three Baton Rouge Police Officers July 2016.

(Top Photo Courtesy of Wikimedia/Bottom Photo Courtesy of The Daily Caller)

10: The Creation of a Sovietized Black America

Photo of Lovett Fort-Whiteman, head of the American Negro Labor Congress (ANLC) and the *only* African-American who died in Stalin's Gulag in Siberia Russia in 1938. (Courtesy of Wikimedia)

So far throughout this book, we have learned that the main overall objective of Marxist Men, is to create a utopian world where Communism/Socialism would be carried out by the few collective elites, to control every bit of human nature over the many. The repetitive nature of this statement must be emphasized repeatedly, for others to understand the true colors of those advocating such a proven oppressive ideology. Communists create narratives and propaganda campaigns to exploit an issue, whether true or not to further their agenda. By doing this, Marxist Men along with their duped

Progressives/Liberals, pushes the envelope hard as they can during the sometimes made-up crisis, providing a concentrated, continuous effort of agitation, hate, and discontent to sway public opinion. Once they control public opinion their way, it will be easy for them to achieve what they want, in the long term. Every Communist campaign started are specifically intended to arouse, influence and mobilize as many people as possible to create the façade that what Marxists want, is the majority opinion of the public, when it is not.

Marxist Men target prominent professions and use the people in them to create such a massive exploitation value of such members, as the crust of their agitation operations.[1] People working in such professions include, Religious Clergy, Public Educators, Lawyers, Scientists, and Artists have been used as political prostitutes as vehicles to drive home Communism's worldwide domination plan. By zeroing on the biggest and most popular personalities, millions of people inside the United States of America will feel, deceptively, that such agitation is more important than anything other issues going on at the same time. Marxists Men specifically target Hollywood Actors, Music Entertainers, Trade Union members, Workers and Foreign-born persons to create even more agitation and protests to destroy opposition of those opposing the Communist view.

Black Men, Women and their dependents are ripe for exploitation by Marxist Men for those working in such industries, as well as those Blacks who are emotionally driven to believe anything and everything that they see, hear or are told, whether such information is true or not. Black Americans that fit into these categories are considered "perfect targets" to Marxist Men because it takes so little work for those weak-minded enough to jump onboard and support Communism without even having knowledge is to understand that they are being used. [2]

For decades, since the 1920's and beyond, Blacks in America have been used by Marxists of all skin colors, including their own, to manage their exploitation operations, using lies and deceptive banners like "**Civil Rights**", "**Social Justice**", "**Equality**" and "**Systematic Racism**". These lies have been so effective and successful on the psyche of Black folks in the past and even in the present, that Marxist Men target Black Americans, even more nowadays, to drive their agenda further than they ever had in the past. Mostly, it is because of the successful elections of America's first Marxist Man and the 1st Black President named Barack Hussein Obama in 2008 and 2012.

Since then, Blacks Americans of all economic and educational levels have swallowed the bait thrown out by Communists like a Catfish in a freshwater pond!

When the Bolshevik Revolution occurred in March 1917, installing Russian Dictator Vladimir Lenin, Moscow had become the chief capital city and operation of **Global Communism ("Globalization")**.

Between 1919-1989, Moscow under the KGB and Communist International Conventions have operated the Marxist Plan of Action both financially and metaphorically to spread and implement worldwide Communism. The United States of America became their largest and final target for complete subversion into Communism. However, since 1989, the capital city of Global Marxism has divided into distinct cities; New York, New York (The U.N./CPUSA) and Chicago, Illinois (CPUSA).

Early on, it was determined that all people of cultures and skin colors now needed to be psychologically subverted, including Blacks, to create a "Soviet America". In between the set-up, create and operation of CPUSA, both Black and White Communists within American borders, have advocated in the past and even now, the establishment of a "*Soviet Negro Republic*" within "*Soviet America*".

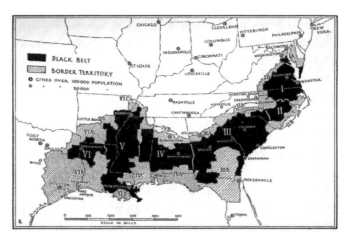

BLACK BELT AND BORDER TERRITORY

The Call Goes Out

Sometime in July 2016, this author was reading an article posted online by Breitbart news site, titled "*EXCLUSIVE-New Black*

~ 169 ~

Panther Leader: Blacks Need to Migrate to Five Southern States, Form 'Country within a Country'".[2] Upon reading this article, written by Aaron Kline, who interviewed the New Black Panther Leader/Minister of Defense, Babu Omowale on his New York City radio show, boasted that five states located in the Southeastern section of the United States belong to the so-called "Black Nation"; Louisiana, Mississippi, South Carolina, Alabama and Georgia. Mr. Omowale claimed that America's Black Community needed to migrate back to the after-mentioned states by "taking control of the economies in those states." He further goes on to say during Aaron Kline's interview that "if Black People move in, most definitely White People will move out. So, it's not a hard process for us to have our own country within a country."

Really Babu Omowale?

It's a pathetic shame that folks like him, not only don't have a clue about anything dealing with basic economics, but this Marxist idea has been done long before he was ever born, what during the early 1990's? All negative comments aside from this author, the nonsense of establishing Blacks their own country within the United States is nothing new, but was tried during the 1920's, 1930's and 1940's, advocated by the original Black Panther Party during the 60's and 70's under Huey P. Newton, and Malcolm X when he was the Spokesman for the Nation of Islam. This idea was floated, even more, advocated by the latter organization, egged on by its leader, Louis Farrakhan, as late as the mid-1990's![2,3,4]

The one thing that each of these so-called ideas about Black Americans having their own country with a country have in common; rhetoric. That's all Mr. Babu Omowale and those folks who think just like him is just that; rhetoric, or talk! Each time this idea has been advocated for, it has failed miserably. The main reason for such outlandish talk is a deceptive tactic to not only support Marxist Men's idea that Blacks can have their own country, falsely but to reverse segregation of today's American Blacks, to meet the goal of Karl Marx. The goal that says that for Communism to work, the old society, called Capitalism must be undone in its entirety and reshaped by the "Almighty State".

In other words, Blacks need to revert-back to Segregation to make things 'equal' again. Insanity!

What was termed as *"**The Soviet Negro Republic**"* was first envisioned not long after CPUSA was established in 1919 in Chicago, Illinois, by Black Poet and well-known Black Journalist of the time named Festus Claudius "Claude" Mc Kay. Mc Kay was born in Jamaica and emigrated to the U.S. in 1912. After attending Tuskegee Institute (now-Tuskegee University), he transferred to Kansas State University, located in Manhattan Kansas.[5,6] He became interested in the works of another African American, W. E. B. Du Bois. an outright Communist, after reading Du Bois book *"**The Soul of Black Folk**"*. Though he was brilliant academically, Mc Kay decided to leave Kansas State University and move to New York City. It was there when he married his wife Eulalie Lewards and began writing his books.

While he was living in New York City, Mc Kay began to be involved with both Socialists and Marxist-Leninist Radicals, which included Caribbean authors Cyril Briggs, Richard B. Moore and Wilfrid Domingo.[7,8] Mc Kay began to write for Marcus Garvey's *"**Negro World**"* newspaper for Garvey's United Negro Improvement Association (UNIA) in 1918.[9,10] After many trips overseas, Claude McKay visited Moscow Russia from November 1922-June 1923, to attend the Fourth Congress of the Communist International (COMINTERN). While there, he gained access to meet with many inner circles of men of Leon Trotsky, Nikolai Burkrain, and Karl Radek. After returning from Soviet Russia, McKay wrote an article in the NAACP's magazine called *"**The Crisis**"*, where wrote about the glorious welcoming reception that he received during his visit there.

McKay became somewhat a "spokesman" for Black Americans to the Russian KGB Agents and was tasked to describe the conditions of the Negro Population in America in detail and even write about it, in which he did. McKay, without knowing that his Soviet hosts were duping him to write such a piece, so they can use it for a more sinister purpose, in the form of propaganda, to be edited and distributed throughout Africa, often told the questioners during such conversations, that he blamed such racism here in the U.S. of Blacks on Capitalism and Imperialism.

In response, McKay and his counterpart from the African Blood Brotherhood (ABB) Socialist front group, Harry Haywood, recommended to the Communist International (COMINTERN) that money, manpower, and a large propaganda campaign where necessary, to mobilize millions Black Americans, particularly in the South, to join the revolutionary cause.[11, 12, 13, 14,15] COMINTERN approved the request shortly afterwards and gave $300,000.00 American Dollars ($3.41 Million Dollars in 2016) to CPUSA to begin the psychological subversion process of Black Farmers and Sharecroppers throughout the South.

The Communist International further determined, in both 1927 and 1928 conventions in Moscow, that Black Americans working as Farmers and Sharecroppers were considered a separate class of people, therefore, they would make up the Working Class or Proletariats of the coming World Communist Revolution. The Farmers and Sharecroppers were also important in creating a *"Soviet Negro Republic"*; _a country within a country._

During the 1928 COMINTERN Convention, the organization needed a group of Black Men to head up a separate committee to operate, manage and even provide the allotted funding via CPUSA for this subversion of Blacks in the South to become successful.

The Gang of Eight and John Pepper's American Negro Problems

In 1925, COMINTERN selected the first eight American Black Men, which we will call "The Gang of Eight" from within the Communist Party in America to be sent to Moscow, to undergo extensive Marxist Men training at the Lenin School. This facility, operated by Russian Premier Joseph Stalin's Committee of State Security, known around the world as the KGB, the school was made to psychologically subvert these eight men to propagandize and create agitation within the targeted population, to mobilize them to accept and join the Communist Revolution _at all costs_. Of this so-called gang, the major players who attended this training were;

> *Lovett Fort-Whiteman, founder of the American Negro Labor Congress (ANLC)*

> *James W. Ford- High ranking member of the Chicago-based American Negro Labor Congress (ANLC)*

> *William L. Patterson- Ranking member of the Civil Rights Congress (CRC) and later-on, Head of the International Labor Defense (ILD)*

> *Otto E. Huiswoud- Charter member of CPUSA and ranking member of the African Blood Brotherhood (ABB) and a contemporary of Harry Haywood*

Harry Haywood- Leading figure of CPUSA and high-ranking member of the Young Communist League and African Blood Brotherhood (ABB) figure

Cyril Valentine Briggs- An African-Caribbean Writer, Communist Political Activist, and another high-ranking ABB member.

Richard Benjamin Moore- ABB ranking member

Otto Hall- Contemporary of Lovett Fort-Whiteman and ranking member of the American Negro Labor Congress (ANLC)

Of the above eight Black Men, Lovett Fort-Whiteman, per a Time Magazine Article dated November 9, 1925, titled "***Black and Red***", described Fort-Whiteman after he gave a fiery speech in Chicago "The Reddest of the Blacks."[16]

However, James W. Ford and another Soviet-trained Black man, James S. Allen, will make a second attempt to create a Sovietized Black America in the South 20 years later. Until then, a Hungarian-Jewish Communist will write an article, on orders from COMINTERN, which will bring the idea of the first attempt to psychologically subvert and create the atmosphere to make the "Soviet Negro America" almost into reality. His name was Józef Pog`any, a.k.a Joseph Pogany, better known as "***John Pepper***". [17]

Artist rendition of Josef Pogany a.k.a. John Pepper, Author of the article "*American Negro Problems*" in 1928, creating the call for the Negro Soviet Republic in the South of the United States.
(Courtesy of Wikimedia)

Since the establishment of the Negro Commission inside the Communist International in 1925, a Hungarian-Jewish Marxist named Józef Pogany came to the United States in 1922 to originally assisting internal strife within CPUSA, between fractional Socialist members and Financial handlers.

His job was to also assist CPUSA in subverting an increasing Hungarian Immigration population in Chicago also, which soon became a heated relationship between Pogany and CPUSA leader William Z. Foster. As their working relationship deteriorated, Foster requested that Pogany is recalled to COMINTERN and sent away from the organization. In 1926, the request was approved and Pogany traveled back to Moscow Russia. COMINTERN ordered him to work in their propaganda Information Department, in which he wrote an article *"American Negro Problems"* under the moniker John Pepper.

John Pepper's article, written in 1928, sounds eerily familiar in language, delivery and context that mirrors the same propagandized rhetoric that Marxist Men and CPUSA voices today. One thing about the dangerous ideology of Marxism and their propagandists constantly do; they recycle the same words or "verbal stimuli" repeatedly in a rebranded version.

The reason why they constantly recycle the same rhetoric, because, in order to make their gullible target of people to psychologically believe what they say, you keep repeating it, until they, the targets, have no other point but to accept it as fact. Words like "Self-Determination", "American Imperialism", "Hegemony" and many other words fill Pepper's article that is pure fiction. Of course, Marxist Men like Pepper are who they are; liars.[18]

For example, on page 2 of American Negro Problems, Pepper wrote;

"The struggle against white oppression of the Negro masses is a tart of the proletarian revolution in America against capitalism. The American working class cannot free itself from capitalist exploitation without freeing the Negro race from white oppression. What Marx said about the United States is still true; 'Labor cannot emancipate itself in the white skin where in the black it is branded.'"[19]

Understand, that John Pepper was a White male from Hungary and in the above quote proves one more thing that Communists are;

hypocrites! Despite the obvious, Pogany's message was ***effective*** and this is what matters the most to Marxist Men. The article goes on to make the case only to the Black Farmer and Sharecropper in the "Black Belt", because as he states,

"...the millions of Negro Farmers of the 'Black Belt', [are] living under the most oppressive conditions, 'half-feudal, half-slave'...".

He goes on to say that American Negroes need to struggle for their right of a nationwide self-determination:

"Self-determination means the right to establish their own state, to erect their own government if they choose to do so. In the economic and social conditions and class relations of the Negro people there are increasing forces which serve as a basis for the development of a Negro nation (a compact mass of farmers on a contiguous territory, semi-feudal conditions, complete segregation, common traditions of slavery, the development of distinct classes and economic ties, etc. etc.)."

If you noticed, that John Pepper's message was only geared towards the so-called "half-feudal, half-slave" Black farmers and sharecroppers in the South. That's because they were ripe to be exploited emotionally, as victims of White Capitalism, at full value to help the Communist's worldwide domination. What makes this even more dangerous is that the targeted people, the Black farmer/sharecropper, will never ever be a part of this new 'self-determination' state as freedmen.

Why?

Because in reality, Marxist Men like Caucasian John Pepper did not say to the masses being told this lie is that their conditions will never get better, it will only get worse. As a matter of fact, by creating a **"Soviet Negro Republic"** inside a **"Soviet America"**, in practicality, will only segregate the Black poor farmer/sharecroppers of the South from the rest of the country, which is be counter-productive objectively when it comes to the so-called "equality" non-sense Pepper advocate in writing. Also, notice that Pepper stated *'if they choose to do so'* when the targeted population, can establish their own government.

The question that needed to be asked at the time and even now, if this situation was to occur, what would happen if they, the Black poor in the South didn't choose to establish their own government? The answer to that is simple; one would be established *for them*, on purpose by the Communists which will not have *any* Black representation whatsoever!

Of course, that not what John Pogany wanted those in the South it to ask about in his American Negro Problem lies. The job was to mentally subvert his targeted audience and portray them as victims, to drive them to create their own nation emotionally without thinking rationally. What's even more amazing about this publication by Pogany/Pepper article is that he mentions the rise of what he terms the "Black Petit-Bourgeoisie". He states;

"The very fact of segregation of the Negro masses creates the basis for the development of a stratum of small merchants, lawyers, physicians, preachers, brokers, who try to attract the Negro industrial bourgeoisie...This Negro bourgeoisie is closely tied up with the white bourgeoisie; [and] is often the agent of white capitalists...Politically, the Negro bourgeoisie is participating, to a growing degree, in the so-called 'commissions for interracial cooperation.' These committees {he claims} exist in eight hundred counties of the south and are spreading all throughout the 'black belt'. But the ideological and organizational bearer of the national racial movement of the Negroes is today rather the intelligentsia and petit-bourgeoisie."[20]

What Pogany/Pepper advocated in his writing that the **Negro Bourgeoisie** is just as equal to the **White Bourgeoisie** inside "Imperialistic America". Both classes of people must be destroyed in a violent revolution by the Proletariat class of Black farmers/sharecroppers, in accordance with the ideology of Karl Marx and Friedrich Engels. Unfortunately, this point has been carried on by inner-city Blacks in America for the past almost 90 years, who they see that the successes of their own people, the same Black Lawyers, Doctors, Merchants etc., as champions of Capitalism and are not a part of the '*revolutionary struggle*' that they have been mentally subverted to believe by Marxist Men.

One thing Communists are successful in doing when subverting a population or race. Once they create a false narrative and it doesn't catch on to the targeted population in accordance with their plans, they will not give up their agitation campaigns. As mentioned before in this chapter, all Marxist Men will do is wait for the opportunity to present themselves, repackage their mobilization campaign and try again, with even more voracity than ever before. The same happened here with the "Soviet Negro Republic".

The Soviet Negro Republic and the Harlem Renaissance

Renaissance is loosely defined as a period in human history, where a vigorous artistic and intellectual activity takes place to either revive or renew the spirit of a certain culture or population.[21] As in the case of American History, Black Americans experienced this mood revival and spiritual renewal in what was called the "***Harlem Renaissance***".

This era of Black Cultural revival occurred between the years 1918-1937. In this span of 19 years, which accounted for almost one generation of American people, a mass movement of Black talent emerged in the nation in all areas of Liberal Arts; from music in the form of Jazz, Blues, Theatrics, Literary Arts, to Comedy (known as the 'Chitlin' Circuit), Movies and other areas of staged performance. Some coined the Harlem Renaissance, as the "New Negro Movement", the term created by Writer, Educator and flamboyant Marxist Man, Alain Leroy Locke.[22, 23, 24]

What was even more fantastic during this span of time, was the geopolitical environment of the time, in which a plethora of famous talent painted the American Mainstream. In 1919, Congress and several states passed the 18th Amendment of the U.S. Constitution, prohibiting the manufacturing, importation, exportation, possession, sale, and distribution of Alcohol beverages.[25]That same year, America's involvement in World War I was ending, which sparked an environment what was called ***"The Roaring 20's"***. The 1920's was a decade where the American Economy was going strong, the 19th Amendment of the U.S. Constitution followed shortly thereafter in 1920, giving Women the right to vote in every election throughout the country.[26]

Also during this era, America's Italian Mobs were running every aspect of illegal activity, from prostitution, narcotics and illegal manufacturing and bootlegging of liquor, in clubs from Chicago, St. Louis to New York City, especially the independent city of Harlem, where numerous of night clubs or "speak easies" operated every night that attracted thousands of White patrons to pay thousands of dollars to listen, watch and is entertained by Black talent.

Entertainment venues such as the Cotton Club, the Savory and hundreds of other places showcased Black American female artists such as Singers Bessie Smith, Ella Fitzgerald, Josephine Baker, Ma Rainey and Clara Smith. Popular Black American Male artists had their start into fame during this timeframe, like Joe "King" Oliver, Paul Robeson, Duke Ellington, Cab Calloway, Edward "Kid" Ory and many others. In literature, Poet/Writer Langston Hughes, Jean Toomer, Zora Neale Hurston highlighted this era also.[27]

Based on a major explosion of artists and talent that showcased Mainstream America during the Renaissance, many writers of the day and historians of the present, billed this time as a great movement of a race of people, built on self-determination, that "transformed Blacks from a social disillusionment to racial pride." *The Roaring 20's* was also a time in American History when the height of "***The Great Black Migration***" occurred.[28]

This happened where American Blacks left the mostly agricultural-driven Southern United States and relocated in mostly manufacturing-Northern and Border State Cities, looking for work and opportunity to create a better life for themselves and their families. Another major issue that came to the forefront during the Harlem Renaissance; Communist influence and subversion by Black Marxist Men and their dupes to convert their own race and culture to support The Marxist Theory for worldwide revolution.

One way to subvert performers of Black entertainers was to educate such men and women to accept Marxist-Leninist principles, by duping them that such a system would benefit them at the end. Once that has been accomplished, and these duped persons have fallen for the lies and deception of such duping techniques, then these dancers, singers and actors/actresses are then paraded in front of the media to be exploited at full value. It is at this point, where these brainwashed entertainers will come out publicly and support Marxist Men agenda of the time, like a trained parrot.

And who is responsible for training such naïve entertainers to believe in the Marxist lie? The same people within the Entertainment Industry, who are leaders of the industry itself who are also Marxist Men. These "leaders" often provide Mentors and/or Coaches to Black Actors, Music Artists and Producers, so they can hone-in the after-mentioned performers' skills and showmanship presentation on stage; to draw larger audiences. Once these audiences have become attracted to these duped entertainers' award-winning performances, the Mentors will then provide additional training to those who are being mentored, subverting them even more into accepting Communist ideology.

The ultimate-goal of this training, is not just to provide better entertainment to the public in future performances, but to duped such artists, and make them "**Community Activists**" so they can come out in the open and advocate for socio-economic "change" by promoting Communism, which they have been told, will make things 'fair', 'equal' and 'destroy racism' once and for all. In other words, these brainwashed Black Entertainers, become parrots of Marxist Men, to sell such drivel to their massive audience, who they, the Dancers, Singers, and Comedians had mentally brainwashed to support them. By this time, the subversion has been so complete, that such Entertainers do not even realize, that they are being used like a cheap political prostitute, to help Marxist Men further their agenda, for worldwide domination, that they, the Black Entertainers themselves, will never be a part of.

As in the case of the 1930's, these duped Entertainers will use the aura of the Harlem Renaissance of "**Black Pride**" and "**Self-Determination**", for artists to promote "**Negro Equality**" during their public notoriety, and the outright called for the creation of a "country within a country"; a Soviet Negro Republic.[29] Three of the biggest renaissance Marxist Men dupers were **W. E. B. DuBois**, co-founder of the NAACP and led Editor of **The Crisis**, Poet/Writer **Claude McKay**, and Singer/Actor/Star-Athlete **Paul Robeson**.   Other Black Entertainers, Novelists, Poets Editors and Playwriters of the era, that have been subverted in similar fashion, included;[30-40]

>   *Countee Cullen (Playwright and Author)*
>
>   *Daisy Turnbull (Actress-Husband of Poet Sterling Allen Brown)*
>
>   *Canada Lee (Actor)*
>
>   *Chester Himes (Writer)*
>
>   *Theodore Ward (Playwright)*
>
>   *Sterling Allen Brown (Poet)*

Lena Horne (Great Actress and Singer)

Ralph Waldo Ellison (Writer)

Billy Strayhorn (Composer and Band Leader of Duke Ellington)

Wallace Thurman (Flamboyant Novelist/Contributing Editor of the Socialist Publication the Messenger)

Jean Toomer (Poet/Author. Claims that he was African-American, but was Caucasian)

Arana Bontemps (Writer)

Frank Marshall Davis (Journalist and Editor of the Atlanta Daily World, Chicago "Red" Star and Honolulu Record)

Zora Neale Hurston (Writer. Left CPUSA in 1954, became Blacklisted in the Entertainment Industry and became a vocal opponent of Communism)

Photo of Claude McKay, the originator of COMINTERN's plan to create the Soviet Negro Republic and Mentor to several of the Harlem Renaissance Performers. (Courtesy of Wikimedia)

As CPUSA continued their march to create a worldwide revolution in other areas of American society, they continued to use African Americans as pawns in the process. An additional way they conducted their subversive activities, was by inundating the media within the Black Community, or the **Black Press,** to funnel their propaganda to the masses of people in print form.

Remember, this is the 1930's; there were no such things like Television, Social Media and the Internet back then. However, the lines of communication were just about as fluid as they are now, apart from the after-mentioned items. Newspapers and editorial articles by numerous of Black-owned and Communist-supported publications, such as Frank Marshall Davis's "*Atlanta Daily World*", Langston Hughes's poetry written inside the "*Baltimore Afro-American*", Cyril Briggs "*Crusader*", DuBois's "*The Crisis*", Richard Nathaniel Wright's "*New Masses*" and hundreds of others. These publications contained thousands of pages of writings that were filled with Marxist propaganda.

Books being sold on the market, purchased by and/or read by Black Americans inside Public Libraries, were also filled with such lies and disinformation. Examples of such publications, included W.E.B. DuBois's "*Black Reconstruction in America*", Richard Nathaniel Wright's books, "*Uncle Tom's Children*", "*Black Boy*", and "*Native Son*", and others who plant such lies in-order to sell their non-existent, non-racism lie of glorious Communism. For example, when Langston Hughes wrote in an article in "*New Masses*" in 1932, he infamously stated;[41, 42, 43]

"Put one more 'S' in the USA to make it Soviet. The USA, when we take control will be the USSA".

After appearing in a series of performances at various Southern Black Universities around 1933, the flamboyant Hughes immediately left the U.S. and visited Stalin's Russia, whom he solely admired in his poems and newspaper commentaries. After returning a few weeks later, he wrote of his trip;

"There [in Russia] seems to me that Marxism had put into practical being many of the precepts which our own Christian America had not yet been able to bring to life."

He further wrote;

Goodbye Christ, Lord Jehovah, beat it away from here
Make way for a new guy with no religion at all
A real guy named Marx, Communism, Lenin, peasant, Stalin,
worker, me

What you just read above was the **_real_** Langston Hughes! A person who was psychologically subverted to believe in the lie that Karl Marx, who he [and many others] thought was the greatest and most brilliant human being ever to walk the Earth.

When in reality, Hughes's hero **_never_** owned or operated a company or organization, **_never_** made payroll to pay employees a wage, **_never_** conducted any accounting practices and **_never_** held a job-ever! On top of that, Marx was financed by a Bourgeoisie's Son, Friedrich Engels, who owned a manufacturing corporation, while keeping every bit of his monies from his wife and kids, whom he kept in abject poverty and misery for the rest of their natural lives!

Yet, Langston Hughes revered Karl Marx as a God! However, don't think for one-second that those inside the African-American Community of the 1930's and 1940's wasn't listening to Hughes's rhetoric and saw his words as being true. They did.

They also saw other poets, authors, and other Harlem Renaissance entertainers through the same telescopic lens as Hughes and CPUSA took advantage of this at full value.

In 1938, Marxist Man Author Richard Nathaniel Wright wrote and published his short story book titled "**_Uncle Tom's Children_**", which was based on factious and often overhyped stories of White mob lynching of Blacks in the South.[44, 45]

Critics of the book at the time described Wright's book as being graphic, loaded with violent descriptions, purposeful human mutilation of blood, guts, and gore. The book, they concluded, was so graphic, with made-up human nature practices, that the stories were written was absolute lies, to instill emotion and fear to those Blacks reading it. Another critic voiced that Uncle Tom's Children contained four short stories, in which three of them contained such murderous violence by the after-mentioned mob, that all four stories the book in conclusive, were killing everyone in every aspect of the book![46]

Wright's publication had its effect, in a positive way for CPUSA recruitment efforts to draw Blacks within their organization.

The targeted population of Wright's book, was the Black Communities located in the North, such as New York, New Jersey, Massachusetts and other states/cities, where for the most part, never seen, lived nor experienced such racial attacks in the South; especially the magnitude that Wright wrote them in his book. It was just such false perceptions of reality, that drove Blacks in the North to join the Communist Party and their tentacles of front groups by the hundreds, under the guise of **"Civil Rights"**, **"Ending of Racism"** and **"Equality"** of all the races and economic classes of people.

Other writers during the time included author Zora Neale Hurston,[47, 48] who published ***"Their Eyes Were Watching God"***, the flamboyant Alain Locke's ***"The New Negro"***, Countee (pronounced Count-Tay) Cullen's ***"Color"***, ***"Copper Sun"***, ***"The Black Christ and Other Poems"***, were only a handful of books like Wright's propaganda publications, in which CPUSA took advantage of. There were other entities prior to the outbreak of World War Two, that Black Marxist Men and their White Marxist counterparts, spent huge efforts to agitate and subvert masses of Black Americans into accepting the false premise of equality of Communism/Socialism.

One last area that the Communist Party had some influence, but with very little success in controlling and subverting it, was in the world of Sports. The main reason why they didn't have any success, because of competition with the realm of athletics, usually wrote their own history. Second, the American Sports environment of the 1930's did not have as many Athletes who were African American. However, that would change after two of the most-influential Black Men in American Sports History, would dominate their profession in the 1930's and 1940's, which will enhance Black national pride and identity, plastered by both the White and Black media.

Take, for example, Joe Louis, a.k.a. ***"The Brown Bomber"***.[49, 50, 51] Joe Louis is considered as one of the greatest Professional Heavyweight Boxing Champions of all-time, long before legends like Muhammad Ali, "Smokin'" Joe Frazier and others. Joe Louis was born in Chambers County, Alabama near the Alabama-Georgia state line, on May 14, 1914. Louis became a nationwide sensation when he defeated Maximillian 'Max' Baer (father of Max Baer Jr. of Beverly Hillbillies TV fame) in September 1935. He also fought exciting, yet brutal-outstanding fights against Adolf Hitler's own Max Schmeling in June 1936 and 1938. Prior to the outbreak of World War Two for the United States, the ***"Brown Bomber"*** also fought a hard battle against William David "Billy" Conn, also known as the ***"Pittsburgh Kid"*** in May 1941, winning in a knockout during the 13th Round.

Another great African American competitor in the arena of Sports was Olympian Jesse Owens. Owens, born in Oakville Alabama, the youngest of ten siblings, and as a teenager, attended Cleveland Ohio's East Technical High School.[52, 53] While attending school there, Owens became so popular as an instant track star, upon graduating, attended Ohio State University (OSU). Even though he did not attend Ohio State without a scholarship, Owens began to work numerous odd-jobs to pay for his way through college. It was there when he came under the tutelage of a White former track star himself-turned-coach Larry Snyder, who mentored Owens. Under Snyder's coaching, Jesse Owens performed so well on the track, that he earned the nickname the "*Buckeye Bullet*".

After graduating OSU, Owens was selected in 1935 to compete in the Summer Olympics, located in Berlin Germany. Along with him, other African Americans track-stars trained and then traveled along with Owens. Black Athletes, such as James Du Valle, Ralph Metcalfe, and Mack Robinson (Brother of legendary Hall-of-Fame Baseball Player Jackie Robinson) dominated the track competition.[54, 55, 56, 57]

With Adolf Hitler himself in attendance watching the game after the United States won their competition, this didn't sit well with the German Dictator, who was upset that Owens won the Gold Medal and departed the stadium. By the end of the games, Jesse Owens won four gold medals in the 100 meters, 200 meters, long jump and the 4x100 meter Relay, Mack Robinson won the Silver Medal after Owens in the 200-meter run, while Du Valle and Metcalfe, earned Silver and Bronze medals for their performance respectfully.

Dominating both White and Black Press headlines, while they returned home, Owens, Metcalfe, Du Valle and Robinson became heroes in the Black Community. Unfortunately, not everybody celebrated these men and their accomplishments, One-man did not want Jesse Owens to compete and another man, *the President of the United States, Franklin D. Roosevelt, never invited Owens and his teammates to congratulate them at the White House!*

As for the former, prior to competing in Germany, NAACP Executive Secretary, Caucasian Walter Francis White, wrote a letter to the American Olympic Committee in December 1935, advocating that Owens should not participate in the Olympics. White stated in his letter, that since Owens was an African American, who promoted "racist

America", a country which he (White) considered, as being a racist regime, to compete against another racist regime in Germany.

The Olympic Committee totally ignored White's letter, as they should have, and labeled the NAACP's head as being 'Un-American' and a Communist Agitator. The reader must understand, that the NAACP Executive Secretary Walter White, publicly stated that;[58, 59]

"I am a Negro, my skin is white, my eyes are blue, my hair is blond. The traits of my race are nowhere visible to me...I am not White. There is nothing within my mind and heart which tempts me to think I am."

White was also a Journalist who wrote for such Marxist-driven publications, such as **New Masses**, **The Crisis**, **The New Republic**, **The Nation**, **The Chicago Defender** and the **New York Herald-Tribune**.

NAACP Executive Secretary Walter Francis White, who called for Jesse Owens and other Black Athletes to protest and not compete in the 1936 Summer Olympics in Berlin Germany.
(Courtesy of Wikimedia)

In retrospect of the ever-increasing Marxist subversion in the United States via CPUSA from Communist International (COMINTERN) in the Soviet Union, many politicians in Washington D.C. have been taking notice of such activity within our borders.

By 1938, the Federal Government itself was being infiltrated on every level and within every federal agency by Joseph Stalin's KGB and COMINTERN-trained agents under the Franklin Delano Roosevelt (FDR) Administration. By placing such agents and covert operatives hired by the Federal Civil Service, their goal was to subvert employees and their leaders into believing Marxist-Leninist ideology, ferment hate and discontent with the administration, then take over the federal government by a violent revolution from within.

This was not and is not speculation; it was true. If the FDR Administration would hae got overthrown, _**The Soviet America**_ would have been formed, and within it the _**Soviet Negro Republic**_ in the South, all under the leadership of Soviet Premier Joseph Stalin!

The House Un-American Activities Committee (HUAC)

Chairman Dies of the House Committee on Un-American Activities (HUAC), center, proofs his response to President Roosevelt on October 26, 1938. Roosevelt came out publicly and denounced the committee.
(Courtesy of Wikimedia/Library of Congress)

As the 1930's ground on, with the Communist agitation campaigns in both the North and in the South in full-swing, the Scottsboro Boys case weaved its disastrous and multi-dimensional track through the Alabama State judicial system, Roosevelt's New Deal initiatives and the possible outbreak of World War, the American Communist Party and its tentacle organizations, were very busy in their subversion processes nationwide. Despite their heavy activity throughout society and within both State and Federal Governments in the United States, there became one entity, that was taking copious notes of CPUSA's illegal activities; The House of Representatives.

So, in 1938, multiple members of Congressmen decided that enough is enough of this Communist subversion, formed an investigative committee named *The House Committee on Un-American Activities Committee (HUAC)*. HUAC was formed to be a long-term standing committee within the House of Representatives, that had Judiciary subpoena power, which held hearings on all un-American activities, such as NAZI and Communist sympathizers, regardless of race, color or creed, in the effort to both slow down and attempt to put a halt to all such activities to overthrow the U.S. Government.

HUAC was created on the idea and results of three previous congressional committees which were created with the same purpose in mind. These entities were *"The Overman Committee"*, which lasted from 1918-1919, chaired by North Carolina Senator Lee Slater Overman, *"The Fish Committee"* in 1930 chaired by Republican Congressman Hamilton Fish III of New York and *"The McCormack-Dickstein Committee"* from 1934-1937 chaired by Democrat Congressmen John William McCormack of Massachusetts and Samuel Dickstein of New York.[60,61,62] The first House Un-American Activities Committee was chaired by Texas Congressman Martin Dies Jr., which began to hold hearings on Communist subversion of Southern Blacks in the South, now known as *"The Dies Committee"*.[63,64]

One of the first hearings held by "The Dies Committee" subpoenaed one William Odell Nowell, a Black man who was a former member of CPUSA and one of its high-ranking officers from 192-1936. Nowell testified in front of the committee on November 30, 1939, that he had traveled to Russia as a representative of CPUSA and met with members of COMINTERN's Negro Department from 1928-1930.

During the trip, COMINTERN formulated a new program to separate the Negro from the rest of the country, to create a separate Negro state and form its own government in the South to run it. He testified that a Communist International "Executive Committee" directive was issued to CPUSA, ordering them to organize and mobilize Blacks to carry out the new program. The directive ordered that CPUSA directly target Black Farmers/Sharecroppers from Virginia to the Mississippi Delta and pepper the population using lies, deception and pointed propaganda campaigns so that Negroes in this area were to become a "revolutionary class" of people, to ally themselves as the Proletariat.[65]

William Odell Nowell further testified that this Soviet Negro Republic was planned to be a "buffer state", operated under Soviet leadership. The plan called for the weakening of the U.S. either by an Economic Depression, War with Russia itself of by manufacturing some other crisis, that can arouse a great deal of hate and discontent throughout the nation. Nowell stated that "this would be the time to strike", the time for CPUSA to utilize this position to set up a Negro republic in the South. By creating such agitation, anger and discontent to Southern Black Farmers located in "The Black Belt", they were to revolt against Capitalism and the Bourgeoisie class (both Black and White), while at the same time, a similar agitation and anger campaign was being conducted in the North's Industrial Cities.

Negroes at this time would be called the National Minority, who will bring up the rear during the Communist Revolution in America, which will serve as the catalyst to weaken the entire U.S. Geopolitical system. Essentially, the Russians were to use the Negroes in both the South and in the North as sacrificial lambs, putting their lives on the line during a bloody and violent revolution, in which only the Communist Party would benefit at the end.

After "*The Dies Committee*" ended in 1944, HUAC continued as a standing committee in 1945. Under Public Law 601, passed by the 79th Congress the same year, members of the committee had a mandate to follow when they began their operation. Their mandate consisting of nine committee members were to investigate suspected threats of subversion and/or propaganda that attacked the American form of government granted by the U.S. Constitution.

During one hearing conducted on December 1, 1953, another former CPUSA high-ranking officer and Young Communist League member, Louis Rosser, testified to HUAC confirming William Odell Nowell's testimony in 1939. Rosser initially joined the groups, because he was led to believe (falsely of course) that they were fighting against racial discrimination for Black folks. Rosser, a Black Man himself, testified that in 1932, CPUSA gathered a group of Black Intelligencientas, Harlem Renaissance Entertainers, himself and others to visit the Soviet Union and create a film for COMINTERN to be used as propaganda.

In this group, artists such as Langston Hughes, Paul Robeson, author Richard Wright, actor Canada Lee and many others, was to make a scripted movie to falsely show a distorted, Soviet view of the conditions of Blacks in America. The film was supposed to be distributed to African and Asian countries being subverted by COMINTERN, using the plight of Black Americans to support their argument that Communism would be the way to equality, not Capitalism. The filming of the movie was canceled when they arrived in Russia because some of the members of the entourage correctly saw what the Russians were doing with the film, so they refused to make it. These same members who refuse to participate, Rosser stated to HUAC, are the same people who continue to fight against Communism in America.

Rosser also further confirmed that the **Soviets wanted to eagerly segregate the American Negro Population in the South, by instilling disunity within themselves, other races and cultures, causing confusion and discontent based on their emotions. By doing this, at the end, a revolution would be initiated within the Negro Community, causing a rash of unspeakable violence between them, until the entire American Negro population would have been destroyed in large numbers. It was then, that the remaining Black population will be subjected to the authority of the Soviet Union under Dictator Joseph Stalin**!

The same Russian Dictator and author of the Great Purges in Russia between 1936-1939 that killed well over 1.2 million people. Included in the death count, were COMINTERN's Joseph Pogany (A.K.A. John Pepper) and former President of the American Negro Labor Congress (ANLC) and COMINTERN's Negro Committee Member **Lovett Fort-Whiteman**; **the only Black American to die in a Soviet Union Labor Camp/Gulag Prison system in 1939 from cold exposure, Exhaustion from Hard Labor and malnutrition located in Siberia.**[66,67,68]

Communist Party Propaganda "Target Marketed" for African Americans 1945
by the National Economic Council

Second Attempt at Creating a Soviet Negro Republic

The plan to create the Soviet Negro Republic within the United States of America did not stop during the outbreak of World War II. The plans to create a separate country for Blacks in the United States, operated by Marxist Men of CPUSA via Moscow Russia was put "__on-hold__" until after the war ended. However, behind the scenes, such planning continued, by CPUSA Front Groups like the National Negro Congress (NNC), the American Negro Labor Congress (ANLC) and the Young Communist League (YCL).

All three organizations were operated by both African-American and European-descent American Marxist Men working for CPUSA and its tenets groups. One of the lead planners was a person, named **Sol Auerbach** (A.K.A. **_James S. Allen_** and Co-Author of **The Negroes in a Soviet America**), who not only approved of some of the subversion plans, but also took it upon himself to advance the second attempt of establishing a Soviet Negro America to a new level.[69] Even though Auerbach considered himself as a "**_progressive_**", his actions told a different story.

Born in Philadelphia, Pennsylvania in 1906 to Russian-Jewish immigrant parents, after graduating high school, he attended the Ivy League School University of Pennsylvania. It was there, where Auerbach was one of the first Ivy League students in the United States selected to become a member of the American Student Delegation to Russia in 1927. After that visit, Auerbach became a hardcore duped radical Marxist. His views, attitude and outright protests got him kicked out of school in 1928 and here he turned to the Communist Party to work. Since he studied Journalism in school, Auerbach began to write for the Communist Party's newspaper *"The Daily Worker"* and editor of the International Labor Defense (ILD)'s publication *"Labor Defender"*.

In 1929, Sol Auerbach traveled to the Soviet Union to attend the Communist International's Lenin School of Soviet Propaganda, returning to the United States in 1930 and took the name James S. Allen as his alias. Shortly after returning, Auerbach/Allen became the editor for CPUSA's first Southern Newspaper named *"The Southern Worker"*, which was produced by him and his wife Isabelle in Chattanooga, Tennessee. However, to throw off the local police authorities and FBI agents who began to shut down the publication, Auerbach/Allen made it known that the publication was being made in Birmingham, Alabama instead. To provide additional cover for the newspaper, both Sol and Isabelle printed their editions of the paper to coincide with the printings of the popular Ku Klux Klan publication named *"The Montgomery Advertiser"*.

The motive behind The Southern Worker was to spread Soviet Marxist propaganda through the Black Belt of the South to agitate, once again, and motive Black Farmers/Sharecroppers to riot against the Bourgeoisie and join in the Communist revolution. However, Auerbach/Allen and CPUSA did not anticipate one major problem; the Ku Klux Klan (KKK) in the South. By ideology, the Klan did not like giving Blacks an equal footing in creating "equality" among the races, especially among the White races in the South at the time. They were just as extremists as CPUSA were! But, the Klan also did not like Jewish and other Immigrants from Europe, because they were considered "dirty" and was a threat to the KKK in controlling money and power, in increasing numbers in the South. In turn, not only Auerbach/Allen had to conceal his propaganda newspapers and other communications that he and other Communist Party members were doing, in their effort to subvert Southern Blacks.

The other reason why Auerbach/Allen concealed his communications, was because of the numerous threats he faced, which would have labeled him and CPUSA as enemies of the state, by local authorities, state authorities, FBI agents and the Ku Klux Klan together! The Klan took it upon themselves, to even post advertisements throughout the Black Belt intimidating Southern Blacks for even subscribing or attending any meetings that were held by the Communist Party.

One of many posted "bills" or advertisements that discouraged and intimidated Blacks throughout the South for attending Communist Party meetings during the latter's drive to create the Soviet Negro Republic.
(Courtesy of Marxist.org)

By late 1931, with the Scottsboro Boys case about to become a media spectacle, the Harlan County Kentucky Miner's Strike looming in the distance, Auerbach/Allen was recalled back to New York City, stopping his fledging and non-profitable newspaper that people became too frightened to subscribe. After serving as the Communist Party's representative in the Philippines, between 1936-1939, after World War Two, Auerbach/Allen and Black CPUSA high-ranking officer and Marxist Man James W. Ford pinned a book, published by the Communist Party called "*The Negro in Soviet America*" in June 1935.[70]

For example, in Chapter One of The Negro in Soviet America, the Black Marxist, CPUSA Executive Committee member and former Communist Party Vice-Presidential Nominee in 1932, 36, and 1940, James W. Ford and Auerbach/Allen, ridiculed Booker T. Washington's solution of Black racial pride and self-sufficiency to compete against their White counterparts in America. They wrote;[71]

"Booker T. Washington once said; 'No race that has anything to contribute to the markets of the world is long in any degree ostracized".

Ford and Allen went on;

"He thought that Capitalism would permit the Negro to develop business and manufacturing and increase his ownership of land. In this way, he believed, the Negro could achieve an important economic place in the capitalistic world. His whole philosophy was based upon this belief..." {It wasn't, however}

The Marxist Men continued;

"'agitation for social equality, he [Washington] said, would be extreme folly.' Let each Negro train himself in industrial pursuits or in business hew a place for himself in Capitalistic America, and only then will he be treated with respect..."

Ford and Allen stated next; ***"But what has this led to?"***

What has this led to? Maybe what Booker T. Washington has suggested led to a more prosperous, innovative and individual success of the Black Community to come together and work for the common good, despite the odds? This is exactly what happened, between 1866-1930. However, the propagandists of CPUSA didn't think so. They continued;

"Let us consider the question of land ownership. During the Civil War and immediately after, the Negroes thought they would obtain the land-'Forty Acers and a Mule. But nothing of the kind happened."

Of course, their assessment of the Black Condition in the South of the Post-Civil War era was an absolute lie! They failed to grasp the fact, that after the War, which freed the Slaves, the creation of the Freedman's Bureau, the Civil Rights Act of 1866 and the 13th, 14th and 15th Constitutional Amendments, gave all formerly enslaved Blacks in the South, the opportunity to not only own land, but be a part of the political process and vote.

These items and even more, too numerous to describe here, also have given Blacks the opportunity to be educated in ways that only a few Black Americans enjoyed in the South, prior to 1861. In other words, what Ford and Allen want their readers to falsely believe, is the falsehood, that despite the Black Community's advancement as a people and as a race since the end of the Civil War, they are still psychologically enslaved to Capitalism, which is responsible for racism, bigotry and segregation that Blacks faced throughout "Imperialistic America".

What Ford and Allen suggested, that in-order to get rid of all the racism, bigotry and segregation caused by so-called Capitalism in America, Blacks need to rise-up, mobilize behind the Communists and help overthrow the state governments in the 'Black Belt' South. By doing so, if the Black people "want to" elect their representatives in government, upon taking over the Black Belt South, they could.

That's a lie-in-itself.

However, once the take it over in the South is complete and has ushered in a Socialist, then-Communist society, then everything in society would be "fair" and "equal" for all. Everything would be operated, once again, under the auspice of Soviet Dictator Joseph Stalin, located in Moscow.

Another CPUSA Executive Committee member, **New Masses** Editor, Potemkin Progressive Harry Haywood, wrote in his first book "**Negro Liberation**", written in 1948, in Chapter Seven, titled "**The Negro Nation**", stated;[72]

"…. The fight for self-government in the 'Black Belt' is the fight for the right of Self-Determination, by the Negro Nation…The right of Self-Determination…applies the application of democracy in the sphere of relations between nations, the elimination of the forcibly imposed distinction between oppressed and oppressing nations; it means the abolition of all sundry privileges of one nation over the other. Specifically, it means simply the right of the people of a nation to determine their own fate, or destiny, free from forcible intervention from without by the people of another nation…"

Haywood finish with this note;

"Finally, Self-Determination means the recognition of the sovereignty of a people in all matters affecting their internal life as well as in matters involving their relationships with other peoples or nations. This is then, is the content and principle of the right of self-determination."

In layman's terms, Harry Haywood describes self-determination in regards to the Soviet Negro Republic, as a utopian dream! In a true

Communist society, the supreme rule of the people (the definition of sovereignty) is the Proletariat and only after the Dictator of the Proletariat has come and only when the "Almighty State" has withered away. As Friedrich Engels has stated "then it will be possible to talk about freedom"

As the 1930's continued-on into history, a tragic situation would occur, which will further promote CPUSA's plan to create a Negro Soviet America in the Southern states, with the help of the media. This incident will transform a small town in the northeastern part of Alabama, named Scottsboro, which will thrust events there onto the national scene. One which the Communist Party would take the liberty to exploit at full value, regardless of human lives that will be directly affected by their intrusion. This is the story of the Scottsboro Boys case.

11: The Scottsboro Boys and the Communist Party Intrusion

Photo of the nine Scottsboro Boys in jail prior to their first trial in April 1931. (Courtesy of Wikimedia)

One of America's most tragic incidents in 20th Century American History involved nine Black Male Teens, which cumulated as the case of the Scottsboro Boys of the 1930's.[1,2,3] Many books, articles, and even movies have been written, performed and told the story of a racial incident that occurred on March 25, 1931, at Paint Rock, Alabama.

The teenagers named Clarence Norris, Charlie Weems, Haywood Patterson, Ozie Powell, Willie Roberson, Eugene Williams,

Olen Montgomery, Andy Wright and Roy Wright, were falsely accused of raping two White Teenagers named Victoria Price and Ruby Bates.[4] The case of the Scottsboro Boys had the equal amount of the main street media press back then comparative to the O.J. Simpson trial of the mid-1990's. However, the comparison between the two cases stops right there. The Scottsboro case was way different in many ways and it added a different dimension for the ideas for some to help create the Soviet Negro Republic.

During the early part of the 1900's, the United States of America had its share of poor people, in a country numbering 122,775,046 in 1930, a lot of the poor population, especially within the rural areas of country, to "**hitch**" ride onboard half-full or empty boxcars on trains which crisscrossed the country, which would take them to other places to seek work or new adventures of life. Called "**Hoboing**", using such transportation was not only risky, because of the same poor, criminal and/or fugitives from justice were using the same mode of transportation, but riding trains in such manner was both illegal and dangerous.[5] Since not everybody at the time could afford a car, plus the fact that what we know today as the interstate highway system, wasn't created and built until almost 30-years later. For the early-1930's, the sensible and easiest way to travel, besides via bus, were trains.

On that day, the two previously mentioned White girls were hitching a ride on the same train that the nine Scottsboro boys have been riding. The train, which was traveling from Chattanooga, Tennessee to Memphis, also had contained several White male teens hoboing on the same train as well. Sometime during the trip, a fight broke out between some of the Black teenage boys and the White ones, in which the latter was thrown off the moving train at a high rate of speed. Once the White male teens recovered from being thrown off, they made their way to the nearest train station nearby and informed the station master of what happened. The boys told the station master that they were in a gang fight with a bunch of Black teens and got thrown off the train by them. The station master informed the train's next stop, which was a town called Paint Rock, Alabama outside of the Huntsville-Decatur, Alabama metropolitan area.

As the train pulled into the station, many local, White militia men waited for the train to stop and apprehend the Negro boys in question. Not all the Black Teens were involved in the fight with the White teen boys, were together. Some were in other boxcars and didn't know what was going on. Some of them didn't know each other, but they were about to get well acquainted with each other sooner than later.[6] The Negro boys, nine of them in total were gathered up by the militia, who were armed with guns, arrested the boys and transported them to the nearby Scottsboro, Alabama Jail. Once at the jail, the Black teens were told why they were arrested for; the gang raping of the two White girls Victoria Price and Ruby Bates.

Photo of Ruby Bates (l) and Victoria Price (r)
(Courtesy of Wikimedia)

Understand, this was the 1930's of the Southeastern United States, De Jure Segregation or "Jim Crow" laws prevailed. Any interracial contact between the races was considered taboo by many within the population, but not all. In this case, the former was more accepted than the latter, especially was news began to spread like a wildfire in a California forest, of the Black boys being arrested and charged with gang raping two White girls. Such news enraged White Segregationists, which caused an enormous mob of vigilante groups to gather outside the Scottsboro, Alabama Jail.

This crowd of people, which included men, women and children were ready to take the law into their own hands and met out severe punishment to the nine Blacks as their own prosecution, judge, and jury. As news spread of the posse of vigilantes gathering outside the jail, via news radio, the Governor of Alabama, Benjamin M. Miller, activated and called out the National Guard to protect the teens, as they surrounded the jailhouse, reestablishing order outside.[7]

Because of the mass hysteria caused by the media coverage of the nine Black teens, which continue to spread, pressure by the vigilantes gathered outside of jailhouse building and local citizens began to mount against local authorities to defuse the situation quickly. The Scottsboro Police decided to take advantage of the free publicity that the situation offered and publicly announced that swift justice for the boys will be forthcoming. They weren't the only ones who saw the opportunity to exploit an already tragic situation, to instead, further their cause of creating the Soviet Negro Republic in the South. The other entity was the Communist Party and they exploited the situation at more than full value when they join the cause to defend the nine Black Teens. One Marxist, Sol Auerbach/James S. Allen, was heard the news on his radio in his Chattanooga apartment. He immediately phoned CPUSA and requested to mobilize lawyers of the International Labor Defense (ILD), who were Marxist Men themselves, to represent the boys in court. The Scottsboro case could not have come at a perfect time for CPUSA. The drive to create the Soviet Negro Republic in the South began to falter, so this incident has breathed new life in the cause of a Proletariat revolution for "Mother" Russia.[8]

However, the Communist Party should have stayed away from the Scottsboro case completely. Because of their intrusion into representing the nine Scottsboro boys, the Lawyers with the ILD almost destroyed the case completely, which almost included the boys' lives in the process. As Auerbach/Allen joined the media in writing about the case as a cause for Black Famers to revolt against the racist oppression of the American Judicial System in the "*Southern Worker*", the case took many dramatical twists and turns that almost ended the nine boys lives by public execution! International Labor Defense lead attorney for the case, Samuel Leibowitz did not make a favorable impression to Segregationists in the South.

Locals labeled him a "Jewish-Communist-New York-Yankee" and that he and his legal team he brought with him were either too old, too-drunk or too-incompetent to adequately represent the Scottsboro Boys. The boys themselves did not make to situation any better themselves, as some began to admit guilt, while some began to deny any participation in the act, while the press inserted their views into the case. Add-on insult to injury, local authorities under pressure of all the publicity being waged, tried to move the case as fast as possible, in which they did. Within five days of being arrested, charges were made against the boys and jury selection of all-White citizens were put together, to make the trial began and end as quickly as possible.

After the first trial began April 6, 1931, and within two weeks, eight of the nine Scottsboro Boys was convicted of rape of the two

White Girls, except for one, Leroy Wright, who was 13 at the time and was a Minor. Because Wright was an underaged Minor, the jury sentenced him convicted to Life Imprisonment. The story does not end there. ILD quickly filed for Appeals, which was quickly made and the second trial of the nine Scottsboro Boys commenced in March 1933, this time with a change of venue. The second case was heard in nearby Decatur, Alabama. This second trial ended with the all-White Jury convicting Haywood Patterson to the Death Penalty, but the Judge in the case, Justice James Edwin Horton overturned the conviction.

In the meantime, the Communist Party used one of their best tools in their arsenal to help propagandize, not only the fate of the Scottsboro Boys but the case for the creation of a Soviet Negro Republic; the Media. Starting May 7, 1933, a continuous precession for marches and demonstrations littered the American landscape about freeing the Scottsboro Boys, as a third trial was conducted, ended in a mistrial, word was spread about the two girls recanting their story. Both Victoria Price and Ruby Bates claimed that the rape charge was coerced by the militia men at the Point Rock Train Station, and both claimed that they were really Prostitutes, who didn't want their actual lifestyle known to the public. They also admitted that by sticking with the original accusation of rape, they were paid a good amount of money.

The Scottsboro case was heard again for the fourth time, in 1936, ended in a verdict in longer prison sentences. Eventually, various aspects of the case, as ILD began to have separate court trials for several the Black boys, which eventually made it all the way to the U.S. Supreme Court in 1935. Here, only Norris and Patterson's convictions were overturned. The other convictions for the rest of the Scottsboro Boys were ongoing. However, in some form or fashion, all the boys were still convicted to serve various numbers convictions and each serving increasing amounts of prison time. Four of the nine, Olen Montgomery, Eugene Williams, Willie Roberson and Roy Wright, after being confined in jail for over six years, Alabama Governor David Graves dropped all the charges against them.[13, 14]

Photo of Montgomery, Williams, Roberson, and Wright charges dropped and freed from Jail. (Courtesy of Wikimedia)

All nine of the Scottsboro Boys meeting with International Labor Defense (ILD) Lawyer, Samuel Leibowitz prior to the first court trial in April 1931. (Courtesy of Wikimedia)

The Communists Take Advantage of a Sad Situation

As the Scottsboro Boys fiasco began to take shape, CPUSA led by Earl Browder, sent out an all-points-bulletin to all Marxist-driven publications and its front groups, such as the;

American Civil Liberties Union (ACLU)
National Association for the Advancement of Colored People (NAACP)

International Labor Defense (ILD)

Church League for Industrial Democracy (CLID)

Methodist Federal for Social Services (MFSS)

that world attention on the outcome of the Scottsboro case, whether favorable to the boys or not didn't matter. The case was going to be used as a catalyst to mobilize thousands of Negroes inside trade unions, upper-class professions, and poor Blacks into marching for the revolutionary cause, to create a Soviet America and the Soviet Negro Republic throughout the South.

Browder's goal, matching Communist International's Negro Department in Moscow, was to bring hell, hate, and agitation to move the entire Black population to their agenda. Of course, CPUSA had plenty of help to support their propaganda campaign during the Scottsboro case, such as Poet Langston Hughes, Entertainer Paul Robeson, Hollywood Actress Lena Horne and many other Harlem Renaissance performers. Proceeds from giving such performances in support of the Scottsboro case were given to the ILD who is representing the boys in Alabama!

(An example of the Emergency Scottsboro Defense Committee, a select-CPUSA Committee formed to help influence the Scottsboro Boys Case)
(Author's Collection)

Groups such as the NAACP at first, joined with the Communist Party supporting the Scottsboro Case. However, back in the 1930's, the NAACP aligned itself mostly with the Republican Party, especially when it came to social and legal issues such as this. The organization also teamed up with the editor of *The Atlanta Independent*, Ben Davis Sr. who was the Conservative rival to the Marxist publication *The Atlanta Daily World*, edited by the future 44th President of the United States,

Barack Hussein Obama's mentor, Frank Marshall Davis Jr. The front-page headline of the Atlanta Daily World on January 1, 1932, read;

"Will Communist Sacrifice Eight Boys to Propaganda?"

Notice that the headline stated eight of the nine Scottsboro Boys. CPUSA knew that the ninth defendant, Leroy Wright, was just a Minor, so in their eyes, not much CPUSA could do to sell their propaganda campaign to Mainstream Americans.

However, there have been some serious discussions within the upper hierarchy of the NAACP about whether they should team up and assist CPUSA and ILD with the Scottsboro Case. Most members viewed the Communists as a predatory organization, who hid their true intentions under the veil of words such as "Social Justice" or actions similar in scope to the NAACP, on the outside. Unfortunately, CPUSA under the orders from the Communist International, had penetrated well-organized, well-intended groups like the NAACP, the Young Men's Christian Association (YMCA) and Young Women's Christian Association (YWCA) with Marxist Men and their duped flock of ideological sheep in tandem, to subvert their members into towing the Communist line.

For example, one of the NAACP top-ranking members, William Pickens, wrote a letter to the Communist Party's publication "***The Daily Worker***", on NAACP Letterhead, offering money and support to the International Labor Defense (ILD) to help pay for the legal expenses for the Scottsboro Boys. In his letter, with an enclosed check, that was to be forwarded to the ILD, Pickens's letter stated towards the end;

"The one objective for final security is the absolute and unqualified unity and cooperation of ALL WORKERS {Pickens' emphasis} of all the exploited masses."

His letter no doubt stated its true intentions as to whom he was **_really_** supporting and it **_wasn't_** the Scottsboro Boys! Like CPUSA Commander Earl Browder stated in his all-points-bulletin, it didn't matter what the outcome of the numerous trials and appeals and legal ramblings that the nine teenaged Black Boys were going through in Alabama. Pickens's only issue was that the Communist Party exploit this case fully and to recruit many Blacks to fill the ranks of CPUSA, to agitate the "workers" into furthering the cause of a worldwide revolution against the United States. However, other Black leaders did not agree with Pickens and publicly stated so. The most prominent critic of the Communists within the NAACP was Acting Secretary and future leader of the NAACP Roy Wilkins.

Wilkins saw right through the hogwash that CPUSA was trying to promote, by using an already tragic case of Black Civil Rights violations of the Scottsboro Black teens, to promote their own agenda, to overthrow the Federal Government. Wilkins wrote Earl Browder at the Communist Party and told them that the NAACP wanted **NO part** of their agitation campaign. Roy Wilkins wasn't alone. Herbert Hill of the NAACP expressed his views to the Communists more bluntly, by saying;

"American Communist Party interest in the Negro can be neither genuine or sincere..."

Hill further concluded that;

"Whenever the interests of Negroes come into conflict with the political interests of Russia, the Communists abandon Negroes like rats on a sinking ship."

Hill's assessment was spot on. At the end of the Scottsboro trials, even though none of the boys were executed, the same cannot be said the same for the 2-3 million-plus people being killed in Stalin's Soviet Union during the "Great Purge" at the same time. Eventually, all the boys had suffered long jail and prison times, during the ensuing court trials and never-ending appeals. Also, all the Scottsboro boys suffered mentally and physically which greatly affected them for life, because of the media spectacle and the Communist Party's intrusion into the case. Even today, the lies of CPUSA still exists in various forms, to include the false notion by those in academia, that the Scottsboro Boys case was the beginning of the American Civil Rights Movement, which was about to occur later on.

THEY ARE WRONG!

There was **NO JUSTICE** for the nine Black Scottsboro Boys at the end! The only beneficiaries of this tragic and pathetic event were the Communist Party! Segregation in the South continued for another 20-plus-years, the nine boys mental state and livelihood was forever ruined, but CPUSA and the Communist International succeeded in recruiting and mobilizing more Blacks into their ranks for the "cause" for Communism.

Lastly, to add insult to injury, one of the White Teens in the case that accused the boys of rape, Ruby Bates, became an advocate and highly paid speaker for the International Labor Defense (ILD) Organization; the same organization that both represented the boys and almost botched the entire Scottsboro Boys case, that could have sent them all to be executed. Of course, to the Communist Party, unlike true patriotic Americans, the only allegiance that their American members pledged to support and defend, was to Stalin's Russia as planned and written by Karl Marx and Friedrich Engels! As World War Two began to ratchet up in intensity, with most of the Scottsboro Boys serving jail time, CPUSA's increased their activities as well, which will help define the Social and Political atmosphere that would cumulate into what would be known as *The Cold War*.

Photo of a planned, orchestrated protest by the Communist Party in response to the Scottsboro Boys Case of the 1930's in Washington, DC.
(Courtesy of Marxist.org)

11: Communists and Socialists Influence on Big Labor Unions

"To hold a Man down, you have to stay down with him."[1]

Booker T. Washington

From the beginning of the Great Depression in 1929, under Republican President Herbert Hoover, until the beginning of World War Two, Communists, Socialists, Populists and Progressives ruled over every aspect of the American workforce. From Manufacturing to the halls of Universities and Colleges, the severe economic downturn caused by the Stock Market Crash provided a great opportunity for such conditioned criminals to exploit an already tragic and sad situation, affecting every American living at that time.

With severe unemployment around the country, African Americans were especially vulnerable to such exploitation. Because the American Black Population were the hardest hit population affected by the economic crisis, anything that sounded good publicly by such organizations, like the NAACP, would have got many people in the community's attention. During that time, low-paying jobs that called for unskilled laborers in the manufacturing, construction, mining and lumber industries, overnight disappeared or ceased production.[2,3] Since the Stock Market Crash, there was not a demand for their products, because of the lack of finances, which allowed employees to be laid-off because companies couldn't afford to pay their workers. No one had money, meaning no one can buy products that they needed, which meant that there became no need for such products to be produced, ending a severe decrease in the workforce.

As more jobs became scarce, any employment openings available, which were little as compared to the previous decade of the 1920's, competition between Blacks and Whites fighting for those same jobs, sometimes becoming physical in nature, attempted to undercut each other to obtain those same employment openings which were left to be filled. With a total Unemployment Rate between 1929-1941 of 16.04%, the Black unemployment rate of nearly 50-percent and a White Unemployment rate was around 30-percent.[4,5] For many, any opportunity to work became a blessing and a will to survive to put food on the table for their families. The White Population in America also suffered just as much as their Black counterparts, however, both races attempted to take advantage of each other, even if it was done by criminal means, to obtain such employment during the beginning years of the Great Depression.

In the summer of 1930, a group of Downtown Atlanta Georgia African-American Bellhops were falsely arrested for disorderly conduct, jailed and fined, causing their employers to completely fire them from their positions and immediately hiring White Men to fill those vacant positions. In Baton Rouge Louisiana, White Segregationists launched a reign of terror on Black Railroad Firemen, killing ten and wounding dozens of others, to force them to not work on the rails. The vigilantes, who did the heinous murders in cold-blood, without remorse, wanted those vacant job positions can be filled by unemployed White Men.[6]

While such incidents were taking place, the Communists and Socialists knew that the time was ripe to conduct their exploitation campaigns. By using different avenues in the media, such as writing books, printing union literature, posting Bills on power poles in the streets and advertisements on public transportation buses and streetcars, Communists and Socialists became effective in their propaganda campaigns.

Such advertisements contained words and phrases, blaming Capitalism for the Great Depression. Marxist Man, Moscow-dupe Reinhold Neibur, pinned his book in 1932 titled "**Moral Man and Immoral Society**", toted the Communist-line in Stalin's Russia that Capitalism was dead. Along with article and editorials written in the "**American Black Press**", began writing about the end of Capitalism as well, calling for the economic system of Communism to replace it. Inside their editorials, their opinions, wrote that Communism was a more "profitable in production and solution" to America's economic ills, where "no racism existed" and everybody received "equal money for equal pay".[7] Such propaganda, used by Marxist Men became lucrative offers to consider by those in the Black Population, who believed that such lies were really factual in nature.

By creating an effective marketing campaign, using the press and media, both Communists and Socialists, began to work the emotions of those who dearly suffered from the Great Depression. Their timing for such propaganda was, extremely brilliant. After all, money was extremely tight, work was almost non-existent, and families needed to pay their bills put food on the table and pay rent. The latter was experienced many times, when Black families living in the inner-cities of Harlem New York, Chicago Illinois, St. Louis Missouri, Detroit Michigan, Gary Indiana and other places, began to hold '**Rent Parties**' in their flats. Here, friends, families, and neighbors held private parties among themselves, charging their guests money, to partake in the entertainment. These activities were done, so that families could have enough to pay their rent due, at the end of the month.[8] Such socioeconomic environments of the day triggered by the end of the decade, 1939, would spark one of the largest Communist mobilization campaigns of the 20th century

Outside the Harlem Renaissance, Scottsboro Alabama and the economic suffering from the Great Depression, the largest of the Communist Propaganda Operations that took place on American soil up to that time, involved Labor Unions. During the 1930's and early-

1940's, Labor Unions became hot beds of Marxist-Leninist activity, which increased in crescendo, in a way that no one had ever seen before until the American Civil Rights Movement of 1960's. Since African-Americans were becoming vocal in their demands for civil rights and equality by the time of the Presidential Election of 1932 commenced, they began to advocate for equal wages for work and the shortening of work hours, and 'fair treatment and housing' in the industrial cities of the North and Agricultural regions of the Deep South. Using such media to relay their vocal displeasure of the economic situation, methodological agitation tactics, used by both the Communist and Socialists Parties of the United States, were started, to spark racial division and discontent throughout American society, ending in Federal Government intervention. What role did African-Americans play during these agitation campaigns? They were right in the middle of these campaigns, on both sides of the aisle, which would eventually come to a head during the era.

The agitation campaigns started on March 6, 1930, when both Communist and Socialist Parties announced to the public, on that particular day, they advocated that all workers, Black, White and Indifferent, hold protests and demonstrations on what was called "**International Unemployment Day**".[8,9] Under the banner "Work or Wages" and "Fight, Don't Starve!", such protests led to civil disobedience and open-rebellious actions between the protesters and the police, which spread across every major city in the U.S. The St. Louis Post-Dispatch and Washington Post carried headlines on their front-page titled;

"Reds Clash with Police in Front of White House".

In Chicago Illinois, over 100,000 people protested, while in Boston Massachusetts, 50,000-plus protesters gathered in that city's Downtown area. In Milwaukee Wisconsin and Detroit Michigan, an equal-number of protestors clashed with police in those cities as well. In New York City, demonstrators protesting in Lower Manhattan attempted to rush the doors of City Hall, while New York City Police in cars, trucks, and horseback, repulsed the protestors with tear gas, clubs, nightsticks and even bare-fisted confrontations. Such rioting in the after-mentioned cities resulted in hundreds of injuries and thousands arrested and jailed. This was just the beginning.[10,11]

That same year, CPUSA organized what was called "***Unemployed Councils***", which operated in almost every major city in the country. These councils provided subverted Marxists dupes to demonstrate in front of apartment buildings, houses where landlords lived with their families, to humiliate, intimidate and often scare land lords to not evict families from their homes.

In some instances, when a family was evicted and, and their personal belongings were placed outside on the curb of the street, neighborhood watches notified the councils. It wasn't long after when the families were evicted, such Unemployed Councils sent a cadre of men, known as "Goons" over to the place of the evicted families and moved their personal articles back in the apartment that they were just thrown out of. These Goons were sent afterward to find the land lord responsible for the eviction and let them know in no uncertain terms not to evict these families again, "or else". Such actions seem similar in fashion to the Italian Mafia operations.

Whatever such actions by the "Unemployed Councils" did, to protect evicted families from living out in the street, became instantaneously effective. So much pressure and lawlessness that the councils welded, that land lords were hesitant to evict tenants from their homes for fear of the councils' actions. For example, on the Southside of Chicago, it became a rare event to evict some families out of their flats. Some have stated;

"It was not unusual for a mother to shout at her children, when they were getting thrown-out of their place, to say 'run quick and find the Reds!'"

In the 'Black Belt' South, Marxist-Leninists under the orders of the Communist Party and Socialists attempted to organize *"The Black Peasantry"*, where union agitators and Unemployed Councils sought to rally rural Blacks in a similar fashion as in the industrial North. In May 1932, Young Communist League (YCL) Executive Secretary, Lenin School-trained, Mulatto Angelo Herndon, tried to organize a demonstration of young Black-unemployed workers to protest at the Georgia State House, in Atlanta. The protest was broken up by Atlanta Police, which Herndon and a few demonstrators were arrested and charged with trespassing and numerous other charges.

The biggest charge which was levied at Herndon himself which authorities charged Herndon with, that he violated an unknown law, that dated back to 1866. This law, which stated that if a person has been accused of starting an Insurrection against the state government, if found guilty, the sentence was to serve a minimum of 20-years in Georgia State prison. The Communist Party got involved in what is known as "**The Angelo Herndon Case**", CPUSA's International Labor Defense (ILD) Lawyers defending him, appealing the case all the way to the Supreme Court, which overturned the conviction.[12,13]

The Southern Tenant Farmers Union (STFU) and The Sharecroppers Union (SCU)

Members of the Sharecroppers Union (SCU) mobilizing in Arkansas in 1937
(Courtesy of Wikimedia)

In Alabama, CPUSA attempted to rally and mobilize steelworkers in Birmingham, Black Sharecroppers in the countryside and Cotton Field Day-Laborers to protest and demonstrate. This group called for better wages, shorter work hours and better living standards. Most of these protests were broken up by local police, who at the time were also local area White Segregationists who, did not like Blacks "getting out of line", but also hated Red Commies at the same time.

Members of CPUSA agitated the Field Day-Laborers, and when the time came when Segregationists arrived to put down such insurrections, the same Marxist Men which started the protests, left the Black Laborers to solve their own problems with the local authorities, when such protests were broken up, by the police. This has been proven time-and-time again. Of course, this did not deter some local Sharecroppers to join the Reds in starting trouble each time, and each time Communist Party members were right there accepting new members.

In March 1931, CPUSA members in Alabama formed both the Southern Tenant Farmers Union (STFU) and the Sharecroppers Union (SCU) in Tallapoosa and Lee Counties Alabama next to the Alabama-

Georgia border.[14,15,16] Both unions' membership consisted mainly of both Black and White Communist Agitators, manning senior leadership positions, as they began to organize and assist local Black Sharecroppers, Tenant Farmers and Agricultural Laborers to demand the same thing that the previously-held protests in Birmingham, of fair wages, better working and living conditions. The STFU became the largest CPUSA-led union organization in the Deep South during the 1930's. The Southern Tenant Farmers Union conducted several protests and demonstration campaigns located throughout the South, protesting for Day-Laborers for "fair wages", better working conditions and shorter work hours, similar with other unions across the nation.

STFU was so successful, that by 1936, its membership rolls bloated to over 25,000 members, two-thirds being of American-American and had opened regional union offices in Arkansas, Southern Missouri, Oklahoma, Tennessee and Texas.[17] However, STFU didn't last long. The union's meetings and protests were constantly raided by local and state police departments, causing shootouts between officers and union members, bare-knuckle brawls, nightstick confrontations and tear gas engagements. Such raids caused well-over 100 injuries, 200-plus arrests and more than 50-plus union members being sent to Federal Prison.

After internal leadership strife, decreasing union membership rolls, and STFU's failure to merge with another CPUSA-operated union, the United Cannery, Agricultural, Packing and Allied Workers of America (UCAPAWA) led by Communist Professor Donald Henderson, the STFU was doomed. After a final and unsuccessful demonstration and protests of evicted Black Sharecroppers in New Madrid County, Missouri in January 1939, by the end of the year, the Southern Tenant Farmers Union ceased to exist.

The Sharecroppers Union (SCU) fared somewhat better than STFU during the 1930's, but not by much. SCU was formed under the leadership of Mark Coad, An African-American Marxist-Leninist, trained by the Lenin School in Moscow, Russia, was originally from Charleston, South Carolina. One he got the union organized, he made an all-out effort to recruit the local population to boost the union's rolls. Within a month-in-a-half, the Sharecroppers Union contained over 800 members the end of May 1931.[18,19]

However, trouble began to brew immediately between the union and local authorities. In July, Police and County Sheriffs raided one of the SCU meetings at Camp Hill, Alabama. Within minutes of the raid, an all-out shootout war took place in broad daylight, which took the life of a Sharecropper and wounding two union officials. For fear of his life and local White Segregationists retribution, Mark Coad fled the state of Alabama successfully. The leadership of the SCU fell into the hands of Young Communist League (YCL) member Eula Gray, teenaged-daughter of Sharecropper Union co-founder Tommy Gray.

Since the deadly shootout at Camp Hill, SCU decided to go underground for a period, with its agitation campaigns, to avoid even more bloodshed. By July 1932, a new Union Secretary was appointed by the name of Al Murphy, a Black Marxist-Leninist from McRae Georgia. Soon after Murphy took over of union operations, the organization had about 600 members on its rolls, which significantly dropped soon after the Camp Hill incident. Under Murphy's direction, the Sharecroppers Union began to arm its members with rifles, shotguns and portable machine guns, all brand-new and all paid for by CPUSA. Eventually, members would use them to defend themselves against local authorities.

In December 1932, more trouble came for SCU and its members, when local police and county sheriffs raided a union meeting, this time in Reeltown, Alabama. During the intense 45-minute exchange of gunfire between both parties, three SCU members were dead and five other members were wounded. The deaths of Sharecroppers Chifford James, John Mc Mullen, and Milo Bentley followed a wave of police raids, arrests and beatings of SCU members throughout Tallapoosa and Lee Counties, that ended in jail time, convictions and prison time for many of those caught by police. Of the people who were not caught up in the arrest and police raid melee, were, of course, Sharecropper Union leadership members, who escaped arrests.

By 1934, faced with mass-scale land evictions of Sharecroppers across the 'Black Belt', due to the first "New Deal" legislation that was put into place under the Roosevelt Administration, SCU membership began to rebound and increase in number slowly, but not to the level that it once attained when Mark Coad was in charge. As it was then, and even now, any organization operated as a tentacle of the American Communist Party, usually inflated their membership numbers, on purpose, with the intent to publicly make such entities bigger than what they really were.

Al Murphy's inflation of SCU's membership numbers was no exception.

In June 1933, Murphy reported that the Sharecroppers Union boasted nearly 2,000 members and by the fall of 1934, its membership rolls swelled to over 8,000. However, despite Murphy's claim that the membership increased as more people were being evicted from their land, meeting minutes, logs and eyewitness testimony contradicted both Murphy's claims and union membership numbers.

In all actuality, The Sharecroppers Union maintained about 700-800 active members. It is interesting to note, that between 1933 and 1935, SCU was never successful in their efforts to recruit even one White Sharecropper to join their ranks, even though they had the full support of local White Sharecropper and White Tenant Farm owners supporting the union's activities.[20,21]

In 1935, a new leader arrived to take the helm of the union, who went by the names Clyde Johnson, or Thomas Burke, or Al Jackson. Johnson-Burke-Jackson was a White Communist from Minnesota, that was trained at the Lenin School in Moscow Russia, who also was sent by CPUSA to conduct community organizing activities in the cities of Birmingham Alabama, Atlanta and Rome Georgia.

Comrade Johnson attempted to take The Sharecroppers Union out of the underground and make it into a viable, public service union and aligned its leadership as such, so that outside law enforcement agencies would not be aware of their subversive activities that the union continued to conduct. His leadership circle, called "The Executive Committee", was steered by Black Marxist-Leninist Hosie Hart, who was originally from Tallapoosa County, as president of this committee.

Together, Johnson-Burke-Jackson and Hart pushed The Sharecroppers Union to be recognized as a legitimate organization, by even going as far as publishing their own newspaper *The Union Leader*, throughout the Black Belt of the South. Unfortunately, the organization's past reputation with Law Enforcement Officials, White Segregationists Groups and even many African-American Sharecroppers, saw the union as just another Communist Front Group, who was only there for their own benefit, not the benefit of the American Worker. These issues along with internal strife between the executive committee and SCU members provided the catalyst to sound the death knell of the union itself.

During the Spring and Summer of 1935, SCU began to stage numerous agitation protests and demonstrations during the April-May Cotton Pickers Strikes, and the Cotton Choppers Strikes during August and September, being conducted in both Lowndes and Dallas Counties Alabama. However, the criminal activities that the SCU were conducting, such as paying the protestors and union members large sums of money per-day to demonstrate, caused an immediate and deadly response from Law Enforcement and Segregationists, once again. In both countries, protestors and police went toe-to-toe with each other, cumulating in numerous shootouts, beatings, and fistfights, which caused the lives of six strikers from gunshot wounds and scores of people injured.

As these incidents took place, Johnson-Burke-Jackson and Hart expanded SCU's influence throughout rural Mississippi and Louisiana, even opening an office in New Orleans to manage their operations in those states. By this time, seeing the published reports of SCU's activities and all-out confrontations with the Police and Segregationists, not many Black Sharecroppers and Tenant Farmers wanted to join the union.

Minus the intimidation tactics by local Ku Klux Klan and Knights of Columbus (KC) Segregationists, the SCU foundered and by 1937, CPUSA disbanded the union and sent its executive committee members to other organizations to continue their agitation efforts. At the end, some asked what did the Sharecroppers Union succeeded at during their six-year reign of existence?

The answer to that question was ***nothing***, but take legitimate issues, make them bigger than what they really are, via protests and demonstrations, prompting a response by police and disappearing in think-air when the clashes turned violent and deadly.

This was and still is the Communist mantra into creating racial divides to advance their agenda. As the Great Depression wined on, more of the same would happen, to the point where such Communist Party influences extended to the Oval Office at the White House itself.

Election of Franklin D. Roosevelt as President and his New Deal Initiatives

With the Great Depression in full-swing and running into its third year of economic calamity, the Presidential Election of 1932 was key, into which political party, was going bring the country back from the financial depression. The election hinged on who was going to re-instill hope for the future back into the American people. With what was called "*Shanty Towns*" or "*Hooverville's*" popping up around major industrial centers of America, including the World War I Veteran Protests in Washington D.C., called "*The Bonus March*", everybody was looking for a savior to get them out of hard times.[22,23]

African American Family living in a "Hooverville-type" housing structure in St. Louis, Missouri circa 1930. (Courtesy of Library of Congress)

The 1932 Presidential Election became one of the most interesting campaign battles and one of the most popular elections to date in the 20th Century. The Presidential Nominees consisted of Democrat Franklin Delano Roosevelt and Republican Incumbent President Herbert Hoover. Affectionately called "**FDR**", Roosevelt was a well-known Governor of New York, serving from 1928-1933. President Hoover decided to run again for a second term, against the advice of some of his party members, because of most of the American public, blamed him for the Great Depression.

Between the end of the American Civil War and the 1932 Presidential Elections, Black Americans voted overwhelmingly for the Republican Party in Presidential Elections, but with the never-ending media coverage of labor union strikes, lack of jobs, protests, demonstrations severe economic downturn and an unemployment rate of over 20-percent, doomed Herbert Hoover any chance of getting re-elected.

There were third-party candidates, who were running against Roosevelt and Hoover during the 1932 election also. This included the following;[24,25]

Communist Party's Candidate and CPUSA head William Z. Foster

Marxist Man Vice-President Nominee James W. Ford (The first African American nominated for any political party for Vice-President in U.S. History)

Socialist Party Candidate Norman Thomas
James H. Maurer

Prohibition Party Candidate William David Upshaw
Frank S. Regan

Liberty Party Candidate William Hope Harvey
Frank Hemenway

Socialist Labor Party Candidate Verne L. Reynolds
John W. Aiken

Farmer Labor Candidate Jacob Coxey
Julius Reiter

What is interesting to note, the 1932 Presidential Election was the last time in American History for 84 years, where a large percentage of African-Americans will ever vote for a Republican candidate again.

The results of the election were staggering, giving newcomer Franklin D. Roosevelt the victory in a super landslide from both the Electoral College and the Popular Vote.

Of the 528 total Electoral College votes, Presidential Candidate Roosevelt won 472 votes and 22,821,857 popular votes. The Incumbent President Hoover won only 59 Electoral College Votes and 15,761,841 Popular Votes. Coming in third, behind the Socialist Party Candidate Thomas, was CPUSA's Foster/Ford ticket only garnered zero Electoral

College Votes and only 102,991 Popular Votes. The American people have chosen Roosevelt as their savior from the Great Depression.[26]

As for the Black Community, upon the swearing-in of the newly-elected President Roosevelt (FDR) in 1933, FDR's first order of business was to attempt to get the United States out of the Great Depression. His administration began to create and enact his *"**New Deal**"* initiatives, which on the outside, was supposed to get the country out of the Great Depression, by creating Federal Government programs to put people back to work and improve the economic environment of the country. In-actuality, the New Deal ended up being a massive expansion government, with Marxists and Socialists-operating as heads of all the federal government agencies of the Executive Branch.

The New Deal was broken down into two versions. The **First New Deal** acts were enacted between 1933-34 and the **Second New Deal** acts, which were enacted between 1935-1939. What each of these acts, the Federal Government expanded tenfold, created vast amounts of regulations, via committees and boards of unelected officials, with the intent to rule every industry and every aspect of American life.

Each of the New Deal Programs/Acts is as follows;[27,28,29,30]

The First New Deal:
The Emergency Banking Act of 1933-Establishing the Federal Deposit Insurance Corporation (FDIC)

The Economy Act of 1933-Establishing monetary policy using Keynesian Economics

The Securities Act of 1933-Establishing the Securities and Exchange Commission (SEC)

The Public Works Administration (PWA)

Resettlement Administration (RA)

Rural Electrification Administration (REA)

National Youth Administration (NYA)

Civilian Conservation Corps (CCC)

Tennessee Valley Authority (TVA)

Farmer's Relief Act of 1933

Agricultural Adjustment Act of 1933 (AAA)-Part I

The Second New Deal:
The Works Progress Administration (WPA)-Establishing the largest Federal Government Works Program in U.S. History

Social Security Act of 1935

The National Relations Act of 1935-Establishing the National Labor Relations Board (NLRB)

Revenue Act of 1935-Establishing a 75% Income Tax for those making more than $1 Million Dollars in revenue

The Housing Act of 1937-Establishing the U.S. Housing Authority and the Department of Housing Urban Development (HUD)

Fair Labor Standard Act of 1938-Establishing the National Minimum Wage

Agricultural Adjustment Act of 1938 (AAA)-Part II

Throughout the 1930's, Communist Agitators continued to use, abuse and in some cases, sacrificed the lives of African-Americans during FDR's Administration, under the banners of '***Fair Wages***', '***Equality***', '***Equal Work***' and '***Civil Rights***'.

Even as the administration massively expanded the role of the Federal Government, the New Deal programs were just as discriminatory and based on skin color than ever before. For example, when Congress passed the Agricultural Adjustment Act of 1933 and 1938 (AAA), was a federal law that in-order for the government to pay farmers their subsidies, the U.S. Department of Agriculture (USDA) mandated that the Farmers had to reduce agricultural production of planting food on a part of their land and kill-off excess livestock, to reduce crop surplus, which will effectively raise the value of crops in the market.

The result of the AAA meant that Sharecroppers, especially in the agricultural Deep South and in the Border States, who were largely African-Americans, enabled Tenant Farmers regardless of skin color, to evict the Sharecroppers from their part of the farm to comply with the AAA law. Those Blacks who were evicted, called the AAA law, *"The Negro Removal Act"* similar to the *"Indian Removal Act"* 100-years before, creating an enormous homeless problem of African-Americans, which forced them to move to the big industrial cities in larger numbers than the Great Black Migration did at the same time.

African American Sharecroppers line up on the side of U.S. Highway 60
in New Madrid County, Missouri January 1939
(Courtesy the Library of Congress)

Other New Deal laws and acts, openly discriminated against Blacks working on federal government projects, such as the Works Project Administration (WPA) and the Tennessee Valley Authority (TVA) public works system. The latter, placed Blacks in segregated berthing units and segregated work crews, to include both its administration and settlement programs. An anonymous TVA official, wrote in 1935 when he was asked about why such segregated units were put in place, he responded;

"You can raise all the rumpus you like...We just aren't going to mix Negroes and White Folks in any village in TVA."

Nor did FDR supported the NAACP-supported and Republican-sponsored Anti-Lynching Law in 1934, despite dozens of state governors, including the state of Florida's Governor David Sholtz. Even though FDR publicly denounced Lynching, he refused to endorse the bill by saying;

"The Southerners...are chairmen of occupying strategic places on most of the Senate and House committees...If I come out for the Anti-Lynching Bill now, they will block every bill I ask Congress to pass to keep American from collapsing."

This was the ***real*** Franklin Delano Roosevelt. There is more, especially when it comes to the American Workforce affecting African-Americans during the 1930's.[37,38]

In July 1934, one of the largest labor strikes involving African-Americans occurred, when the United Textile Workers Union (UTWU) throughout the South, demanded higher wages of $13-15 per week, a 30-hour work week, union recognition and reinstatement of worker's jobs who were fired for their union activities. Negotiations between the Communist-led UTWU and the Roosevelt's National Labor Relations Board (NLRB) broke down when top-ranking union members refused to meet with them.

Workers began to strike on July 18, 1934, in Huntsville Alabama, which expanded to the cities of Florence, Anniston, Gadsden, and Birmingham. The strikes caused greater than 400,000 textile workers, to stop work and protest throughout the South. Which greatly affected that industry's regional production.

Add-on agitation protests led by Communist Agitators, who were on the payroll of CPUSA, some companies began to hire strike breakers or "picket line crossers", to keep production going. These moves resulted in violence against these workers, causing four deaths on September 2; two in Triton Georgia and two in Augusta Georgia. Six picketers were shot and killed by responding law enforcement officers and picket-line crossers in Honea Path, South Carolina on September 6.

More violence, riots, clashes between law enforcement, local citizens, picket-line crossers and corporation owners against striking workers, resulting in hundreds of injuries. As the textile strike spread to the New England states, on September 11, Rode Island Governor activated the state's National Guard and set them to the city of Salyersville, when thousands of strikers, began to block the existing strikebreaker workers from leaving the textile factory there, which broke out into more violent clashes between Guardsmen, Police and the Strikers. This caused the Governor Theodore Francis Green to declare Martial Law there.[39,40,41]

Such labor strikes like the one that hit the Textile Industry, spread to other industries of manufacturing, including the Automobile Industries like Ford and General Motors plants in Michigan. "Sit-Down" Strikes, conducted by the United Auto Workers of America (UAW), demonstrations conducted by Hollywood unions in California, against Walt Disney Corporation in 1941 by the Screen Actors Guild and more became the crust that defined President Roosevelt's second term in office. However, such strikes and labor issues did not deter African-American support of the President.

In-reality, Blacks accelerated their likability and support of the Roosevelt Administration, despite the outright racism they faced in the New Deal programs. Blacks increased their support in favor of FDR, even when he did not support the Anti-Lynching Bill being pressed through both Houses of Congress on Capitol Hill. One reason for such support was that a few rural Blacks located in the Border and the Southern States benefited in some ways off the government loans and grants given to them to create agricultural settlements.[42]

New Deal initiatives in the Northern metropolitan areas, provided African-Americans thousands of jobs during the latter-half of the 1930's, which further advanced such support to the President, which included Public Housing Vouchers and the building of new high-rise and low-rise homes in cities like St. Louis, Chicago and Cleveland Ohio.

Roosevelt Public Works Administration (PWA), spent huge sums of taxpayer-funded money to build schools, hospitals, and other projects in Black neighborhoods, which African-Americans had used in their everyday lives. By 1939, social welfare programs enacted and operated by the Federal Government created a temporary upward mobility for Blacks in the North. An unknown Black Supporter of President Roosevelt was quoted in the Chicago Tribune in 1940 was quoted by saying;

"Let Jesus lead you and Roosevelt free you!"[43]

It's interesting to note, not to think that the FDR Administration wasn't taking note of the many praises of Black Americans had for their dear leader during the 1930's. It would have been political malpractice if they didn't. However, Franklin D. Roosevelt took the high praise and exploited at full value, along with his wife, Eleanor Roosevelt, Secretary of the Interior Harold Ickes and FDR's personal assistant, Marxist Man

Harry Hopkins, into creating what was called Roosevelt's "Black Cabinet" in Washington D.C.

Roosevelt's "Black Cabinet" Minstrel Show

Outside of the Harlem Renaissance, The Scottsboro Boys Case and Communist Propaganda campaigns, using the free press and union literature to spread their rhetoric, garnered the praises from America's Black Community, Eleanor Roosevelt went as far to recruit for her husband a "Black Cabinet" as a show to garner and gain even more African-American support.

Officially called "***The Federal Council of Negro Affairs***" (FCNA), was a group of Black men and women consisted of 45 highly-distinguished members of African-American Elites, many who held Marxist views of the world and had ties with CPUSA, was created to fill Executive Cabinet posts and New Deal Agencies within the Federal Government.[44,45]

Formed in 1936, on the surface, the façade of Roosevelt's all-Black Cabinet seemed to appear good and wholesome, that allowed African-Americans throughout the country to finally conclude that they had a man in the White House, who championed equal rights for them. Using the media to stoke such support, the psychologic value of seeing an all-Black cadre of highly-intellectual and influential men and women to become the right-hand of FDR's initiative to champion Black Civil Rights had a successful effect. Some of the top members of the FCNA along with their cabinet positions included;

> *Mary Jane McLeod Bethune- National Youth Administration (NYA)*
> *Dr. Ambrose Caliver- Department of the Interior*
>
> *Dr. Roscoe C. Brown- Public Health Service (PHS)*
>
> *Dr. Robert C. Weaver- Federal Housing Authority (FHA)*
>
> *Joseph H. Evans- Farm Security Administration (FSA)*
>
> *Lawrence A. Oxley- Department of Labor (DOL)*
>
> *Henry G. Hunt- Farm Credit Administration (FCA)*

However, remember, what's on the surface may seem harmless and good, but underneath that façade, lies a brick wall with no masonry attached to it, which is bad.

What FDR's Black Cabinet did do, was become an optic campaign used to shore up support for Roosevelt's Democrat Party. The members of the cabinet were used to prove to everyday African-Americans that they indeed have a friend in the White House.

In 1936, Roosevelt was up for re-election also, so for him to appoint such a distinguished bunch of high-society, highly-educated Blacks, was key into stealing the Black Vote on November 9, 1936, against Republican contender Alfred Landon. Some of these Black Cabinet members worked with CPUSA boss Earl Browder, Socialist Candidate Norman Thomas and Populist Candidate William Lemke, the latter was more radical than Bowder ever was.

Other than putting brown faces on the front of FDR's Administration, not much work was done by the FCNA group. Some Black Organizations called the members *"a bunch of window-dressers"*, that was just symbolic in appearance than in action. NAACP head Roy Wilkens went further than that;

"[they] had never existed before...The Negro had never before had this penetration into the government that he had under Roosevelt...Thanks to the Black Cabinet, Blacks felt that they were getting through to the man."

Whatever the case maybe, what the Black Cabinet did for President Roosevelt, was to give the political advantage over any of his opponents during the next Presidential Elections in 1936 and 1940. On the flip-side, however, one must give the FDR Administration credit, for the successful optical illusion that they presented to the African-American Community.

Such perception showed three distinct things. One, it showed that by the time the 1930's ended, the Democrat Party, was now the "political party" for Black Americans now, instead of the Republican Party, for the first time since the end of the Civil War.

What FDR and his henchmen in the White House did, was to make Black Americans dependent on the Federal Government for their well-being, instead of individual efforts within their own community. To do this effectively, all the Democrats had to do is to put brown faces of so-called "Black Community Leaders" and "Black Intelliencia" into false "positions of power" within the Federal Government, to make many in the Black Community feel good for once, under the false pretense that Blacks do have a man in the White House who will look out for them.

Secondly, both the Democrat Party, called "Progressives" and the Communist Party watching behind them, understood intimately, that the African-American people in the United States can be easily duped and persuaded to do anything that the after-mentioned groups tell them to do, without much effort. The end-result was that the Black Community will wholeheartedly mobilize in large numbers, to do their bidding. Whether-or-not such actions will cost them their lives.

Third, by manipulating African Americans' emotions via propaganda, lies and blatant falsehoods, Progressives in the Democrat Party and Marxist Men in the Communist Party, can easily sell to the Black Community a can of snake oil, and they will buy it without any questioning its source. With such duping, Blacks can now be and will be used like pawns in a chess game from 1936 onwards, for such exploitation value both politically and ideological agendas.

Since using the 'Black Cabinet' propaganda gain so much success as a Public Relations (PR) stunt to emotionally sway the Black Community to vote Democrat instead of Republican, that it assisted FDR to win the 1936 Presidential Election in a bigger landslide than he won in 1932. Roosevelt won 523 Electoral College Votes against his opponent, Republican Alfred "Alf" Landon's eight votes. As for the Black vote, Franklin Roosevelt carried 56-percent of Knoxville, Tennessee Black vote, 75-percent of Pittsburgh, Pennsylvania Black votes, 81-percent of New York City's Black vote and 90-percent of the Black vote in the Midwest.[46,47]

President Franklin D. Roosevelt's "Black Cabinet" members 1936
(Courtesy of the Library of Congress)

African Americans in World War Two

As a world conflict began to rear its ugly head over the horizon of the United States of America, the late-1930's and the first two years of the 1940's, the Great Depression ended up making the country an isolationist nation. As world events took shape around the world, from Japan to China, to Soviet Russia and Germany, the Roosevelt administration attempted to stay out of a World War which was brewing. It's well-known that in Germany under Adolf Hitler and the Nazis, that Germany began his systematic repression of his own people. Many of them were Jewish, Homosexuals, Christian, and non-German persons, by placing them in concentration camps located throughout the German countryside.[48,49,50]

While at the same time, CPUSA's hero in the person of Joseph Stalin, commenced a repression campaign of its own. Between 1936 and 1939, called "**The Great Purge**", Stalin's henchmen murdered high-ranking Communist Party officials, high-ranking Government Officials, Peasants (the Proletariats) and Soviet Russian Army Leadership. By using hundreds of Gulag Prison Camps spread out throughout the Russian countryside, people by the dozens were subject to public executions via firing squads, lynching and hanging persons from tree limbs, throwing them from the roofs of public buildings and more.

Those who went to the Gulag died from epidemic outbreaks of diseases, mass starvations, exposure to super-frigid Siberian temperatures and exhaustion from hard labor. This Gulag list included a handful of Americans who began to live under the so-called lie of "equality" and "no-racism" under Communism in Soviet Russia. The same system that, just a short time ago, they were brainwashed to accept. In all, Joseph Stalin was responsible for the deaths and murders of over 2-3 million people, subtracted from the Soviet population.[51,52,53]

In Italy, under the dictator of Benito Mussolini, a large police state was created, which Mussolini secret police carried out mass 'liquidations' of dissenters and all opposition to the unchecked power of his government administration caused the murder of over 300,000 Italians by the hands of *"The Almighty State"*.[54,55]

For Black Americans, like every other American in the United States, the Roosevelt Administration sheltered the public from such atrocities being done throughout the world, causing them to ignore such important issues. They have been told, through the media, the Federal Government had everything under control. That didn't happen and on December 7, 1941, the Imperial Japanese Navy, attacked Pearl Harbor Hawaii, killing over 2,300 people during the hours-long attack. One of the heroes of the attack was an African American from Texas, who served as a Mess Attendant First-Class, named Doris Miller.

Seaman Miller was serving onboard the U.S. Navy Battleship USS West Virginia (BB-48) when the Japanese struck. Miller tried to shield his Commanding Officer, Captain Mervin S. Bennion from shrapnel and attempted to treat the officer's wounds, which the officer succumbs to them. While the ship's Captain died from his injuries, Doris Miller took a 25-millimeter chain gun, nearby on the Bridge Wing of the West Virginia from dying White Sailor who was fatally wounded, manned the gun and began to fire back at the attacking Japanese planes, shooting down four of them, unofficially out of the sky.

After the third wave of attacking plane departed the carnage, Seaman Miller, after being blown overboard because of the heinous explosion of the nearby Battleship USS Arizona (BB-39), was picked up by other White Sailors who were manning a Motor Whale Boat and began to help them fight numerous fires that were burning in "Battleship Row". For his outstanding action and devotion to duty, Mess Attendant First-Class Doris Miller was awarded the Navy's highest award for valor, the Navy Cross from fellow Texan Admiral Chester W. Nimitz onboard the flight deck of Aircraft Carrier USS Enterprise (CV-6) in Pearl Harbor.[56,57]

As World War Two commenced, involving the United States after the wake of the Pearl Harbor Hawaii attack, African Americans became to be involved in both the military and civilian aspects, to support the war effort. Unfortunately, Blacks were prevented to join the United States Marine Corps, Coast Guard, and Army Air Forces initially, while in the Navy and Army, they were only tasked to serve in support occupations, such as constructions, food service, and supply corps.

Despite these odds, Black Americans joined the war effort eagerly, by the dozens, some joined and didn't wait for the Draft Board to contact them to join. As the war, ground on, Blacks began to fill jobs that other military personnel was doing all along, from infantrymen to medics and Commissioned Officers. In the U.S. Navy, Black Sailors began to work in Engineering, firing the big guns on its ships and fought along with and dying right along with their White counterparts fighting the enemy.

An all-Black 5-inch Gun Crew onboard a U.S. Navy Destroyer in the Pacific during World War II. Each man in this photograph received the Navy's Bronze Star for action against enemy planes they shot down in the South Pacific, 1944.
(Courtesy Navy Heritage)

In 1943, under the urging of his wife Eleanor Roosevelt, President Franklin D. Roosevelt ordered the U.S. Army Air Corps to create an all-Black fighter unit, officially called the 99th Fighter Squadron. Under the capable command of Army Air Corps Colonel Benjamin Davis Jr., USAAC, this squadron was known affectionally as the "*Tuskegee Airmen*".

On the civilian side of the war effort, the Great Depression officially ended; not because of Roosevelt's New Deal Programs, but by becoming an isolationist country, and being forced to join her allies to fight the world at war. For African Americans, the economy began to boom once again, the quality of life began to get better and jobs and work were plentiful for people to apply for with the numerous defense and construction jobs being created to support both Pacific and European Wars. However, problems did exist in the 1940's when it came to race and don't think for a second, that the Communist Party, NAACP, and other Marxist-driven organizations did not take advantage of the situation to start some type of trouble, to get their way.[58,59]

One issue that came to a head, was the Selective Service Draft. For religious reasons, people who were Jehovah Witnesses became Conscientious Objectors to the military draft. Failing to not just register for the Draft, but refuse to be Inducted into the military when being drafted, without having valid circumstances, punishment can range from paying fines and serving a minimum of five-years of jail time.

By the end of World War Two in August 1945, over 6,000 Jehovah Witnesses were arrested and sent to prison for five years for what was called "dodging the draft". Draft dodging was also prevalent among the Caucasian-founded Nation of Islam, where members not only refuse to sign up for the Draft but refused to be Drafted into the military, then pledged no allegiance to the United States of America; the same country which members benefited off-of, both economically and socially.[60,61]

Members of the Nation of Islam (NOI), now under the leadership of Elijah Muhammad, refused the Military Draft also, citing things like;

"Why would we go and fight for America against a racist country like Germany, when our own country are racists against us?"

The NOI firmly stated in no uncertain terms, that they owed no allegiance to the United States of America, causing some of its members to be arrested, fined and serving jail time, including Elijah Muhammad himself. Elijah failed to register for the Draft on May 8, 1942, in Washington D.C. and fled the city. Weeks later, he was arrested in Chicago, Illinois and charged with eight-counts of Sedition (Inflammatory speech given to start an insurrection), because he told his followers **_not_** to register for the draft. Elijah Muhammad was convicted on all eight-counts and served four years in the Federal Penitentiary in Milan, Michigan, between 1942-1946.

The era of World War Two, 1939-1945, was also the era of the Second Great Black Migration (1940-1970), where Black families relocated from the agricultural Deep South to the Industrial Cities in the North, Border-States and Western Cities, such as Los Angeles, San Francisco, San Diego, Oakland California and Seattle Washington metro areas. As Blacks migrated to the already overcrowded Industrial Cities, both the Communist Party and the NAACP increased its recruitment efforts and membership rolls ten-fold.

Both organizations began to create their own propaganda campaigns, calling for African Americans to mobilize against racial discrimination abroad. Even Swedish Marxist Man Gunnar Myrdal wrote in his 1944 book *"An American Dilemma"*, where he argued that such racial discrimination practices being used against them, violated deeply held precepts for which the nation was then shedding its blood. Even Public Service Unions, began to join in the rhetoric to mobilize Black folks emotionally, to protest and conduct demonstrations, so they can access good-paying jobs in new defense plants, created nationwide.[62]

Socialist A. Philip Randolph, head of the Brotherhood of Sleeping Car Porters, called for Blacks nationwide to openly protest and march on the segregated-city of Washington D.C. on July 1, 1941, to force the Roosevelt Administration to end racial discrimination in war industries. Remember, these are the same African Americans who just two-years prior stated;

"Let Jesus lead you and let Roosevelt free you!"

They must have found out that the President did not free them from racial discrimination as they were promised by Roosevelt and his "Black Cabinet" subliminally in 1941!

President Roosevelt saw that A. Philip Randolph and a White-Blond-Black man of the NAACP named Walter White and other Black organizations were serious about the march on Washington, he decided to make the move to pacify such leaders of the America's Black Community. On June 25, 1941, President Roosevelt signed *Executive Order 8802, "Prohibition of Discrimination in the Defense Industry"*, created the Fair Employment Practices Committee (FEPC), where a selected number of bureaucrats in Washington D.C., to do the following;

Centralized all governmental contracting and negotiations with the Office of Personnel Management (OPM)

Create and enforce fair housing practices at the job gate

Create on-the-job training programs for African American hires

Tell such contractors to avoid racial and religious discrimination upon hiring.

Because of this "swift-action" by President Roosevelt, A. Philip Randolph and Walter White canceled the march on Washington. Claiming victory, the National Urban League (UNL) head Lester Granger rejoiced by stating "Employment is a civil right!".

Oh really?

In the real-world scheme of things, FEPC was weak. Executive Order 8802 establishing the committee was only a temporary measure, that was only designed to last until the end of World War Two.

Second, the President created the Executive Order on the basis that Randolph and White had a large following of African Americans, who were going to make the march on Washington a real event, creating a media spectacle. This was something which Roosevelt wanted to avoid altogether.

To counter this problem, he had to convince the public, that the Executive Order was the answer, to stamp out racial discrimination in the defense industry. However, the Armed Forces, Federal Civil Service, and State Employment Agencies were still operating segregated units and still employed tactics of racial discrimination.[63,64,65]

In major production centers, such as Philadelphia Pennsylvania, another needless bureaucratic committee created by the Roosevelt Administration, The War Manpower Commission (WMPC) and FEPC, forced the Philadelphia Transit Company (PTC), a private entity, that they must promote eight of their African American workers to become Streetcar Operators, whether-or-not they had the skills or training to assume the task.

Of course, this action did not sit well with both the owners of the company and its White Workers. To have the Federal Government to intervene into a private company and dictate what they do inside their operations, was beyond the pale for PTC, so on August 1, 1944, workers decided to strike. The strike in protest against Federal interference effectively shut down that city's transportation and its wartime industries.

The loss of millions of dollars of wages and production caused Philadelphia's defense industries to speak out publicly about their displeasure of the transit workers to strike. President Roosevelt, who was on the west coast at the time of the strike, ordered the War Department (predecessor to today Department of Defense) led by Secretary of War Henry L. Stimson, to mobilize 8,000 U.S. Army Troops and send them to Philadelphia.

Once there, Stimson ordered Major-General Philip Hayes of the Army's Third Service Command, to take over the Philadelphia Transit Company and operate the system. The strike officially ended quickly on Sunday, August 6th, which allowed PTC workers to go back to work the following morning of Monday, August 7th. Not one shot was fired by the Soldiers and no riots were created.[66]

President Roosevelt's Second Bill of Rights: The Communist Plan to Control American Citizens

President Franklin Delano Roosevelt, speaking to Congress and the Public about the
Second Bill of Rights on January 11, 1944.
(Courtesy of the National Archives and Records Administration)

Since the Socialist Party made its unofficial entrance into the American psyche, during the 1890's, Socialist in the United States, followed by the Communist Party in 1919, had advocated that the United States Constitution and the Bill of Rights, have become outdated documents, that have become irrelevant in modern times. An article published in the ultra-Marxist publication, The Huffington Post, printed an editorial on June 3, 2014, written by Galanty Miller, which makes such an argument true, by saying sarcastically and incoherently;

"People continue to treat the Constitution as if it's some all-knowing mystical force, beamed to us from outer space by omniscient alien gods who were absolutely certain of the universal, never-changing fact that Senators should serve six-year terms, rather than five..."[67]

There also have been instances inside American public schools, where Six-grade students are taught to destroy the U.S. Constitution and the Bill of Rights because they are outdated. In return, teachers will have them complete assignments to turn-in their assignment, with their own lists they think, should be "The Bill of Rights", with the ultimate objective to replace the current founding documents.

The Educators emphasize to their students, that they must keep in mind of the 21st Century American society we live in! Even in pop-culture, unless it benefits them, both of our founding documents, are said to be flawed, because they have been brainwashed to accept that the persons who wrote them were Slave-owners, and they did not care about the 'common man' and they were bigots, racists, and rich-statists. These lies are what they have been taught to believe.[68,69,70]

Such lies and misinformation are even advocated by a current-sitting, Supreme Court Justice of the United States. Justice Ruth Bader Ginsburg, while in Cairo Egypt on January 30, 2012, told the Egyptian government, which was creating a new constitution after the Muslim Brotherhood coup, ousting Egypt President Hosni Mubarak from power, stated;

"I would not look to the U.S. Constitution if I were drafting a constitution in the year 2012. I might look at the constitution of South Africa. That was a deliberate attempt to have a fundamental instrument of government that embraces human rights, have an independent judiciary. It really is, I think, a great piece of work that was done."[71,72]

These words are coming from a Justice of the United States Supreme Court, whose job is to interpret the U.S. Constitution as written and rule whether or not the cases put before her and her colleagues on the court are within the realm of validity of the constitution, that she had sworn to protect and defend!

Outrageous, isn't it?

This rhetoric has been debated over-and-over again, ever since 1919, since their main objective is to overthrow the Government of the United States, in the form of a violent and bloody revolution, Marxist Men and outright Socialists have targeted both documents and sometimes misinterpret them, to advance their agenda to usher in Socialism, then full-Communism which follows next. However, President Franklin D. Roosevelt and probably along with his personal assistant, Marxist Man and possible Soviet KGB Agent Harry Hopkins, wrote something that Leftists can and have agreed on.

It's called the "*__Second Bill of Rights__*", and it was first presented to the American people, when President Roosevelt made his radio broadcast to Congress and the nation on January 11, 1944. He called for the implementation of the Second Bill of Rights because he saw that the current Bill of Rights, written in 1791, has proved to be inadequate in the modern-age and expansion of the country.

Roosevelt also called for the new Bill of Rights to be immediately implemented directly after the end of the Second World War, so that the American people can have "*equality*", seek the "*pursuit of happiness*" in the name of "*security*". These words have been articulated before, by the likes of Joseph Stalin, Adolf Hitler, and Mao Tse Tung. FDR outlined eight specific "*__Rights__*" that will reach that aforementioned goal of equality and pursuit of happiness in the name of security of the people once implemented. The transcript of Roosevelt's speech is as follows;

"It is our duty now to begin to lay the plans and determine the strategy for the winning of a lasting peace and the establishment of an American standard of living higher than ever before known. We cannot be content, no matter how high that general standard of living may be if some fraction of our people—whether it be one-third or one-fifth or one-tenth—is ill-fed, ill-clothed, ill-housed, and insecure.

This Republic had its beginning, and grew to its present strength, under the protection of certain inalienable political rights—among them the right of free speech, free press, free worship, trial by jury, freedom from unreasonable searches and seizures. They were our rights to life and liberty.

As our nation has grown in size and stature, however—as our industrial economy expanded—these political rights proved inadequate to assure us equality in the pursuit of happiness.

We have come to a clear realization of the fact that true individual freedom cannot exist without economic security and independence. "Necessitous men are not free men." People who are hungry and out of a job are the stuff of which dictatorships are made.

In our day these economic truths have become accepted as self-evident. We have accepted, so to speak, a second Bill of Rights under which a new basis of security and prosperity can be established for all—regardless of station, race, or creed.

Among these are:

The right to a useful and remunerative job in the industries or shops or farms or mines of the nation;

The right to earn enough to provide adequate food and clothing and recreation;

The right of every farmer to raise and sell his products at a return which will give him and his family a decent living;

The right of every businessman, large and small, to trade in an atmosphere of freedom from unfair competition and domination by monopolies at home or abroad;

The right of every family to a decent home;

The right to adequate medical care and the opportunity to achieve and enjoy good health;

The right to adequate protection from the economic fears of old age, sickness, accident, and unemployment;

The right to a good education.

All of these rights spell security. And after this war is won we must be prepared to move forward, in the implementation of these rights, to new goals of human happiness and well-being.

America's own rightful place in the world depends in large part upon how fully these and similar rights have been carried into practice for all our citizens. For unless there is security here at home there cannot be lasting peace in the world."

One of the main objectives of both Communist and Socialists, besides control of the people, is to regulate every aspect of human activity being conducted by everyone each day, as they, the almighty collective, see fit.

Even Karl Marx in the Communist Manifesto admitted, that in-order for full-Communism to take place, control of the people and forcing them to get rid of the old society, must be done. What Communists and Socialists have in common, is that by subverting the masses into thinking that everything that they do, they have the "**_Right_**", to do, even if it is criminal, instead of the masses of people have the "**_opportunity_**" to achieve their full potential in life. Because if the latter existed, the Communist and Socialists cannot and will not be able to control you.

Therefore, Marxist Men hate the Bill of Rights in the U.S. Constitution, unless it fits their agenda because they see that document as being a hindrance to their goal of creating a worldwide revolution and the ultimate control of Man period. Don't believe me? Noam Chomsky, a Marxist Man who is considered by the Communist Party as one of the foremost intellectual activists today, wrote about this in his book "**_Who Rules the World_**". He concludes the book with this paragraph;

"…'Who rules the world?', we might also want to pose another question; 'What principles and values rule the world?' That question should be foremost in the minds of the citizens of the rich and powerful states, who enjoy an unusual legacy of freedom, privilege, and opportunity thanks to the struggles of those who came before them, and who now face fateful choices as to how to respond to challenges of great human import…."

Understand what FDR's Second Bill of Rights *really mean*.

What it means, is that the ***Almighty Federal Government***, operated by a cadre of Marxist Men, wielding immense power over the entire population, **will dictate what you do, where you live, how much you will grow on your land, that they essentially own, to include your business that you sell goods, will be rationed in accordance to the State and how much you can sell!**

The Almighty Federal Government, therefore**, will also tell you what size of home you can live in, what kind of home you should live in, determine what type of "adequate" health care you will receive, if any as determined by this collective bunch of Marxist Men, who will also determine what type of decent living you can have, up to the point where how many children you and your spouse can bear!**

Just think about this.

If you are not scared about what FDR's Bill of Rights really mean, and it's gaining traction by the Communist Left in this country, nothing will scare you and self-genocide will commence to the Marxist Men's target population; African Americans.[73,74,75]

https://youtu.be/Ey5i5WObUgQ

"Riots, demonstrations-street battles-detachments of a revolution army-such are the stages in development of the popular uprising."

Vladimir Lenin

Everything mentioned in the previous chapters detailing Communist influence inside the Black Community, all accumulated to a head during the American Civil Rights Movement of the 1950's and 60's.

It was at this stage in American History, that Marxist-Leninist Ideology, began to immerse itself into every aspect of Black society. From trade unions to churches, to the Public Education System and of course, the Black Entertainment Industry, the Communist Party, its numerous front groups and their supporting "civil liberties" associations, ratchet up their agitation campaigns, to mobilize millions of Blacks to fight for 'equality' and destroy 'discrimination' in America.

Such wording and ideas were noble in causation, due to the fact, that both De Jure and De Facto Segregation, employment inequality and many other social issues were going against some living within the Black Community of the time. However, Communists love to project optical illusions, under the pretense of fantastic goals or slogans in- order to, psychologically subvert the masses into believing their lies and criminal activities.

However, slogans such as 'equality', 'social justice', and 'fight against racial discrimination', was just a ploy by the Communist Party to make it **_look like_** that everybody wanted to work together as a team with the same goal in mind. Behind the scenes, that wasn't the case; they were **_lies_**. What is interesting to note about the Communist Party and their Marxist Men façade of wanting to bring everybody together, was to in-plant as much hate, discontent, public protests and even violence, in-order to control every aspect of human activity, using noble causes, such as the U.S. Civil Rights Movement, then transform the cause into something that it wasn't supposed to be.

It must be remembered, that CPUSA along with the Communist International in Moscow, adding their many front groups, only target a section of the population of people, exploit real world situations and use them to their advantage, while hiding their real intentions of a worldwide revolution, behind the shield ***actual*** human atrocities!

Human atrocities which were perpetrated by Progressive, Racist and self-ideological Anarchists, which stoked the flames of emotion, to hype up their rhetoric that society was on a downfall into nuclear war, NAZI-like death camps and oblivion. In reality, it was the Communist Party that succeeded in mobilizing the Black Community, by the thousands, to be used as 'useful idiots' to help Marxist Men within CPUSA, to continue their march towards a Global Communist society, which in the end, Black America will ***never*** be a part of.

The American Civil Rights Movement Gains Steam- Truman's Executive Order 9981

The starting point of the American Civil Rights Movement is inaccurately credited to the day, where the Supreme Court of the United States handed down its decision, desegregating America's Public-School System. The date in question, was May 17, 1954. On that day, the Court ruled upon hearing the famous ***Brown vs. Board of Education*** lawsuit, which rendered a 9-0 decision in favor of Brown, that stated that segregation of public schools in America was unconstitutional, in accordance with the Equal Protection Clause of the 14th Amendment of the U.S. Constitution. However, the Civil Rights Movement ***did not*** start with the SCOTUS decision, but almost 6 years prior to that.

The Civil Rights Movement ***should be accurately credited***, to the date of July 24, 1948, under the direction and leadership of Democrat and Anti-Communist President Harry S. Truman. On that day, President Truman signed ***Executive Order 9981: Desegregating the Armed Forces of the United States***. It was this order, which set the stage for the most controversial and violent movement for Blacks to gain their civil rights as equal citizens in America, since the American Civil War almost 100 years earlier.

Truman's **Executive Order 9981**, was the result of the President's avocation of African-American Civil Rights that was put into action directly after World War Two.[1]

By 1940, The U.S. Census indicated that there were 132,164,569 people were living in America and within its territories. Of that total, approximately 12.9 million people were African-American, which represented only 9.8% of the overall population number.[2] From the outbreak of U.S. involvement during World War Two, 2.5 million Black males were drafted to serve in the armed forces, which over 1 million of that number served in every military organization, with a small amount serving with the Marine Corps by December 31, 1945.[3]

During that time, African-American Women served in the military also. 72 Black Women served as Commissioned Officers in the United States Navy and Army, serving in a variety of positions from Administration positions to Nurses during the war. The author himself, besides having many distinguished family members and relatives who served in the military as Black Americans, my Paternal Great-Aunt served as one of the 72 African American Women commissioned in the U.S. Navy during World War Two, serving for 3.5 years and being honorably discharged in mid-1946.[4]

Though Truman's predecessor, President Franklin Delano Roosevelt created Executive Order 8802, establishing Black Employment within Defense Contractor organizations during the war and establishing a *"Fair Employment Practices Commission"* (FEPC) to enforce the provisions, FDR's Executive Order didn't go far enough to address other areas of African-American Civil Rights in other entities and institutions throughout the nation. By the end of WWII in the Summer of 1945, FEPC actions expired and were abolished by Congress in its entirety.

Black Americans who had served in World War Two, after its end, with FEPC gone, continued to serve in a segregated military, in units at home and abroad. President Truman seeing that conditions in the U.S. Armed Forces and Federal Employment (Blacks were banned from the latter under a previous Presidential Order by Democrat President Woodrow Wilson in 1913) wanted both Federal Government entities racially integrated.

In December 1946, President Truman appointed a 15-member panel to look into desegregating the military service and federal employment, with the goal, unlike FDR, to find a permanent solution on desegregation. The President tasked the panel to formulate recommendations to end the after-mentioned problem in its entirely, and commissioned the **President's Commission on Civil Rights (PCCR).** The panel who were appointed had the dubious task to end such racial segregation in America. PCCR's members were;[5,6,7,8]

> *Charles E. Wilson- President of General Electric Corporation and Commission Chairman*
>
> *Charles Luckman- President of Lever Brothers Corporation*
>
> *James B. Carey- Secretary-General of the Congress of Industrial Organizations (CIO)*
>
> *Boris Shiskin- Economist of the American Federation of Labor (AFL)*
>
> *John S. Dickey- Present of Dartmouth College*
>
> *Frank R. Graham- President of the University of North Carolina*
>
> *Francis J. Haas- Roman Catholic Bishop of Grand Rapids Michigan*
>
> *Henry Knox Sherrill- Presiding Bishop of the Episcopal Church*
>
> *Rabbi Roland B. Gittersohn*
>
> *Sadie T. Alexander- City Solicitor of Philadelphia (Black Female & First African-American appointed as City Solicitor)*
>
> *Channing H. Tobias- Director of the Philips-Stokes Fund*
>
> *Morris L. Ernst- American Civil Liberties Union (ACLU) Lawyer*
>
> *Francis P. Matthews- Former head of the Knights of Columbus*
>
> *Dorothy M. Tilly- Field Secretary for the Southern Regional Council*
>
> *Franklin Delano Roosevelt Jr.- Third Son of former President Franklin Delano Roosevelt Sr. and First Lady Eleanor Roosevelt, formerly decorated WWII Navy Officer and Lawyer*

Governed by *Executive Order 9808*, PCCR set about its task to, not only end racial segregation in America's military, but they were tasked to come up with recommendations to slowly tear down and began to dismantle the institution of racial segregation, both De Jure and De Facto Segregation entities throughout the country.[9,10] The committee corresponded with over 250 organizations, held hearings and received hundreds of advice and recommendations from many individuals from a broad range of professions.

The Committee sought out academic advisors and professors from highly distinguished Historically Black Universities (HBU) such as Howard University in Washington D.C. and Hampton University in Virginia. PCCR solicited advice and information from veteran advocate groups, such as AMVETS, American Legion, and the American Veteran's Committee, in-regards to African-American Civil Rights. They also held hearing and sought input from over 40 experts and advocates of Black American Civil Rights, to include the head of the Brotherhood of Sleeping Car Porters, A. Philip Randolph, NAACP Secretary-General Roy Innis and many others.[11,12]

After meeting with each other 10 times between January and September of 1947, the committee drafter their final report, titled "*To Secure These Rights*" the following month of October. Truman's Presidential Committee on Civil Rights, the first of its kind ever appointed by a President of the United States since Reconstruction, recommended 34 major political and social recommendations, which called for sweeping Federal Government intervention in order, to once and for all to abolish racial segregation throughout the country. Some of PCCR recommendations were;

The Right to Safety and Security of the Person regardless of their station in life

Install and enforce Anti-Lynching Laws of both Blacks and Whites

Eliminate Police Misconduct, especially when it comes to minorities

Strengthen the Civil Rights Division within the Department of Justice and provide them with legal and subpoena power to enforce civil rights violations

Eliminate Involuntary Servitude within America's workplaces, when it comes to Race, Culture, Gender and Economic level

The Right to Citizenship and its Privileges regardless of Race, Culture and Economic Level

Advocate and enforce American Citizens and those who are trying to assimilate and become American Citizens the right to vote in elections, hold public office and have an effective voice in the nation's affairs

The elimination of Poll Taxes, Literacy Tests which disfranchised Blacks to vote in American Elections, especially in the segregated South. PCCR stated that such Poll Taxes were unconstitutional.

The Right to Bear Arms for every citizen of the United States regardless of Race, Gender and Economic Status, to defend themselves, their families and their country

The Right of Freedom of Conscience and Expression

Military personnel and Federal Civil Service Employees must remain loyal to the United States of America, regardless of position, rank or grade of service

Assist in destroying the enemies of the United States both foreign and domestic

The Right to Employment, based on qualifications of the individual and not because to Race, Culture, Gender or Disability

The Right to Education and eliminate racial segregation in both Public and Private Schools in America, including the South

The Right to Housing, the freedom to rent, purchase or buy a home without discrimination

The Elimination of 'Restrictive Covenant'

The Right for Health Service and eliminate in its entirety segregation of medical facilities and organizations throughout the nation

The Right to Public Services and Accommodations, by eliminating racial discrimination of public services, government help benefits, and hotel/sleeping accommodations

President Truman was very satisfied with the report from the committee and gave the report to Congress in February 1948. He made the argument to Congress at that time and pleaded for them to take immediate action, to create legislative bills and internal committees to enact laws that PCCR recommended.

Of course, President Truman's advocating to desegregate American society was met with some very serious and fierce opposition, from Southern Senators in Congress and the Black Press who were a part of the Communist Party.

The latter concluded that they were left out of the decision-making process of PCCR and felt that Truman should have solicited them for advice first prior to the committee's finalized report. Senators in opposition immediately threatened to Filibuster every bill put before them that had ***anything*** to do with desegregation, regardless of institution or entity PCCR and Truman proposed.

This created a showdown of monumental proportions which would pit the nation's political parties against each other, and form what will be called "***Dixiecrats***" which will shake up the 1948 Presidential Election and spur on more of the American Civil Rights Movement yet to come.[13,14]

The "Dixiecrats", Truman's Opposition Against Desegregation

One of the most vocal opponents who publicly denounced President Truman's Presidential Committee on Civil Rights' that recommended immediate actions to desegregate the country, were the same people of the same political party that Truman himself, had represented as President of the United States; the Democrat Party, ***especially*** Southern Democrats. This political party has been known throughout American History, since at least the 1820's under Democrat President Andrew Jackson, to have blocked any and all legislation that attempted to destroy the Institute of Black Slavery in America. After the Civil War, it was the Southern Democrats who formed terror groups, such as the Ku Klux Klan (KKK), White Liners and other organizations, which disenfranchised African-Americans, using death and intimidation tactics throughout the South before 1890.

It was these groups, backed up by the Democrat Party in the South, who drove racial segregation in the Southern and inside the Border States during the 19th and early 20th Century America; **_not the Republicans_**. The Democrats who advocated, support and in some circles, were active members of racist groups such as the KKK, who called themselves "Segregationists" actively prevented Blacks not to have the same or share in the same privileges that they enjoyed. So, when the SCOTUS case, **_Plessy vs. Ferguson_** in 1898, Segregationists solidified their position on every level of government, in blatant violation of the U.S. Constitution and against the Civil Rights of Blacks and Minorities, period!

Copy of the Dixiecrat advertisement in 1947.
(Courtesy of MediaMatters.org)

When Democrat President Harry S. Truman came along after FDR's death, created a committee which called for the Civil Rights for Blacks, the Southern Segregationists/Democrats wasn't all too happy with the platform that gave Black Americans equal rights and opportunities that they themselves enjoyed. This attitude was led by a group of Southern Democrat politicians in the Congress, to protest Truman's desegregation plan for the country. Twelve Congressional Senators split from the Democrat Party and created a third political party called "Dixiecrats". The Dixiecrats were led by then-Democratic

Senator J. Strom Thurmond of South Carolina, that included other Senators listed below;[15,16,17]

James Eastland- Democrat Senator-Mississippi

Richard E. Russell Jr.- Democrat Senator-Georgia

Thomas G. Bilbo- Democrat Senator-Mississippi

J. William Fulbright- Democrat Senator-Arkansas
(Mentor to future President William J. "Bill Clinton)
Spessard L. Holland- Democrat Senator-Florida

Claude D. "Red" Pepper- Democrat Senator-Florida

Walter F. George- Democrat Senator-Georgia

John C. Stennis- Democrat Senator-Mississippi
(Took the seat of Senator Bilbo after that Senator's death in 1948)

Absalom W. Robertson- Democrat Senator-Virginia

Olin D. Johnston- Democrat Senator-South Carolina

J. Lister Hill- Democrat Senator-Alabama

The Dixiecrats platform was to campaign for a decentralized government, while simultaneous stated that they "have a passionate defense for their racial hierarchical society".

Their plan was to have a two-prong attack going into the Presidential Election of 1948. The first objective was to decry any-and-all attempts by both Harry Truman and Republican Presidential Nominee/Candidate Thomas E. Dewey from proposing anything regarding desegregation.

Secondly, the Dixiecrats was to deny both Democrats and Republicans the majority of the Electoral College. By going on a third-party ticket, with then-Democrat Senator Strom Thurmond as the nominee and Mississippi Governor Fielding Wright as Vice-President, they hoped that they can capture 127 Electoral Votes from the heavily Black populated South in the "Black Belt". If they succeeded, the 1948

Presidential Election would be decided by the House of Representatives in Congress to decide who would be the next President of the United States, which would have become a media spectacle.

__In other words, there wasn't any "Southern Strategy"! It doesn't exist! This so-called "Southern Strategy" malarkey is another lie created and manufactured by the United States Communist Party__.

Fortunately, besides the Racial Segregationists who objected to desegregation, such as the Southern Democrat Elites, members of the Ku Klux Klan, White League and White Liner groups, the Dixiecrats have very little support; especially from the African-Americans residing in the Black Belt. In one incident, on the front-page of July 24, 1948, St. Louis Post-Dispatch under the headline;
"Grand Dragon Predicts 'Blood in Streets' if 'Yankee bayonets' are used to Back Truman Civil Rights Program".

At the same time, some other southern newspapers echoed the same rhetoric that the St. Louis Post-Dispatch did. For example, the front-page article from **The Anniston (Alabama) Star**, dated July 25, 1948, announced that the Dixiecrats campaign will be based on

"State's Rights", and will to

"preserve the real Jeffersonian Democrat Party".

The Anniston Star, in the same article, interviewed Senator Thurmond stating;

"We are not running a white supremacy, racial-hatred or class prejudice platform, but on the issue of state's rights."

In reality, not many leaders in the Southern States agreed with the Dixiecrats platform.[19,20,21]

North Carolina Governor Robert Gregg Cherry, stated that he did not support the Thurmond/Wright ticket because he saw the protest and split in the Democrat Party as being;

"An abortive, tragic, and silly 'Southern Secession'".

Editors of the **Raleigh News and Observer** adamantly dismissed the Dixiecrats who's attitude was;

"As arrogance that has been rivaled only by their stupidity."

The paper also stated that North Carolinians were not interested in abandoning the traditional Democrat platform by joining the Dixiecrats who they, the editors called **"Rebels"**.

The most surprising detail that Truman's Civil Rights Commission's proposal had caused, by some odd reason, was the **absolute silence from the Black Press!** One would wonder why they would miss a golden opportunity to promote handsomely the President's Civil Rights proposal, that would have given many actual "equality" and possibly could have started the process to dismantle the evil racial segregation that had plagued the African-American Community nationwide. Why were they silent. There is a reason.

The reason being that the American Negro Press (ANP), which was a tentacle of the Communist Party had its own problems to deal with, especially when it comes to the House Un-American Activities Committee (HUAC), which were investigating ANP and other organizations in-regards to their subversive activities promoting Communism.

However, not everyone in the Black Press went silent on the issue Truman's Civil Rights Proposal. The American Negro Press hated Harry Truman from the outset, because of his foreign policies he enacted to stand up against Stalin, Mao, Ho Chi Minh, and the Kims in Korea. So, when another 1948 Presidential Candidate who decided to run on a third-party ticket, Henry A. Wallace became their man.

The Progressive Party Opposition to Truman

Henry A. Wallace was more than just another Presidential Candidate for the American Negro Press; *he was an outright Communist himself*. Wallace had previously served as President Roosevelt's Secretary of Commerce, who fiercely opposed Truman's foreign policy practices just as the Black Press did. Wallace was fired by Truman, which allowed him to voice his resentment of Truman's policies by being hired to his new job at the Marxist publication New Republic. By the time that the summer of 1948 arrived, as Truman began to add-on his Desegregation of the U.S. Military and Federal Civil Service into the Democrat platform, Wallace chose to run as another third-party candidate to challenge him.

Thus, The Progressive Party was born. Wallace chose Idaho's Senator Glen H. Taylor as his Vice-Presidential running mate, which whipped the Black Press into a happy frenzy. The Progressive Party platform was more like a regressive party platform. Wallace advocated more big government policy overreach, such as Universal Health Insurance, full-voting rights for African-Americans and the end of racial segregation, even though when he was Secretary of Commerce, he opposed these very things he promised his Black supporters.[22,23,24,25]

Henry Wallace campaigning for the 1948 Presidential Election for the Progressive Party. (Courtesy of Past Daily.com)

Seeing these promises, Wallace used his popularity with help from the Communist Party to launch a spirited, media frenzy campaign throughout the South, where large numbers of Blacks were seen with him or next to him at every Progressive Party event. Leftist Black publications, such as the **Baltimore Afro-American**, **Atlanta Daily World**, and NAACP's magazine **The Crisis** featured front-page headlines of Wallace's events. Papers like the after-mentioned, stated that Wallace;

"Was down for the struggle to end racism for Blacks everywhere" one editor wrote.

The Progressive Party's rallies in the South was met with some stiff resistance from segregationists everywhere he went. At one event in Burlington, North Carolina, a segregationist's crowd gathered around his rally and began to pepper Wallace, Taylor and their Black supporters with eggs, tomatoes, and bottles. Wallace lost his temper when this happened and jumped into the crowd grabbing one of the perpetrators throwing the items.

Despite all the hoopla that the Wallace/Taylor ticket aroused, some in the Black Press figured that the ticket was a long shot that the Progressive Party candidates will be elected President of the United States. However, it wasn't all the hype of The Progressive Party's campaign and anti-segregation views that brought down Henry A. Wallace, but Wallace himself and the things that he did prior to running for President doomed his campaign.

For one, there have already been questions about Wallace's mental health and state. He often went on delusional ramblings during his campaign speeches, which were long and often boring. Nearly 10 years prior, Wallace wrote what was called "**The Guru Letters**", that showed that he believed in outlandish religious beliefs and that he was the ultimate center "the guru" or teacher of such religious beliefs.

Besides his mental capacity, Wallace was being investigated for Communist subversive activities by HUAC, where he also hired Harry Magdoff as his campaign advisor and speechwriter. The death knell for Wallace's Progressive Party campaign, when the House Committee on Un-American Activities produced evidence that Magdoff was a Soviet-trained KGB Propagandist and a card-carrying member of CPUSA, things that Wallace could not deny.

At the end, President Truman won the election, the Black Press was not too happy, and the President signed **Executive Orders 9980** and **9981** on July 26, 1948, ordering the immediate desegregation of both the Federal Civil Service Employment and the United States Military respectfully. Executive Order 9981 reads in part;

"...There shall be equality of treatment and opportunity for all persons in the Armed Forces without regard to race, color, religion or national origin."

The order goes on to say;

"This policy shall be put into effect as rapidly as possible, having due regard to the time required to effectuate any necessary changes, without impairing efficiency or morale."

The order further established an advisory committee to examine rules, regulations, procedures, and practices to make the military fully integrated. Amazingly, only one Black newspaper headlined Truman's Executive Order, desegregating the Military and that was from the Chicago Defender. It must have shocked the African-American Press for a few minutes to learn that what their nemesis, President Harry S. Truman, put his promise on paper and began to enforce it, instead of empty promises put out by Henry A. Wallace failed Progressive Party campaign.

Of course, Executive Order 9981 was not accepted right away and there was pushback by many uniformed generals of both the Marine Corps and the Army, to include Army General Omar N. Bradley and Commandant of the Marines Corps Randolph Pate. By the outbreak of the Korean War, however, the military was fully integrated.

U.S. Navy Ensign Jesse LeRoy Brown 1st African-American Naval Aviator to fly combat missions over Korea, during the Korean War, 1950
(Courtesy Navy Heritage and History)

All-integrated U.S. Army Unit based in Germany in 1949.
(Courtesy of Wikimedia)

The First Supreme Court Decision: Shelley vs. Kraemer 1948

Since President Harry S. Truman's historic Executive Orders to desegregate both the Military and Federal employment, other issues regarding the tearing down of the brick wall of Segregation was taking place at the same time. Recall that Truman's Committee on Civil Rights identified multiple issues, which needed to be addressed and immediately tackled for integration of the country to place. One of their recommendations had to with *Restrictive Covenants*.

Restrictive Covenant is a provision written in a deed or contract of property, that limits certain uses of the said property deeded.[26] In layman's terms, owners of that property can designate such pieces of land, that either has existing houses built on them or planned houses proposed of being built in the future, can only be used for sold or rented for a specific purpose. That specific purpose is written in that contract.

In the days before cities and counties began to use what it's called **"Zoning Ordinances"**, restrictive covenants were used as a tool that restricted the uses for land owners and buyers.

In the early-to-mid 1900's, in communities where either De Jure or De Facto Segregation of the races existed, Restrictive Covenants were used to limit a specific race or culture from either buying or occupying such land. Some believed that such restrictions were justified to keep the value of such properties in neighborhoods from going down.

Other reasons that were used, is to keep such land areas in the hands of White persons, who did not want their property to be bought by another race or culture. In some cases, Restrictive Covenants were also used to keep certain neighborhoods Black.

The first Civil Rights case regarding Restrictive Covenants that had a major impact on American society was in 1948 in the City of St. Louis, Missouri. Understand, that at the state of Missouri was considered, what was called a "***Border State***", meaning that it bordered between states that were considered the Northern States and the Southern States. The Northern States practiced either De Facto Segregation or no segregation at all, vice in the Southern States that practiced De Jure Segregation. Typically, the Border States, minus the District of Columbia, practiced De Facto Segregation.

In the story of **Shelley versus Kraemer**, this issue really began in the year 1911. The neighborhood inside the City of St. Louis, which covers the area of 4500 to 4630 Labadie Avenue, bordering;

> ***North Taylor Avenue to the east***
> ***Cora Avenue to the west,***
> ***Includes both sides of the street on Labadie Avenue***
> ***And all property comprising of that area (Highlighted in Red)***

Map of the St. Louis Missouri Neighborhood regarding Shelley vs. Kraemer Restricted Covenant Case 1948.
(Courtesy of Google Maps)

Was sectioned off into 39 lots to be occupied by residents. Thirty of the 39 lots owned at that time, had Restricted Covenants language written into their contracts. Dated February 16, 1911, contracts of those 30 lots of the said land, specifically prevented African-Americans or "Mongolian in Race" persons to either buy or own land for a term of 50 years, ending in 1961. Despite the fact, that five lots of the original 39, were already owned by Blacks, one who has lived on the same plot of land dating back to 1882; almost 30 years earlier.[27,28,29]

The Shelley House at 4600 Labadie Avenue in St. Louis, Missouri
(Courtesy of Wikimedia)

Mr. Jim "J.D." Shelley, his wife Ethel (Lee) Shelley and their five children, who were African-Americans, had moved from Starkville, Mississippi to St. Louis, Missouri sometime during the early 1940's. They relocated during the middle of The Great Black Migration (see Chapter 5), they came to St. Louis to look for better-paying work and provide a better life for him and his family. After renting various apartments for a few years, they decided to buy a house, found one they liked that was built in 1906 at 4600 Labadie Avenue in 1945.

The property was being sold by a Mr. Bishop, who was selling the house originally owned by Mrs. Josephine Fitzgerald. Shelley bought the house and signed the deed to the property from Mr. Bishop on August 11, 1945. As the Shelley family began to move into their new home, one of their White neighbors, Mr. Louis D. Kraemer and family who lived at 4532 Labadie Avenue, told the family that Blacks were not allowed on that property because of the clause Restrictive Covenant, which did not allow Blacks to occupy the property. The Restrictive Covenant clause was not disclosed to the Shelley family when he bought the property from Mr. Bishop, who held the property in the care of Ms. Fitzgerald.

Kraemer sued the Shelley family, stating that they could not legally take possession of the property because of his race. The Shelley's' hired one of the most prominent Black St. Louis Lawyers at practice of the time, George L. Vaughn, to fight the lawsuit, stating that the Restrictive Covenant was never disclosed to them, by law, based on a property created nearly 34 years prior.

The Shelleys also counter-sued to say that Restrictive Covenants, based on race, is unconstitutional and a blatant violation of the equal protection clause written in the 14th Amendment of the U.S. Constitution. While the state of Missouri District Court ruled in favor of the Shelleys in 1946, the Missouri State Supreme Court reversed the lower court's decision the following year. The legal team for the Shelley family, led by their outstanding lawyer George L. Vaughn immediate filed an appeal. Now it was up to the United States Supreme Court to decide whether-or-not Restrictive Covenants based on racial lines were legal or not.

The **Shelley vs. Kraemer** case was combined at the Supreme Court level with **McGhee vs. Sipes** case from Detroit Michigan. The McGhee family had a case which was similar in Restrictive Covenant rules in their city. Their Attorney was Assistant-Lead of the NAACP Legal Counsel Thurgood Marshall and his assistant Loren Miller. The combined cases were the first Supreme Court case, where the U.S. Office of the Solicitor General, Philip Pearlman, filed an **amicus curia** (Friend of the Court) in support of the Shelleys.
On January 15, 1948, the cases were argued in front of six of the nine Justices, they were;

> *Chief Justice Fred M. Vinson*
> *Associate Justice- Hugo Black*
> *Associate Justice- Felix Frankfurter*
> *Associate Justice- William O. Douglas*
> *Associate Justice- Frank Murphy*
> *Associate Justice-Harold H. Burton*

Associate Justices Stanley F. Reed, Robert H. Jackson, and Wiley B. Rutledge abstained themselves from the case and took no part in the decision. The questions that lay in front of the case were;

Are Racially-based Restrictive Covenant legal as dined in the Equal Protection Clause of the 14th Amendment of the U.S. Constitution?

And if so, can they be enforced by law?

On May 3, 1948, The Supreme Court rendered their decision and reversed the respective State Supreme Court decisions of both Missouri (Shelleys) and Michigan (McGhee). Chief Justice Fred M. Vinson rendered the court's opinion;

"The historical context in which the Fourteenth Amendment became a part of the Constitution should not be forgotten. Whatever else the Framers sought to achieve, it is clear that the matter of primary concern was the establishment of equality in the enjoyment of basic civil and political rights and preservation of those rights..."

Chief Justice Vinson continues;

"...from discriminatory action on that part of the States based on considerations of race or color. Seventy-five years ago this court announced that the provisions of the amendment are to be construed with this fundamental purpose in mind. Upon full consideration, we have concluded that in these cases the States have acted to deny petitioners the equal protection of the laws guaranteed by the Fourteenth Amendment. Having so decided, we find it unnecessary to consider whether petitioners have also been deprived privileges and immunities of Citizens of the United States. For the reasons stated, the judgment of the Supreme Court of Missouri and the judgment of the Supreme Court of Michigan must be reversed."

REVERSED. [author's emphasis]

The Supreme Court had ruled the Restrictive Covenants on the property based on race was unconstitutional.

The Shelley Family, not long after the case, moved into their hard-fought won house and property at 4600 Labadie Avenue. The 1906-built two-story Rowhouse was designated as a National Historical Landmark on December 14, 1990. J.D. Shelley passed away at the age of 92 in 1997 the city of St. Louis, Missouri.

The Shelley case was the 1st major Civil Rights case to gain major public attention. The case also set the stage of the next Supreme Court case which, along with President Truman's Executive Actions on Desegregation, has lit the fuse to the social bomb in which will define, shape, and drive at times too far, the next twenty years of what was called the American Civil Rights Movement.

However, before the latter movement was to begin, one major issue persisted throughout the country, which reared its ugly head, at a time, that threw the accomplishments which the *Shelley vs. Kraemer* SCOTUS decision on Black Civil Rights to the back burner.

Called the Smith Act Trials, this incident not only allows the American Public to be more aware of this deadly ideology called Communism but put the spotlight on CPUSA, whose main job was to overthrow the U.S. Government in the form of a bloody and violent worldwide revolution.

The Smith Act Trials 1948-1958

As the Shelley vs. Kraemer case wound up being heard in front of the Supreme Court, assisting of tearing down racial discrimination in ownership of property, Marxist Men both Black and White took center stage to account for their illegal, Marxist-Leninist activities. Most people know this era today as the "**Second Red Scare**", while others call it "**McCarthyism**", named after the courageous and incredible Republican Senator from Wisconsin, Joseph McCarthy. However, another part of American History that is not taught to the younger generation, was the "*Smith Act Trials*".[30,31]

Recall during the late 1930's, where numerous members of Congress became concerned about the multitude of public demonstrations, protests, and riots that went on throughout the country, operated by CPUSA and its hosts of splinter groups. When the Dies Committee was formed in 1936, later becoming the permanent House Committee on Un-American Activities (HUAC) after 1944, their job was to send out the Federal Government Investigative Agencies, such as the FBI, the Army Security Agency (ASA) to seek out and bring to justice those individuals who were violation of the Smith Act.

One of their main-focus targeting members of CPUSA were card-carrying members, loyal followers and Marxist Men-trained, duped Progressives inside the Party, and determined whether-or-not, their goal was to overthrow the U.S. Government on behalf of Joseph Stalin's Soviet Russia.

The Smith Act of 1940, officially called the Alien Registration Act of 1940 (ARA), started off as a Bill called House Resolution 5138, introduced by Virginia's Democrat Representative Howard W. Smith on June 29, 1939. After much debate, re-write by members of both Houses of Congress, the Bill passed the Senate on June 22, 1940. President Roosevelt signed the Bill into Law on June 28th of the same year. On the ***Federal Register, the Smith Act of 1940 is listed as Title 8, of the United States Code (U.S.C.) as Aliens and Nationality.*** In short, the Smith Act contained three-separate Titles in the law;

Title I. Subversive Activities
Title II. Deportation
Title III. Alien Registration

Ironically, it must be noted, that the Smith Act or Title 8 of the U.S.C., is still being used today and has become a hotly-debated political topic in recent years regarding Illegal Aliens. However, for the express intent and purpose of this book, only Title I will be the main topic of the discussion.

Title I of the Smith Act sets criminal penalties to include fines and punishment for up to 20-years in prison and denied Federal Government Employment up to five years for anyone accused of the following;

"...intent to cause the overthrow or destruction of any such government, prints, publishes, edits, issues, circulates, sells, distributes, or publicly displays any written or printed matter advocating or propriety of overthrowing any government of the United States by force or violence, or attempts to do so; or...organizes or helps or attempts to organize any society, groups, or assembly of persons who teach, advocate, or encourage the overthrow or destruction of any such government by force or violence; or becomes or is a members of, or affiliates with, any society, group, or assembly of persons, knowing the purposes thereof."[32,33]

After signing the Smith Act of 1940 into law, President Roosevelt swiftly transferred the Immigration and Naturalization Service (INS) from the Department of Labor (DOL) to the Department of Justice (DOJ). By doing so, the move sent its intention to the public, that the Federal Government had seriously considered that the influx of Illegal Aliens entering the country at the time, has posed a serious threat to national security. Fortunately, the FEDS did not have to wait long to start enforcing the provisions of the Smith Act, especially Title I of the law.[34,35]

In 1941, FBI Agents raided the Minnesota Offices of the Socialist Workers Party (SWP), a Leon Trotskyite organization that controlled various aspects of Teamster Unions in over 30 cities. The arrest netted the following members;

James P. Cannon
Carl Skogland
Farrell Dobbs
Grace Carlson
Harry De Boer
Max Geldman
Albert Goldman

And twelve-other party members. On December 8, 1941, all seven above-listed Socialist Workers Party members and another five leaders, were sentenced to consecutive 16-month prison sentences.

In 1942, the FBI raided and arrested members of the Crusader White Shirts (CWS), a Fascist/Marxist organization located in Eastern Tennessee, whose members infiltrated the U.S. Military to spread their ideology within the ranks, in the effort to start a military coup. If they were successful, the CWS would have started the process to overthrow the U.S. Government in a violent, bloody revolution. The leader of the Crusader White Shirts was George W. Christians, who wrote in the organization's newspaper in 1934;[36]

"It is the privileged role of the Art Smiths, the William Pelleys, and the George Christians to lay the cornerstone of Fascism. It is in their rudimentary organizations that the Petty Bourgeoisie receives its first elementary schooling in a dictatorship. It is from the Smiths, and the Pelleys that it learns to scrap its democratic scruples, to hate the Jew as the Mephistopheles responsible for depressions and to detest the Communist as the companion of the Devil..."

The leader of the American Fascist/Marxist group the Crusader White Shirts (CWS).
(Courtesy of Appalachian History)

It's leader, pictured above) and several members of the group were arrested, jailed sent to trial and convicted of violating the provisions of the Smith Act of 1940 and were sentenced to five years in the Federal Penitentiary on June 8th of that year.

The biggest and largest trial regarding the violations of the Smith Act was yet to come.

In 1945, under the directions of President Harry S. Truman, who assumed the Presidency after the death of Franklin D. Roosevelt, and his new Attorney General Tom Clark, ordered the Federal Bureau of Investigations (FBI) and Army Intelligence Agency (AIA) to begin monitoring, infiltrate and gather evidence on the American Communist Party members, who blatantly violated the very language of the Smith Act. Such surveillance became necessary, to bring up charges to prosecute CPUSA members, whose explicit goal was to overthrow the U.S. Government in a bloody, violent revolution, to usher in Communism.

In 1946, FBI Director J. Edgar Hoover and his force compiled an astounding 1,800-page report, sent to Congress, particularly HUAC, that outline overwhelming evidence on CPUSA's Senior Leadership's operations and Hollywood influence.

It should have been no surprise to anyone within the FBI, including Hoover himself, that CPUSA's existence, along with its multitude of splinter groups located from the African American

Community in New York City to almost every aspect of Hollywood Industry in California. The goal of CPUSA was to advocate the overthrow of political power in Washington D.C. and fundamentally transform the United States into a Soviet Satellite country under Stalin.[37]

As the Cold War began to heat up, between the Soviet Union's unchecked reign throughout Eastern Europe, Mao Tse Tung's advancement in the hostile takeover of China and Ho Chi Minh creating his Communist crisis in Formosa (Vietnam)in 1947, Congress began to act on Hoover's report, who by then had numbered into nearly 3,000-pages.

The House Committee on Un-American Activities began to issue subpoenas to the first people on the list in which they intend to take out; Hollywood California's Entertainment Industry. Of the 79 people which HUAC subpoenaed to appear in front of the committee, only ten showed up, with their lawyers in tow. Dubbed the *"Hollywood Ten"*, then consisted of;

Alvah Bessie-Screenwriter

Herbert Biberman- Screenwriter and Director

Lester Cole- Screenwriter

Edward Dmytryk- Director

Ring Lardner Jr.- Screenwriter

John Howard Lawson- Screenwriter

Albert Maltz- Screenwriter

Samuel Omitz- Screenwriter

Adrian Scott- Producer and Screenwriter

Dalton Trumbo- Screenwriter

Many of the Hollywood Ten were high-ranking members of the **Screen Writer's Guild**, which were infested with Marxist-Leninists and their psychologically subverted dupes.

Nineteen more members of the Screen Writer's Guild were supposed to appear in front of the House Committee, but they refuse to cooperate. As the men above appeared, with the media watching and listening, most of the Hollywood Ten refused to answer questions that were levied at them by committee members, that they were members of the Communist Party.

Of course, they denied that they were, except Dalton Trumbo; HUAC presented evidence that he had traveled to Moscow in 1932, along with Langston Hughes, Paul Robeson, and others to write the plot of the propaganda movie that the Communist International wanted them to make depicting the plight of African Americans in the United States.

Trumbo denied that allegation. The men's lawyers defended their clients, stating that anything that they said to defend Soviet Russia was a part of the 1st Amendment of the Constitution; Freedom of Speech. At the end, all ten were found In Contempt of Congress and each of the men served between six-months and one-year prison terms, along with fines of $1,000 each ($10,000 each in 2016 currency).[38]

After the Hollywood Ten appeared before HUAC, other Hollywood Writers, Actors, Entertainers, Accountants and Interns were all subpoenaed by Congress and took the Oath, to tell the truth. Below is a partial list of such Hollywood personnel that appeared either in front of the committee itself or provided written testimony;

Paul Draper- Actor/Dancer

Paul Green- Playwriter/Screenwriter

Lilian Hellman- Playwriter/Screenwriter

Canada Lee- Actor/Singer

Paul Robeson- Actor/Singer/Athlete

Edwin Rolfe- Actor

Richard Wright- Author

Lena Horne- Actress

Burl Ives- Singer

Langston Hughes- Poet/Writer

Orson Wells- Screenwriter/Actor

Edward G. Robinson- Actor

Pete Seeger-Singer/Musician

Theodore Ward- Playwriter

Eddie Albert- Actor

Ossie Davis- Actor

Ruby Dee- Actress

Earl Robinson- Songwriter

J. Edgar Hoover wasn't done yet. HUAC wasn't done yet either.

The biggest show was about to begin and it involved directly CPUSA itself. This time, instead of these next few members going in-front of Congress, Hoover and AG Clark decided to take them to a court of law. The Federal Prosecutor designated for the task was John F. X. Mc Gohey and the case will be tried in the U.S. District Court of Southern New York, located in Lower Manhattan. A sealed indictment was issued on June 29, 1948, and by the end of July, twelve members of the Communist Party's National Board were arrested, handcuffed and jailed pending trial. The people arrested by FBI Agents included;

Benjamin J. Davis Jr.- Chairman of CPUSA's Legislative Committee and New York City Council Member. The oldest son of the Georgia Republican, Newspaper Editor and staunch Anti-Communist Benjamin J. "Ben" Davis Sr.

Eugene Dennis A.K.A. Tim Ryan B.K.A Francis Xavier Waldron- CPUSA General Secretary

William Z. Foster- CPUSA National Secretary. Due to medical problems, he was never tried in court but was still punished with the rest.

John Gates- Young Communist League (YCL) Head

Gil Green- CPUSA National Board Member

Gus Hall- Member of CPUSA's National Board

Irving Potash- Furriers Union Official and CPUSA's National Board Member

Jack Stachel- Editor of CPUSA's publication Daily Worker

Robert G. Thompson- Head of CPUSA's New York City Office

John Williamson- Member of CPUSA's Central Committee

Henry M. Winston-Member of CPUSA's National Board

Cal Winter- Head of CPUSA's Detroit Office

Even though J. Edgar Hoover wanted the entire 55-member National Board of CPUSA to stand trial and indicted on charges of violating the Smith Act, Mc Gohey wanted just the main characters of the Communist Party instead. Regardless, things were about to get interesting.

Of the twelve-members indicted by the District Court, two of the men, Benjamin Davis Jr. and Henry M. Winston, were both African Americans and wielded immense power and prestige within the Black Community. Since both advocated for equality, they were now about to get their share of it, along with their White partners in crime.

Immediately after their arrest, the 11 of the 12 CPUSA members trial became a media spectacle. However, the prosecution had an enormous following and positive support from the American Public.

Most of the latter, did not like Red Communists in the United States because they figured out that CPUSA wasn't a Civil Rights Organization (this claim would later change in the next five-to-six years), but a mouthpiece for Joseph Stalin and his henchmen in Moscow Russia.

Unfortunately, the Black Press and numerous Communist Organ publications did not see things the way the American People saw the trials. In their demented minds, they became critical of the trial, calling it "Mc McCarthyism" and a "Witch-hunt" by Attorney General (AG) Tom Clark. Both Washington Post and New York Times called the Smith Act Trials a "circus act", that was not warranted nor needed.[39,40,41,42]

During the first day of the Smith Act Trials, which started November 1, 1948, the presiding Judge overseeing the case, Judge Harold Medina, over 400-plus Law Enforcement personnel were present to maintain order, both outside the Foley Square District Court building and inside the court room itself. While protestors were demonstrating outside supporting the CPUSA men, counter-protests were conducted across the street, who were advocating that the men go to jail for their subversive activities against the Federal Government.

Two of The Smith Trial CPUSA Defendants:
Robert Thompson and Benjamin Davis Jr. surrounded by pickets as they leave the New York City Federal Courthouse in October 1949.
(Courtesy of Wikimedia/New York World Telegram and Sun)

Numerous witnesses for the prosecution testified in court, including FBI Informants which infiltrated CPUSA Angela 'Angie' Calomiris, A.K.A. Angela Cole, Herbert Arthur Philbrick, and several former Communist Party members. One of the latter, Louis F. Budez, was once a CPUSA National Committee Member himself and intimately knew those being tried.

During the proceedings, numerous of outbursts occurred in the audience watching the trial, causing needless interruptions of court room operations, while police took such distractors and threw them out of the courthouse by force. Several times, Judge Medina, hearing the case had to take charge of the courtroom because of the outbursts by the audience and by the defendants themselves, including the Black Marxist Man Henry Winston.

One day during the prosecution's testimony, Winston shouted at the Justices;

"More than 5,000 Negroes have been lynched in this country, so when are you going to try the sons of bitches for that!"

Immediately Winston was found in Contempt and Winston with his lawyer was jailed and fined for such outbursts. Too many of the justices on the court, it appeared to them, that CPUSA was intentionally making an all-out effort to cause a mistrial. When they are on trial, that is usually the case. But the Communist Party had other avenues that they attempted to do throughout the Smith Act Trials.

The Communist Party mobilized their followers to start a heavy letter writing campaign, addressed to President Truman at the White House, and Judge Medina at his office and to his personal address, requesting for the charges to be dropped for the men.

Western Union Telegrams were also sent, some written in a hostile manner, threatening violence and retribution of the 11 men were convicted.

Outside the District Court Building, the environment was no better.

As Anti-Communist and Pro-Communist protestors clashed violently, rioting and civil disobedience consumed Lower Manhattan streets around the Foley Square Court House, causing a million dollars in property damage, and injury 140 people, including CPUSA defendants Irving Potash and Benjamin J. Davis Jr. on September 4, 1949.

The latter were pummeled with glass bottles and rocks, breaking their car windows as they drove off through the crowd. Soon everything would be over as the Defense finally rested their case on October 14, 1949. The sequestered Jury began deliberations whether-

or-not to sentence the men. After seven-and-one-half hours of deliberations, the jury came out with the verdict. It read;

"*Guilty on all charges*"

CPUSA Lawyers representing the men were stunned. In their view, publicly, there was no way that their clients were working to overthrow the government. *After all, it is their constitutional right and freedom of speech, to denounce the United States as a racist country and the cause of the world's ills.* {sounds familiar]

They contend, falsely, that Soviet Russia's economic, social and political system, is the solution to the world's problems, that would eventually make everything fair and equal for all, that has abolished racism, especially for Blacks living there. It's nonsense!

Judge Medina handed down the sentences for the 11 CPUSA members that appeared in the Smith Act Trials;

10 of the 11 defendants to serve prison time for five-years

All 11 were fined $10,000 each ($100,600 each in 2016)

Robert G. Thompson, a decorated veteran of World War II was sentenced to three years

William Z. Foster, who was hospitalized during the trial, was fined $10,000

Lawyers for the defendants immediately filed appeals so the case would be heard at the Supreme Court. However, President Truman, J. Edgar Hoover and Tom Clark were satisfied with the outcome of the trial.

The Aftermath of the Smith Trial

As CPUSA's lawyers began the appeal process, the organization's front group the Civil Rights Congress (CRC), posted bail for the 11 defendants in the amount of $260,000 ($2.6 million in 2016 dollars). After reviewing the lower court's ruling, on July 2, 1951, the Supreme Court upheld the lower court's decision and ordered immediate sentencing of all 11 defendants. Out of the original 12 accused, William Z. Foster paid his fine $10,000 fine and escaped incarceration altogether. Seven of the eleven who physically stood trial at the Southern District Court of New York, reported as ordered to serve out their sentences. The other four CPUSA men, Henry Winston, Gil Green, Robert G. Thompson and Gus Hall, did not report to receive their punishment and went into hiding.[43,44,45,46,47,48,49,50,51]

Of course, this had complicated things more for the accused who went into hiding and became a fugitive from justice. Gus Hall was the first one to be captured. In October of 1951, Hall was captured by U.S. Marshalls with the help of the Mexican Federalizes hiding in Mexico City. He was there trying to arrange transportation to travel to the Soviet Union. After all, this is where his loyalties lie.

Gus Hall's prison sentence was increased from five years to eight years behind bars at Fort Leavenworth, Kansas. After he was released from prison, Hall rejoined the Communist Party, rebuilt the organization and advocated for the immediate implementation of FDR's Second Bill of Rights.

After having run unsuccessfully as the **Communist Party Candidate from President of the United States in 1972, 1976, 1980 and 1984**, he was still spreading Marxist-Leninist ideology on college campuses nationwide. During his run for President, it is interesting to note that Gus Hall chose Jarvis Tyner (now the current Executive Vice-Chairman of CPUSA) as his running mate in 1972 and 1976 and the Marxist-Leninist Angela Davis in 1980 and 1984. Even in the Communist Party, despite some loyalty by African Americans, Blacks are still considered *"second-class citizens"* to those of European-descent.

As for Robert G. Thompson, the WWII war-hero was captured by Federal Marshalls hiding from justice in California in 1952. Thompson's time in the Federal Penitentiary was a hard one. Like Gus Hall, Thompson's sentence was extended three-years because of his fugitive status. While incarcerated at the Federal Penitentiary in Terre Haute, Indiana, a group of Yugoslav inmates attacked him in the prison chow hall and brutally beat him unconscious, fracturing his skull in the process after being hit repeatedly by a steel pipe by one of the attackers. Released from custody in 1956, Thompson returned to CPUSA and help plan the future Anti-Vietnam War Protests, which will be soon coming forth in the middle-1960's. Thompson died of a fatal heart attack in October 1965.

Henry Winston, was sent to prison, served out his time there, including the three extra years that were added to his original five-years from him avoiding justice in 1961. In poor health, due to a Brain Tumor which was removed while incarcerated in 1960, nevertheless, returned to CPUSA. Upon his arrival, the Black Winston was elected as Chairman of CPUSA in 1966. However, his failing health became his downfall, and after seeking 'free healthcare' in third-world countries of Nicaragua, the Honduras without success, Henry Winston died of Brain Cancer in the Soviet Union at the age of 75 in 1986.

Eugene Dennis, A.K.A, Francis Xavier Waldron, served his time for violation of the Smith Act of 1940, released in 1955 and of course, returned to CPUSA to serve as Executive Secretary. He died in January 1961 of Cancer. The same can be said about John Gates, A.K.A. Solomon Regenstrief, served his time in prison and returned to CPUSA.

However, Gates/Regenstrief, upon his return, was appointed Editor of the Communist Mouthpiece Publication the **Daily Worker**, until 1958. That year, he resigned from the Communist Party, stating that CPUSA could not gain its independence away from the Communist International. Unfortunately, and probably unknown to Gates, CPUSA wasn't supposed to gain their own independence, that's why its members took orders from COMINTERN's Central Committee. They were supposed to lead a worldwide Communist Revolution together! After living a long life, away from the spotlight, Gates/Regenstrief became a Research Assistant for the International Ladies Garment Workers Union (ILGWU), retiring in 1986. He died at his home in Miami Beach Florida in May 1992 at the age of 78.

Black Communist and Marxist Man Benjamin J. Davis Jr., served his time in prison at the Federal Penitentiary in Terre Haute, Indiana too. Prison life wasn't kind to the former-New York City Councilman either. As he was mopping a cell block floor, he was viciously attacked and injured by numerous White Supremacists inmates in 1953 and hospitalized for a few weeks. The group who attacked him stated that the reason why they attacked him, was that Davis was complaining about racial discrimination in the prison and began to complain to the prison staff about such incidents and were naming those accused of such conditions.

After his release in 1955, he too rejoined the Communist Party and became one of the organization's mouthpieces, giving speeches at major Ivy League Universities, such as Columbia, Harvard, Yale Amherst,

Oberlin and the University of Minnesota. Davis was arrested again, this time in 1964 for giving speeches advocating for a worldwide Communist Revolution to overthrow the U.S. Government, in violation of the Mc Carran Internal Security Act of 1950. At the time of his arrest, Davis was campaigning for the New York State Senate but died before being tried in court. Benjamin J. Davis Jr., who also wrote his book while in prison *"The Communist Councilman from Harlem"*, died August of 1964 from Lung Cancer.

As for Jack Stachel, he was incarcerated at the Danbury Federal Penitentiary in Danbury Connecticut, until he was released in 1955. As like the others, he returned to CPUSA and was given one of the organization's top leadership positions, the National Trade Union Commission (NTUC). He was elected as the Communist Party's National Executive Secretary in 1957, the National Board Executive in 1961 and the National Administrative Committee in 1962. Stachel died from Heart and Kidney Disease in December 1965.

John Williamson, after serving his five-year sentence for violation of the Smith Act of 1940, was deported back to his native Scotland and lived there, working heavily for the United Kingdom's Communist Party. He died there in 1963 of a Massive Heart Attack. It was in the U.K. where he pinned his book *"The Dangerous Scot: The Life and Work of an American 'Undesirable'"*, released in 1965.

Irving Potash, served his five-year prison sentence starting in 1951 and was released in late 1955. Immediately after his release from federal custody, Immigration and Nationalization Service (INS) deported him back to his native country of Czechoslovakia. He returned to the United States illegally and began to work for CPUSA, becoming National Labor Secretary, passing away in February 1963.

Gill Green, who was one of the last Smith Trial defendants who was a fugitive from justice, was captured by Federal Agents on February 27, 1956. He was sent to prison, with added time and was released on July 29, 1961. After incarceration, Green returned to CPUSA as Chairman of the New York Office. There, he helped organized the Anti-Vietnam War Agitation Campaign. He was elected to serve on the Communist Party National Committee in 1966, serving until 1969. That year, Gill Green ran afoul with Gus Hall and other CPUSA executive leadership personnel, because of his outspoken views against the Soviet Union invasion of Czechoslovakia, causing him to resign his position. However, being the loyal Soviet Compatriot that he was, he remained as a member of the Communist Party, until he died in an Ann Harbor, Michigan Nursing Home in May 1997.

Lastly, Carl Winter served his time in prison from 1951 to 1955. Upon release, he returned to Detroit Michigan as head of CPUSA's Detroit Office, serving there until 1965. In that year, Winter was promoted to serve as the New York Correspondent for the organization's newspaper *The Daily Worker*, while also holding several high-ranking positions up to becoming Chairman of the National Board. He died there in New York City in 1981.

What the first Smith Act Trials set in stone, was that it pitted the everyday patriotic American against an ever persistent, agitative community of American Communists. The former, who wanted the United States to maintain its Superpower status and spread peace and Free-Market Economic Principles throughout the World so that everybody can achieve and succeed in endeavors in whatever they chose in life. The latter, are persons who instead, want the United States to be psychologically subverted into accepting Communism, a deadly, yet non-reality form of economic production, produced "by all" as written by the likes of Karl Marx and Friedrich Engels. A deadly proposition, which has been shown (and continues to do so) not to work and has been proven to have killed millions of innocent lives.

As for the Black Community in America, the Communist Party have had success in recruiting younger and younger generations of people and teaching them the basic principles of Marxist-Leninism, on college campuses and in the public schools. However, as HUAC continued its trek into publicly bringing the spotlight on those who held Marxists beliefs, using the Smith Act of 1940 as a guide and a new, more strenuous law called *The McCarran Act of 1950*, officially named the *Internal Act of 1950*.[52]

Named for the Congressman, Democrat Pat McCarran of Nevada in August 1950, the latter Law (*Title 50 U.S.C. Chapter 23-Public Law 81-831*) stated (in-part);

"An act to protect the United States against certain Un-American and subversive activities requiring registration of Communist organizations…"

The law established the Subversive Activities Control Board (SACB) within the Attorney General's Office, to not only monitor and enforce organizations such as the Communist Party of the U.S.A. to register, but to assist in other entities within the government, such as HUAC, to determine if, such groups and organizations operate in the manner to overthrow the government.

One of the first people to be indicted for violations of both the Smith Act of 1940 and the McCarran Act of 1950, was a Black Woman named Claudia Jones. Jones A.K.A. Claudia Vera Cumberbatch, was a Trinidadian-born Journalist and high-ranking Communist Party leader, who was heavily involved in the subversion of Black Americans of her day. In 1936, was a member of the Young Communist League (YCL) and promoted on the editorial staff of the CPUSA mouthpiece publication *The Daily Worker*, and the *Weekly Review* in both 1937 and 1938 respectively.[53,54,55]

During World War Two, Jones became one of the high-ranking members of the American Youth for Democracy (AYD) and Editor of the organization's monthly journal Spotlight. The Dies Committee, in 1943 had identified the AYD as a Marxist front group on the payroll of the Communist Party. In 1946, Jones was elected Executive Secretary of the Woman's Commission of CPUSA and elected again to head its National Peace Council. Claudia Jones is known for her editorial written in 1949 in the Communist Magazine Political Affairs, titled *"An End to the Neglect of the Problems of the Negro Woman!"*. She wrote;

"The Bourgeoisie is fearful of the militancy of the Negro Woman, and for good reason. The Capitalists know, far better than many progressives seem to know, that once Negro women begin to take action, the militancy of the whole Negro people, and thus the anti-imperialist coalition, is greatly enhanced..."

She continues:

"Historically, the Negro woman has been the guardian, the protector, of the Negro family...As a mother, as Negro, and as a worker, the Negro woman fights against the wiping out of the Negro family, against the Jim Crow ghetto existence which destroys the health, morale and very life of millions of her sisters, brothers, and children..."

She concludes;

"Viewed in this light, is not accidental that the American bourgeoisie has intensified its oppression, not only of the Negro people in general but of Negro women in particular. Nothing so exposes the drive to fascination in the nation as the callous attitude which the bourgeoisie displays and cultivates toward Negro women."

Amazing, that the same words that Claudia Jones stated in 1949, verbatim is still being stated by African American women in 2016 America!

Of course, her speaking engagements which she conducted, for a price, while serving as Secretary of the Women's Commission of CPUSA, gathered some attention with the Hoover's FBI.

After gathering evidence of her speeches and actions, along with the rest of the Communist Party's leadership, she was arrested, charged, tried in court and convicted for violation of the Smith Act of 1940 in 1948. After 24-months in Federal Prison, she was released.

Unfortunately for her, Jones returned to her Communist Party activities. Since she was not a Naturalized U.S. Citizen, the FBI arrested her again in December 1950. After her case was reviewed by the Immigration and Naturalization Service (INS), she was ordered to be jailed as an Illegal Alien and ordered to be deported back to Trinidad-Tobago. With her lawyers from CPUSA, Jones contested her deportation order and was released from jail pending appeal.

In response to her so-called *"imperialistic harassment by the fascist U.S. Government"*, she was again arrested for her outspoken views on Marxism, which became even fiercer than the last previous ones she had given, Jones was again arrested, this time for violation of the McCarran Act of 1950.

In 1951, she was tried in a court of law with eleven other CPUSA members, that included Elizabeth Gurley Flynn, found guilty for conducting illegal subversive activities on behalf of the Communist Party and convicted to spend 5 years in the Federal Women's Penitentiary. She and the other CPUSA members immediately filed for an appeal. On October 22, 1954, the Supreme Court of the United States refused to hear the case and she was sentenced to the Federal Reformatory for Women in Alderson West Virginia. After spending one-year and one-day in prison, she was released in October 1955 and immediately deported. However, the Trinidadian-Tobagonian

Government refused to accept her return, so in December 1955, she was instead deported to the United Kingdom.

Photo of Claudia Jones, the outspoken Communist of CPUSA.
(Courtesy of Marxist Leninist.wordpress.com)

Finally thrown out of the United States, once she got to the UK, her activities resumed. She joined the British Communist Party and began a ten-year run on giving speeches, writing editorials for various Communist Publications and traveling to Red China, where she met face-to-face with Chairman Mao Zedong.

Claudia Jones has been in failing health for over three-decades when she was infected with Tuberculosis and possibly Syphilis as a young adult. She had her first Heart Attack while jailed in New York in 1951 at the age of 36. By the time, she reached the age of 49, she was doomed physically. On December 24, 1964, Claudia Jones suffered a Massive Heart Attack.

Before her death, she asked the British Communist Party to be buried next to her hero, ***Karl Marx***, in Highgate Cemetery in London. On January 9, 1965, that wish was granted and she was buried next to her psychological mentor.

The irony of Claudia Jones was this; she did not know that as a Black Woman of African-descent, she requested to be buried next to a White man, who considered African Slavery as being justified because of its "extrinsic value of labor".

Today in the 21st Century, not many people have ever heard of or even been taught that it was President Harry S. Truman's Committee on Civil Rights that help jumpstart the American Civil Rights Movement. Acting on their recommendations, Truman won the Presidency in 1948 and put into practice desegregation processes, which further gave new energy to the movement.

When in July 1948, the signing of Executive Orders 9980 and 9981, desegregating both Federal Employment and the Armed Forces, his committee and many others who were involved in President Truman's Administration, created the first overall action that helps jumpstart the American Civil Rights Movement. The **Shelley vs. Kraemer** Supreme Court decision, given two months prior to the Harry Truman's Executive Orders, gave the movement judicial power to fight racial segregation at its core. Black folks in America have taken noticed and so did CPUSA. The next Supreme Court decision which came in 1954, will not be as celebrated by many, both Black and White but will set off the bomb, of social events in which still see and that have affected us today.

Brown vs. Board of Education of Topeka, Kansas

There's been a plethora of publications, scholarly articles, books, movies and other forms of media, that have consistently covered, one of the most controversial Supreme Court cases in American History; **Brown vs. Board of Education**. The above-mentioned media have been noble in deed, upon outlining how the Supreme Court decision changed the social landscape regarding Civil Rights for African-Americans. However, there is one aspect of the SCOTUS case which the above publications have missed; the deception and communist influence regarding the Brown vs. Education and its aftermath. These are the things that will be presented here for you, the reader will be amazed as to what really occurred during that time, that was hidden from the public.

Long before Kansas became the 34th State admitted to the union on January 29, 1861, and prior to the outbreak of the Civil War, one major question existed when it applied for statehood; should Kansas be admitted as a Slave State or not.

After numerous incidents between the territorial residents between Slave Abolitionists and Pro-Slavery advocates, by 1861, the question was answered. Kansas will stay as a Free State.

In 1859 though, since Kansas has been populated with many people from the Slave-holding Southern states, including many within the territorial government, passed a law in 1859, that allowed the Kansas Public Education system to be segregated along racial lines. Twenty years later, in 1879, the state of Kansas passed the **Kansas Permissive Law of 1879**, which allowed individual school districts to choose whether to segregate their schools or not.

It wasn't mandatory for the school boards to enforce the law. The law allowed that cities within the state that had a population greater than 15,000, should have separate schools for African-Americans, Whites, and even Native-Americans. Places that have less than 15,000 persons in their population, the cities, towns, and counties shall have flexibility as to whether they have schools that should be separated by race.

Fast-forward to the mid-Twentieth Century, where the Black population of the state of Kansas has tripled in size of African-Americans. The population spike was due to two separate Great Black

Migrations from the South; one directly after the American Civil War which ranged from the years 1866-1890 and the second one from 1910-1950.

As the overall population increased, the more of the population wanted the schools to desegregate. However, there were some who did not want desegregation to happen. In 1896, a Supreme Court decision, **Plessy vs. Ferguson** stated that **"separate but equal accommodations"** on Public Transportation was constitutional and did not violate the 14th Amendment. What Kansas did, as did the rest of the states both in the North, Border States and in the South, was to create two separate but equal educational facilities. One for Blacks, One for Whites.

The Schools for Blacks were mostly staffed by Black Teacher and Black Administrators, as the White ones were staffed just the same, but with White Teachers and Administrators. Before 1948, Kansas has been one of many states that have been sued to have its public-school system to be desegregated.

One lawsuit has been successful in 1941 when the Kansas Supreme Court ordered that Kansas Junior High Schools were to be desegregated, which was done. However, this wasn't enough and one man began the process, where his dislike for the "separate but equal" stance would take on a whole new meaning and fundamentally transform the Civil Rights Movement from a slow, diligent process to hypersonic speed in just four years. This man's name was McKinley Burnett.

McKinley Burnett was born on January 9, 1897, to Mr. Henry Burnett and Mary Ann (Holland) Burnett in Oskaloosa, Jefferson County, Kansas. Both of his parents have interracially-mixed ancestry of Black and White. McKinley was one of a total of 15 siblings, 2 which died young. Despite growing up in a small rural town located northeast of the capitol city of Topeka, Kansas, where he has personally experienced racism, even while he served in the U.S. Army in WWI.

Burnett claimed that after serving in the Army, he experienced large amounts of racism and segregation when he worked for the Veterans Administration. He later joined the Topeka Chapter of the NAACP and swiftly rose through the ranks of the organization.

Mc Kinley Burnett became President of the local chapter in 1948. One of his first acts after becoming the chapter's President, he vowed that he was going to desegregate Topeka, Kansas Public School System. Between 1948 and 1950, he wrote many letters of correspondence, attended every school board meeting that the city's Board of Education, demanding to allow Black children attend schools with White students of their peers. Each time the Board of Education told him no.

Topeka Kansas of the day, like many other cities within the state, lived in and worked in businesses that were interracially mixed. The difference, when it came to both Black and White students were that Black students attended all-Black Schools, while White students attended all-White Schools. The disparity of having a separate but equal school system was the fact that some schools were located in close proximity to neighborhoods that were Black and White lived, while the all-Black schools were located blocks or miles away, that required the former to walk a few blocks, and take school buses to attend. Between 1950 and 1951, Burnett personally recruited 13 African-American families and their combined total of 20 children, were sent to force Topeka's schools to desegregate. One of these families recruited were the Oliver Brown family.

Oliver Leon Brown, who would later-on became the main plaintiff in the **Brown vs. Board of Education** case, was born in Springfield, Greene County, Missouri in August 1918. He worked as a Welder for the Atchison-Topeka-Santa Fe Railroad Corporation and was an Associate Pastor of St. Marks African Methodist Episcopal (AME) Church. Along with his wife, Leola (Williams) Brown and the couple's two daughters, Linda and Cheryl, the Brown family became one of the

13 families who agreed to help Burnett try to integrate the schools. In 1951, Oliver's daughter Linda was a third-grader who attended an all-Black Elementary School, named Monroe Elementary. In the same neighborhood, however, another elementary school was located just six-blocks away from the Brown's home, named Sumner Elementary. The reason why Linda could not attend Sumner, was because that school only accepted White students.

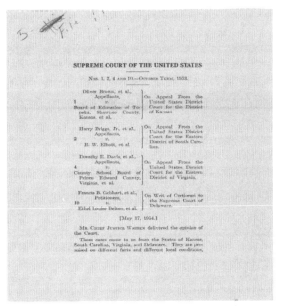

Brown vs. Board of Education Decision of 1954.
(Courtesy of Our Documents.Gov)

During the 50th Anniversary of the Supreme Court decision of Brown vs. Board of Education, both of Oliver Brown's children and their mother was interviewed on PBS Television's News Hour anchored by Bill Kurtis. The youngest child at the time of the initial court filing, now Cheryl Brown-Henderson, who was head of the Brown Foundation, stated on the program;

"The neighborhood we lived in was an integrated neighborhood along First Street and every morning the African-American children that lived along that stretch, that block or two, would head off [to school] in one direction, and the White children will head off in another direction. And for the children, I don't think it was problematic. You know, kids are very accepting of how they live. The African-American schools were good schools. The facilities were built by the same person [as the White schools], so we're not talking about

substandard facilities with leaky roofs and outhouses like they were in the South. The Teachers were well-trained. Many of them had advanced degrees. So, we aren't talking about a poor education. You know, we are not talking about having to walk miles because, in South Carolina, the children walked 10 miles. In Topeka, they [African-American children] walked a few blocks and caught a bus. So, we weren't talking about real hardships here. We were talking about the principle of the thing."

During the fall of 1950, Burnett asked the 13 families along with their collective children, to go to various White-only schools around town and try to enroll them. Oliver Brown took his daughter Linda to attempt to enroll her at Sumner Elementary nearby. On the program, Linda Brown Thompson recalled this visit;

"...I remember going inside and my Dad spoke with someone and then he went into the inner office. I could hear voices and hear his voice raised as the conversation went on. And then, he immediately came out of the office, took me by the hand, and we walked home from school, and I just couldn't understand what was happening, you know, because I was sure that I was going to get to go to school with Mona, Guinevere, Wanda and all my playmates."

Linda's playmates were from the neighborhood they lived in. Oliver Brown's Wife, now-Leola Montgomery next explain;
"He came back and reported to me what had transpired; That the Principal over there told him it wasn't he who was against the integrated schools, but it was the school board and there wasn't nothing he could do about it at the time."

Cheryl Brown-Henderson continued the conversation;

"So, at that point the plaintiffs, after the test, you know, pretty much got to go back to their everyday lives. It was left to the legal team to come up with all the legal strategy and do all the research to put together the case..."

Consulting with the NAACP Headquarters in Baltimore, Maryland, McKinley Burnett talked to the NAACP led Defense Attorney, Thurgood Marshall. On February 28, 1951, with the help of two of Topeka, Kansas local attorneys, Charles Bledsoe and John Scott, who served as legal counsel and Lucinda Todd, who served as Secretary, filed a lawsuit on behalf of the 13 Plaintiffs to desegregate the city schools. The Plaintiffs were;

Oliver Leon Brown (The only Male Plaintiff)

Darlene Brown

Lena M. Carper

Sadie Emmanuel

Marguerite Emerson

Shirley Fleming

Zelma Henderson

Shirley Hodison

Maude Lawton

Alma Lewis

Iona Richardson

Vivian Scales

Lucinda Todd

The case was officially entered in the judicial record as ***Oliver Brown et al. v. The Board of Education of Topeka, Kansas***. The main idea of the lawsuit was not just to fight to integrate Topeka's Public-School System, but to make the case to challenge the 1896 Supreme Court decision of ***Plessy vs. Ferguson***, which upheld that states can make laws requiring Separate but Equal accommodations for Black and Whites. In other words, the main thrust of the case was to tear down and nullify the "Separate but Equal Clause", previously mentioned.

The "Doll Experiment" and Case Decision

5.

RACIAL IDENTIFICATION AND PREFERENCE IN NEGRO CHILDREN   By Kenneth B. Clark and Mamie P. Clark

PROBLEM

The specific problem of this study is an analysis of the genesis and development of racial identification as a function of ego development and self-awareness in Negro children.

Race awareness, in a primary sense, is defined as a consciousness of the self as belonging to a specific group which is differentiated from other observable groups by obvious physical characteristics which are generally accepted as being racial characteristics.

Because the problem of racial identification is so definitely related to the problem of the genesis of racial attitudes in children, it was thought practicable to attempt to determine the racial attitudes or preferences of these Negro children—and to define more precisely, as far as possible, the developmental pattern of this relationship.

PROCEDURE

This paper presents results from only one of several techniques devised and used by the authors to investigate the development of racial identification and preferences in Negro children.[1] Results presented here are from the Dolls Test.

Dolls Test. The subjects were presented with four dolls, identical in every respect save skin color. Two of these dolls were brown with black hair and two were white with yellow hair. In the experimental situation these dolls were un-clothed except for white diapers. The position of the head, hands, and legs on all the dolls was the same. For half of the subjects the dolls were presented in the order: white, colored, white, colored. For the other half the order of presentation was reversed. In the experimental situation the subjects were asked to respond to the following requests by choosing one of the dolls and giving it to the experimenter:

1. Give me the doll that you like to play with—(a) like best.
2. Give me the doll that is a nice doll.
3. Give me the doll that looks bad.
4. Give me the doll that is a nice color.
5. Give me the doll that looks like a white child.
6. Give me the doll that looks like a colored child.
7. Give me the doll that looks like a Negro child.
8. Give me the doll that looks like you.

Requests 1 through 4 were designed to reveal preferences; requests 5 through 7 to indicate a knowledge of "racial differences"; and request 8 to show self-identification.

It was found necessary to present the preference requests first in the experimental situation because in a preliminary investigation it was clear that the children who had already identified themselves with the colored doll had a marked tendency to indicate a preference for this doll and this was not necessarily a gen-

Condensed by the authors from an unpublished study made possible by a fellowship grant from the Julius Rosenwald Fund, 1940-1941.

[1] Other techniques presented in the larger study include: (1) a coloring test; (2) a questionnaire and (3) a modification of the Horowitz line drawing technique. (R. E. Horowitz, "Racial Aspects of Self-identification in Nursery School Children," *J. Psychol.*, 1939, VII, 91-99.)

The Doll Experiment was originally conducted by Kenneth and Mamie Clark in the 1940's
and was used by NAACP Supreme Court Lawyers to argue in Brown vs. Board of Education
(Courtesy of Our Documents.gov)

On August 3, 1951, The U.S. District Court in Kansas City, Kansas ruled in favor of the Board of Education of Topeka, stating that Kansas Public School System did maintain Separate but Equal Education for both Black and White Students throughout the state. The NAACP immediately filed an appeal before the October 2, 1951, deadline for the cost of $5,000.00 ($ 45,700.00 in 2016 dollars), which was raised locally by the NAACP Local Chapter and other nearby NAACP Chapters. At the Supreme Court level, the Brown vs. Board of Education case was merged with four similar cases, that were filed at the SCOTUS level. These cases were;

Briggs vs. Elliot (South Carolina)

Davis vs. County School Board of Prince Edward County, Virginia

Gebhart vs. Belton (Delaware)

Bolling vs. Sharpe (Washington D.C.)

Since all five cases were NAACP-sponsored and legally represented cases, Thurgood Marshall argued the cases in front of the Supreme Court for the Plaintiffs, while Assistant Attorney General under President Dwight D. Eisenhower, Paul Wilson, argued the cases for the Defense. These cases were argued in front of the Justices under the new leadership of the recently appointed Chief Justice Earl Warren, when Chief Justice Fred Vinson passed away on September 9, 1953, on December 7, 1953.

The strategy used by Marshall and his legal team argued that segregation **_PERIOD_** had a psychological impact on students who were attending separate but equal education schools. To prove this theory, the NAACP enlisted the testimony and research that were provided to the Justices that were conducted in 1939 and 1940 by the Husband and Wife Psychology team of Kenneth B. and Mamie P. Clark. Called the "Doll Experiment", this research to show how negatively segregated education mentally affected African-American student's self-esteem and self-identification.

The Doll experiment was conducted when a child of elementary age, was presented with two different dolls; one White with Yellow/Golden hair and one Black with Brown/Black hair. Besides the skin color and hair colors, both dolls were the very same. When the child being tested were presented with the dolls in person, the Clarks would ask the child open-ended questions for the child to answer back, such as;

a. *Which doll would you play with?*
   i. *Which doll was the best?*
b. *Which doll looked bad?*
c. *Which doll had the nicer skin color?*
d. *Which doll looks like a White child?*
e. *Which doll looks like a Colored child?*
f. *Which doll looks like a Negro child?*

g. *Which doll looks like you?*

Psychologist Kenneth Clark conducting the "Doll Experiment" in 1940.
(Courtesy of The Root)

The Doll Experiment questions above was to reveal preferences (questions 1-4), indicate knowledge (questions 5-7) and the last question, was to show self-identification. The whole study was based-off Mamie Clark's Howard University Thesis, which was used to support the argument that racism is internalized early in age within the African-American community due to segregation of the races.

NAACP Legal Defense Attorney Thurgood Marshall used it when arguing the Brown vs. Board of Education case, that having segregated educational institutions, the long-term effect on a child's self-esteem and self-concept can and will end up causing that person to have an aura of self-hate later in life.

Finally, on May 17, 1954, the Supreme Court made its decision was rendered by the nine Justices of the Supreme Court;

Chief Justice- Earl Warren (Rendered the majority opinion)

Associate Justice- Hugo Black

Associate Justice- Stanley F. Reed

Associate Justice- Felix Frankfurter

Associate Justice- William O. Douglas

Associate Justice- Robert H. Jackson

Associate Justice- Harold H. Burton

Associate Justice- Tom C. Clark (Former Attorney General under President Truman)

Associate Justice- Sherman Minton

Under a unanimous opinion of the court, 9-0 decision, the Supreme Court ruled that the "***Separate but Equal***" provision outlined under the 1896 ***Plessy vs. Ferguson*** and in the Public Education System goes against the 14th Amendment of the U.S. Constitution's Equal Protection Clause. In other words, Separate but Equal accommodations are **_unconstitutional_**. The Plaintiffs of the five-combined Supreme Court case of ***Brown vs. Education*** won an outstanding victory!

The Aftermath of the 1954 SCOTUS Decision

Locally, the Supreme Court decision desegregating Topeka Kansas Public School System almost amounted to nothing. What it did accomplish on the local level, was that both Linda Brown and Cheryl Brown, to include many other African-American children in Kansas can now go to the same schools and receive their education right along with their White counterparts.

However, despite the ***Brown vs. Board of Education*** historical decision, the Kansas Permissive Law of 1879 segregating the state's school system was **_only applied_** to elementary grades.

Topeka's High Schools have been integrated since 1871 and Topeka's Junior High Schools have been integrated since 1941. Athletics of the former became integrated in 1949. When hearing of the SCOTUS decision, McKinley Burnett stated: "Thank God for the Supreme Court". During the PBS interview, Oliver Brown's wife recalled what she did after hearing the Supreme Court decision;

"I was waiting. I remember I was home doing the family ironing that day when the decision was handed down. I was home, all the kids were in school, my husband had gone to work, and I'm home doing that. And when it [the Supreme Court decision] came over and they said that it had been…segregation had been defeated, oh boy, I think I was doing the dance there at home by myself. (laughs) I was so elated. I could hardly wait until my kids and my husband got home to relate to them."

Cheryl Brown-Henderson stated;

"What the Brown decision did was it broke the silence. It made the country start talking about racism and segregation and discrimination and second-class citizenship and all of those things. Because if you look at Brown and everything that came after the Civil Rights Act ten years later in 1964; the voting rights act one year later; even before that, after the Montgomery bus boycott, the Supreme Court decision that ended the practice of segregation, you know, in transportation-all of those things emanate from the Brown decision."

What Cheryl Brown-Henderson stated that "it broke the silence" on racism, segregation, discrimination and second-class citizenship is not debatable. Those conditions to end such practices have been vocally loud ***long before*** the **Brown vs. Board of Education** decision in 1954. Maybe not as much in the state of Kansas, but many other places, including in the North where a subtle version of racial segregation existed, called De Facto Segregation, have been protected with a public outcry for decades prior to the case.

What the Brown decision ***did accomplish***, however, was that it brought out the most vile, evil and often-violent agitation of the masses of the negative opposition of desegregation in modern American History.

Lastly, the Brown case was reopened twice at the Supreme Court level for various reasons, which the following chapters this book will cover. ***Unknown to the American Public, especially to the Black Community, that the Brown vs. Board of Education case was finally closed by the Justices in 1999!***

It was that year, the Supreme Court officially closed the case and found that all segregation in public education has been eliminated...45 years later!!

May 17, 1954 Supreme Court Decision on *Brown vs. Board of Education*
(Courtesy of Our Documents.gov)

The Backlash of the Decision

Brown vs. Board of Education caused such an uproar and criticism in the public, where not everyone accepted the decision and they said so verbally!

Upon hearing the SCOTUS decision, Virginia's Senator Harry F. Byrd Sr. organized a large movement of his constituency to shut down that state's Public Education System before they integrated them. Senator Byrd Sr. also had the backing of the Virginia Legislature, who created the **"Stanley Plan"**, named after Virginia's Governor Thomas B. Stanley, that pushed for a package of legislation of 13 statutes, to legally ensure racial segregation continued in the state, despite the SCOTUS decision.

In North Carolina, in response to Brown vs. Board of Education, in August 1954, Governor William B. Umstead created a "Governor's Special Advisory Committee on Education", headed by prominent Farmer, Businessman, and former state house speaker Thomas Pearsall.

The committee was made of 19 members, to include 12 Whites and seven Blacks, with the responsibility to determine whether-or-not North Carolina should or should not integrate its schools.

The committee concluded that it would be impossible to integrate all North Carolina's schools. In the meantime, the committee designed what was called "**The Pearsall Plan**". The plan required that the North Carolina General Assembly enact a Pupil Assignment Act, in which was completed the same year, where school districts could use a-race-neutral criteria, preventing further action to desegregate its schools and allowing African-American students for attending all-White schools. In Texas, the state's Attorney General, Ben Shepperd, organized a public outcry via the media, that he will stand firm and not force schools to desegregate, regardless of what the Supreme Court decided.

In the May 24, 1955, issue of the **Orlando** (Florida) **Sentinel** Newspaper, it was reported that the Florida House Legislature approved a state constitutional amendment to permit country-by-country abolition of the Florida Public School System. The idea behind the move is by closing down the entire state's school system to the general-public and change them into Private Schools, lawmakers there can evade enforcement of desegregating schools in the state that was mandated by the Supreme Court.

The bill was sponsored by State Representatives Prentice Pruitt of Jefferson County and Sam Gibbons of Hillsborough, Florida, would not just stifle desegregation of Florida's schools, but the state will save money and not have to pay for the facilities and curriculum changes for their schools to integrate.

A May 18, 1954, edition of the **Anniston** (Alabama) **Star**, the front-page headlines read as such;

"Vast Problems Face South"

"Study Begun in Dixie Ruling"

"Race Ruling Causes Mixed State Views"

"Segregation End Seen Years Off"

On the same date, this time in Jackson, Mississippi, the city's main newspaper of the time read as follows;

> **"State Seek Answer to Adverse Ruling on School Desegregation"**
>
> **"'Go-slow' Attitude Urged by Governor in Court Decision"**
>
> **"Hint Effective Date of Decree May Be Delayed"**

The only city in the South who unanimously accepted **Brown vs. Board of Education** mandate was Greensboro, North Carolina. Under the chairmanship of D.E. Hughes Jr., the school board announced publicly that it will follow mandate that the Supreme Court ruled to desegregate its schools. However, other Greensboro citizens weren't that accepting.

The latter filed a plethora of lawsuits in court to stop that from happening. Violent protests followed each year when the city finally decided to carry out desegregation of its schools; in 1971! After almost 20 years of constant fighting and indignation between its Black and White citizens, including court rulings, riots, violence, deaths and injuries, Greensboro, North Carolina finally had integrated schools.

However, there were more events like this which required the force of military action, in some cases in-order to force cities to integrate their schools. Some of these cities will be discussed soon. But there is one unknown issue, that some educators of history and politics selectively left out when it comes to explaining the impact of Brown vs. Board of Education of 1954.

The Northern cities within the United States **_did practice_** and followed the 1896 Supreme Court decision of Plessy vs. Ferguson, Separate but Equal clause too, but in a totally different way. By 1955, one year after the decision, cities like Chicago, Detroit, St. Louis, Cleveland, Baltimore and others had not desegregated their schools either. Even though, like in Topeka, Kansas, these cities followed De Facto Segregation, which no matter how you look at it, it was still a form of segregation based on racial lines. As a matter of clarity, Harlem New York, for example, had not one new Public-School Facility built in that city since the beginning of the turn-of-the-20th Century. Fifty-plus years later, their schools, were badly in need of repairs, were staffed by inexperienced Teachers and administrators, had leaky roofs, broken plumbing and were just as bad, if not worse than schools in the rural South. Public Schools like the ones in the cities of St. Louis, Gary Indiana, Chicago Illinois, Cleveland Ohio and more, in 1955, still had school buildings in operation, with racially segregated students attending them that were built in 1875!

Brown vs. Board of Education (II)

Unfortunately, the May 17, 1954, ruling by the Supreme Court ending segregation in public education did not just end there. After the initial decision, the states of Florida, North Carolina, Arkansas, Texas, Oklahoma, Maryland, South Carolina and Virginia, ask the court to re-open the brown case, requesting monetary relief and timeline clarity as to how long they needed to desegregate their schools. Commonly called the **Brown (II) case**, oral arguments were presented in front of the Justices between April 11th through the 14th, 1955. The states were also asked at what level of government or judiciary entity will be responsible to enforce the original Brown ruling.

On May 31, 1955, the Supreme Court rendered its decision on the **Brown (II) case**. Chief Justice Earl Warren rendered the opinion of the court;

These cases were decided on May 17, 1954. The opinions of that date, declaring the fundamental principle that racial discrimination in public education is unconstitutional, are incorporated herein by reference. All provisions of Federal, State, or local law requiring or permitting such discrimination must yield to this principle. There remains for consideration the manner in which relief is to be accorded."

Chief Justice Warren continues;

"... the courts will require that the defendants make a prompt and reasonable start toward full compliance with our May 17, 1954, ruling. Once such a start date has been made, the court may find that additional time is necessary in the public interest and is consistent with good faith compliance at the earliest practicable date...."

"The cases are remanded to the District Courts to take such proceedings and enter such orders and decrees consistent with the opinion as are necessary and proper to admit to public schools on a racially nondiscriminatory basis with all deliberate speed the parties to these cases..." [Author's emphasis]

The *Brown (II)* decision sent shock waves through the NAACP and other so-called Civil Rights groups like a lightning bolt from the sky!

Essentially, Separate but Equal education is unconstitutional as with the original order by the Supreme Court, but the court never gave a timeline for school districts to desegregate! Instead, *Brown (II)* allowed the school districts to provide "good faith" in compliance of desegregating at the "earliest practicable date"; set by themselves! Enforcement of the original Brown case were left up to the District Courts. Again, Chief Justice Earl Warren wrote:

"at stake is the personal interest of the plaintiffs in admission to public schools as soon as practicable on a non-discriminating basis".

This statement was interpreted as Black students can gain admission into a formerly racially divided school, in accordance with the original order at the earliest date in which the school's districts should be set up and have ready to integrate under the thumb of the District Courts. Meaning this, Blacks students can enroll in a once all-white school when the school districts are ready in "good faith" to accept them. This is also where "all deliberate speed" comes into play.

Thurgood Marshall, when filing and arguing the original Brown vs. Board of Education case, stated that "all public schools for Negro children will be desegregated within five years of the decision". Marshall was he wrong in that assessment and things were about to get worse, and probably on purpose.

Others interpreted the *Brown (II)* decision as a kick in the pants.

What it did was it gave the schools districts almost unlimited time to stall out and/or have the flexibility whether to desegregate or not, regardless of the original Brown decision. Case-in-point can be illustrated of what happened in Prince Edward County, Virginia immediately after the *Brown (II)* decision. The U.S. District Court whose jurisdiction covers the county told the board members that it did not need to desegregate immediately. The country continued to operate separate but Equal schools until 1959.

On February 2, 1959, the U.S. District Court ordered the state of Virginia to desegregate its schools in accordance with both Brown decisions by the Supreme Court. Seeing this beforehand, Prince Edward

County Board of Supervisors ceased all funding to the Public-School System and closed it down completely.

From 1959-1964, the county's school became **"Private White-only"** schools, which were taught by former Public Education Teachers who used to teach at the segregated schools prior to them shutting them down. As for the African-American Children; they had NO schools to go to in their county to receive an education! They either funded their own transportation to school in other countries or communities surrounding Prince Edward County or they didn't go to school at all; for 5 years!

When Virginia finally gave in under pressure from the U.S. Government in 1965, the state only allowed a few Black students to attend integrated schools. It was estimated that in the same year, of the 230,000-plus Black Students residing in Virginia, only 12,000 went to desegregated schools. Local school boards like Prince Edward County attempted to selectively admit certain Blacks students into their schools by a written test or some other way, which were deemed illegal. However, by the mid-to-late 1970's, Virginia schools, including the ones in Prince Edward County, were fully integrated.

Outside of the states that provided push back against desegregation of public schools, one of the little unknown facts not mentioned in the historical context of both Brown cases, where the pushback coming from the African-American community.

Yes, Black Americans voiced their displeasure with the Supreme Court decisions of **Brown vs. Board of Education** for various reasons.

One critic was Sadie T. Alexander, by 1955 was the former City Solicitor of Philadelphia, Pennsylvania and one of the distinguished members of President Truman's Committee on Civil Rights (PCCR).

Alexander mentioned that until Blacks achieved more educational and economic success in Black Public Schools and Universities, the Supreme Court decisions essentially will begin the destruction of America's Black Educational System at its core, that many people have worked so hard to create. Well-known Harlem Renaissance Writer, Folklorist and Anthropologist Zora Neale Hurston, wrote a scathing but essentially true editorial in the **Orlando Sentinel** dated August 11, 1955, titled **"Court Can't Make the Races Mix"**. In this article, she states in part;

"Now a great clamor will use certain quarters that I seek to deny the Negro children of the South their rights, and therefore I am one of those 'Handkerchief-head Niggers' who bow low before the White man and sell out my own people out of cowardice. However, an analytical glance will show that this is not the case."

Hurston Continues;

"If there are not adequate Negro schools in Florida, and there is some residual, some inherent and nonchangeable quality in White Schools, impossible to duplicate anywhere else, then I am the first to insist that Negro Children of Florida be allowed to share this boon. But if there are adequate Negro schools and prepared instructors and instructions, then there is nothing different except the presence of White people."

Hurston goes on inside her editorial that the above reasons, she regarded the ruling of the U.S. Supreme Court decision to desegregate the nation's public schools was done to insult her race, the African-American race than honoring it. Hurston goes on to write;

"It is most astonishing that this should be tried [desegregating of public schools] *just when the nation is exerting itself to shake off the evils of Communist penetration. It is to be recalled that Moscow, being made aware of this folk belief, made it the main plank in their campaign to win the American Negro from the 1920's on."*

Remember the action by CPUSA and COMINTERN of creating a "Soviet Negro Republic"?

Zora Neale Hurston went on and adamantly accused Blacks of supporting the SCOTUS decisions and those belonging to the Communist Party of getting a White wife or husband to supply the expected demand that the party place on them. In other words, the entire hype of Brown vs. Board of Education was to spur up agitation, by using what she calls "tragedy of color' to garner sympathy. Essentially, she was right on the money with the assessment. One can only revisit the 2004 PBS interview with the Brown family, in which Cheryl Brown Henderson stated that in Topeka, Kansas;

"The African-American Schools were good schools. The facilities were built by the same person, so we're not talking about

substandard facilities with leaky roofs and outhouses like they were in the South. The teachers were well-trained. Many had advanced degrees. So, we aren't talking about a poor education...In Topeka, they walked a few blocks and caught a bus. So, we weren't talking about real hardships here. We were talking about the principle of the thing."

The principle of why there should be two separate but equal educational schools teaching the same thing was the problem that the NAACP wanted to point out, which in turn would have caused hate, discontent, and agitation of the public, that would have further the Communist cause. Hurston in her editorial also believed that the Supreme Court decision was also used to be a distraction to take people's attention away for what was really important, the Communist subversion of Blacks in the United States.

Ex-Communist and International Labor Defense (ILD) member William Patterson, also shared the opinion of Zora Neale Hurston. Being on the inside and dealing daily with CPUSA, COMINTERN in Moscow and other Marxist entities, voiced that the **Brown vs. Board of Education** ruling was essentially a Communist agitation campaign, using real-world social issues to use Blacks as "cannon fodder" to promote division between the races, hidden under the name of Civil Rights. This same idea of subversion to divide the races even further along racial lines was also echoed by former FBI Secretary Julia Brown, who stated;

"Racial differences was America's most weakest point, for the Communist Party to divide our differences. They have and continue to use any and all opposition to the point of submission."

The perception that the Communists wanted to portray during the American Civil Rights Movement, was to use the media, the churches, the schools, and the unions to agitate the masses of people in-order to control public opinion. By doing this, Marxist Men can show, falsely, that most of the American people agree with the few agitators that they see in the media, even though the few selected agitators who were being used themselves as useful idiots, their job is to stoke the flames of racial division, using real-life incidents. Marxist Men also want to show the entire World, that African-Americans in the United States popularly support these agitation campaigns, even though not every African-American agreed with these agitators.

As the old saying goes that "***Perception is only 9/10ths of Reality***".

In the next few chapters, the after-mentioned quotation will be one of the main focal points that will define the next phases of civil rights campaigns, in-order to shape and mold the American Civil Rights Movement. These campaigns will be operated by three-separate factions, whose ideology will spin the entire movement into a totally new direction. The end-result of which will get people are killed, severely injured, property destroyed, new laws and regulations will be created, right along with the false intentions by some to instill deception, lies and hidden effects are still felt in today's 21st Century America.

15: Two Factional Groups: The American Civil Rights Movement (III)

"There are two ways to circumvent, or trample over, a constitution, however ingeniously contrived maybe its democratic precepts. One way is to arouse public fear and hatred to a point where all concepts of minority protection, or right of dissent, get swept away in a tide of emotion...The second way to abrogate a Constitution is to amass enough police or military power to force your will upon society."

Carl T. Rowan

Anarchy is defined by the breakdown of law and order; a chaotic reign of terror, mob-rule, and rioting; the collapse of the government. This definition describes in the historical context of the American Civil Rights Movement within the next decade, between 1955-1965, which is considered by some, the peak of the movement within itself. It was during this timeframe, the Civil Rights Movement splintered into four-separate factions, two of them Black, two of them White.

The first one was the **Nonviolent groups** led by the late great Dr. Martin Luther King Jr., Rosa Parks, Ralph Abernathy, Stokely Carmichael and many others. This faction believed that nonviolent protests and community involvement would ultimately end racial segregation for all.

The second faction of the Civil Rights Movement is the **Revolutionary Groups**, who preached violence, hate, and discontent with the plan to force their will on society through violent means. These groups, were led by the likes of Nation of Islam (NOI) leader Elijah

Muhammad, NOI Speaker Malcolm X, the Black Panther Party (BPP) led by Huey P. Newton and Bobby Seale, were being supported directly by CPUSA and COMINTERN in Moscow.

The third faction, during the movement, were groups that have been well-known during the latter-half of the 1960's and early 1970's; the **Anti-Vietnam War Protestors**. Groups such as Students for a Democratic Society (SDS), The Weather Underground (WU) are just some of the many groups that were trained and funded by CPUSA.

The fourth faction, are the **Segregationists**. These are groups in which we all know very well, even in the modern-day public psyche. Groups such as The Ku Klux Klan (KKK), White League, White Liners and other White Supremacy groups, made up of White Americans, who consistently tried their dam nest, using intimidation tactics, violence, and sometimes absolute murder, to stop the other three factions from succeeding in their quest to change the legitimate social structure in America. To be clear, there are great differences between the third and fourth factions of the movement. ***The latter faction was led by Segregationists, who occupy positions of political power, via the Democrat Party.***

Their aim is to use their political and law enforcement clout to erase any-and-all attempts of integration of the races. This includes politicians in the like of Tennessee Governor Albert Gore Sr. (Father of former Vice-President Al Gore), James "Bull" Connor, Arkansas Governor Orval Faubus and many other people.

For the sake of time and space, this book will only talk about two of the four factional groups during the American Civil Rights Movement, after ***Brown vs. Board of Education***.

As 1955 trots on towards the end of the year, with both Brown cases still stewing in the public's mind, one incident would light the fuse of the bomb, which will pit all four of the aforementioned-factions against each other for the next 20 years, in the name of African-American Civil Rights; The Montgomery Alabama Bus Boycott.

National City Transit of Montgomery, Alabama General Motors bus number 2857. The exact bus where American Civil Rights Leader Rosa Parks was arrested on December 1, 1955.

(Courtesy of Wikimedia/Henry Ford Museum)

The Non-Violent Movement

What brought to the mainstream American radio and television screens, the first factional group of the Civil Rights Movement came on Friday, December 9, 1955, in the Southern City of Montgomery, Alabama. On that date and long afterward, the incident of the Montgomery Bus Boycott is considered the pinnacle of the movement of itself, which brought to fame three African-American Civil Rights Leaders; Dr. Martin Luther King Jr., Rosa Parks, and Ralph Abernathy.

Alabama, like many other Southern States, operated their societies under De Jure Segregation. This is where both Blacks and Whites had their own, but often unequal sections standards of living, where Blacks could only live in this neighborhood and Whites lived in that neighborhood, etc. When it came to using public transportation, ticketing, passes and seating accommodations were divided by skin color.

The metropolitan area of Montgomery Alabama was like the after-mentioned; everything was all divided by race. For example, at a major transportation hub in the South of 1955, public bathrooms, drinking fountains and waiting areas were all divided by skin color, with signs that read, *"White Only"* or *"Colored Only"*.

In places like Montgomery Alabama, which was a major transportation hub and a largely populated city that had a sizable population of low-income Blacks, this was the theme of everyday life in the segregated South.

Many families in Montgomery's Black Community, were on the low-income scale, so they had to rely on the use of public transportation as their mode of travel. As a matter of fact, 75% of the city's Black population used the city's buses that way. Traveling between home, going to and from work, to shop, to eat and other places to conduct their everyday activities, this was the environment.

On the flip-side, some of the White residents in Montgomery had the benefit and access to cars and trucks to conduct their daily business, so the number of Whites taking the same public transportation system were a lot less, but they still chose to ride that system. When African-Americans did use the city's public transportation system, they usually rode in the aft-section of the streetcars and buses. Of course, during peak hours of the day, especially during the time of significant national holidays such as Christmas and New Year's, the city buses or streetcars often became overcrowded with more White passengers than Black ones.

When that was the case, as the number of White passengers increased, the Black passengers already seated at certain sections of the bus or streetcar, had to give up their seats to Whites who didn't have seats, thereby allowing them to either stand up or attempt to move further back of the streetcar or bus. To alleviate this problem, before the start of the boycott, Black passengers had to choose one or two things to alleviate this condition. The first one being, while riding the bus or streetcar along the route, if the numbers of White passengers increasingly dwindled, Black passengers could reclaim their seats that they have given up or two, stand up until it was time to get off the bus or streetcar at their chosen stop.

In 1955 Montgomery Alabama, Transit Busses were split into three sections, from front to back. As in the illustration, the front-seats of the bus was reserved for Whites, the middle-section were considered 'neutral' seating and the back of the bus were for Black riders at all times. There have been incidents in Montgomery, Alabama prior to that time, when National City Transit Company, who operated the Montgomery City Buses, enforced a ridership rule, which allowed Blacks to enter the bus at the front door, pay their fare, get off the bus and re-enter the bus via the back door, which was normally used as an exit. That rule was changed shortly afterwards, because of hundreds of complaints that were levied against the company, accusing the bus drivers, who were mostly White, of driving off, leaving Black passengers at the stop, directly after the Black rider paid their fare at the front door, before they could re-enter bus at the back door.

Also prior to 1955, several incidents occurred in numerous Southern Cities, like Montgomery Alabama, where buses or streetcars became so overcrowded, that when the driver told some of the Blacks to move further back of the vehicle so more Whites can board, some Black passengers refused to obey the request.

These passengers were arrested, thrown in jail and/or paid a hefty fine for their act of rightful defiance. This resulted in several lawsuits which were levied at transportation companies, which were moved through the court system, several of them being won. However, this one particular-incident stood out among all of them, on the cold December 9th of 1955, the beginning of the Montgomery Bus Boycott, which lasted until the following year.

The Montgomery Alabama Chapter of the NAACP, led by Edgar Daniel "E.D." Nixon, who was also the head of the Montgomery Alabama Chapter of the Brotherhood of Sleeping Car Porters Union, planned to do something about desegregating that city's transit buses.

This had to be achieved by creating an agitation campaign, "a test case", using a scripted, real-life incident, to stir up the public's emotion, create a public outcry, spread through the media. The goal was to force other public transportation companies throughout the South like National City Lines to desegregate their systems too. This had to be planned methodically and on purpose for the end-result to occur. It was in Montgomery Alabama is where the Nonviolence Movement faction started within the Civil Rights Movement.

E.D. Nixon chose his NAACP chapter member Rosa Parks for the job to create the hysteria to desegregate the buses. She would be used in the so-called "test case", to see if such actions can be held in other Southern cities. At the time of the boycott, the then-42-year-old Rosa Parks was a full-time Seamstress that earned $23.00 per week ($373.00 in 2016) and worked as the local chapter's NAACP as a Secretary.

She was sent by E.D. Nixon for Marxist Agitation Training at the Highlander Folk School (now- Highlander Research and Educational Center), then-located in Monteagle, Grundy County, Tennessee before 1955. What E.D. Nixon needed was for Rosa Parks to get arrested challenging segregation on Montgomery Alabama buses, to mobilize the Black Community and file lawsuits against National City Lines for outright racism. By doing this, a severe backlash would be caused, by stirring up public anger and emotional uprisings among the population, with help of the media, further causing the bus company to lose money and reverse their rules on Segregation. For the actors, it was the perfect plan; and written history showed that it worked.

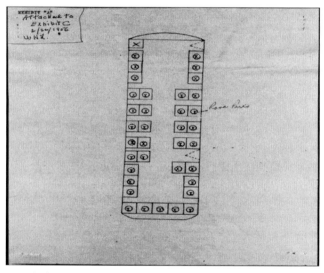

Diagram of where Rosa Parks' seat on bus number 2857 December 1, 1955
(Courtesy of National Archives and Wikimedia)

On December 1, 1955, Rosa Parks played the role of a tired African-American Woman, who have worked a long day of being a Seamstress near downtown Montgomery. She caught the Cleveland Avenue bus, number 2857, which was driven by long-time National City Lines Bus Operator James F. "Jim" Blake. Parks got on the bus and sat in the second-set of longitudinal rows of seats, next to the window, facing out the right side of the bus. After making several stops along the route, additional passengers were being picked up, which allowed the bus to become crowded. In the section where Ms. Parks was seated, three other Black passengers were seated in the same section as well. When Jim Blake made another stop, a White male passenger boarded the already crowded bus, he turned from his seat and requested the Black passengers (to include Rosa Parks) to relinquish their seats, move to the back of the bus, so the other White passengers can sit in them. As the other three Black passengers located near Rosa Parks, made their way towards the back of the bus as best as they could, Ms. Parks refused to move.

In a Washington Post interview with the bus driver that day, Jim Blake, dated July 24, 1989, as told to Paul Hendrickson, that he called his supervisor to report the incident. Mr. Blake denies written accounts of the incident, accusing him of cursing at Ms. Parks that day and calling her names to get her to move to the back of the bus. Jim Blake recalled, that his supervisor asked him;

"Did you warn her Jim?"

After telling his supervisor that he did, he was told by the same person;

"Well then, Jim, you do it, you got to exercise your powers and put her off, hear?"

Jim Blake did just that. The Police responded to the site within a few minutes, took her off and arrested her. Blake maintained his innocence until the day he passed away from a Heart Attack in 2002, that he did not call the police on Ms. Parks. They just responded. He further stated during his interview that;

"I wasn't trying to do anything to that Parks woman except do my job. She was in violation of the city codes. What was I supposed to do? That damn bus was full. I had my orders. I had police powers—any driver for the city did. So, the bus was filled up and a White man got on and she had his seat and I told her to move back and she wouldn't do it."

Jim Blake swore a warrant for the Montgomery police to arrest her and took her to the city jail. He worked for the transit company after he was drafted in the U.S. Army during World War II as a truck driver and was hired shortly after returning from the European Theater in 1948. Jim Blake retired from the company in 1974. He admitted during the interview that he and his family, (he had a Wife and three children) received thousands of death threats on the telephone from members of the Montgomery Alabama's Black community day and night for weeks after the incident.

When two Police Officers arrived, they put Rosa Parks in handcuffs, took her off the bus and escorted her to the waiting police car. While in route to the car after being arrested, in her Autobiography written in 1992, she asked one of the policemen this question;

"Why do you all treat us [Blacks] bad?"

The officer looked at her, shook his head side-to-side and responded;

"I don't know ma'am. I don't know. But the law is the law."

After she was processed at the police station, she was formally charged with violating Montgomery, Alabama City Ordinance Chapter 6, Section 11; Failure to obey person in charge of a vehicle. She was fined a total of $14; $10 fine and $4 processing fee.

That same night after Park's arrest, one of the local NAACP splinter groups, the Women's Political Council (WPC), led by its President Jo Ann Robinson, an English Professor at Alabama State College (Now-Alabama State University), used the school's mimeograph machine all night and printed over 35,000 handbills (flyers).

The idea behind the flyers were to distribute them throughout the Black Community of Montgomery, advertising Rosa Park's arrest. The handbills also called for a 1-day boycott of all Montgomery Alabama public transit buses the following Monday, December 5, 1955. Mrs. Robinson used some of her Black students to help her print the handbills as well as assisted her in its distribution. The students were tasked to put up these flyers around the city's Black Schools, go door-to-door handing them out, post them on trees, telephone poles, inside of homes, inside the Black churches and in their parent's homes everywhere. With 75% of the Black Community using the transit buses in the city, it was bound to gain some quick attention and it did.

That Sunday, December 4, 1955, every Black church in the Montgomery Alabama area, preached about the news of Rosa Parks arrest advocating their congregations to support the 1-day boycott of the transit buses the following day. By the end of the day of December 5th, not one National City Lines bus transported one Black passenger that day.

Some thought that protesting for one day, wasn't enough, a bigger boycott was needed to provide a bigger, more public-driven impact on the city of Montgomery, the National City Lines Company, the entire South's segregation enforcement and to the world. One 26-year-old African-American Minister who was originally from the city of Atlanta, Georgia, who was hired as an Associate Pastor at the Dexter Street Baptist Church a few months prior to Rosa Park's arrest, who will lead one of the first Nonviolent protest faction groups ever during the American Civil Rights Movement. His name is Dr. Martin Luther King Jr.

Rosa Parks, with Dr. Martin Luther King Jr. in the background during the Montgomery Bus Boycott in 1956

(Courtesy of Wikimedia/Public Domain)

As the call went out throughout the Black community for a bigger, more substantial boycott, the Senior Pastor of the city's largest African-American church, The First Baptist Church, Reverend Ralph Abernathy Jr. was first approached with the idea and he had just the man in mind to lead one, his friend Dr. King.

Abernathy wasn't any small-time minister. He was the Dean of Men at Alabama State University and had gained the utmost respect from both the Black Community and some of Montgomery, Alabama's non-segregationists White Community as well. Since he was a mentor to Dr. King, the men formed the Montgomery Improvement Association (MIA) as the main boycott operation entity to run the much bigger bus boycott to soon come.

Outside its leadership, the MIA was formed using members from the Southern Christian Leadership Conference (SCLC), which was being funded by the Southern Conference Educational Fund (SCEF). SECF in-turn was a branch of the Southern Regional Council (SRC), which was a branch of itself of Communist Party (CPUSA), which was run off the orders of the Communist International (COMINTERN) based in Moscow, Russia! The Women's Political Council (WPC) was a branch of the local NAACP, led by E.D. Nixon, in which Rosa Parks was a mentor for the local branch of the NAACP Youth League. The connection gets better as we continue on in the chapter.

Since E.D. Nixon was out of town conducting business, he did not want Abernathy nor King to plan or do anything with the MIA until he returned-back to Montgomery. Without Nixon's presence, the planning for the bigger boycott continued to push on. When E.D. Nixon returned, with Dr. King in charge of the protests, Nixon became MIA's Treasurer and Abernathy became MIA's President and Chief Organizer. Another member of the Clergy has added to the leadership circle of the Montgomery Improvement Association also. His name was the Reverend E.N. French and these four men made up the organization, held meetings at various churches to strategize the protests, which was set to start on Friday, December 9, 1955.

On that day, Dr. King, Rosa Parks, WPC President Jo Ann Robinson and founder/former President of the Women's Political Council, Mary Fair Burks, began the first few Nonviolent marches. As the boycott of the buses continued day-after-day, a major financial impact began to wear on the bus company, National City Lines. The company itself continued to run their normal scheduled operations for the first few weeks after the start of the protests. However, soon the company realized that running empty buses, was not only costing the company large sums of money in the form or revenue (money coming into the company), but the boycott impacted the driver's payroll, increased maintenance costs on the buses, that later turned the majority White bus drivers against the company and the city itself. This prompted the Mayor of Montgomery, William Armistead "W.A." Gayle, to call a meeting with the MIA to negotiate an end to the boycott. It was a moot point.

On February 1, 1956, at its headquarters in New York City, the NAACP Legal Defense Fund Attorneys made up of Robert L. Carter and Thurgood Marshall, began to complete the paperwork for a lawsuit against Montgomery's Mayor W.A. Gayle. Carter and Marshall enlisted the help of local Montgomery Black Attorney Fred Gray and White Attorney Clifford Durr.

The lawsuit was filed accusing the City of Montgomery Alabama and National City Transit Company for violating the Equal Protection Act under the Fourteenth Amendment of the Constitution. By creating rules, regulations and city ordinances regarding enforcement of segregation of the public transit system by race, the Mayor and the bus company were violating the civil rights of African-Americans. The Plaintiffs of the suit were made up of numerous Black women who have had been arrested by the Montgomery Police Department, for not giving up their seats on buses like Rosa Parks. The Plaintiffs of the case were;

> *Claudette Colvin-Member of the NAACP Youth Council, who was a pregnant 15-year-old teen who was arrested in March 1955 for not giving up her seat on a bus when requested.*

> *Aurelia Browder-Namesake of the lawsuit, Associate Professor at Alabama State University and member of the Women's Political Council.*

> *Susie McDonald-Ranking member of the Women's Political Council.*

> *Mary Louise Smith-Ranking member of the Woman's Political Council, ranking member of the NAACP Youth Council, who was arrested and charged for refusing to give up her seat on a Montgomery bus in October 1955.*

Jeanette Reese-Ranking member of the Women's Political Council and the NAACP Youth Council, who was arrested and charged for refusing to give up her seat on a Montgomery bus in November 1955. However, she dropped out the lawsuit voluntarily for fear of her life and her family's life after numerous death threats received by her by Segregationists.

The lawsuit, officially entered in the legal and history books as **Browder, et al v. Gayle, et al**, which was filed in U.S. District Court the same day. After hearing arguments on both sides in April 1955, the three-Judge Panel ruled in a 2-1 decision that segregation on Montgomery Alabama city buses and the city ordinances were unconstitutional, violating the 14th Amendment. The Lawyers immediately filed an appeal for the case to be heard at the Supreme Court-level. After hearing the case during the summer of 1955, the Supreme Court Justices handed down their decision on November 13, 1956, upholding the lower- court's decision.

The Montgomery Bus Boycott was a success!

On December 20, 1956, Mayor Gayle was handed the court order to desegregate the transit buses immediately, which they did the next day.

Life Magazine cover photo of Reverends Dr. Martin Luther King Jr. (l) and Ralph Abernathy, riding on a Montgomery Alabama Transit Bus shortly after the boycott, in 1956.

(Public Domain)

The Aftermath of the Nonviolence Faction

When the city of Montgomery Alabama signed a new ordinance that allowed Blacks to ride the city buses in any seat they wished, along with White passengers, the 381-day boycott was a resounding success, which led to other desegregation initiatives on public transit buses throughout the South. Dr. Martin Luther King Jr., Rosa Parks, and Ralph Abernathy became household names, who then became the faces in the public eyes in the struggle for civil rights for African-Americans nationwide. Unfortunately, the behind-the-scenes story does not end here, regarding the Nonviolence Movement.

Despite the worldwide fame in which the media had given to the Montgomery Improvement Association and the Women's Political Council, the boycott sparked other similar movements in other countries. In 1957, a bus boycott was conducted in the Alexandria area of Johannesburg, South Africa and in 1963, another bus boycott began in Bristol, England. Both boycotts ended in successful outcomes, even though they were conducted on different issues other than just segregation, unlike the case in Alabama. There was a downside which was spawned in the aftermath of the Montgomery Bus Boycott.

The backlash of the protests was swift, violent and oftentimes, were effective. Such acts of Anarchism were dominated by the area's White Segregationists, against the protestors. On December 23, 1955, an unknown assailant fired a shotgun through the door of Dr. King's residence. The next day, Christmas Eve, a group of White Segregationists harassed and severely beat a Black teenager, as she exited one of the city's buses during the boycott, causing major injuries, in which she recovered from. On December 28, an unknown assailant began to fire sniper fire into two-separate city buses, wounding one pregnant Black female in both of her legs. That wasn't all that happened.

During the evening of January 10, 1956, several fire bombs were detonated in Montgomery, that damaged Ralph Abernathy's own First Baptist Church, the Mount Olive Baptist Church, the Bell Street Church as well as the home of the Reverend Robert S. Graetz. The latter bombing targeted Graetz's home because he was a White minister who supported and participated in the marches during the bus boycott. On January 23, 1956, a group of Ku Klux Klan (KKK) members, kidnapped an innocent 24-year-old Black man named Willie Edwards Jr., who was beaten and tortured inside their car for hours and forced him to jump off the 125-foot drop of the Tyler-Goodwin Bridge, into the Alabama River, killing him.

Edwards body wasn't recovered until three months later, which by that time was too badly decomposed to determine the exact cause of death. After conducting two-separate trials of the Klansmen who did the act, one in 1976 and one which lasted two years from 1997-1999, no one was ever convicted for the murder of Willie Edwards Jr. On January 30, 1956, Dr. King's house was again attacked, this time by a bomb which was set off by Segregationists while his Wife Coretta Scott King, two of their children and a congregation member of the Dexter Street Baptist Church where at the home.

After hearing the news, Dr. King immediately drove home and arrived to see that his family was safe. Shortly afterward, a mob of Dr. King's supporters gathered outside of the King home, with bats, bottles, pipes, and guns, ready to retaliate against the White Segregationists who perpetrated the act. Dr. Martin Luther King himself went outside and gave a speech, convincing the crowd not to use violence against violence.

Also during the 381-day boycott of the city's buses, Dr. King and 89 MIA and WPC leaders and protests participants, were arrested and indicted on charges of interference with local business ordinances and trespassing. Rosa Parks, in-particular the instigator of the bus boycott, along with her husband and family, left Montgomery in face of numerous death threats they received. Rosa Park herself was blacklisted from ever working in the city again. As mentioned earlier, the bus driver, Jim Blake received numerous calls of death threats levied against him by many in the Black Community to his family as well.

Some say that the Montgomery Bus Boycott was a successful venture that provided big steps for the freedom of the African-American Community. However, this is extremely debatable, considering the entire outcome of the nonviolent protests. Subjectively, if one can look at the overall impact of the boycott on both a national and international stage of events during the late-1950's and early-1960's, a sensible conclusion can be almost made to support that theory. What Dr. King, Ralph Abernathy, E.D. Nixon and Rosa Parks did, sparked more bus boycott protests in far-away places such as

Johannesburg, South Africa in 1957 and Bristol, England in 1963, but that was it. As far as the Black Community within Montgomery Alabama in-itself had very little to gain from the protests, besides desegregating the city's bus transit system.

Until the Civil Rights Act of 1964 and The Voting Rights Act of 1965, De Jure Segregation went on as usual in that city. What the Nonviolence Movement protests also succeeded in doing, was bringing media attention and motivation to the American Civil Rights Movement cause and provide the basic imprint for demonstrations in the future.

Lastly, there is this observation when looking back at the Montgomery Bus Boycott; The Red Communist Observation. Not to get things confused, **_Dr. Martin Luther King Jr. was not a Communist nor was he a Socialist in character and action._** He was none of that. However, Dr. King in the long-term, became a dupe in the overall Marxist-Leninist Establishment, which were echoed in the hollow halls of the CPUSA, its numerous splinter groups that both funded and provided human labor for the Montgomery Improvement Association (MIA), the Women's Political Council (WPC), and the Southern Christian Leadership Conference (SCLC).

Dr. King once said about the accusations that the American Civil Rights Movement was a Communist drive to subvert the United States and overthrow its government;

"There are as many Communists in this freedom movement as there are Eskimos in Florida."

He didn't either know or chose to ignore the fact, that Marxist Men love using real-life situations, and using real-life dupes to further their "cause" to dominate the World.

Consider this.

On May 1, 1957, Dr. Martin Luther King attended a meeting held at the Highlander Folk School in Monteagle, Tennessee and met with some shady characters who were very much underneath the House Committee on Un-American Activities' (HUAC) radar for some time, because of their Communist affiliations. Those who attended with Dr. King at this meeting are as follows;

Myles Horton-Founder of the Highlander Folk School and key Communist Party Organizer for the state of Tennessee

Aubrey Williams-Former head of the National Youth Administration (NYA), friend of FDR's Chief of Staff Harry Hopkins (who was later determined to be a spy for the Soviet KGB) and high-ranking officer of the Southern Conference Education Fund (SCEF)

Abner Berry-Former Communist Organizer for Harlem New York and one of the Editors of CPUSA's publication The Daily Worker

James Dombroski-Co-Founder of the Highlander Folk School, Co-founder of the Conference of Younger Churchmen (CYC) and then-Executive Director of the Southern Conference Educational Fund (SCEF).

Dr. Martin Luther King Jr. giving a presentation to members of the Highlander Folk School in May 1957.

(Courtesy Marxist.org)

The men were there to plan and lay the groundwork for future nonviolent demonstrations throughout the South. It is a bit surprising that Dr. Martin Luther King Jr., the champion of the American Civil Rights Movement associated himself right next to openly-admitted Marxist-Leninists. To get a better understanding, of the entire idea of the Nonviolence faction of the Civil Rights Movement, one have-to understand its main purpose and it wasn't just a movement for civil rights and equality for African-Americans, even though it was advertised as such.

In 1965, Dr. King explained the four-goals of the Nonviolence movement;

"The goal of the demonstrations in Selma as elsewhere is to dramatize the system of injustice and to bring about the presence of justice by a method of non-violence. Long years of experience indicate to us that the Negroes can achieve this goal when one of four things occur. First, non-violence demonstrations go into the streets to exercise their constitutional rights. Second, Racists resists by unleashing violence against them. Third, Americans of conscience in the name of decency, demand Federal intervention and legislation. Fourth, the administration under mass pressure initiates measures of immediate intervention and remedial legislation."

These were the goals of the Nonviolent organizations, such as SCLC, WPC, MIA and much more soon to be created and the gist of the American Civil Rights Movement.

However, when an organization or organizations have been created either by the Communist Party or its tenants, once these entities have become useful and have completed their objectives, ***they are no longer useful to "the cause" anymore***. The best way to remember how Communists exploit their duped masses of people, who call themselves Liberals or Progressives; ***"once you have been useful, you are no longer useful to them anymore"***.

When that is the case, and it has always been the case, the best way to destroy a large, powerful group is to ferment internal strife among each other. In other words, pit one group against the other and see which ones will implode on itself. Consider the timeline of the Nonviolent faction of the Civil Rights Movement and what they accomplished after the 1955-56 Bus Boycott in Montgomery, Alabama;

The formation of the Southern Christian Leadership Conference (SCLC), with Dr. King as President in 1957 in Atlanta, Georgia

The 1957 Civil Rights Act signed into law by then-President Dwight D. Eisenhower on September 9, 1957, despite a large Senatorial Filibuster by Southern Democrats.

Little Rock, Arkansas Central High School Integration, called the "Little Rock Nine", ended up as a showdown between President Dwight D. Eisenhower and Arkansas Governor Orval Faubus, September 23, 1957.

The 1957 Durham, North Carolina Sit-in Protest at Royal Ice Cream Parlor, June 23, 1957, sponsored by the NAACP Youth Council.

July 19, 1958, Wichita, Kansas Sit-in Protest at Dockum Drugs.

August 19, 1958, Oklahoma City, Oklahoma Katy Drug Store Sit-in Protest, sponsored by the NAACP Youth Council.

February 1, 1960, Greensboro, North Carolina Sit-ins Protests at both Woolworth and S.H. Kress Drug Stores.

The February 13-May 10, 1960 Nashville, Tennessee Sit-ins throughout the city, sponsored by the Nashville Christian Leadership Conference (NCLC), a branch of the Southern Christian Leadership Conference (SCLC). NCLC was one of the biggest, but most-known Sit-in protests of the entire American Civil Rights Movement and was led by NCLC President James Lawson.

In April 1960, at Shaw University in Raleigh, North Carolina, the Student Nonviolent Coordinating Committee (SNCC) was founded. SNCC would be a branch of the Nonviolent faction SCLC, but its operations were tied directly with the NAACP Youth Council. SNCC's first President was Marion Barry, the future four-time Mayor of Washington D.C.

On January 31, 1961, the last of the Nonviolent Sit-ins was conducted in Rock Hill, North Carolina on January 31, 1961. This protest was sponsored by North Carolina's CORE Field Secretary Thomas Gaither.

After all the organized protests of Sit-ins, the "Little Rock Nine" who integrated that city's Central High School, under Federalized U.S. Army National Guard and the 101st Airborne Division based at Fort Campbell, Kentucky, two Civil Rights legislations, the Nonviolent groups did not accomplish much as they thought they should have, during that five-year timeframe. However, starting with a "test-run" on a Greyhound Bus, on April 22, 1961, a new campaign of agitation began and will always be known in American History as *"The Freedom Riders"*.

The Freedom Riders

Outside of Brown vs. Board of Education Supreme Court Rulings in 1954-55, the Nonviolent movement after the Montgomery Bus Boycott in 1956, continued to meet ever increasing the number, and sometimes often deadly attacks by Segregationists groups. As 1961 began, one of the most-violent attacks is yet to come, aimed specifically to those persons who volunteered, Black, White and indifferent, who chose to become willing participants in such campaigns. The Freedom Riders became that target.

The idea of the Freedom Riders came in early 1961 when CORE and SNCC teamed up to force integration on interstate travel. As part of the overall **"Freedom Summer"** campaign, the objective of the rides was to protest racial segregation at bus stations and waiting rooms throughout the South. The riders themselves were to defy both De Jure and De Facto Segregation in the Border states and through the South, by riding on Greyhound and Trailways buses chartered specifically to carry the riders, who were integrated by seating. Blacks sat with Whites, White sat with Blacks etc. Despite what the Bus Boycott did in Montgomery Alabama, that protest did nothing for the South in general. They still followed the **"Separate but Equal"** rule on Interstate travel. CORE and SNCC wanted to break through that system, region wide.

The first Freedom Ride took place on a Greyhound bus on April 22, 1961, departing East St. Louis, Illinois with the destination of Sikeston, Missouri. There were 18 CORE members who took this trip, to include CORE's leader James Farmer, future-Congressman, CPUSA card-carrying member and Civil Rights Activist John Lewis, future-Environmentalist and Feminist Genevieve Hughes, future-Greenpeace activist Albert Smith Bigelow and high-ranking CORE member and former U.S. Marine Corps/Korean War Veteran Edward "Ed" Blankenheim.

What the riders did not expect, when they publicly announced the rides this early in the campaign, was the resistance that they faced. Not counting all the White Southeast Missouri Segregationists who lined the route of the trip, and there were many, found out when they arrived at the Sikeston Bus Station. Of the 18 "Freedom Riders", 15 of them were arrested for protesting after being refused service at the station's restaurant. After being arrested and beaten with police sticks and fists by the Sikeston Missouri Department of Public Safety (DPS), jailed and fined heavily for their actions, some of the CORE riders began to question the risks involved in conducting such rides. One of the CORE members asked that;

"if bus protests end in arrests in Missouri, what can be expected when Freedom Rides get to Georgia and points South?"

It wasn't going to take long for that question to be answered.

To further prove what Dr. King was talking about in 1965 and to provide the answer of one of the riders arrested in Sikeston, Missouri, the notion that the Nonviolent protests were about provoking violence by those in opposition to racial integration, was going occur between May 4 and May 22, 1961.

Two buses, one Greyhound, and one Trailways bus left the Washington D.C. terminal, heading south, destination New Orleans, Louisiana. Onboard these buses, 13 Freedom Riders sat (seven Black, Six Whites) to include CORE's President James Farmer, Genevieve Hughes, ranking-member of SNCC William E. Barbour, John Lewis and Ed Blankenheim.

A group of buses and "Freedom Riders" leaving New York City heading down South in protesting Segregation on Inter-state travel in 1962.

(Courtesy of Wikimedia)

The plan called for the ride to go through the states of Virginia, the Carolinas, Georgia, Alabama, Mississippi and ending in New Orleans Louisiana. The riders, once they reached New Orleans, they were going to participate in a Civil Rights rally planned there. However, the trip took a lot longer than they, the riders could ever imagine.

When driving, and stopping in Virginia, only minor trouble was encountered, in the forms of insults and swear words. The buses continued their travel into North Carolina, where some of the Freedom Riders were arrested in Charlotte for violating the interstate travel laws and segregation policies.

It's worth to mention here, that as the buses began to lose freedom rider passengers, more freedom ride passengers were waiting to take the place of those number of men and women, Black or White, were there to take their place. A carefully, crafted and calculated plan.

When the buses reached Rock Hill, South Carolina, John Lewis and some other Freedom Riders were beaten by White Segregationists in Rock Hill, South Carolina. Still, other Riders were beaten and arrested when the buses came to stop at Winnsboro, South Carolina. However, the biggest assault by White Segregationists was about to come, as the buses traveled further South into "Dixie".

At the head of this soon-to-be big assault on the Freedom Riders would be no other than the man himself, Birmingham Alabama Police Commissioner and Democrat Politician Eugene "Bull" O'Connor. Together with Ku Klux Klan supporter and member, Sergeant Timothy "Tim" Cook, both worked with the region's KKK organizations to coordinate a planned ambush-style attack on both buses. The plan called for one attack in Anniston, Alabama and another one in Birmingham.

The plan also called for the attempt to disable the buses in some form or fashion, take the Freedom Riders off the buses and attack them brutally to send a message to the nation, that such protest rides will not be tolerated in the South; especially in Alabama. Lastly, the plan called for the police not to respond to the attacks for 15 minutes once the beatings occurred.

As the Greyhound bus began to leave Anniston, a mob of White Segregationists began to surround the bus and tried to prevent it from leaving the station. The mob then began to slash the tires of the bus with knives, damaging its tires.

The bus, despite the damage, got through the mob, drove for a couple of miles and stopped, as the bus couldn't drive anymore on the slashed threads. Then, another group of Klansmen began to attack the bus, using Molotov Cocktails which were thrown through the windows of the bus, setting the vehicle afire.

As the Freedom Riders began to flee through the front door, Klansmen barricaded the door to prevent the passengers from escaping, trying to murder them by burning them alive. After one of the gas tanks exploded on the bus, the Klansmen unbarricaded the doors and the passengers began to rapidly escape the carnage, even though they were being beaten and kicked by the Klansmen prior to law enforcement and fire departments intervened on the situation. Luckily, no one was severely injured, but they were shocked and frightened as to what happened.

They were lucky.

Photo of the bombing of the Freedom Rider Bus outside of Anniston, Alabama in 1962. (Courtesy of Library of Congress)

The next assault was in Birmingham when the Trailways bus pulled into the bus terminal and all-hell broke loose. As the Freedom Riders exited the bus, Klansmen armed with baseball bats, iron pipes and bicycle chains savagely began to beat with such veracity, that many of the riders had to be hospitalized. Reporters at scene witnessing the attacks were beaten as well and their equipment was destroyed.

The beatings that these riders suffered were so brutal, one of the White Freedom Riders had to have over 50 stitches placed in his head. As the report of the attack reached the White House in Washington, D.C. President John F. Kennedy and his brother, Attorney General Robert F. Kennedy, the latter called CORE, SNCC, and SCLS to begin "cooling off period" of such demonstrations, because of the terror that the Segregationists were imposing on the riders.

Of course, this was during the Cold War, when Soviet Russia under President Nikita Khrushchev, along with its propagandized media touting "**racist America**". The Kennedy Administration was simultaneously receiving hundreds of letters and phone calls from the local Black populations where the Freedom Riders and Nonviolent Demonstrations were occurring, stating that they were receiving a domino-effect violence from White Segregationists long after the so-called "civil rights leaders" have left the area. **The latter complaint, had the Black Community fed up both the "Civil Rights" agitators and the White Segregationists, to the point where they were going to take the law into their own hands, using violence with violence.**

That was the whole idea of the American Civil Rights Movement; to cause anarchy no matter what the price was, including the taking of innocent lives, long after the Marxist Agitators have left the scene of action.

Their job as to also ferment racial division, among everyone, using actual legitimate grievances of the Black Community, to create a civil war to bring the country into crisis and install Socialism, which in the words of Charles E. Smith of the John Birch Society in 1970 "Communism follows Socialism, like night follows day."

Again, Ella Baker, founder of SNCC and by the time of the Freedom Rides commenced, she became Executive Secretary of the Southern Conference Education Fund (SCEF). SCEF was already labeled by HUAC in 1958 after they changed names to the current one, as a Communist front group, so while she served in that capacity, Ms. Baker has been quoting for saying this;

"Remember, we are not just fighting for the freedom of the Negro alone, but for the freedom of the human spirit, a larger freedom that encompasses all mankind."

Think about that. Understand the irony. The entire American Civil Rights Movement was not, and in-reality has not been a movement to free Blacks from the institution of "Separate but Equal" accommodations, but to create so-called freedom of all mankind, under the veil of "Equality" and "Civil Rights"; using Black bodies as sacrificial lambs in the process! The entire operation was funded by Soviet Russia and American Marxist Men, to overthrow the U.S. Government and instill Communism in the United States of America!

Remember, by 1961, every Civil Rights organization was being operated, funded and driven by the Communist International (COMINTERN) in Moscow, CPUSA in Chicago, NAACP in New York, with training at the Highland Folk School in Monteagle Tennessee. From there, funding was being secured for such agitation campaigns via the **Ford Foundation**, the **Rockefeller Foundation**, the **Milton S. Eisenhower Foundation** and Marxist Men donations from subverted Marxist-Leninists like Saul Alinsky, James Dombrowski, Abner Berry and Noam Chomsky to name a few.

This money has changed hands through organizations like the Southern Regional Council (SRC), to the Southern Conference Educational Fund (SCEF), to the Southern Christian Leadership Conference (SCLC), the Student Nonviolence Coordinating Committee (SNCC), and the Congress of Racial Equality (CORE).

Other large groups of participants of the Nonviolence movement during the Civil Rights era were the Mississippi Freedom Democratic Party (MFDP), the Council of Federated Organizations (COFO), the Regional Council of Negro Leadership (RCNL) and hundreds of other groups, containing thousands of people either willingly or not-willingly knowing what they were doing, will eventually enslave them all.

This is just one of four-separate factions. The next faction had so much influence and publicity during the era, that many of the tactics are being seen today, by Communist front groups such as Black Lives Matter (BLM) movement and the New Black Panther Party (NBPP).

Revolutionary Groups: The Black Power Movement

Black Panther Black Power Symbol.

Former Russian Dictator Vladimir Lenin once stated;

"Riots, demonstrations-street battles-detachments of a revolutionary army-such are the stages in the development of the popular uprising."

~ 317 ~

This is the fundamental core and the ultimate-goal of instilling full-Communism into a country like the United States of America; by creating a violent revolution.

The perception which Communists want everybody to believe during the troubling-time of the 1960's and, as in 2017, was to use the media, the churches, the schools and the unions, to agitate the masses to control public opinion.

They do this with the absolute intent to manipulate the outcomes of such agitation campaigns to their liking. Remember from the previous chapters, that Karl Marx, despite him being convinced by Socialists, that the "Almighty State", which is suppose-to wither away, he concluded that a violent revolution between the Proletariat and the Bourgeois classes is unavoidable as was inevitable. So, one has to ask, what is the best and efficient way to foment a Communist Revolution here in the United States? The simple answer is this. Marxist Men will;

1. *Take an actual tragic situation or grievance, make it appear to be 100-times bigger than what the situation really is,*

2. *Dump raw-human emotions into the mix, create the impression a developing crisis,*

3. *Fan the flames of such emotional-driven anger, hate, and discontent if front of the media by design,*

4. *Then call for government intervention to stop it*

Sound familiar? It is the same concept over-and-over again, but the way such sensitive issues are exploited and packaged as such, changes.

Just like the Nonviolent faction of the Civil Rights Movement, this same concept in which Dr. King had outlined in 1965, was also the blueprint for the Violent faction of the movement. If one was to look at the historical record objectively, after the Nonviolent protests conducted by SCLC, SNCC and other groups, you never have seen nor read anything about mass-riots in the streets of major metro cities of America until about 1965, right?

Wonder why?

Minus a bit of overlap in dates and times as to when the call went out into the public, to start what was called "a violent revolution" via "Black Power", a-quite-of-bit of planning must have to be accomplished first and considered in-order for the outcome to be effective enough to manipulate public opinion and support the cause. To understand this concept, of evil and obvious manipulation of facts pertaining to real events, one just have to look at the definition of planning in a business sense. After all, to create a revolution in a country like the United States, it has become an often-profitable business to do such acts. The business definition of Planning is;

"A basic management function involving the formulation of one or more detailed plans to achieve the optimum balance of needs or demands with available resources. The Planning process [Includes] (1) identifies the goals or objectives to be achieved, (2) formulates strategies to achieve them, (3) arrange or creates the means required, and (4) implements, directs, and monitors all steps in their proper sequence."

Once Dr. King's Southern Christian Leadership Conference (SCLC), (CORE) headed by James Farmer, (SNCC), and other groups were conducting Sit-ins, Freedom Rides and Nonviolent protests to integrate schools to include the conduction of voter registration drives in the South, the phase of training and planning was already being conducted for the next phase of the so-called "*revolution*".

The story will begin in the great state of North Carolina with an unknown figure in Black History and American History in general. His name is Robert F. Williams.

Robert F. Williams, former President of the Monroe, North Carolina chapter of the NAACP

In May 1961.

(Courtesy of Wikimedia/King Archives)

Not many people in the United States of America, Black White or in different ever heard of the name of **Robert Williams**. Unless you have been a student or a researcher of history, no one teaches that Williams became the first African-American to teach and physically use violence as an answer to the White Segregationists violence against Black Americans, long before the Black Panther Party and other organizations existed, regardless whether Nation of Islam Spokesman Malcolm X preached it.

Unfortunately, despite what has been taught in the public education system, most of the African-American Community agreed mostly with William's type of answer to the race problem than those of Dr. Martin Luther King Jr.

Robert Franklin Williams was born on February 26, 1925, in Monroe, North Carolina, a small community just southeast of the major city of Charlotte to Emma (Carter) Williams and John L. Williams. His Father was a railroad boiler washer and his Paternal Grandmother was a former Slave, named Isabel (Tomberlin) Williams.

It was William's Grandmother and Grandfather who gave Robert his first rifle at a young age and inspired him to become like his Grandfather. The gun was owned by his Grandfather, Sykes Williams, who was a staunch Republican Campaigner and Publisher of the Newspaper "*The People's Voice*", who had defended himself against White Supremacists for decades because of his passion for uplifting the Black population and his love for American-way of life.

By the age of 18, Williams has seen a lot for his age. Seven-years earlier, he had witnessed police brutality by a White Segregationist Cop, who was beating a Black Woman in public with no remorse. Between 1940-1943, he migrated to Detroit Michigan and witnessed riots and civil unrest because of labor disputes between newly arriving Blacks from the South who were trying to fill the jobs that Whites of the North refuse to give them.

He was drafted in 1944 and served at Camp Johnson, Marine Corps Base, then-outside of the main Marine Corps Base of Camp Lejeune, North Carolina, where he was discharged after serving in Korea in 1955.

Once he returned to his hometown, he went and joined the local NAACP Chapter in Monroe, which at this time, had a population of about 10,882, about ½ of the population being almost even between Whites and Blacks. Williams, along with Dr. Albert E. Perry, local Black Physician, and NAACP Vice-President, re-worked the local chapter's membership and recruitment efforts and their numbers began to swell in membership.

Once that was accomplished, in 1957 Williams led efforts to integrate the areas public swimming pools, using Nonviolence demonstration. White Segregationists counter-protested and someone fired a shot, but no one on either side was hit, even though the city's police were in the area. After hearing rumors around the Black Community and gather some information from the White Community, Monroe began to enlarge their KKK Chapter as well. With a population of just under 11,000 in 1960, some estimated that well over 7,000 were members of the Klan.

This fact put Williams on notice and he applied to the **National Rifle Association (NRA)** to charter a local rifle club in Monroe exclusively for Blacks. He was granted the charter and named the Monroe Chapter of the NRA the *"**Black Armed Guard**"*, and had a membership between 50-60 men and women to include his wife Mabel and former military veterans.

When the NAACP National Board of Directors were notified about Williams being granted a charter by the NRA for a Gun Club, they assumed that he was advocating for violence, in which the NAACP publicly acknowledged that they don't support violence as the means of desegregating the South. The board censured Williams for his conduct, which didn't go well in the eyes of either Williams or the local chapter. He explicitly told the NAACP Headquarters in New York City, that his Gun Club was for self-defense only.

He also told them that he does not want to declare a war with the White Racists and opposed such actions. When Williams began to make his intentions public, his NAACP Chapter began to receive thousands of weapons of almost every kind and monetary support from other across the country, both rich, poor and famous persons as well, to continue to operate his gun club there. Soon afterward, his name was about to be put in the spotlight.

Robert Williams Spotlight as a Black Nationalist/Red Communist

Outside of the state of North Carolina's debacle, which accumulated into what was called "**The Kissing Case**", Williams really became popular in August of 1961 during the beginning of CORE's Freedom Rides. At the beginning of that year, the fiery NAACP leader was censured by the NAACP National Board of Directors in New York City once again, for his public outcry of "meeting violence-with-violence" rhetoric, which went against the Nonviolent principles of the NAACP organization itself.

Williams responded back to the board, that since there have been numerous attempts on his life, by the larger-in-number Ku Klux Klan organization, he was only going to meet such attacks for "self-defense purposes". He also made it clear to the board, that that the Federal Government refused to protect his community from constant racial attacks on the Black Community, so he encouraged them to do the same thing he was done against the White Segregationists; defending themselves.

In his book, written while he was in exile in the Castro Brothers Cuba, Williams wrote;

"Racists consider themselves superior beings and are not willing to exchange their superior lives for our inferior ones. They are most vicious and violent when they can practice violence with impunity."

Williams further wrote;

"It has always been an accepted right of Americans, as the history of our Western states proves, that where the law is unable, or unwilling, to enforce order, the citizens can, and must act in self-defense against lawless violence."

As Williams and his NAACP chapter continued their civil rights protests when the city itself became one of the battle grounds of the Freedom Ride Campaign. In Early August 1961, CORE sent a contingent of "Freedom Riders" into Monroe, who were to replace the riders that were already on the bus when it stopped in the city. CORE also decided to test the Freedom Ride Campaign right into the heart of Monroe, North Carolina as a destination stop, against objections from the National Board of the NAACP. Williams and group quickly gave the Freedom Ride guests hospitality when they arrived in Monroe. Then both organizations began to protest in solidarity of the Freedom Ride Campaign, located outside of the Union County, North Carolina Courthouse (in which Monroe was the county's seat). On August 17, the first buses arrived in the city and all-hell broke loose on the riders by the local police.

As a matter of fact, the Freedom Riders were brutally attacked with bats, pipes, clubs, chains and even pistol-whipped with the butts of guns by Klansmen, under orders of the police. On August 27, CORE's leader James Farmer was brutally attacked that day and was knocked unconscious when one of the attackers hit him with the butt of a rifle, prior to being taken to jail, along with other riders and demonstrators. Later-on that day, Police and Klansmen formed roaming vigilantes and began to shoot at any African-Americans who they came across.

They even went into the Black Neighborhood, shooting at anything that moved, burning crosses on residents' lawns, while yelling and cursing at the residents. What the group did not expect, was a violent response in return. Blacks of Monroe were in a virtual shootout with Klansmen of Monroe, making the town a virtual war zone.

During the entire summer, Williams had armed every resident with handguns, rifles, semi-automatic and fully-automatic weapons. During the melee of gunfire, loud back-in-forth yelling and swearing between both parties, an old White couple who was not from the Monroe, North Carolina area were driving through the city, when they got caught up in one of the detours that local police had set up earlier in the day, that led them straight through the Black section of Monroe.

As the gunfire subsided a bit, the elderly couple drove smack into an angry crowd, who surrounded their car. A handful of NAACP members made their way through the crowd, got the couple out and away from the melee for their safety and brought them to William's house.

However, the angry crowd was looking for some revenge, especially since the crowd was all African-Americans and they were still in a shootout with Klansmen. Williams knew that the couple would have been beaten badly by the angry mob if he would have let them go right away. He did offer the couple that they can go free immediately, but only when it was safe for them to leave the area. In the meantime, Williams and a few other NAACP members quickly took the couple to another safe house nearby, so they could leave the Black neighborhood safely without harm, which they did almost an hour later.

It didn't take long for word to spread to authorities about what had happened to the Elderly White Couple that Williams and his NAACP members saved. As facts began to spin out of control, the authorities began to charge him and his wife, Mable Williams, with kidnapping the elderly White couple and immediately called Governor Luther H. Hodges for them to use the state militia.

The FBI was called as well and they issued a warrant for his arrest hours later. In the meantime, Robert Williams, his wife Mabel and their two children quickly packed up and left Monroe quickly. Feared that he would be lynched once the state militia arrived, he fled the state and took a chartered plane two days later to the island of Cuba, from Quebec Canada, via Mexico to seek refuge.

NAACP lawyers, immediately in the following days of William's departure, began a frenzy to de-escalate the situation as soon as possible. The Lawyers, led by NAACP Civil Rights Lawyer Conrad Lynn told the jailed Freedom Riders not to practice their "Jail-no Bail" mantra in Monroe, for fear of their lives if they remained in the county jail. Amazingly, the local law enforcement, after seeing the entire Black Community come together and defend themselves against the Klansmen with guns and ammunition, wanted the de-escalate the situation too.

During the Freedom Riders' court hearing, the Judge found the riders guilty of trespassing and violating segregation laws of the state of North Carolina, but immediately suspended their sentences, except one person. John Lowry, one of the Freedom Riders and Mae Malloy, an associate of the local NAACP chapter, went to trial for assisting Williams for so-called "kidnapping" the elderly White couple who they saved from certain danger. Both Lowry and Mallory received lengthy prison sentences, in 1962, which they each served less than three years. In 1965, their convictions were vacated due to the exclusion of Blacks from their jury trial selection.

The Rise of the Black Power/Black Liberation Movement

Once Robert Williams fled the country and sought exile in Cuba in 1961, it was here where he and his wife began their conversion to accept the Marxist-Leninist ideology, and began to politicize the next phase of the American Civil Rights Movement.

Prior to William's arrival in Cuba, other Caribbean nations/territories have been inundated by Marxist-Leninist Ideology as well. This was done via Soviet KGB Agents and their subverted dupes who underwent Marxist training at the Lenin School in Moscow, just like the duped Americans had done in the past. The goal of these countries was, of course, to psychologically subvert their population of people into accepting, Socialism/Communism. Places such as Central America, Mexico, South American countries of Brazil and Argentina, conducted such successful conversion operations in their quest to encapsulate the rest of the world around the United States and make her that final target to complete their worldwide revolution.

Seeing Williams as an opportunity to spread Marxist-Leninist propaganda, via racial division, they made him and his family's life as comfortable as possible on the island. The plan was to use the Williams' as exploitation value of his new views of Marxist-Leninism, broadcast those new views of instilling an American Revolution.

While in Cuba, he pinned his popular book **Negroes with Guns** published in 1962. Under both Fidel and Raul Castro, Robert Williams was given a radio broadcast program, called "**Radio Free Dixie**", where he condemned the Nonviolence Agitators of the Civil Rights Movement as "**_ineffective_**" in the overall struggle of the Black race. He urged African-American military personnel stationed throughout the South, that while being armed, it's their only chance to become free to stop people like the White Segregationists for treating them "worse than dogs."

As revenge against the Kennedy Administration's failure, to oust the Castro Brothers via the failed "Bay of Pigs" Invasion, President Fidel Castro gave Williams' their own published newspaper to smuggle into the United States called **The Crusader**.

CPUSA saw this as a stab in the back, as to why Williams was given a more broader propaganda campaign audience than they had ever dreamed of since 1918! This had caused some tension in the relationship between Williams and CPUSA's head Gus Hall, which has been written by The Crusader's Chief Editor via Conrad Lynn in May 1964;

> "...the U.S.C.P. {U.S. Communist Party} has openly come out against my position on the Negro struggle. In fact, the party has sent special representatives here to sabotage my work on behalf of the U.S. Negro liberation. They are pestering the Cubans to remove me from the radio, ban THE CRUSADER and to take a number of other steps in what they call 'cutting Williams down to size'...."

Apparently, the excuse that CPUSA had admitted in private meetings and conversations, explained that the strained relationship between them and the fiery Williams in Cuba, was this; they feared that Williams's message was becoming **too effective** in its purpose to support an equally violent revolutionary movement. In other words, they couldn't control Williams. They, CPUSA, wanted all the glory and be the main force behind the destruction of the United States of America; not Williams.

Of course, they did not admit this in public, it was only discussed behind closed doors.

However, what the Communist Party **did** admit to the public, was that Williams's broadcasted rhetoric of Blacks fighting back against White Segregationists with guns was going to divide the 'working class' in the U.S. along 'racial lines'. This is laughable to say the least because the **_whole idea of subversion_** to install Socialism/Communism was to **_divide people along racial lines_** in first place, then create some type of civil war between them!

Gus Hall had to be in shock, to the point where CPUSA was willing to take out Williams's radio program and discredit his newspaper editorials, as Williams explains in his letter to cut him down to size. Nobody outside of CPUSA were to be better propagandists unless they came straight from them. Since Williams's messages were having a desired result within the American Black Community, and CPUSA couldn't control him, they had to do something about it. Some have noticed, that as Blacks throughout the South and even in the Northern industrial cities were using guns and ammunition to fight back White Segregationists, that the segregationists themselves began to dramatically cut back in their blatant acts of violence against the Black Community.

Robert Williams, in the same May 1964 letter, mentioned this to Conrad Lynn;

"The whole thing is due to the fact that I absolutely refuse to take direction from Gus Hall's idiots…"

This meant that regardless as to what the Communist Party were trying to do to destroy or discredit Williams, he was still going to fight against CPUSA whether-or-not they liked it or not.

Between 1965 and September 1969, Robert and Mabel Williams left Communist Cuba and settled in Communist China (dubbed 'The People's Republic of China'), then being ruled by the ruthless Chinese Dictator Mao Zedong. Between the year, he lived in China and 1967, **Williams became a Propagandist for Chairman Mao and traveled to Hanoi, Vietnam numerous times where he advocated violence against "Imperialistic America". He made public speeches to the North Vietnamese Army (NVA) and the Vietnamese Guerillas (Viet Cong), urging them to kill American soldiers in South Vietnam, because of the U.S. onslaught of the country.**

By 1969, with a new U.S. Presidential Administration, Republican/Socialist Richard M. Nixon, began to warm relations with the Red Chinese and eventually, making them a part of the United Nations in 1972.

Robert and his Wife Mabel, returned to the United States in Detroit Michigan, were arrested and immediately extradited to his native North Carolina. After much legal rambling, delays, and technicalities, Robert and his wife went on trial in December 1975 for the kidnapping charges of the Elderly White couple in Monroe 14 years earlier. Both were acquitted of the charges by the state of North Carolina and they returned to Michigan, where Robert died at the age of 71 of Hodgkin's Lymphoma on October 15, 1996.

Second, after the dramatic media spectacle to make a martyr out of the murder of NAACP Mississippi Field Secretary Medgar Evers on June 12, 1963, followed by the bombing of the 16th Street Baptist Church in Birmingham Alabama September 15, that killed four little Black girls and wounding 22 others, caused many to wonder what good had the Nonviolent protests done for the Black Community?

Other than causing a backlash of violence which caused the needless death and injuries of innocent people going about their everyday lives, which has the Nonviolent movement done overall? Some people in the Black Communities throughout the South began to ask that very question. Some of them began to voice their displeasure with the Civil Rights Leaders such as Dr. King, in the local newspapers, Television and on the public stage. One of the largest and most vocal critics of Dr. King and his cadre of Civil Rights leaders was none other than Nation of Islam Spokesman Malcolm X. In 1963, Malcolm X stated his dislike of Dr. King's Nonviolence demonstrations;

"The only revolution based on loving your enemy is the Negro Revolution...That's no revolution!"

In a letter, dated July 31, 1963, written by Malcolm X addressed to Dr. King, Malcolm proposed to him that a conference should be formed, that consisted of every faction of the Negro people, either leading or participating the Civil Rights Movement. The objective of such round table of men and women were to sit down and rationally discuss the 'race problem' and come up with solutions to solve it. In that letter, Malcolm X wrote;

"If Capitalistic Kennedy and Communistic Khrushchev can find something in common on which to form a united front despite their tremendous ideological differences, it is a disgrace for Negro leaders not to be able to submerge our "minor" differences in order to seek a common solution to a common problem posed by a <u>common</u> <u>enemy</u>."

Unfortunately, Dr. King did not consider such advice of Malcolm X to create a conference of Black leaders because he himself knew that the original purpose of the Nonviolence demonstrations in the South was not to solve the 'race problem', but to ratchet up the racial division between people and instill Socialism. Besides Malcolm X and Robert Williams, there were many other Black Americans, in the North and South, who more aligned themselves with the ideology of Malcolm X and Robert Williams, than Martin Luther King.

This belief even transcended down to the local level also. However, there was one person would not have his name placed in the halls of American History as a fighter for Civil Rights in America. The latter person did not have the large public audience or major mainstream media like Malcolm or Williams, but he did have a large following inside his own community. His name was Perry Smaw.

Perry Smaw was born in March 1879 in Hollow Square, Hale County, Alabama. He made his living as a Farmer, marrying his wife Sophia "Sophie" (Mcalpin) Smaw in March 1898 and raised a large family of 11 children. Fast-forward to 1965. Perry Smaw began to see what the Nonviolent faction of the Civil Rights Movement really was; to intentionally cause trouble for the local Black population, once their so-called "desegregation" protests were done and completed. Seeing such protests happening in the area he lived in and raised his family for decades in downtown Greenville, Butler County, Alabama. For months, he adamantly spoke out against such Communist Agitators who were hiding behind the veil of African-American Civil Rights in the local newspapers, community meetings and inside local churches.

Smaw's message was so attractive to the local Black Communities surrounding nearby Montgomery Alabama, that Marxist-Men sent their dupes to silence Mr. Smaw, permanently. One night in August 1965, while he was at home, Perry Smaw was assaulted by an intruder that broke into his small, wooden home.

The assailant told Smaw that he was sent to the old man's house to cut his tongue out. As a struggle between them ensued, the 86-year-old Smaw was head in the head with a cast-iron frying pan, so hard and with so much force, that the handle of the pan broke off. As Perry Smaw was clinging to life, the intruder pulled the old man's tongue out and cut it with a butcher's knife that was so sharp, that his tongue to cut all the way back to the Perry Smaw's tonsils!

Smaw survived the attack and was alive for five-days until he succumbed to his wounds on August 25, 1965. An investigation was conducted to search for Perry Smaw's killer, who has left the area. It has been speculated, with a nearly 95% accuracy, that Black Civil Rights members, who of course were Marxist-trained dupes, who themselves a member a part of CPUSA's many networks of splinter groups, ordered Perry Smaw killed, because he too became *too* effective in calling out the hypocrisy of the leaders of the Civil Rights Movement.

In the minds of CPUSA, they have done the pretty-damn good job by waging a consistent drive of major agitation campaigns, of Bus Boycotts, Sit-ins and Freedom Rides. They have conducted these campaigns, despite the needless death and destruction of innocent people caught in the crossfire, between the protestors and the segregationists.

Ideally, the Communist Party could care less if such domino-effect of White Segregationists violence was caused by their "Civil Rights Leaders", in-order to divide the races even further, using the Black bodies to become mentally enslaved to do their bidding. They call that *"the end justifies the means"*.

By 1964, as the Nonviolent protests began to draw up its final plans to form a much larger and bigger march, between the cities of Selma and Montgomery Alabama, organizers of the march, led by the likes of the Southern Christian Leadership Conference (SCLC), SNCC, NAACP and other groups, the first faction of the Civil Rights Movement were well on its way to complete their first objective (first phase) in transforming America, by forcing the Federal Government to intervene.

That came later-on the same year when in September, the *Civil Rights Act of 1964* was signed into law by President Johnson and Dr. Martin Luther King won the prestigious *Nobel Peace Prize*. However, no matter how successful the splinter groups of the Communist Party were in their attempt to transform the American Government, from a representative Republic into a Socialist/Communist satellite country, CPUSA had another obstacle to breach.

One person's actions, Robert Williams, continued to hamper Gus Hall's Marxist Men and their efforts to carry out their next pre-planned mission too prematurely. Remember, in Marxist ideology, opportunity, and timing to conduct subversion operations is very important to create a revolution inside the United States. What men like Malcolm X, Robert Williams and people such as Perry Smaw have done, would have had CPUSA's diabolical scheme and plans regarding their true intentions of waging the Civil Rights Movement would have been blown wide open!

If that situation did occur, not only exposure of their real intent would compromise future operations concerning their implementation of Socialism, but CPUSA's tentacles of front groups will become publicly discredited. Therefore, no one in the American population would even trust them anymore, causing failure.

Marxist-Men never consider themselves as failures, no matter what the costs may be in prevent such an incident to happen. However, it is quite-obvious to note, that the Communist Party wasn't ready to implement Phase Two of their plan to subvert America to accept Communism, via a violent revolution, because they were still managing the outcome of phase one, the Nonviolent revolution!

Inspiration for Black Power Revolutionaries

During the same timeframe that Robert Williams and his family fled to nearby Cuba, bubbling under the surface out of the view of public scrutiny, CPUSA were training violent revolutionary activists, at the Lincoln School in Chicago, the Lenin School in Moscow and at the Highlander Folk School/Research and Education Center in Tennessee for **Phase Two**.

Persons being trained at these Marxist/Community Organizing facilities were being mentally subverted in Marxist-Leninist ideology to rage an internal civil war against the federal government. These students made up the core factions of Black and White Revolutionaries, which will be discussed in the following chapters. Once these activists training was complete, they were to go onto college campuses nationwide, or in the streets of the inner cities, to ferment hate and discontent of the American system, to dupe others to follow along with them and began to overthrow the U.S. Government power structure at its base. Their main objective is to physically conduct and carry-out an actual violent revolution on American soil. During this phase of the Civil Rights Movement, new groups were successfully formed, becoming additional tentacles of CPUSA and COMINTERN.

Their goal was to use a multitude of small-arm weapons, bombs, civil disobedience and inner-city riots to force their will on society to accept Socialism/Communism. Even though these groups still used the same-old rhetoric in the public eye, that they were "*organic in nature*" and had "*grassroots*" participation of many in the population.

In other words, such groups in Phase Two did the standard Communist practice; create the public perception that a significant portion of the American people supported their cause when in-reality they didn't.

Using the mainstream media to push these lies and deception, these revolutionary groups pushed their agenda to openly advocate that the Capitalist system was filled with systematic racism, chauvinism, homophobic tendencies and they reject the "American way" of life.

These groups made the argument, that by overthrowing such an unfair political system and replace it with Socialism, eventually Communism, that these social-economic systems would make everything ***fair and equal***.

These activists were subverted to believe that under Socialism/Communism, there would be no racial bigotry, class differences and everybody will work for the community and not for themselves.

Sounds familiar?

On top of this, these stupid, blind and rationally inept glorious revolutionaries were still hiding under the disguise of Civil Rights for Blacks, in-order to justify their heinous actions. Phase Two of CPUSA's plan were sub-divided into six-different sub-groups;

> *Black Nationalists*
>
> *Black Separatists Groups*
>
> *Black Power Groups*
>
> *Afrocentric*
>
> *Black Supremacy Groups*
>
> *Black Anarchists Groups*

Black Nationalists and *Black Separatists* are ideologically different. ***Black Nationalists*** follows the principles outlined by Martin R. Delaney, who advocate for Black Self-Determination, racial pride, justice, and identity.

On the other hand, ***Black Separatists*** consider themselves hindered in advancement in American society by a White majority. **Their ideology is simple to understand; those African-Americans who**

believe that in-order for their people to advance in society, they have to separate themselves from White society. Both physically and geographically.

In other words, they want to segregate themselves away from other races and culture. Black Separatists preaches that Blacks should have their own nation, "***within a nation***" {sounds familiar} for themselves. Separatists want their own so-called Soviet Negro Republic per se.

Black Power Groups practice and preaches Black pride in oneself, within the black community, within the culture, within societal advancement, and in Black family values. To explain Black Power in two words, those words are "**Black Autonomy**".

Afrocentric Groups believe in a similar ideology like Black Power, with the exception that groups who consider themselves Afrocentric, align themselves with the people and culture in Africa. Such alignment includes various African Tribal history, their diets, embracing their culture, heritage, spirit and their struggles.

On the other end of the spectrum, you have African-American groups who consider themselves powerful revolutionaries who consider themselves the supreme beings on Earth. Called ***Black Supremacists***, one can look at such groups as the opposite of White Supremacy Groups, such as the Ku Klux Klan, Skinheads, and other groups.

Black Supremacy Groups consider themselves as superior to all other races and culture!

This includes Blacks who are ***not*** a part of them. These groups are not ashamed to let the entire world know what their objective is.

Finally, we have ***Black Anarchism***. These are dangerous groups that came out of the American Civil Rights Movement who strictly follows Marxist-Leninist ideology to a T. Black Anarchists oppose the very existence of the "**Almighty State**", just as Karl Marx did over 160-years before. They favor a non-hierarchical society who argues for the class struggle, against racism and oppression brought about the Bourgeoisie society.

Malcolm X, along with the militant radical Leftist Robert Williams, became heroes to these new Black and White Revolutionaries towards the end of the 1960's. With the war in Vietnam took place in Southeast Asia, where President Kennedy, then afterward, President Johnson, increased the U.S. Military involvement there, the U.S. had been wrapped up in a constant string of emotional turmoil for several years.

Add-on the Civil Rights Movement which was being transformed from Nonviolent protests, into a violent one, the geopolitical environment inside the United States became ripe to exploit the American people's emotions at face value by the Communist Party. This violence and revolution have just begun, which will remain constant for the next 10-years ending well into the late 1970's.

The second conflagration of Phase Two of the so-called "**Black Revolutionaries**" began in a small little mid-Atlantic community, named Cambridge Maryland. Nestled on the Eastern Shore in the state of Maryland on the east bank of the Chesapeake Bay, the city at that time had about 12,000 citizens and was the county seat of Dorchester County. The actions that occurred in the years 1963 and 1967, would both determine the new route where the Civil Rights Movement was heading and the latter would help define what the Civil Rights Movement was about; Federal Government Intervention.

Gloria Richardson, a resident of Cambridge and a recent graduate from Howard University in nearby Washington D.C., became indoctrinated in Marxist-Leninist ideology while attending school there. After graduation, with a Bachelor's Degree in Sociology, she returned to her hometown, to become a community activist for SNCC, the Communist organization who began to drop their nonviolent stance and advocate for a radicalized, Marxist revolutionary stance on Black race issues, after the Freedom Ride debacle.

Photo of Gloria Richardson, head of the Cambridge Action Movement in 1962. (Courtesy of Vanderbilt University)

Richardson created the Cambridge Action Movement (CAM) in 1962, whose goal was to desegregate businesses and public places in the city. It is worth noting that in the early 1960's, Cambridge Maryland like many cities in the surrounding state, to include the major metropolitan area of Baltimore, where following De Facto Segregation practices, where racial discrimination wasn't written by law but followed instead by society-as-a-whole.

As a matter of fact, one of Cambridge's Black Aldermen rejected Richardson's complaint that there was major racial segregation in the city. Many of the city's councilmen told her "that most of everything here in Cambridge was integrated, and nobody complained to me about anything usual". Apparently, he didn't get the picture of what Ms. Richardson was really trying to accomplish. He failed to grasp that it wasn't about helping Blacks gain freedom, but instead, agitate the situation enough to allow the Federal Government to become involved and regulate everything in-regards to human activity, yes even in Cambridge Maryland.

Richardson began to organize protests in front of business establishments, such as restaurants and convenience stores using Blacks residing in Cambridge and outside protestors from Baltimore, from the Suburbs Washington D.C. and from within the city of Washington D.C. itself. Their intention was to, of course, instigate trouble between law enforcement and the protestors to create the illusion that it was the Police who protected these segregated businesses from poor Blacks who wanted to patronize them.

Similar as to what Karl Marx has said about law and order; that police and laws were designed to protect the Bourgeoisie' wealth from the Proletariat. As designed, many of these protests ended in arrests, which garnered media attention which spread around the world, as Cambridge Police charged the protestors of unlawful assembly, trespassing, resisting arrest and impeding access to public buildings. These actions by CAM caused Mayor Calvin Mawbray to ask Richardson to stop the protests, which will in-turn, will stop the arrests by police.

Gloria Richardson refused the Mayor's request and warned the mayor that there will be even more protests and violence will occur with them against the police if the demonstrators were provoked. It didn't take too long for that situation to occur and spin out of control. On the afternoon of June 11th, the town erupted into an outright anarchical riot and disobedience, as young teenagers, who probably were not from Cambridge Maryland, began to throw rocks, bricks, and glass soda bottles through the windows and doors of White-owned businesses.

In response to this violent outbreak, a shootout with guns began as Blacks engaged Police in an all-out gun battle, to the point where Maryland's Governor, Democrat J. Millard Tawes declared Martial Law in the city and activated the Maryland National Guard to patrol the streets of Cambridge to silence the melee. By then, Attorney General of the United States, Robert F. Kennedy, along with Governor Tawes and Cambridge Mayor Mawbray, offered Richardson and her organization CAM some sort-of a treaty to end the violence.

The following month, in Harlem New York, numerous riots and anarchy took place causing enormous property damage between July 16-22, 1964 when New York City Police (NYPD) Officers were involved in the shooting death of Black resident James Powell.

The 10-day riot, sponsored by both the NAACP, CORE and CPUSA financing it, resulted in 465 people arrested, 500-plus people injured, one death and over $1 Million Dollars in property damage ($7.74 Million in 2015 dollars). This wasn't it. Two-days after the

Harlem Riots, another one broke out in upstate New York in the city of Rochester.

These riots, which lasted from July 24-25 of 1964 was started when a 19-year-old Black male teen, who was intoxicated from alcohol from a block party, began to display irrational behavior. After giving him a field sobriety test, which he failed, Rochester Officers arrested him.

As usual, rumors began to fly that Police officer abused the Black teen after his arrest and booking at the Police station, causing rebellion to break out in the city. New York Governor, Republican Nelson Rockefeller, called in the state's National Guard to quell the riot and restore order. In the meantime, during the National Guard deployment into the riot area, one of the transport helicopters went down and crashed, killing three Soldiers onboard.

At the end, the riot caused the deaths of four people, including the three National Guardsmen), 350 people injured, 1000+ people arrested, 204 stores were looted and damaged or burned to the ground, costing $2 Million Dollars-worth of damage. What was striking about the Rochester riot, was that 70% of the rioters who were arrested and jailed were NOT residents of the Rochester metro area.

Sounds familiar? It does.

The month after Rochester New York, a race riot broke out in "The City of Brotherly Love", Philadelphia Pennsylvania. Unlike the previous riots discussed, the demographics of Philadelphia (called Philly in slang terms) were much different than others, because the city had a very large substantial African-American population. That year, it was estimated that Philly had a total of 400,000 Blacks out of 600,000 population total overall. However, for months and days leading up to the riot, especially after seeing the results of the Rochester New York, Harlem New York, and Cambridge Maryland riots, tensions between the Police and residents became intense and rumors were spread of oftentimes false accusations of Police Brutality.

On August 28, 1964, an African-American woman named Odessa Bradford, was in the car with her boyfriend arguing with him. As the argument heated up in intensity, Bradford who was the driver, suddenly applied the brakes to the car in the middle of the busy intersection of 23rd Street and Columbia Avenue.

Answering to complaints that a couple was in a car fighting among themselves in the middle of the intersection, Police responded to the scene. One Black Officer, Robert Wells, and his partner, White Officer John Hoff, approached the occupants of the car and verbally told them to remove themselves out of the middle of the intersection. Broadford refused and began to argue and fight with Officers Wells and Hoff, in which they pulled her out of the car physically, slammed her on the hood of the car and arrested her.

Seeing this, another unknown African-American male, probably her boyfriend or a bystander, intervene between Bradford and the officers, thereby starting a physical confrontation between Officers Wells and Hoff. Soon, backup police began to descend on the scene, prompting more onlookers of the situation. Officer Wells and Huff, finally handcuffed Bradford and the other male, put them inside a police car and transported them to jail. In the meantime all hell broke loose at the intersection of 23rd Street and Columbia Avenue.

In the meantime, false rumors began to circulate around North Philadelphia, where many of the city's African-Americans resided. Rumors that told that White Police Officers had beaten to death a pregnant Black woman in the middle of the intersection of 23rd Street and Columbia Avenue in broad daylight. This lie provoked an angry and serious emotional response which turned into crowds of people that protested the Police, which turned into abject rebellious behavior. This caused businesses primarily located along Columbia Avenue to become targeted for looting, property damage as well as setting many of the businesses that were looted afire.

Philadelphia Police responded quickly to the unruly rioting and set up barricades and perimeter controls to limit the riot area from spreading. However, hours after the riots started, long after the Police Department began to confront the rioters, Mayor James H.J. Tate ordered the police to back off the rioters and contain them, not confront them, thinking that the rioters will begin to stand down by themselves without being provoked by law enforcement. That decision proved to be wrong and for the next two days, the burning of businesses and property destruction continued unabated.

When the riot did end, on August 30, 1964, 341 people were injured, 774 people were arrested on numerous charges and 225 businesses, majority of them White-owned, but some Black Businesses were destroyed as well, costing the city over $5 Million dollars ($38 Million in 2016 dollars).

Later investigations of the riot revealed that Black Nationalists and Black Muslims instigated the riot and spread the lies of between a pregnant Black Female and the Police. The city Black Christian ministers had called for calm and tried to de-escalate the rioters. Unfortunately, the largest and biggest riots were still to come, which will forever scorch the landscape of the United States of America and put into question, the true motives behind the American Civil Rights Movement. Was it about "Civil Rights" for African-Americans or was it more sinister behind closed doors, which the intent to create a Soviet-style Revolution to install Socialism/Communism into the U.S.

The burning of businesses in Watts, California in 1965.

(Courtesy of Wikimedia)

The Watts, California Riots of 1965

Watts California was originally founded as a part of a Mexican Land Grant, named Rancho La Tajauta, which became farmland for grazing cattle for beef production. Not long after the area become an incorporated city in 1907, the name Watts came into being, because 10 acres of the land encompassing the current 2.2-mile city was occupied by Pacific Electrical Power, which was called the Watts facility. As the area continues to grow in number, in a special election on April 2, 1926, residents there voted to merge the town into the ever-expanding city of Los Angeles to the east. Therefore, Watts became a municipality of the City of Los Angeles located then in the South-Central area.

Fast-forward 39 years. Watts California, like the rest of its neighboring municipalities, like Compton, Inglewood, Long Beach, Carson and the city of Los Angeles expanded greatly and experienced a major population explosion due to the nearby shipbuilding and repair facilities, Aircraft Industries located there before, during and after World War II. South-Central Los Angeles population to include Watts, increased its population ten-fold, because of the Second Great Black Migration (1941-1970) of African-American families relocating to the West Coast from the Segregated South. As the population increased in the area between races, discrimination among them and differences between them began to escalate also.

By the year 1965, tensions mounted between the Black residents of Watts, Los Angeles Police Department (LAPD) and California Highway Patrol (CHP). With mounting accusations of police brutality on the Black minority in South-Central Los Angeles, another explosive power keg began to be lit, which will eventually explode into one of the largest, deadliest and costly riots in American History, The Watts Riots of 1965.

On August 11, 1965, CHP Officer Lee Minikus was on a patrol one evening on Avalon Boulevard near 116th Street, when he observed an African-American male, driving a 1955 Buick, driving erratically, from lane-to-lane. When he pulled the car over, he encountered one Marquette Frye and his brother Ronald. When Officer Minikus smelled alcohol on Marquette Frye's breath, his suspicion proved to be correct that he was intoxicated, while driving a motor vehicle, and requested backup on his radio. At the time, Officer Minikus began to give the driver a field sobriety test to confirm his accusation of drunk driving.

While this was being conducted, Marquette's Brother, Ronald, left the scene and ran home to tell their mother what happened. The

Frye brother's mother, Rena Price was at home which was nearby where the drunk driving incident took place. Upset about the incident, Ms. Price left the house and ran towards the scene with Ronald to see what was happening.

In a Los Angeles Times interview in August 1990, the then-retired CHP Officer Lee Minikus recalled the incident that "it was just a normal, routine traffic stop." He further explained, that he never knew that his actions that night would spark one of the worst urban riots ever to take place in American History.

Meanwhile, Marquette Frye had failed his sobriety test and was very cooperative with law enforcement officers, until his mother Rena Price arrived on the scene. This is the point where things spiraled out of control. In the initial police report filed by the California Highway Patrol, Officers at the scene noted that once his mother arrived at the scene, Marquette's demeanor immediately changed from one of being cooperative with law enforcement to an angry, hostile one.

Conflicting stories between all those who were involved vary from one person to another. Ms. Price stated in an Orlando Sentinel interview in 1985, that one of the backup patrol officers had pushed her in the back, and that's when she responded by jumping on the back of another patrol officer at the scene, causing still another patrol officer to pull out his shotgun. Other accounts differ from what she recounted 20-years later.

Another account from one of the officers on the scene stated that when Ms. Price arrived, she began to cuss out and berate the patrol officers that her son was being arrested unjustly and then proceeded to jump on one of the officer's back, tearing his shirt, as other officers move in on her to subdue her. Whatever the cause of the riots maybe, her actions began an all-out assault on CHP officers, which Ronald Frye became a part of the fighting too.

Marquette Frye was subdued by receiving a police baton to his head, which stunned him, and all three were placed in handcuffs and arrested on numerous charges and whisked away to jail. As this incident was taken place, a crowd of onlookers appeared to watch the action and immediately shouted and yelled at the officers their displeasure with the way they were handling the Frye brothers and Ms. Price.

All of this was going on, when once again, rumors began to spread about CHP officers *"roughed up a pregnant Black woman"* {sounds familiar}, which formed angry crowds and mobs of people to begin to vent their frustration in the form of a rebellious, disobedient riot.

Businesses were being looted, cars were being overturned, fights between the police and the rioters began to fly, gunfire erupted between the rioters and the police, which then were re-enforced by LAPD, other CHP officers, and Los Angeles County Sheriff Department deputies. The rioting area wasn't just going on in the 2.2 square mile area of Watts but expanded to include all of South-Central Los Angeles cities, of Compton, Inglewood, Long Beach, Carson and many other places, which expanded to an area of roughly 50-square miles.

As firefighters was trying to access the burning businesses and buildings, they were greeted with sniper fire from the rioters hidden on top of roofs, in between trees and walls and fences of residential areas, causing the Los Angeles Fire Department to back off the riot area until it was saved for them to go in a fight the numerous conflagration fires, that began to spread rapidly.

LA Mayor Democrat Sam Yorty requested additional help to silence the riots from California Governor Edmund G. "Pat" Brown {Father of current California Governor Edmund G. "Jerry" Brown}. Governor Brown did so, but not fast enough, causing heavy criticism from the mayor about the slow response from the Governor. On August 13th, Governor Brown activated the California National Guard to deploy to the riots area, with 3,000 Soldiers and the riots finally quelled on August 16th. The next day, the National Guard element pulled out of Watts and the rest of South-Central LA signaling the end of the melee.

In the wake of the Watts Riots, Mayor Yorty publicly accused Black community leaders that conspired with Communist Agitators, that they were the parties responsible that escalated the riots, by stoking fear, hate and discontent in relations between the Watt's residents and the city's police and fire departments. **Mayor Sam Yorty criticized the**

American Civil Rights Movement overall, saying that the entire action of the movement was not created to help African-Americans gain their civil rights as American Citizens, but to install Marxist-Leninist ideology throughout his city and the rest of the country to start a violent revolution.

The end count of the Watts Riots was staggering. 34 people lay dead, 1,032 were injured, 3,952 people were arrested, 1,000+ buildings were damaged or destroyed in its entirety. The overall riot cost the city of Los Angeles, California a whopping $40 Million Dollars ($970 Million Dollars in 2016 money). However, the 1965 Riots caused issues within Watts and South-Central LA in general, as street gangs, drug abuse, and distribution, worsening poverty, and public-school illiteracy still are affecting the area 52 years later.

16: Riots, Assassinations, and Mayhem- the American Civil Rights Movement (IV)

"Once the Socialists come to power, they will stay in power and keep the people fighting among themselves in order for the revolution to take place."
Leonard Patterson
Former Head of the Young Communist League

By the time the riots in Watts, California ended, both the Civil Rights Act of 1964 and Voting Rights Act of 1965, the violent revolution was well on its way inside America's borders. Between the Spring of 1966 to the Summer of 1967, there were **eight-major racial "revolutionary" riots**, which were billed as fighting the "system" to gain civil rights for African-Americans, when in fact, it didn't. In all-actuality, these so-called revolutions ended up being more detrimental to America's Black Community in both the long- and Short-term socially, mentally and economically, as planned. The name and cities where such anarchy that took place as are follows;

June 12-14, 1966- Chicago, Illinois "The Division Streets Riots"

July 2, 1966- Omaha, Nebraska Race Riots

July 12-15, 1966- The Chicago, Illinois "West-Side Riots"

July 18-24, 1966- Cleveland, Ohio "Hough {pronounced huff} Riots"

August 27, 1966- Waukegan, Illinois, Race Riots

August 30-September 4, 1966- Benton Harbor, Michigan Riots

September 6-8, 1966- Atlanta, Georgia "Summerhill and Vine City Riots"

November 12, 1966- West Hollywood, California "Sunset Strip Curfew Riots"

By the Spring of 1967, geopolitical events were not just limited to other parts of the world where the United States of America had no direct involvement, but there were other events in which we did have some major involvement both abroad and at home. As the Spring rolled into Summer, events such as the further escalation of the war in Vietnam was in full-swing, Boxer Muhammad Ali's (formerly Cassius Clay) World Heavyweight Championship Belt was stripped from him by the National Boxing Association in Houston, Texas. The latter happened because Ali refused to register for the draft, or what he called "A White Man's War".

At Howard University on March 21, 1967, in Washington D.C., a known hotbed during the 1960's for Marxist-Leninist Indoctrination of its students and a Historically Black University (HBU), experienced campus unrest and protesting, when U.S. Army General Lewis Hershey was giving a speech to Howard's ROTC unit.   General Hershey, at the time, was Commanding General of the Federal Government's Selective Service System at the Pentagon, known as the Draft Board, which was interrupted by Blacks students yelling "America is the Black Man's Battleground".

Dr. King himself, begin to change his stance from a Nonviolent movement to one of an open protest stance against America's involvement in the Vietnam War. This became public on April 4, 1967, in New York City.

The following month of May 2, 1967, armed members of the Black Panther Party (BPP) stormed the California State Capitol Building, in Sacramento, to protest a state bill by lawmakers restricting the carrying of guns in public. Five-days later, on May 6, 1967, over 400 African-American Students conducted a hostile takeover of the Administration Building of Cheyney State College (now Cheyney University of Pennsylvania), to protest racial harassment of the college's students by Pennsylvania State Troopers, discrimination in housing and other issues, led by the local chapter of the NAACP. There were many other incidents that happened that led up to the events of what is now called "***The Long Hot Summer of '67***".

During the Summer of 1967, starting in June, Communist Agitation Campaigns in the form of revolutionary riots plagued the American landscape throughout the time-period. Such incidents led by the Communist Party via the Communist International in Russia were all being financed and in many ways manned by either Marxist-Leninist subverted activists themselves and/or their duped "useful idiots" called Liberals. The latter population of people, bought into the lies, deception, and distortions of facts, were led to believe, that the anger that they projected in front of the cameras of the media, was being done to help Black Americans obtain equality and put down discrimination.

Again, behind closed doors, that wasn't the case. However, this belief led to well over 159 protests and outright anarchical rioting, costing many lives, damages to businesses, both Black and White-owned, and large sums of money from state and local municipal accounts.

The following below are just brief accounts of just a handful of the riots that were sparked between the months of June through September of '67;

Avondale Riots in Cincinnati, Ohio lasted between June 12-15, costing one death and 13 injured and $2 Million Dollars-worth of property damage.

Buffalo, New York Riot of 1967, started on June 26 and ended on July 1, leaving with no deaths, 44 injured and costing that city well over $4 Million Dollars-worth of damage.

Newark, New Jersey Riot of 1967, which started on July 12 and ended on July 17. One of the deadliest and costliest urban riots in American History, claimed the lives of 26 people (16 civilians, 8 rioters, 1 Law Enforcement Officer, 1 Firefighter), 727 injuries, 1,500 people arrested and over $10 Million Dollars-worth of property damage.

Plainfield New Jersey Riot of 1967, located just 30 miles from Newark, started on July 14th and ended July 21, leaving one dead (Police Officer), and 100 injuries, costing that city $2 Million Dollars-worth of damage.

Cairo, Illinois Riot of 1967, located 34 miles south of Cape Girardeau, Missouri, at the southern tip of the state of Illinois, at the confluence of the Ohio and Mississippi Rivers, was caused by a prisoner at the city's jail. U.S. Army Private Robert Hunt, was home on leave when he was arrested and taken to jail, where jailers found him hanging inside his jail cell with his T-shirt. The Black Citizens did not believe the story, which touched off three days of protests and rioting, which left no deaths, two injuries, six-fire bombings, 100+ reported shootouts between the police and the Illinois National Guardsmen. Cost of the melee was about $1 Million Dollars.

Milwaukee, Wisconsin Riot of 1967, started on July 30 and ended on August 1st, leaving four people dead, 100 injuries, 1,470 arrests and $1 Million Dollars-worth of damage.

"The 12th Street Riots"

The deadliest of the Summer of 1967 riots was in Detroit, Michigan. In the early morning hours of July 23, 1964, at approximately 3:45 am, Detroit Police Officers raided an unlicensed drinking bar, located in the office of the United Community League for Civil Action (UCLCA).

The office was on one of the floors of the Economy Printing Company Building located at 9125 12th Street, and once they got inside, Detroit Police only expected to encounter only 10-12 partiers. However, to their surprise, the party consisted of 82 people, who were celebrating the return home of a local U.S. Army Soldier, who had recently been deployed to Vietnam.

As the Law Enforcement Officers began to arrest the members of the illegal party, more Police Officers and more police vehicles started to arrive on the scene, causing more attention by many onlookers in the area. Sometime during the arrests, a glass bottle was thrown at one of the arresting officers, which then escalated into additional insults and emotions voiced between the officers and crowd, that then escalated even further into a physical confrontation. These actions further drove the crowd into looting the clothing store next door to the building, and the situation spiraled out of control from there.

Photo of the Detroit Michigan "12th Street Riots of 1967.
(Courtesy of Detroit Journalism.org)

Between that morning on July 23 to its ending on July 27, called *"The 12th Street Riots"*, will go down as one of the most dangerous and explosive riots in American History. Detroit Police force was bolstered by Wayne County Sheriff Deputies and the Michigan National Guard. Mass anarchy filled the air in the city, as businesses were looting, damaged, and burned to the ground set by arsonists during the melee.

Concerts at Detroit's Fox Theater and the Major-League Baseball game at Tiger Stadium were cut short, with instructions broadcasted to their audiences regarding directions and information to avoid the riot areas. Detroit's mayor at the time, Democrat Mayor Jerome Cavanaugh, feared that a major police presence to stop the rioters would have made them, even more, angrier and become more violent, thereby the police department was only allowed to contain the area earlier on, vice confronting the rioters by force. His slow response yielded just the opposite.

By Monday, July 24, and the situation became worse, Mayor Cavanaugh telephoned Michigan Governor, Republican George Romney {father of the future 2012 Presidential Candidate Mitt Romney} for additional assistance. In turn, Governor Romney called President Johnson at the White House requesting federal intervention in the form of U.S. Army troops to help quell the riot.

That same day, the city via the media reported that there were 483 fires going on, 231 acts of robbery, looting, property damages being conducted every hour and nearly 1,000 arrests have been made. Again, Firefighters were trying to gain access to the burning structures inside the riot areas, when they came to the targets of the rebellion.

Firefighters were beaten severely and shot at, while bottles, rocks, bricks and other items were thrown at them, making their job even more dangerous.

U.S. House of Representative and Marxist-Man John Conyers drove himself to the riot area to plea with the rioters to go home, while at the same token he explained to the angry mob of people, that there were members of Congress who supported the rioters, who were just as angry and frustrated of the police than they were. This tactic didn't work, as the unruly crowd began to pelt Congressman Conyers and his car with glass soda bottles, rocks, and bricks, as he sped away from the scene.

The next day, Tuesday, July 25th, President Johnson, along with the Secretary of Defense Robert McNamara and the rest of the National Security Council held an emergency meeting at the White House to discuss the riots in Detroit.

President Johnson invoked the **Insurrection Act of 1807** and the **Posse-Comitatus Act of 1878**, ordered elements of the U.S. Army's 82nd Airborne Division from Fort Bragg, North Carolina to deploy to the city and Fort Campbell, Kentucky's 101st Airborne Division, to boost the Michigan National Guard, Michigan State Highway Patrol, Wayne County Sheriffs and Detroit Police Departments to put down the rebellion.

Another photo of Detroit's 12th Street Riots in 1967.

(Courtesy of Library of Congress)

Some 8,000 Army Paratroopers, an additional 360 Michigan State Highway Patrol Troopers, descend on the scene to stop the anarchical rioting. Within 48 hours, this large contingent force had everything under control. In a scene comparative to a Hollywood movie or when the Soviets invaded Czechoslovakia, armored M-48 Tanks, Personnel Carriers and jeeps transcended on the city of Detroit, Michigan.

At the end, it was estimated that well over 10,000-plus people took part in the rioting, with another 100,000-plus people gather to watch and stir the rioters on. The "12th Street Riots" cost the following;

43 dead (33 Blacks, 10 Whites)

1,189 people injured (407 civilians, 289 suspects, 214 Detroit Police Officers, 134 Firefighters, 55 Michigan National Guardsmen, 67 Michigan State Troopers, 15 Wayne County Sheriff Deputies and 8 Army Paratroopers)

7,231 people arrested (6,528 Adults, 703 Juveniles; ½ of them had no prior arrests)

2509 Stores were looted, burned to the ground
388 Families were homeless or displaced

412 Buildings that were looted or burned had extensive damage to them, they had to be torn down

$40-45 Million Dollars-worth of property damage ($319 Million Dollars in 2016 money)

In addition to the previously-listed riots, additional rioting broke out in the following cities during the Summer of 1967;

Pontiac, Michigan

Flint, Michigan

Saginaw, Michigan

Grand Rapids, Michigan

Toledo, Ohio

Lima, Ohio

Englewood, New Jersey

Houston, Texas

Tucson, Arizona

Birmingham, Alabama

Tampa, Florida

Minneapolis, Minnesota

New Britain, Connecticut

Boston, Massachusetts

Chicago, Illinois

The Long Hot Summer of '67 was finished. The next riot was back in Cambridge, Maryland and it was affectionately known as **"The H. Rap Brown Riot"**.

The H. "Rap" Brown Riots-Cambridge Maryland

The second Cambridge riots, which started on July 24, 1967, was attributed directly to Marxist Man, Black Revolutionary and newly appointed head of SNCC, H. "Rap" Brown. As the media of the time continued to show broadcasts and pictures in newspapers from the inner-city riots from Newark and Plainfield New Jersey to Detroit Michigan, Brown came to Cambridge at the behest of Marxist-Leninist Community Organizer Gloria Richardson.

Brown (now named Jamil Abdullah Al-Amin), because the National States Rights Party (MSRP), a White Supremacist Group, held a rally there in Cambridge prior to holding their National Convention in Baltimore, Maryland. Richardson's Cambridge Action Movement (CAM) organization, began counter-protests in response to the White Supremacists rally going on that day. Brown came from Baltimore, since he was recently appointed the new leader of SNCC, and made a fiery speech to the Black Community as he delivered the following speech;

"It's time black folks stop talking about being non-violent 'cause we ain't non-violent towards each other. Every Friday and Saturday you prove that. You cut up more people among your race than any race. As for being violent, you don't be violent to your brother. Be violent in your communities and it let it end right there. Take your violence to the Honkies..."

He continues...

"Ain't no need in the world for me to come to Cambridge and see all them stores sitting up there and all them Honkies owns them. You got to own some of them stores. I don't care if you have to burn him down and run him out. You'd better take over them stores. The streets are your[s]. Take 'em. They gave you the streets a long time

ago before they gave you houses. Then they gave you the streets. So we own the streets. Take 'em…"

Not long after Brown's speech was given, an hour later, Cambridge Police begin to report gunfire between them and some of the Black Residents the city. Shortly afterward, smoke began to fill the air, as large conflagration fires were started at a Black Elementary School and Black-owned businesses. As Brown returned to Baltimore, upon hearing reports of the rioting in Cambridge, he was quoted as saying that the riots there;

"Is American as cherry pie."

Interesting.

What's even more interesting, is that the same scenario did not play out there in Cambridge, as they did in Newark, Plainfield, Detroit, Watts, Rochester and other places that continue to commit acts of rebellious damage to American cities, in the false assumption called "Civil Rights".

For one, Firefighters learned from other cities that, before they venture into the riot areas, they needed protection from Law Enforcement before going inside the riot areas, to keep firefighting personnel safe. Reports went around to rescue personnel that armed Black residents were not only firing their guns at Police but also at Emergency Personnel too. Thus, the fires continued to burn and spread to nearby buildings and nearby residential areas in the Black Community, without the fire department, unless they were provided security to put out the fires.

By nighttime, the fires burned themselves out, Cambridge Police, Dorchester County Maryland Sheriff's Deputies and Maryland State Highway Patrol diffused the situation and ended the melee. By dawn on the 25th, 16 buildings lay in ruin in a 2-square block area, with damage estimates exceeding $1 Million Dollars.

Where was H. Rap Brown and Gloria Richardson? They were nowhere to be found.

As for the former, by inciting the riot, Brown wasn't going to get away too fast. Governor of Maryland, Republican Spiro T. Agnew, made sure that Brown and Richardson would pay for their deeds for creating Marxist agitation in his state. He informed the FBI head J. Edgar Hoover, who agreed to send out bulletins throughout the Law Enforcement Community seeking to apprehend and arrest Brown and extradite him back to Maryland to face trial.

H. Rap Brown was arrested in September of 1967, charged with arson and inciting a riot, which he jumped bail. He was finally brought to justice in Maryland after being caught during a shootout with the New York City Police in 1971.

As for Richardson? She went underground. She got married and faded away from public life, while still supporting Communist Agitation campaigns for various Black Civil Rights groups.

As for Cambridge Maryland's Black Community? They had to pick up the pieces after the riots and still lived in conditions made worse by such Marxist Men like Brown and Richardson, similar to other major metropolitan cities throughout America. They were left with increased poverty, unemployment, and violent Black-on-Black crime, but on a smaller scale. The Black Revolution in Cambridge Maryland was crushed after Richardson went underground and never surfaced again.

Looking at the number of riots in major cities during his administration, between 1964 and 1967, President Johnson, just as what the Communists hope he would do, called for a federal investigation into the riots, particularly the ones which were the most-deadliest and had the most damage done to them. It is here, where President Johnson signed ***Executive Order 11365***, establishing the National Advisory Commission on Civil Disorders (NACCD), headed by Illinois' Governor, Democrat Otto Kerner Jr. Known as *"**The Kerner Commission**"*, the 11-member panel's job was to thoroughly investigate the causes of the 1967 riots and provide recommendations to prevent future outbreaks of such violence.

The main idea of the commission, in truth, is to create the perception to the American public, that it will be up the Federal

Government to stop these riots from taking place. In other words, if such rioting was to take place, it will be to "The Almighty State" to come to the rescue too and provide solutions to the problem, without addressing the problem first, then find ways or create a plan of action to solve such problems. You can see this as plain as day, when you look at Executive Order 11365, where Johnson tasked the committee to answer three basic questions; *"What happened?"*, *"Why did it happened?"*, and *"What can be done to prevent it from happening again and again?"*.

17: The Communist Plan to Keep the Black Community Enslaved to "The Almighty State"

"Whenever there is the emergence of the new, we confront the recalcitrance [rebellious] of the old. So, the tensions which we witness in the world today are indicative of the fact that a new world order is being born and an older order is passing away"[1]

Dr. Martin Luther King Jr. 1957

It must be recalled in earlier chapters of this book, where Karl Marx, the creator of the Marxist Theory, stated that the old society must be destroyed in its entirety, by creating a violent revolution. The reason why is simple; so, that Man to make a transformation or *"leap"* into the new society called **Communism**. But, in-order for Communism to take effect, Man have-to destroy the old society itself and accept the premise of this new society, whether they want to or not. ***There is not a third choice***, in the matter.

Willful acceptance of this new society is the only way a man can make this new leap into Socialism first, Communism second, even if they have to be forced to comply by Marxist Men and their dupes by the barrel of a gun. This process has been proven over-and-over again in Human History. But in the meantime, a new breed of human being must be created to lead the charge into destroying the old society before such transformation can take place. Here is where Marxist Men come into play. However, Marxist Man cannot do everything by themselves.

The old African proverb states *"It takes a village to raise a child"*. When it comes to the modern-era of the 21st Century, we can safely conclude, that it takes a Police State to raise a village and convert them into accepting Communism or the substituted term named *Globalism.*

The village, meaning the United States of America, have to have a sizable population of what is considered a permanent underclass of citizens, to support and parrot whatever Marxist Men tells them to do, without challenge. Their targets are aimed specifically at Minorities (African-Americans and some Hispanics), to include the Foreign-born, who has been mentally subverted to accept Marxist-Leninist *"liberation"* ideology.

These underclasses of people, must not only accept this lie of "liberation" of Communism but sometimes, they are conditioned psychologically to sacrifice themselves, to lay down their lives in the name of **"equality"** and **"liberation"** (that doesn't exist) for all. This is not funny because many of these people who live inside the United States, some of them are our friends, neighbors, family members, co-workers and yes, even people in positions of power, who believe that such animals exist.

They have been lied-to to accept that they are the victims of the old society, called Capitalism and that in the world of Communism, there will be no racial discrimination, economic inequality, everything is all **"fair"** and **"equal"** among all classes of people, while everybody will happily work to support everybody else and not for their selfish selves. This is absolutely nonsense! Unfortunately, this will be the end-game for America, if we as a people don't wise up and try to recondition this population of a permanent underclass of "Victims", the current society which we live in will turn into a society that will essentially enslave us and/or kill us all!

The Kerner Commission

The blueprint of characterizing this permanent underclass of citizens can be found, by reading the Kerner Commission Report, released by President Lyndon Johnson on July 28, 1967. The 400-plus page report, compiled by the 11-member panel, which included the following members;

Illinois Governor Otto Kerner Jr.-Chairman

NAACP Executive Director Roy Wilkins

New York Mayor Republican-turned-Democrat John Lindsay

Senator Democrat Fred R. Harris-Oklahoma

Senator Republican Edward Brooke-Massachusetts

House of Representative Democrat James Corman-California

House of Representative Republican William McCulloch-Ohio

Founder of Litton Industries Charles Thorton

President of the Steelworker's Union I.W. Abel

Atlanta Georgia Police Chief Herbert Turner Jenkins

State of Kentucky's Commissioner of Commerce Katherine Graham Peden

The authors and data collection processes of the Kerner Commission Report were;

Americans for Democratic Action (ADA) David Ginsburg

The Committee to Defend America by Aiding Allies (CDAAA)

It must be noted, that the authors of the commission's report, that the organization named Americans for Democratic Action (ADA), was a spin-off from another CPUSA/Marxist-Leninist front group The **Union for Democratic Action (UDA)**, which was formed by members of the **Socialist Party of America (SPA)**! **CDAAA was a sub-branch of ADA.** The connection between the two entities is remarkable. The goal of the committee was to consider why the anarchical riots were formed in Watts California (1965), Chicago Illinois (1966) and Newark New Jersey (1967), using the President's three questions.

After seven-months of investigation work, David Ginsburg released The Kerner Commission Report on February 28, 1968.

The Commission blamed the riots in "***White America***", which caused the African-American Community to riot, burn and loot both

White-owned and Black-owned businesses, because of the "lack of economic opportunity" within their community.

In addition, the commission blamed the riots on the "***White Racism***" in the media, going as far as stating directly that;

"The press too long backed in a White world looking out of it, if at all, with White men's eyes and White Perspective."

Sound like a bit of Black Supremacy, doesn't it? Maybe a combination of both White and Black Supremacy. It's a lie of course. In the report, Marxist Man David Ginsburg wrote the famous words which defined the commission's entire purpose, as to the causes of the riots;

"Our nation is moving towards two societies; one Black, one White-separate and unequal".

Based on what many Americans, regardless of skin color, were led to believe during that time {as in now}, that the so-called "American Civil Rights Movement" was to give African-Americans the right to be equal among their White peers, but the final committee report contradicted that premise; on purpose.

By stating that the advancements which Black folks had made during the 20-plus years of numerous sacrifices for themselves in the form of demonstrations, court actions and the like, to obtain that equality and tear down the system of economic and racial injustice, was the committee trying to say that those after-mentioned things did not happen? Or maybe, Ginsburg was saying, that despite these sacrifices, in the Marxist Men eyes, such advances in social status for African-Americans wasn't enough, so it is the job of the "Almighty State" to take control of American society and control everything American citizens do, to make this thing called equality "equal", via Socialistic legislation. Sounds like Dr. Martin Luther King Jr. was right when he pointed this out in 1965.

The Kerner Commission stated that both Federal and State Governments failed America's Black Community because of the lack of adequate housing, public education, and social services policies. They called for the government to create "new" jobs, construct "new" housing, stop De Facto Segregation, and wipe out inner-city ghettos. Finally, the commission's report recommended a "more diverse" and "sensitive" policing in the communities, plus the government should invest in Billions of Dollars in such housing and hiring programs to break up segregation. In addition, the Kerner Commission recommended the following;

Unless sharp changes of factors influencing Negro settlement "patterns" within metropolitan areas, there is little doubt that the trend of Negro majorities living in the ghettos will continue...

To provide employment of the ever-swelling Negro ghetto population, would require opening of suburban areas to Negroes and encourage them to move closer to industrial complexes and centers...

Major cities will have an overwhelming Negro majority in America's population, that by 1985, the suburbs ringing them, will remain largely White, UNLESS [Commission's emphasis] there are major changes in Negro fertility rates, in migration settlement or public policy...

The emphasis should be changed from the previous "progressive" actions that called for publicly-built slum-based on high-rise projects to smaller units on scattered sites...

Not everybody agreed with what the Kerner Commission erratic and contradictory report.

Dr. Martin Luther King Jr., prior to him traveling down to Memphis Tennessee, where he would later be assassinated, called the report a;

"Physician's warning of approaching death, with a prescription of life."

One thing similar aspect of the social construct within the African-American Community back then, just as there is now, more than ever, that a certain portion of the Black Community that have been taught that they have been victims of such abject racism and inequality in America. They have also been taught that their lives will ***never*** get better, regardless of how racial relations have advanced.

The idea of this teaching, of lies and distortion of facts, of course, is to allow the almighty government to dictate what to do in-order to "level the playing field", for them.

This is preposterous and absolutely, pathetic!

What this abject teaching and lies inside the Black Community really means, is that Black America have-to be re-enslaved by the powers there be, so that the Almighty Federal Government, can make decisions for the people of that community, based-off what they, the almighty elites dictate. In other words, the Federal Government must do its best to take care of the Black Community, and not themselves, because with all of this rioting, anger, and discontent, the people are too naïve to govern or take care of themselves. In more realistic terms, by committing reverse enslavement of a race or low-economic of society, it will be the government who will take charge of them and not the people.

This is what the Johnson Administration, CPUSA and all of the so-called Black Revolutionaries of the era, including the Kerner Commission, have been yearning to do for the Black Community for decades. Remember, it is all about control of the masses of people, to bring down Capitalism, preferably The United States of America, to leap to a new society of Socialism/Communism. American Blacks have been used like cannon fodder in-order for this permanent underclass to exist, who will continue to do work for the Marxist Men on top.

What the Kerner Commission report fail to do, is to answer President Johnson's last question; *"**What can be done to prevent it [the riots] from happening again and again"**.* Unfortunately, another martyr of the American Civil Rights Movement will have-to be created, via tragic means, in April of 1968, which will set the tone for that question not to be answered, ever.

The Assassination of Dr. Martin Luther King Jr.

On April 4, 1968, the Civil Rights Leader, Dr. Martin Luther King Jr., was killed when a Sniper's bullet ripped him apart on the balcony of the Lorraine Motel, in Memphis Tennessee. Thirty-six days after the release of the Kerner Commission's report, that man who was responsible for the Nonviolent Movement of the American Civil Rights Era was dead. A tragic event to everyone in America, Black, White and in different mourn the loss of a great man, and with him, the Nonviolent Civil Rights Movement perished along with him.

As news spread of the tragic events of Dr. King's death, the entire country exploded into a fiery landscape that not one person could have seen it coming; except the Communist Party and Communist International in Moscow, Soviet Union. Not to push conspiracy theories a bliss, but in the Black Community back then and some even now, understand or theorize why Dr. King was killed that day.

April 5, 1968, Baltimore Sun Headline reporting the assassination of Dr. Martin Luther King Jr.

(Courtesy of Newspapers.com)

Some speculate that a White Supremacist killed him, which is why the Federal Government went after an unknown person by the name of James Earl Ray.

Ray who held White Supremacist views at the time, was coerced by investigators to plead guilty to the killing of Dr. King in Tennessee. Even though he never went to trial, nevertheless he was convicted of his murder and sent to prison for the rest of his life.

The entire time after he withdrew the plea of guilty after conviction, James Earl Ray up to the time of his death continued to fight for his freedom and consistently stated that he did not kill the Civil Rights Leader and he was set up. Regardless, of this, some conclude that it was either the Mafia who killed Dr. King or people occupying the positions high within the Federal Government.

Unfortunately, no one bothered to ask, if ***the Communist Party had something to do with this tragic event.*** After all, Dr. King's work was done as far as those in CPUSA and within the echelons of the Civil Rights Movement was concerned.

His usefulness to the "cause" was complete.

After the Voting Rights Act of 1965, was signed into law, Dr. King strayed into forbidden territory, that in some peoples' eyes at the time, he never should have gone; ***to protest the war in Vietnam***.

It must be remembered, re-enforced constantly, that once the Communist Party have no use for you, and your objective have been achieved, then there is no more use for you, as far as they are concerned. When Dr. Martin Luther King Jr. led the way, for the 'Almighty State' to legislate and pass both the **Civil Rights Act of 1964** and the **Voting Rights Act of 1965,** to those in various positions of political power, Dr. King's work was completed!

President Lyndon Baines Johnson signing the Civil Rights Act of 1964 into law.
(Courtesy Wikimedia)

This also means that the Nonviolent Movement Faction of the Communist Revolution was completed.

Yet, **_Dr. King decided for himself_**, that he could be used in other areas of the American Civil Rights Movement, which was noble on his part. But, for the American Communist Party, they only saw him as a tool, to be used to further their agenda, to overthrow the Federal Government for Mother Russia, and bring about worldwide Communism, led by them and the U.N.!

The tragic assassination of Dr. Martin Luther king Jr. further concludes that he was a Dupe for CPUSA and it's many tenant groups, hidden under the banner of "Civil Rights", using actual grievances of the African-American population. Unfortunately, that was not in the plans for the American Communist Party. **His job was done and complete; he (Dr. King) had to go, to put it rather bluntly!**

Answer this one specific question. Why would they, CPUSA, allowed him to stray into other areas of their operations? **_Technically, they wouldn't!_** To prove this fact, one have-to revert-back to a previous chapter, how Gus Hall and CPUSA treated Robert F. Williams, when the latter began to become more effective in his message to form a Revolution, without the former's control.

Also, nobody questioned that if a person had to give up their life for the "cause", that would have a major impact on the public's psyche to start a mass civil war or revolution; who would that benefit in the long run? For purposes of reading, this author has chosen to keep that subject open as it stands right there and save the discussion for another publication, **_but this theory must be explored even further_**.

In the meantime, after the media reported the death of Dr. Martin Luther King Jr., well over 100 cities exploded into massive anarchy riots, open protests, and abject revolution-style rebellion. Blacks from the inner-cities of Chicago, Washington D.C., Baltimore Maryland, Kansas City, Missouri, Detroit Michigan, New York City, Pittsburgh Pennsylvania, and Cincinnati Ohio rioted, looted stores, destroyed personal and public property. Fires were lit that either heavily damaged buildings or destroying them because firefighting efforts by the responding emergency personnel were being hampered by rioters, who were either shooting at them, throwing bottles, bricks, rocks, sticks or chains at the rescuers.

As the inner-cities began to burn, most of the trouble causing them, was egged on by Black Revolutionists/Marxist Men, such as H. Rap Brown and Stokely Carmichael. This prompted President Johnson to call-out U.S. Army units from Forts Benning in Georgia, Fort Bragg in North Carolina, and Fort Bliss in Texas, to help put down the rebellious mob causing havoc.

One of the biggest and most costly riots concerning the death of Dr. Martin Luther King Jr., happened right in the backyard of President Johnson himself; Northwest, Northeast and Southeast areas of Washington, D.C. Johnson ordered the use of 13,600 U.S. Army Soldiers, 1,750 National Guardsmen, and elements of 100 Marines to guard and man machine guns in front of the White House and U.S. Capitol buildings.

Photo of the Washington D.C. Riots of April 1968 in reaction to the death of Dr. Martin Luther King Jr.

(Courtesy of Wikimedia)

At the end, the 1968 Riots caused 40 deaths, 3,500 people injured, 15,000-plus arrested and caused almost $500 million dollars-worth of damages ($ 2.6 Billion dollars in 2016 money). In a Newsweek article dated April 22, 1968, written by the well-known author Samuel F. Yette, a young teenager that he interviewed put his feeling about the death of Dr. King and the riots that he participated in days earlier;

"It killed a lot of hopes…but everybody knows that he was out there trying to work this thing out the right way. But after he was killed, I said 'what's the use?' There's nothing left, man. A lot of people feel that way. All hope is gone now. Nobody's going to get out there like he did."

That's what we have been brainwashed to accept. The same premise of a lie, that if we as a Black Community are not led by someone, there is no hope for us. *It is a bald-faced lie! It's a lie back then and it is even a bigger lie even now.*

Remember, there must be a permanent underclass of people to support, parrot and do Marxist Man's work, in-order to get rid of the old society. The chosen population during the American Civil Rights Movement were American Blacks living in the inner-cities. Their re-enslavement of a section of the population in America wasn't over yet.

The National Violence Commission (NVC)

After the 1968 riots, which broke out across the country after the assassination death of Dr. Martin Luther King Jr., to supplement the Kerner Commission's report, Attorney General Robert F. Kennedy, the 1968 Democrat Presidential Candidate, recommended to the president of another commission be formed. Called the National Violence Commission (NVC), the task of this body of bureaucrats was to reassess and re-investigate both the 1967 Riots and the most recent one of 1968. This commission was also tasked to revisit some of the Kerner Commission's recommendations, made public just a few short months ago, the National Violence Commission was a 13-member panel, that consisted of the following personnel;

Milton S. Eisenhower-Chairman, President of the Milton S. Eisenhower Foundation*

Leon Higginbotham-Vice Chairman and U.S. Third Circuit Court of Appeals Judge

Hale Bogg-Democrat House of Representative from Louisiana Cardinal Terrence Cook-Archbishop of New York

Philip A. Hart-Democrat House of Representative from Michigan

Eric Hoffer-Longshoreman, "Philosopher" and Democrat Party Donor

Roman Hruska-Republican Senator from Nebraska

Patricia Roberts Harris-Former Ambassador to Luxembourg

Leon Jaworski-Attorney

Albert Jenner-Attorney

William Mc Culloch- House of Representative from Ohio, who also served on the Kerner Commission

Ernest Mc Farland-Arizona State Supreme Court Justice

Walter Menninger-Founder and President of the Menninger Foundation and Psychiatrist

After an 18-month series of hearing and investigative work, NVC released its findings in December 1969.

The scathing report not only mimic the same findings and recommendations that the previous Kerner Commission report released on February 28, 1968, but the NVC report literally was an outright indictment of the Black and Latino Communities in America! In some circles, the **National Violence Committee report is considered a racist document, which the Federal Government will use to mentally subvert the Blacks Community even further.** One part of the NVC report states, verbatim this in-regards to the inner-city teenage generation;

"...to be young, poor male; to be under-educated and without means of escape from an oppressive urban environment; to want a society claims is available (but mostly to others); to see around oneself as illegitimate and often violent methods being used to achieve material success; and to observe others using these means with impurity-all this is to be burden with an enormous set of influences that pull many towards crime and delinquency. To be a Negro, Mexican or Puerto Rican American and subject to discrimination and segregation adds considerably to the pull of these often-criminogenic forces."

As you can see, the National Violence Committee final report literally and metaphorically, labeled the Minority Community in the United States of America as criminals, **"uneducated"**, **"without means of escape from oppressive urban environment"**, that sees themselves as **"illegitimate"**, who only knows violent means to gain material things.

In other words, the NVC Report stated in broad terms that the African-American Community is stupid, uneducated people, who only knows violence, to gain material items, such as cars, money and valuable property. **This is what *they* thought about Black America!**

They recommended more, as to what kind of government intervention should be done in-order to so-called "**help the poor, young Black male**" in their plight.

The commission recommended that a portion of Federal Government spending in the amount of $20 Billion Dollars ($136 Billion Dollars in 2016 money) per year to be spent on jobs, training and education {Public Education-mind you}. They also recommend that confiscation of handguns, restrictions on new gun ownership to those who the FEDS *"could demonstrate 'reasonable' need"*, and identification of rifle and shotgun owners. {Sounds familiar?} The commission concluded;

"That external assault than from internal decay...The greatness and durability of most civilizations have been finally determined by how they have responded to these challenges from within. Ours will be no exception."

In translation, if you throw money at the problem, without solving the problem, the "State" will control every aspect of your life and everything you do.

Also, when the time comes up, and they ask of you to back them up on something, that in-reality is counterintuitive to your own interests, then you better come to the rescue to cover the "State's" ass, or else they will consider you an enemy! It's only then, the Minority Communities (particularly Black Communities) will become good little Slaves on the Federal Government Plantation.

They will keep this subversion going by throwing such $20 Billion Dollars at these communities in the form of what is called *"government entitlements"* or welfare. What both commissions tried to say, in so many words, that if they give you enough money to keep you subjected to them, for as long as Blacks are psychologically-driven to think, that they will always genetically inferior to other races and cultures. Black will be mentally subverted to believe that they are the permanent underclass, and you, as an African-American will never amount to anything because of the color of your skin.

{Sounds like Black Liberation Theology?}

"The Radicals think they are fighting the forces of the super-rich like Rockefeller and Ford, and they don't realize, that it is precisely such forces which are behind their own revolution, financing it, and using it for their own purposes."
Jerry Kirk
-Testimony with the House Committee on Internal Security (HISC) 1969-

It is amazing to find out, that the very things that Mr. Kirk stated above in 1969, still occurs up to the present-day, of 2017.

As we look around the landscape of America, in the wake of the disastrous eight years of the President Barack Obama's Administration, what some of us have observed and tangibly know, that a minor amount of Super-Rich elitists in this country are financing every Marxist agitation campaigns of today.

Communist front groups, such as ACORN, Occupy Wall Street (OWS), Black Lives Matter (BLM), and now-Organizing for Action (OFA), are being manned and supported by trained personnel, using huge sums of money obtained through Marxist-Leftists donations internally and externally by duped sympathizers. Some of these so-called *"Community Organizers"* like the head of BLM, the Lilly-White Shaun King, and many others, are using at times, homeless people and college students who were trained in agitation centers, to protest and cause mayhem throughout the streets of America.

Such facilities, dressed-up as "education centers", like the Direct-Action Research and Training Center (DART) in Florida or the Organize Training Center (OTC), based in San Francisco California. The after-mentioned Communist Front Groups, organize or "mobilize" thousands of people and pay them large-sums of monies to agitate and protest, various "causes", using names like "**Women Reproductive Rights**", "**Environmental Justice**", "**Earth Justice**" or "**Racial Injustice**". Again, their intent is to spawn hate and discontent, using the Media, to change the perception of reality of the masses, to further their agenda, to usher in Communism.

Some of this money is being allotted by the likes of Marxist Men such as Multi-Billionaire Tycoon George Soros, Former President and First Lady/Secretary of State Bill and Hillary Clinton via their Clinton Foundation or the Ford Foundation operated by Darren Walker. These people and hundreds of others are using the young generation of people, who have not been taught not to think for themselves, as live bait, for their own selfish gains, just as Jerry Kirk had testified to Congress 48-years earlier.

Another force which the Marxist Men of the Super-Rich Elites had benefited from for the past 53 years, was President Johnson's "***War on Poverty***".

What was the "War on Poverty" and "Great Society" and did it ever work in real time? Let's explore the former part of the question first, before answering the latter question afterward.

When announcing the "War on Poverty" to the public, President Johnson stated;

"Unfortunately, many Americans live on the outskirts of hope-some because of their poverty and some because of their color, and all too many because of both. Our task is to help replace their despair. Let me make the principle of the administration abundantly clear. All of these increased opportunities in employment, in education, in housing and in every field-must open to Americans of every color. As far as the writ of Federal law will run, we must abolish not some, but all racial discrimination."

So, in other words, once again it was obviously clear, that it will be the Federal Government's job to end racial discrimination, and not the people themselves.

The following programs were created as a part of Johnson's War on Poverty are as follows;

Job Corps

Community Action Agencies (CAA)

Volunteers in Service to America (VISTA)/AmeriCorps

Head Start Program

Aid to Families with Dependent Children (AFDC)/Temporary Assistance for Needy Families (TANF)

Section 8, Housing Voucher Program

Medicare

What Johnson's War on Poverty really was, is a fake promise that the "Almighty State" was going to **do something** for the inner-city poor, specifically, Blacks, to help solve their problems.

In reality, the "War on Poverty" wasn't designed at the outset to solve anything, for inner-city Black-Americans, but to re-enslave them psychologically to the actions of State.

Job Corps Logo.

For example, the Job Corps Federal Program is a free (Taxpayer-funded) education-based training program, operated by Private Companies on contract with the Department of Labor (DOL). These companies assist troubled teenagers and young adults between ages of 16-24, who didn't finish school because of their "**skin color**" or "**poverty status**". Students can either reside on campus at 126 Corps campuses nationwide or come and go just as they were going to a public school. Students can earn a High School Diploma or General Educational Development (GED) Certification. At the same time, students participating in the program can learn a technical skill where they can get hired by an employer, in an entry-level position.

However, problems immediately began to show within the Job Corps program upon its inception in 1965.

Many people believed that their campuses were modified Concentration Camps for young Black Youths to keep them off the streets and train them for the so-called military-industrial complex.

Another aspect of Job Corps Program problems, which brought numerous of negative limelight public reaction and brought more questions about the program than answers, was the costs associated with it. An enormous cost that offers very little if any, return on investment to the public or to the labor market.

In 1965, the costs for a student in the same age-range of public school was about $500 per student. The same student attending Job Corps cost $6,000 per student in the program! In 2016, the same costs in public school have gone up to an average $20,000 per student while in Job Corps, the costs are $50,000! So where is that money going? You can decide.

Especially when the Department of Labor for the 2016 budget request to Congress, requested $1.7 Billion dollars, with $1.59 Billion dollars for operations. Despite the high costs to the taxpayers, Job Corps has had an awful reputation for 50-plus years, because some speculate that the biggest beneficiary of Job Corps Training isn't the high-risk, troubled student, but the Marxist elites.

The same Communist elites who own big corporations who are in the bed with the Democrat Party were going to receive monetary gains for their businesses and fill their coffers up with taxpayer dollars, because of lobbying efforts to for such lucrative Federal Contracts to operate government programs, like Job Corps.

Some use the term "**Welfare Programs**", but the result is still the same. Private companies such as IBM, Xerox, General Electric and other large companies use the taxpayer money given to them via contracts to operate these entitlement programs, like Job Corps or Community Action Agencies (CAA), without showing any tangible results.

By making the impression to the public, that such corporations were doing something for the so-called minority poor or poverty-stricken inner-city population, Marxist Men running these companies, are operating as instruments of the State, while on-the-flip-side, will continue to protect their interests when it comes to lobbying Congress to influence government policy. Sounds contradictory, to the Marxist Theory, but this is the truth. The same scheme continues into the modern-day of the 21st Century.

An Aero photo of a Job Corps Campus. (Courtesy of You Search.co)

The other reason for the so-called "War on Poverty" to exist, as previously stated, was to pacify (appease) the African-American Community so they can become controlled and enslaved by the Almighty State. This cannot be stressed enough!

This is **_exactly_** what the National Violence Commission (NVC) and the Kerner Commission advocated for in their reports. For the State to help the poor Blacks, and keep them comfortable in the conditions that the community has been reduced to. Here is how it happens.

In order for this appeasement to work, without showing its true intentions, you must at first mentally subvert the African-American Community to accept the ideology of Karl Marx. In the process of accepting Marxism, Marxist Men have-to camouflage the ideology using the slogans "Venceremos" (We Shall Overcome), "Equality", "Liberation" and "Social Justice". How you do this effectively, is through the media on Television on channels such as Black Entertainment Television (BET), News One, the Oprah Winfrey Channel (OWN), Centric and a few other channels.

This subversion is also done via the churches, in the Public-School System, in Hollywood using Black Actors and Entertainers as parrots for the Marxist Men, inside Jails and Prisons, by subversion in learning programs and by convicts who once were Black Radicals, such as H. Rap Brown. Back in the late-1960's and Early 1970's, you had Black Newspapers and Magazines, such as *"Ebony"* and *"Jet"* Magazines, the Nation of Islam's *"Final Call"*, Baltimore Maryland-based *"The Afro-American"* Newspapers and others. Same avenues applied then as they do now. The difference is that we have Social Media outlets and the internet to spread lies, deceptions and propaganda, on top of Newspapers and Magazines.

By providing this smoke screen to hide the true intentions of overthrowing the U.S. Government, Marxist Men will use Black bodies to chant the after-mentioned slogans to protest and sometimes, create violent riots against the Police. These riots, are suppose-to instill fear, intimidation in all opposition throughout multiple cities in the U.S. who decided to go against the Communist Plan of World Domination.

Guess who is there to capture on film all these actions? The Marxist-driven media in order that shape public opinion and provide the deception, that the issue is much bigger and more accepted by a majority of the people.

Once these actions are accomplished, to keep the ignorant masses of the Black Community dumb, ignorant and blind to reality, the so-called *"Black Leaders"* and their input into the mess.

These Black Leaders, who this author will label *"**Poverty Pimps**"*, in the likes of the National Action Network (NAN) leader Al Sharpton based in New York City and the Rainbow Coalition based in Chicago headed by Jesse Jackson Sr. and their minions. Their goal is to continue to ferment distrust and anger within the Black Community to keep the people appeased to the conditions they have been reduced to.

Sharpton and Jackson were not the first to do this, of course. During the American Civil Rights Movement of the early-60's, men like Dr. Martin Luther King Jr., Ralph Abernathy, the flamboyant-Marxist Bayard Rustin via the Southern Christian Leadership Conference (SCLC), Congress of Racial Equality (CORE) and Student Nonviolence Coordinating Committee (SNCC) accomplished this attitude in the Black Community during the Nonviolent Movement.

By the mid-to-late '60s, Men such as Stokely Carmichael, H. Rap Brown, Huey P. Newton, Bobby Seale, Elijah Muhammad via the Black Panther Party (BPP), Black Liberation Army (BLA), NAACP followers of Marxist Robert Williams, and Nation of Islam (NOI). Add-on the caveat of Black Liberation Theology (BLT) being preached from the pulpit of everybody African-American Church in America, such as the African-Methodist Episcopal (AME), Southern Baptist, Pentecostal, Israelites, and Nation of Islam, stoking the racist flame that the White Man is responsible for the "systematic racism" of Blacks in the inner-cities.

VISTA/AmeriCorps

President John F. Kennedy issued Executive Order 10924 on March 1, 1961, establishing the Peace Corps. The concern with events at the time throughout the world, especially in third world countries of Africa and Asia, where governments, who were being subverted by Russian KGB Propagandists to believe that "American Imperialism" and influences were causing a crisis in such countries.

President Kennedy, along with the 87th Congress, wanted to tangibly reverse this lie, so, along with his Brother-in-Law, Sargent Shriver, lobbied Congress to pass the **Peace Corps Act**. President Kennedy signed into law on September 23, 1961, to provide American Volunteers to travel abroad too;

"...promote world peace and friendship through a Peace Corps, which shall make available to interested countries and areas men and women of the United States qualified for service abroad and willing to serve, under conditions of hardship if necessary, to help the people of such countries and areas in meeting their needs for trained manpower."

In 1965, during the Johnson Administration, it was thought that since the Peace Corps became a successful government venture worldwide, a similar organization could be successful here on American soil.

~ 374 ~

Originally called the Volunteers in Service to America (VISTA), the so-called domestic peace corps was created that year as a part of President Lyndon Johnson's "Great Society" Program to fight poverty in the inner-city of America. On the surface, the program's 'good intentions' was to allow college-aged students to sign a contract to give one-year of community service to a non-profit organization (who are receiving funding from the FEDS in form of Grants).

Their task was to fight illiteracy, health services, assist those residing in low-income areas to start businesses, strengthening community actions groups and more. A better way to explain VISTA is simple. It's a Taxpayer-Funded operation, who pays non-profit, Marxist-Leninist ideological organizations to subvert college students into believing that they are doing something for the Black, inner-city poor. Just like other government programs, it not only a slush-fund for these private entities to benefit in the name of 'helping the poor', but it does nothing to solves the problem.

In 1997, VISTA was merged with a new program created by the President Bill Clinton Administration called "*Corporation for National and Community Service*" (NCCC), a private-Taxpayer-funded venture, which oversees, operates and provide manpower for American college-aged students to perform community service.

A group of AmeriCorps/Vista doing exercises in the public. Members are all dressed in their AmeriCorps/Vista-issued uniforms.
(Courtesy of Politico)

Since merging, VISTA was renamed *AmeriCorps/VISTA*, that originally paid volunteers $40,000-50,000 dollars per year to assist in students obtaining their Graduate Degree. However, the policy was changed in 2005, where the same students volunteering under AmeriCorps/VISTA will receive between $11,000-14,000 per year stipend instead, while the same non-profit benefits by employing such volunteers to work and do their business under the lie of "**assisting the poor**".

Head Start Program

The Head Start Program is another "state"-owned and privately-operated entity that's **_supposed_** to give preschoolers in economically-depressed areas, a chance to compete with preschoolers who don't live in economically depressed areas. Created in 1965 as a part of President Lyndon B. Johnson's "Great Society" Program, Head Start was originally planned as a preschool Summer School program to prepare low-income preschoolers to start kindergarten the following year. The program was administered upon inception by the Department of Health, Education and Welfare (HEW), which was the precursor to today's Department of Health and Human Services (DHHS) which oversee the program today.

Unfortunately, shortly after its implementation, Head Start began to change, from an advanced learning program, into a program which studies, document and annotate learning deficiencies of inner-city Black and minority schoolchildren.

By 1969, the Westinghouse Learning Corporation and an Ohio University study published reports that Head Start was a good program to use and promote a nationalized/socialized medicine, in which the program's leader during the Nixon Administration, Edward Ziegler called it;
"**America's most successful educational experiment**."

Head Start Program Logo (Courtesy of DRG News.com)

However, numerous studies conducted by well-known research and policy institutes such as the Hoover Institute, reported as recently as 2010, the Head Start Program's impact on a preschooler's early learning is **_nil_**, when compared to a child of the same age starting kindergarten in public school. With a DHHS 2016 budget of $1.093 Billion Dollars, three-percent of that total, or $59.7 Million Dollars, in which 16% or $7.71 Million which is allotted towards Head Start operating costs, ever wonder whether-or-not the Black Poor hasn't advanced in education, even if as early as 4-5 years of age?

Aid to Families with Dependent Children (AFDC)

The Aid to Families with Dependent Children (AFDC), the forerunner to today's Temporary Assistance for Needy Families (TANF), was originally created under the Social Security Act of 1935, which was signed into law by Democrat President Franklin Delano Roosevelt. The program was intended for children who were deemed by his administration as;

"...deprived of parental support or care because their father or mother is absent from the home continuously, is incapacitated, is deceased, or is unemployed."

The program was designed as a Federal-State Partnership administratively, where cash assistance, in the form of Grants (Taxpayer-funded money), was given to all families who were determined eligible to receive such benefits. Both Federal and States Governments were supposed to contribute to the AFDC program with matching contributions prior to cash being paid out. However, several problems arose from the program immediately, which will hamper the program's reputation even up to the present-day.

AFDC program's 'good intentions', to help the very poor families and single mothers, which led to some beneficiaries to abuse the program, by providing false information, which was not deemed verifiable, to qualify for benefits. This caused some in society, that the AFDC program was a {and still is} a welfare entitlement, to literally gave money to very poor families, allowing members of those families to stop looking for work altogether. When the program was amended in 1965, along with the Social Security Act, the Federal Government allowed individual states to establish their own thresholds of Income Poverty Levels, which is many cases either exceeded the Federal Income

Poverty Level or far below it. This caused a wide variance of benefit payouts state-by-state, even if the eligibility requirements remained the same. For example, if an African-American Family of five in 1970, lived in the state of Missouri, received about $225.00, while the same eligible family in Mississippi would receive $120.00, where those living in Alaska received almost $800.00 per month!

By the 1970's, as the destruction of the family increased in American by Marxist-Leninist ideology, the AFDC program began to show inconsistencies in eligibility requirements, where some people and/or families were receiving program benefits who shouldn't receive them, vice those people/families who needed them, couldn't get it. Especially when AFDC eligibility requirements varied from state-to-state. This caused numerous complaints of fraud being committed by both those who were giving monetary payouts, and the Community Action Agencies (CAA) who administered the payouts, ended in lawsuits, arrests and even revocation from the entitlement program.

Another aspect of the Aid to Families with Dependent Children program was when individuals or families were enrolled in the program, they were automatically enrolled into another Taxpayer-funded benefit program called "**Medicaid**", to include later-on, **Child Care Subsidies**, which were Taxpayer-funded for those beneficiaries who participated in work or job training programs.

Of course, as the rolls of the AFDC increased in the late-1960's and early 1970's, so did the costs of the program's budget. Between the year 1970-1975, AFDC program's budget bloomed from less-than $7 Billion Dollars to over $25 Billion Dollars; an increase of over 35%! In 1997, the AFDC program was merged to the **Temporary Assistance for Needy Families (TANF)**, where cash/funding grants are paid out to the states in-stead of directly to the program's beneficiaries.

Section 8 Housing Voucher Program

The Housing Act of 1937, passed by Congress and signed into law by President Franklin D. Roosevelt, authorized government-subsidized (Taxpayer-funded) housing, for certain groups of low-income families, to include the Elderly and Disabled. **Section 8 of the Housing Act**, governs this process, thus giving the program its street name *"Section 8 Housing"*.

What the program does, that it authorizes payment of rental housing assistance to landlords, for such families to reside in privately-owned apartments, houses or publicly-owned Housing Projects. The program also allows owners/landlords of residential properties to reserve up to 20% of their rental units, to accept low-income families, who are qualified under the program, in any neighborhood that such owners deem necessary.

In turn, Section 8 residents can pay up to a 30% of their yearly Adjusted Gross Income for their housing. The rest of the rent under Section 8 is paid for by the Federal Government or 70-plus percent. The Section 8 Housing Voucher Program, administered by the Department of Housing and Urban Development (HUD), and Executive Branch of the Federal Government. How much does this program costs the Taxpayers, in 2016, was budgeted for the last year of the President Barack Obama Administration, for $21.1 Billion Dollars? This money was allotted to support 4.7 million low-income families throughout the United States.

Medicaid

Medicaid is another government benefit program created by the **Social Security Act of 1935**, which was **amended in 1965**. Created as a part of President Lyndon Johnson's 'War on Poverty' and 'Great Society' programs, to enslave low-income Americans to the 'State', in-order for them to control every aspect of their lives.

The program is Taxpayer-funded, that provides long-term care health care insurance for low-income people, especially African-Americans, that covers both inpatient and outpatient clinical care. Usually, those families who qualify for TANF, also are automatically enrolled to receive Medicaid benefits too.

As with all Federal Government Entitlement Programs, the FEDS partners with the states to provide matching funds to pay the expenses to cover health care services for Medicaid enrollees. The Department of Health and Human Services' (DHHS), Center for Medicaid and Medicare (CMS) administers the entire program. Medicaid, since its inception in 1965, has steadily increased in numbers of enrollment, costing the Taxpayers over $40.68 Million Dollars every hour in 2016, according to the National Priorities Project, which oversees Federal Government spending programs.

Since 2010, with the passage and signing into law by former President Barack Obama, the Patient Privacy and Affordable Care Act (PPACA) or 'Obamacare' has greatly expanded the Medicaid enrollment even more than ever. Over 73.87 million people, out of a total 2016 population of 342. 61 million or 23% of the total population are enrolled in Medicaid. But, of the same Medicaid rolls, African-American enrollment in the Medicaid program topples at 39.6% and 43% of the Black Population of 42.02 million people receive Welfare benefits period! As the population of the United States continue to expand and with less and fewer Taxpayers working to fund such welfare entitlements, the end-point would be a complete collapse of the nation's economy, causing hyperinflation and outright anarchy. Perfect for Marxist Men to exploit to start their worldwide revolution.

19: Conclusion: What's the Point?

"The idea is to create a situation where the people are so frightened of the violence all around them, [eventually] that they would throw their hands up in the air and demand, 'Federal Government, do something'! And the only choice open will be Martial Law."

-Jerry Kirk-

I'm sure some people would ask the question, 'What's the point of this book'?

The point of this book was to bring light and put into focus, both the historical aspect of ideological issues being portrayed right now in the Black Community. The main point of the discussions articulated throughout the publication, can be summed up as this; **Once you give up your individual freedom and liberty to the 'Almighty State', so Bureaucrats at the UN can rule over every aspect of your life, the only thing you will end-up accomplishing, will be the re-enslavement of yourself, your community, your country of the United States of America and assist in your own self-genocide.**

This the Marxist Man's plan and their job to carry out their ideology to instill Communism, wrapped up in the package of Globalism, via a violent/bloody revolution. Karl Marx and Friedrich Engels created it, Lenin, Mao, Jung Un/Ils, Po Pot and Stalin have killed many trying to instill full-Communism into their societies. All of them failed and killed millions. Right- now as of this writing, the countries of Cuba and Venezuela are doing these very things that the previous men had failed at right this very second. By dividing the people along racial lines, Marxist Men will use the sacrifices of the African-American minds, body, and souls, as sheep ready for slaughter on behalf of 'Liberation', 'Equality', 'Social Justice' and 'Fairness'.

The other idea of this publication is to educate those cultures, who are scratching their heads and wondering why a certain section of

Black's in America support, believe in and will die for Marxist-Leninist Ideology. Jerry Kirk, in 1969 was a former member of the Communist front groups of the Students for a Democratic Society (SDS), Black Panther Party (BPP), the DuBois Club of America (DBCA) and Communist Party of the United States of America (CPUSA) answered this very question;

"The Communists, Black Militants, and Revolutionaries will never succeed in overthrowing the government of the United States. But, unless they are stopped, they will scare the American people into accepting Socialism from Washington and Statist rule by the insiders of the establishment. This is what it is really about."

Jerry Kirk's Assessment regarding Marxist Men is right on point. All people have to do, is to have an open-mind and be aware of what's going on in their community, their environment and their country, in order to see what Marxist Men are doing to the United States right before your eyes. Their tactics are nothing new. Their consistent agitation campaigns regarding issues, like Abortion, Religion, Gender, Race, Economic Class, and Law and Order have been in the past and still in the present, are under assault by Marxist-Leninist Ideology; each and every day.

I wrote this book to also educate the African-American Community itself, why a section of those inside our community don't care whether they live or die, or why we hurt or kill each other in large numbers. It has come to a point, where our population numbers as a people are dwindling while other cultures are increasing; including the Foreign-born. **This is not empty rhetoric; it is the truth**. In 2015, the United States Crime Statistics showed that Black kills by other Blacks have increased steadily by 97%, while Blacks who are killed by Law Enforcement is less than 1% and Blacks killed by White Americans have only increased 2%. Ask yourself, why is that? Here's the Answer; we as a community have gone from Independence to Dependence on the "Almighty State's" Plantation. Our dependency on the State to think for us has allowed us to self-destroy ourselves, soon into oblivion, if we don't stop this trend.

At the same time, the U.S. Census data between the years 2000 and 2010 proves this. Between those years, in the year 2000, the African-American Community represented 12.9% of the population, either ***"Black or in combination with other Races"***. The those claiming ***"Black alone"*** that same year was 12.3%. However, by 2010, the African-American Community either claiming "***Black or in combination***" went from 12.9% to 13.6%, an increase of 15.4%. Let's look at 2010. Those persons claiming, ***"Black in combination"*** rose to 13.6%, vice ***"Black alone"*** was reported as 12.6%. Of that combination, between that same ten-year period, within the category of "Black in Combination, the biggest increases are as follows;

Black/White increased by 133.7%

Black/White/Native American increased by 105.7%

Black/Asian increased by 73.8%

Black/Hispanic increased by 62.8%

Black/Native American/Native Alaskan increased by 47.6%

What is wrong with these statistics? You decide.

As you ponder these statistics, our so-called '**Black Leaders**' and their so-called 'Black Organizations', whom this author will label as **'Black Supremacy'** groups, are being financially operated and are being paid by the same super-rich elites that they teach you to hate!

These so-called Black Leadership people include Nation of Islam (NOI) leader Louis Farrakhan, Congressman and Radical NOI Black Muslim Keith Ellison a.k.a. 'Keith X', members of the Congressional Black Caucus, the flamboyant self-admitted Communist Van Jones, and many other people, are psychological dupes who have for their entire lives, bought into the lie of Socialism and Communism ideology.

This also includes the 44th President of the United States, Barack Hussein Obama. Why? Because these are the '***useful idiots***' that Vladimir Lenin has stated, to further this worldwide revolution in which they will never be a part of, at the end! Yuri Bezmenov and the historical context had written thousands of cases of such. Let us not repeat history.

A question needs to be asked. Why would such Capitalists and Business Elites who are running IBM, Xerox, JPMorgan-Chase and many other corporations, would finance and support the economic system of

Socialism and Communism; the very systems that will destroy them? There is an easy answer. The heads of such companies have been brainwashed so-well, that they actually believe that if such oppressive systems come into being, they themselves will profit handsomely off the labor produced by those systems. It's an absolute fallacy and they will never know that at the end, they will be destroyed as well.

"We should measure welfare's success by how many people leave welfare, not how many are added." (Ronald Reagan)

When Vladimir Lenin stated;

"Riots, demonstrations-street battles-detachments of a revolutionary army-such are the stages in the development of the popular uprising."

He was talking about the psychological subversion of the targeted country; in this case, the United States of America. Marx and Engels had called for the overthrow of the 'Old Society' or the 'Bourgeoisie Society', by a Proletariat Revolution. A revolution, that will be bloody and violent.

When you mix what Lenin had stated, coupled with the actions of their contemporaries, such as Joseph Stalin, Pol Pot, Mao Tse Tung and thousands more, plus the four-stage process identified by Yuri Bezmenov in Chapter Six, what do you have? You will have a mixture of societal decay; economic failure and you would have gained the basic understanding of what life is about in our country today. The caveat of this mixture of hate, discontent, violence, instilled by lies, propaganda, and deception via the media, is being done on purpose! The people who are being used and abused to become the sacrificial lamb in the middle of all this drama; African-Americans, other Minorities in the U.S. Population and the Foreign-Born.

Rioters causing property damage during the Baltimore Riots in 2015.
(Courtesy of Baltimore Sun)

Let's be honest about something. When the former President of the United States Barack Obama, campaigned and ran for this position in which he was selected to win in 2008, he operated his campaign on the slogan of '**Hope**' and '**Change**', right? It is also to be recalled that Obama operated his campaign that his job as President would be to '***fundamentally transform***' the country of the United States of America.

The goal of the latter slogan, has a more sinister purpose, that it is extremely important to remember. Every aspect of transforming America into a Socialist/Soviet Union-Communist-type utopia is what Barack Obama meant by 'fundamentally transforming' America. What he did, and what many of us have false accepted, is a part of the Globalist Objective to create a worldwide crisis, in this case, a World War, to instigate a worldwide revolution and usher in worldwide Communism, just as Marx and Engels have planned.

However, for this worldwide revolution to take place, the conditions have-to be ripe for exploitation and an urgent need to have a large, trained and ideological army of people have to be mobilized and equipped for this worldwide revolution to take place. [6]

Yes, you have read the last sentence right! For a revolution to occur, on a massive global scale, as Lenin stated, you must have some sort-of a Revolutionary Army (or Armies), that is well-funded, well-trained and mentally subverting to accept Marxist-Leninist principles very well, to carry out their monument is revolutionary actions.

~ 385 ~

It will be these armies of individual people, who will be the foot soldiers, inside the United States which will launch such a revolution on U.S. Soil.

Who will be the '**lead agent**' of this army of Communist Revolutionaries? Simple, the Communist Party of the United States of American (CPUSA) and its plethora of tentacle front groups, will make up the core constituents of this campaign. Groups such as Black Lives Matter (BLM), New Black Panther Party (NBPP), Organizing for Action (OFA) led by Obama himself, and Antifa, a consolidated mixture of multiple groups of Anarchical, Marxism-driven people, will spearhead this operation.

Their primary objective is to invent and drive a sustainable series of agitation campaigns throughout America, using the media as avenues of communication. The first objective is to change the perception of reality of mainstream America. By doing this, the people will begin to get tired of fighting such wave-after-wave of agitation campaigns, over-and-over again, to the point where we, the American people, Black, White and Indifferent, will just give up and allow such groups to advance their agenda. Just to shut them up.

This cannot happen!

African Americans undergoing Marxist Subversion Training at the Highland Folk School (now-The Highland Research and Educational Center) in the late 1950's.

(Courtesy of Marxists.org)

Once you allow ***BLM, NBPP, OFA, and Antifa*** have their way, with no resistance or pushback to these Marxist-Leninists ideological groups, before you know it, you will be living under Communism and wouldn't even know it happened. Remember, these front groups main objective is to destroy Capitalism and Free-Market Enterprise and replace it under an oppressive system, that has killed millions.

For these groups to continue their wave of agitation, they must be trained on how to conduct such propaganda actions, to help Marxist Men to further their drive towards Communism.

There are actual training institutes, outside of the Public Education System of the United States, that were created to specifically train, equip, and mentally subvert their students to become "**Community Organizers**". A partial list of these institutes, are;

Communist Party of the United States of America (CPUSA)
Slogan- "People and Planet before Profits"
Nationwide in over 30-plus American Cities
www.cpusa.org

Democratic Socialists of America (DSA)
Nationwide
www.dsausa.org

Young Democratic Socialists (YDS)
Nationwide
www.ydsusa.org

Organizing for Action (OFA)- formerly Organizing for America
Slogan- "Your Voice Can Change a Room"
Headquartered in Chicago, Illinois
CEO- Former U.S. President Barack Hussein Obama
www.ofa.us

Highlander Research and Educational Training Center
Monteagle, Tennessee
www.highlandercenter.org

Direct Action and Research Center (DART)
Miami Shores, Florida
www.thedartcenter.org

Organize! Training Center (OTC)
San Francisco, California
www.organiztrainingcenter.org

Sixth and I
Washington D.C.
www.sixthandi.org

Alliance of Community Trainers (ACT)
Austin, Texas
www.trainingalliance.org

Organizing for Power, Organizing for Change (OPOC)
(Apart of the Alliance of Community Trainers)
www.organizingforpower.org

Earth Activist Training (EAT)
Austin, Texas
www.earthactivisttraining.org

Starhawk Tangled Web (STW)
www.starhawk.org

Virginia Organizing
Charlottesville, Virginia
www.virginia-organizing.org

Industrial Areas Foundation (IAF)
Founded by Saul Alinsky in 1940
Slogan- "Faith, Democracy, Relationships, Leaderships and Impact"
Headquartered in Chicago, Illinois
Office locations in 21 States
www.indstrialareasfoundation.org

Voices for Racial Justice (VFRU)
Minneapolis, Minnesota
www.voicesforracialinjustice.org

Camp Wellstone
Nationwide
Boasts 50,000 Alumni

Publicly endorsed by Massachusetts Democrat Senator
Elizabeth Warren
www.wellstone.org

Rainbow/PUSH
Founded by Reverend Jesse Jackson Sr.
Chicago, Illinois
www.rainbowpush.org

For example, CPUSA's mantra states *"People and Planet before Profits"*, though is contradictory, provides an effective message to those who have been taught from day one, not to rationalize for themselves. Their nationwide offices offer training courses to teach Marxism, that can be taken online, by phone and even by classroom instruction!

Similar in scope to your everyday college campus. Other groups such as the San Francisco-based Direct Action & Research Training Center (DART) mantra *"Building the Power of Organized People to do Justice"* and have been affiliated with 22 so-called congregation-based community organizations in the states of Kansas, Kentucky, Florida, Ohio, South Carolina, Indiana, Tennessee, and Virginia. The idea behind the latter Marxist-training Institute, is to subvert the churches, particularly Black Churches, to preach from the pulpit the teachings of Marxism, under the guise of *Black Liberation Theology (BLT)*. [7,8]

Another aspect of these CPUSA-driven Communist front groups is that these organizations and entities are exactly what Obama mentioned in one of his campaign speeches he gave in Colorado Springs, Colorado in 2008. It was here where he called for a civilian security force. He stated in his speech;

"We cannot continue to rely on our military in-order to achieve the national objective we set...We've got to have a Civilian National Security Force that's just as powerful, just as strong, just as well-funded."

Even the New York City-based Action Network (TAN) president, founder and Black Marxist-Leninist Al Sharpton called for similar action in 2015, in the wake of the Baltimore, Maryland Riots, because of the arrest and death of Freddie Gray;

"...The Justice department must step in and take over policing in this country..."

When you have so-called "**Community Activists**" or "**Community Agitators**" advocate for a national police force that is just as armed, equipped and funded like the U.S. Military, it is a guarantee that such forces are not going to fight crime in our streets, but will silence all opposition to the Communist Order.

This mission is one of the overall functions of such protest groups like Black Lives Matter (BLM), NBPP, Antifa and others just waiting to be created and formed to further push the Communist agenda.

Black Lives Matter (BLM) Protest in Portland Oregon in 2017.
(Courtesy of Daily Headlines.net)

This is the "*Social Justice*" and "*Hope*" and "*Change*" that both men had and most likely continue to push for.

Other leaders in recent history had done the same.

Adolf Hitler's SS and Gestapo, Joseph Stalin's KGB, North Korea's State Security Department (SSD) and many others with similar functions. However, in the broader picture, a worldwide Communist Revolution, hidden behind the name of "_**Globalism**_" has taken center stage. If such an enormous violent crisis were to develop in the United States, once the violent change of political and economic power of the country has taken place and a period of Normalcy has taken hold of the country, one must remember this one last fact.

The governing body of the United States will not be in Washington D.C. but in New York City, under the banner of the United Nations (UN)!

It will be here where African Americans or as a matter of fact, any American, who will be left after this Global Revolution had taken place, either we will no longer be alive to see this 'new society' take shape!

The question must be asked; we will be doomed to repeat history and re-enslave ourselves to the *"**Almighty State**"*.

It is here, where we will not have a place to run to, in-order to seek freedom from ***real oppression***.

The United States is the last beacon of hope and freedom. Once the U.S. has been taken over by Communism, we cease being a country. At the end, the entire world will be taken over by oppressive regimes, operated solely by the UN and there will be nothing that we, as a people, will be able to do about it but perish into oblivion.

22

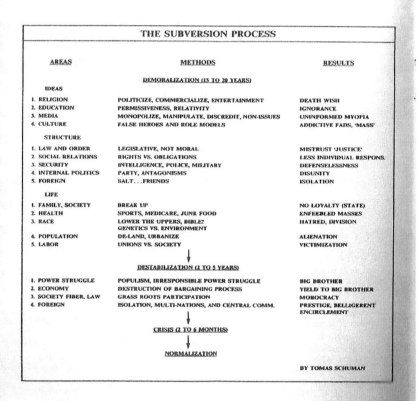

THE SUBVERSION PROCESS

AREAS	METHODS	RESULTS
	DEMORALIZATION (15 TO 20 YEARS)	
IDEAS		
1. RELIGION	POLITICIZE, COMMERCIALIZE, ENTERTAINMENT	DEATH WISH
2. EDUCATION	PERMISSIVENESS, RELATIVITY	IGNORANCE
3. MEDIA	MONOPOLIZE, MANIPULATE, DISCREDIT, NON-ISSUES	UNINFORMED MYOPIA
4. CULTURE	FALSE HEROES AND ROLE MODELS	ADDICTIVE FADS, 'MASS'
STRUCTURE		
1. LAW AND ORDER	LEGISLATIVE, NOT MORAL	MISTRUST 'JUSTICE'
2. SOCIAL RELATIONS	RIGHTS VS. OBLIGATIONS	LESS INDIVIDUAL RESPONS.
3. SECURITY	INTELLIGENCE, POLICE, MILITARY	DEFENSELESSNESS
4. INTERNAL POLITICS	PARTY, ANTAGONISMS	DISUNITY
5. FOREIGN	SALT...FRIENDS	ISOLATION
LIFE		
1. FAMILY, SOCIETY	BREAK UP	NO LOYALTY (STATE)
2. HEALTH	SPORTS, MEDICARE, JUNK FOOD	ENFEEBLED MASSES
3. RACE	LOWER THE UPPERS, BIBLE? GENETICS VS. ENVIRONMENT	HATRED, DIVISION
4. POPULATION	DE-LAND, URBANIZE	ALIENATION
5. LABOR	UNIONS VS. SOCIETY	VICTIMIZATION

↓

	DESTABILIZATION (2 TO 5 YEARS)	
1. POWER STRUGGLE	POPULISM, IRRESPONSIBLE POWER STRUGGLE	BIG BROTHER
2. ECONOMY	DESTRUCTION OF BARGAINING PROCESS	YIELD TO BIG BROTHER
3. SOCIETY FIBER, LAW	GRASS ROOTS PARTICIPATION	MOBOCRACY
4. FOREIGN	ISOLATION, MULTI-NATIONS, AND CENTRAL COMM.	PRESTIGE, BELLIGERENT ENCIRCLEMENT

↓

CRISIS (2 TO 6 MONTHS)

↓

NORMALIZATION

BY TOMAS SCHUMAN

This chart shows the four stages of Soviet ideological subversion: demoralization, destabilization, crisis, and normalization. The methods used by the subverter in the different areas of life produce their desired results in a country that does not resist the subversion process.

The Subversion Process Chart by Yuri Bezmenov a.k.a. Thomas Schuman

Appendix: B

BY. COLUMBIA MISSOURIAN | NOVEMBER 13, 2009

Excerpted from the Columbia Missourian

COLUMBIA — Jarvis Tyner, executive vice chairman of the Communist Party USA, spoke at MU on Thursday and said the election of President Barack Obama opens the door for the left wing, which he feels has allowed itself to be pushed to the sidelines and overcome with progress-impeding cynicism, to mobilize.

"He's only the beginning," Tyner said. "I think he's a transitional president. I think somebody else is going to come in and take it even further." The Communist Party USA

MU students protest the speech of Jarvis Tyner, executive vice chair of the Communist Party USA, with a mock gulag labor camp set up in Speaker's Circle at MU on Thursday.

Tyner spoke to an audience of about 70 people at MU's Ellis Auditorium. He focused on the transitional phase he feels the United States is in because of Obama's election.

Although the president is neither a communist nor socialist, his administration marks the country's movement away from the right-wing governments that have been dominant in the U.S. since the Reagan administration, Tyner said.

He said that while the Democratic Party is not without blame, the Republican leadership has been the source of the nation's problems that include an increase in poverty, a ruined economy, the continuation of global warming, impeded scientific research and the destruction of public schools by No Child Left Behind.

Tyner said he and his party are not completely satisfied with the work Obama has done since taking office, listing the need to withdraw troops more quickly from Iraq, for initiatives to end nuclear weapons and to re-establish trading relations with Cuba...

Read the full article at the Columbia Missourian

CPUSA EXECUTIVE VICE-CHAIRMAN TRAVIS TYNER, SPEAKING TO STUDENTS AT THE UNIVERSITY OF MISSOURI-COLUMBIA NOVEMBER 12, 2009 (COURTESY OF THE COLUMBIA MISSOURIAN)

Appendix C:

**FBI PHOTO OF WALLACE DODD FARD-MUHAMMAD-FORD
(COURTESY OF FEDERAL BUREAU OF INVESTIGATIONS)**

**FOUR PHOTOS OF WALLACE DODD FARD-MUHAMMAD
(COURTESY OF FBI AND TRUTH CONTINUUM)**

Wali D. Fard was arrested in Detroit on Nov. 24, 1932 along with Elijah Muhammad after a Black Muslim killed a man as a "sacrifice" to God. He was ordered to leave the city on May 25, 1933.

Appendix D:

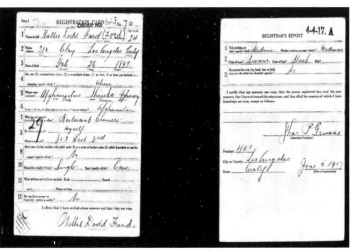

WALLACE DODD FARD-FORD-MUHAMMAD'S WORLD WAR I DRAFT CARD
DATED JANUARY 5, 1917
(COURTESY OF ANCESTRY.COM)

MARRIAGE CERTIFICATE

STATE OF WASHINGTON, } ss.
County of Snohomish,

No. 7697

I HEREBY CERTIFY, That on the 19th day of July in the year of our Lord, One Thousand Nine Hundred and Fifteen at Everett in the County of Snohomish and State aforesaid

I, the undersigned, a **Minister of the Gospel** by authority of a license bearing date the 19th day of July A. D. 1915, and issued by the County Auditor of Snohomish County, did, on the 19th day of July A. D. 1915, join in lawful wedlock

Tony Campagna of the County of Snohomish State of Wash and Pearl Dodd of the County of Snohomish State of Wash

In the presence of

Tony Randall
Minister of the Gospel

John Bump
Mary R Randall

Tony Campagna — Groom

Pearl Dodd — Bride

Filed for Record this _____ day of _____

by _____

FILED
JUL 29 1915
CHAS. H. FICKEL, County Clerk
By _____ Deputy

This Certificate must be filled out and filed with the Clerk of the Superior Court of the County WHERE THE CEREMONY IS PERFORMED, within three months after the ceremony.—See Sec. 2385 of Code.

The fee for recording this Certificate is one dollar, to be paid by the party applying for the License at the time each License is issued—See Sec. 2386 of the Code, as amended in 1886.

**MARRIAGE APPLICATION BETWEEN FRED DODD AND PEARL ALLEN/ENOUF IN 1915
(COURTESY OF THE TRUTH CONTINUUM)**

Appendix F:

Divorce Decree between Fred Dodd and Pearl (Allen) Dodd

(Courtesy of Ancestry.com and The Truth Continuum)

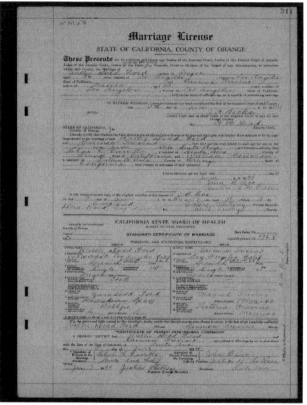

1924 Orange County, California Marriage License and Certificate between

Wallie Dodd Ford and Carmen Trevino

(Courtesy of Ancestry.com)

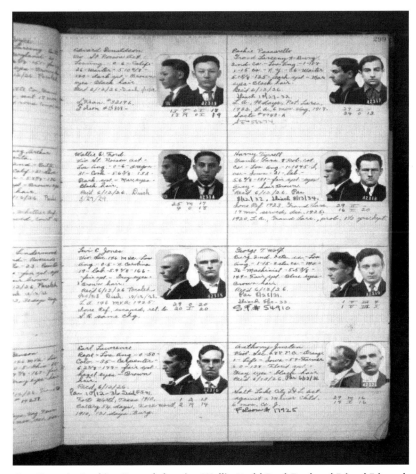

San Quentin Booking Record showing Wallie Dodd Ford-Fard and Friend Edward Donaldson

(Top Left, Donaldson and Ford-Fard)

(Courtesy of Ancestry.com)

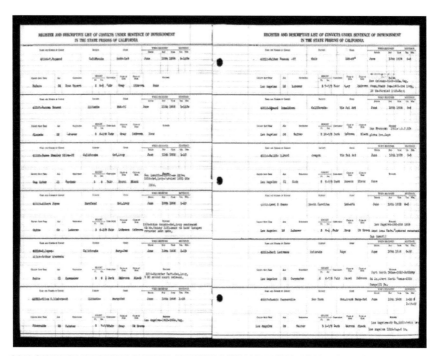

SAN QUENTIN BOOKING RECORD SHOWING WALLIE DODD FORD-FARD AND EDWARD
DONALDSON 1926
(COURTESY OF ANCESTRY.COM)

Appendix I:

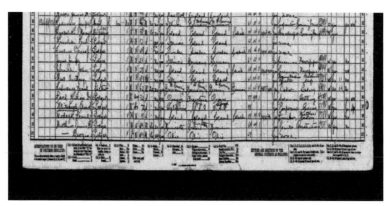

1930 Federal Census of Chicago, Illinois showing a William D. Fard living in the
residence of
Joseph Radwancz.
(Courtesy of Ancestry.com)

November 21, 1932, Detroit Free Press Article regarding the

Nation of Islam member Robert X Harris

(Courtesy of Newspapers.com)

May 18, 1954, Anniston (Alabama) Star Front Page Headline regarding SCOTUS Decision on

School Segregation

(Courtesy of Newspapers.com)

Appendix L:

African American Author and Anthropologist Zora Neale Hurston's Editorial regarding SCOTUS Decision on School Segregation in the Orlando-Sentinel, Thursday August 11, 1955.

(Courtesy of Newspapers.com)

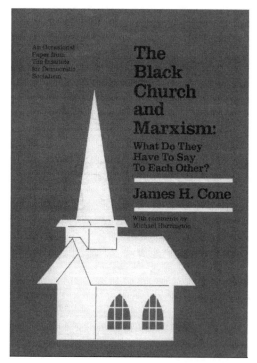

Excerpts from James H. Cone's 1980 book.

(Courtesy of Marxists.org)

April, 1980

THE BLACK CHURCH AND MARXISM:

WHAT DO THEY HAVE TO SAY TO EACH OTHER?

by

James H. Cone
Union Theological Seminary, NY

The black church and marxism have emerged on the North American
continent from separate historical paths and thus have encountered each
other only rarely. Marxism is European in origin and was imported into
the United States in 1851 by Joseph Weydemeyer, a friend of Karl Marx.
The black church is both African and European in origin. It was created
during the late 18th and early 19th centuries when black people refused to
accept slavery and racial oppression as consistent with the gospel of
Jesus Christ. During the early period of their existence in North America,
there was virtually no contact between black churches and marxists. Both
were preoccupied with their own immediate projects, which were sharply
contradicted by the current structures of American capitalism. The
primary historical project of marxists was defined in terms of the
destruction of capitalism and the establishment of a socialist society
in which the means of productive forces would be owned by the people
rather than by an elite ruling class. The primary historical project of
the black church was defined as preaching and living the gospel of Jesus
in order to receive both the gift of eternal life and the courage to
fight against injustice in this world, especially as represented in
slavery and racism.

The different histories of the black church and marxism as well
as their different perspectives on the human condition confirmed their

---

Note: This essay was written for the Democratic Socialist Organizing Committee's seminar on "Religion, Socialism, and the Black Experience," held
at Asbury United Methodist Church, Washington, D.C., April 9, 1980. An
earlier version of this paper was presented in a "Black Theology and
Marxist Thought" seminar at Union Theological Seminary, jointly taught by
Professor Cornel West and me. I wish to convey my gratitude to the
students of that class for their perceptive comments. I also benefited
immensely from the critical observations of my colleague, Cornel West,
whose presentation of the socialist challenge is provocative and appealing.

The importance of the socialist issue for the black church was rein-
forced within my consciousness when I presented this lecture at the Shaker
Heights Community Church's Martin Luther King, Jr. Institute for Racial
Justice, April 25-26, 1980. The black church people of that church and
other blacks attending the seminar responded enthusiastically to my
analysis and encouraged me to pursue the socialism issue.

THE
AMERICAN NEGRO
IN THE
COMMUNIST PARTY

DECEMBER 22, 1954

Prepared and released by the
Committee on Un-American Activities, U. S. House of Representatives
Washington, D. C.

AMERICAN NEGRO IN THE COMMUNIST PARTY CONGRESSIONAL TESTIMONY
(COURTESY OF NATIONAL ARCHIVES)

Author's Notes

Introduction

[1] Woodson, Carter Godwin. *The Mis-Education of the Negro*. United States, Watchmaker Publishing, 2016.

[2] Andrews, Andy. *How Do You Kill 11 Million People?: Why the Truth Matters More than You Think*. Nashville, TN, Thomas Nelson, 2012.

Chapter 1 Truth vs. Deception: An Overview of Karl Marx, Friedrich Engels, and Communism

[1] "Deceit". Merriam-Webster's Dictionary and Thesaurus." *Merriam-Webster's Dictionary and Thesaurus*, Merriam-Webster, Springfield, MA, 2007, pp. 200–201.

[2] "Deception". Merriam-Webster's Dictionary and Thesaurus." *Merriam-Webster's Dictionary and Thesaurus*, Merriam-Webster, Springfield, MA, 2007, pp. 300–301.

[3] Andrews, Andy. *How Do You Kill 11 Million People?: Why the Truth Matters More than You Think*. Nashville, TN, Thomas Nelson, 2012.

[4] "Fascism". Merriam-Webster's Dictionary and Thesaurus." *Merriam-Webster's Dictionary and Thesaurus*, Merriam-Webster, Springfield, MA, 2007, p. 293.

[5] "Marxism". Merriam-Webster's Dictionary and Thesaurus." *Merriam-Webster's Dictionary and Thesaurus*, Merriam-Webster, Springfield, MA, 2007, p. 498.

[6] Bell, Kenton. "Marxism Sociology Dictionary Definition: Marxism Defined." *Open Education Sociology Dictionary*, Open Education Sociology, 2013, http://sociologydictionary.org/marxism/. Accessed 4 Apr. 2017.

[7] "Marxism-Leninism." *Merriam-Webster*, Merriam-Webster, 2017, https://www.merriam-webster.com/dictionary/marxism-leninism. Accessed 4 Apr. 2017.

[8] Skousen, W. Cleon. *The Naked Communist*. Salt Lake City, UT, Izzard Ink, LLC, 2014, pp. 9-13. The Naked Series.

[9] "Georg Wilhelm Friedrich Hegel." *Wikipedia*, Wikimedia Foundation, 31 Mar. 2017, https://en.wikipedia.org/wiki/Georg_Wilhelm_Friedrich_Hegel. Accessed 4 Apr. 2017.

[10] Knox, T. Malcolm. "Georg Wilhelm Friedrich Hegel." *Encyclopædia Britannica*, Encyclopædia Britannica, Inc., 23 May 2011, https://www.britannica.com/biography/Georg-Wilhelm-Friedrich-Hegel. Accessed 4 Apr. 2017.

[11] Landry, Stan M. "From Orthodoxy to Atheism: The Apostasy of Bruno Bauer 1835-1843." *Journal of Religion & Society*, vol. 13, 2011, pp. 1–26., doi:10.4135/9781446216699.n1.
Accessed 4 Apr. 2017.

[12] "Bruno Bauer." *Wikipedia*, Wikimedia Foundation, 28 Mar. 2017, https://en.wikipedia.org/wiki/Bruno_Bauer. Accessed 4 Apr. 2017.

[13] Beiser, Frederick C. *Hegel*. New York, NY, Routledge, 2010.

[14] "Ludwig Feuerbach." *Wikipedia*, Wikimedia Foundation, 30 Mar. 2017, https://en.wikipedia.org/wiki/Ludwig_Feuerbach. Accessed 4 Apr. 2017.

[15] Skousen, W. Cleon. *The Naked Communist*. Salt Lake City, UT, Izzard Ink, LLC, 2014.pp. 13-15. The Naked Series.

[16] "Friedrich Engels." *Wikipedia*, Wikimedia Foundation, 4 Apr. 2017, https://en.wikipedia.org/wiki/Friedrich_Engels. Accessed 4 Apr. 2017.

[17] Leopold, David. *The Young Karl Marx: German Philosophy, Modern Politics, and Human Flourishing*. Cambridge, Cambridge Univ. Press, 2009.

[18] Marx, Karl, and Friedrich Engels. *Manifesto of the Communist Party*. http://www.marxists.org/archive/marx/works/download/pdf/Manifesto.pdf. Accessed 4 Apr. 2017.

[19] Marx, Karl. *Das Kapital*. Miami, FL, Synergy International of the Americas, 2006.

Chapter 2 The Marxist Theory

[1] Marx, Karl, and Friedrich Engels. *Manifesto of the Communist Party*. http://www.marxists.org/archive/marx/works/download/pdf/Manifesto.pdf. Accessed 4 Apr. 2017.

[2] IBID.

[3] IBID.

[4] Skousen, W. Cleon. *The Naked Communist*. Salt Lake City, UT, Izzard Ink, LLC, 2014.pp. 26-30. The Naked Series.

[5] Skousen, W. Cleon. "The Naked Communist." *The Naked Communist*, 1st ed., vol. 1, Izzard Ink, LLC, Salt Lake City, UT, 2014, pp. 33–35. The Naked Series.

[6] IBID. Skousen. Pp. 37-39

[7] IBID. Skousen. Pp. 42-45

[8] IBID. Skousen. Pp. 47-52

[9] Skousen, W. Cleon. "The Naked Communist." *The Naked Communist*, 1st ed., vol. 1, Izzard Ink, LLC, Salt Lake City, UT, 2014, pp. 53–56. The Naked Series.

Chapter 3 Marxism's Means of Production, Class Distinction and Plan of Action

[1] Marx, Karl, and Friedrich Engels. *Manifesto of the Communist Party*. https://www.marxists.org/archive/marx/works/download/pdf/Manifesto.pdf. Accessed 4 Apr. 2017.

[2] IBID.

[3] IBID.

[4] Skousen, W. Cleon. *The Naked Communist*. Salt Lake City, UT, Izzard Ink, LLC, 2014. Pp. 54-60.
The Naked Series.

[5] IBID.

[6] IBID.

[7] "Feudalism." *Wikipedia*, Wikimedia Foundation, 29 Mar. 2017, https://en.wikipedia.org/wiki/Feudalism. Accessed 5 Apr. 2017.

[8] "Feudalism". Merriam-Webster's Dictionary and Thesaurus." *Merriam-Webster's Dictionary and Thesaurus*, Merriam-Webster, Springfield, MA, 2007, p. 300.

[9] Marx, Karl, and Friedrich Engels. *Manifesto of the Communist Party*. https://www.marxists.org/archive/marx/works/download/pdf/Manifesto.pdf. Accessed 4 Apr. 2017.

[10] IBID. Marx/Engels. *Manifesto of the Communist Party*.

[11] Skousen, W. Cleon. *The Naked Communist*. Salt Lake City, UT, Izzard Ink, LLC, 2014. Pp. 69-70. The Naked Series.

[12] IBID.

[13] IBID.

[14] IBID. Marx/Engels. *Manifesto of the Communist Party*.

[15] IBID. Marx/Engels. *Manifesto of the Communist Party*.

[16] Leopold, David. *The Young Karl Marx: German Philosophy, Modern Politics, and Human Flourishing*. Cambridge, Cambridge Univ. Press, 2009.

[17] IBID.

[18] Skousen, W. Cleon. *The Naked Communist*. Salt Lake City, UT, Izzard Ink, LLC, 2014. Pp. 71-72. The Naked Series.

[19] "Matthew 19:24." *Holy Bible: The Old and New Testaments King James Version*, Holman Bible Publishers, 1996, pp. 1503-1504.

[20] Scheeres, Julia. *A Thousand Lives: The Untold Story of Hope, Deception, and*

Survival at Jonestown, Free Press, New York, 2014.

[21] "Jonestown, PBS Documentary (FULL)." *YouTube*, 12 July 2013, https://youtu.be/3HTtLHgU9tY. Accessed 1 May 2017.

[22] Marx, Karl, and Friedrich Engels. *Manifesto of the Communist Party.* www.marxists.org/archive/marx/works/download/pdf/Manifesto.pdf. Accessed 4 Apr. 2017.

[23] IBID.

[24] IBID.

[25] "Horace Greeley-Wikipedia." *Wikipedia, the Free Encyclopedia,* Wikimedia Foundation, Inc, 2017, https://en.wikipedia.org/wiki/Horace_Greeley. Accessed 2 May 2017.

[26] Lawrence, Ken. *Karl Marx on Slavery.* Freedom Information Service, London, 1976.

[27] IBID.

[28] IBID.

Chapter 4 Marxist Man: The Psychopathic Criminal

[1] Marx, Karl, and Friedrich Engels. *Manifesto of the Communist Party.* https://www.marxists.org/archive/marx/works/download/pdf/Manifesto.pdf. Accessed 4 Apr. 2017.

[2] IBID.

[3] Skousen, W. Cleon. *The Naked Communist.* Salt Lake City, UT, Izzard Ink, LLC, 2014.

[4] IBID.

[5] Skousen, W. Cleon. *The Naked Communist.* Salt Lake City, UT, Izzard Ink, LLC, 2014. Pp 171-177. The Naked Series.

[6] IBID.

[7] IBID.

[8] IBID.

[9] IBID.

[10] "Vladimir Lenin-Wikipedia." *Wikipedia, the Free Encyclopedia*, Wikipedia Foundation, Inc, 2017, https://en.wikipedia.org/wiki/Vladimir_Lenin. Accessed 2 May 2017.

[11] Bump, Philip. "Here is When Each Generation Begins and Ends, According to Facts. "*The Atlantic,* 25 Mar 2014,

http://www.theatlantic.com/national/archive/2014/03here-is-when-each-generation-begins-and-ends-according-to-facts/359589/. Accessed 2 May 2017.

[12] "Generation X-Wikipedia." *Wikipedia, the Free Encyclopedia*, Wikimedia Foundation, Inc, 2017, https://en.wikipedia.org/wiki/Generation_X. Accessed 2 May 2017.

[13] "Millennials-Wikipedia." *Wikipedia, the Free Encyclopedia.* Wikimedia Foundation, Inc, 2017, https://en.wikipedia.org/wiki/Millennials. Accessed 2 May 2017.

[14] Skousen, W. Cleon. *The Naked Communist*. Salt Lake City, UT, Izzard Ink, LLC, 2014.pp. 26-30.
The Naked Series.

Chapter 5 The Victim Mentality Syndrome: The Proletariat's Sociological Conditioning

[1] Gardner, John W. "Self-Pity." *Self Esteem,*2017,

https://www.selfesteemawareness.com/self-pity/. Accessed 2 May 2017.

[2] Orloff, Judith. "Strategies to Deal with a Victim Mentality." *Psychology Today*, Sussex Publishers, LLC, 1 Oct. 2012,
https://www.psychologytoday.com/blog/emotional-freedom/201210/strategies-deal-victim-mentality. Accessed 2 Apr. 2017.

[3] Fay, Mary Jo. "Narcissism Victim Syndrome, A New Diagnosis?" *Medical News Today*, ediLexicon International, 17 July 2004,
https://www.medicalnewstoday.com/articles/10872.php. Accessed 2 Apr. 2017.

[4] IBID.

[5] Psyber. "Narcissism and Victim Mentality." *Psychforums*, Psychforums.com, 7 Jan. 2013, https://www.psychforums.com/narcissistic-personality/topic104311-10.html. Accessed 2 Apr. 2017.

[6] Meglamania. "The Mentality and Personality of the Narcissist." *Experts Column.com*, Experts Column, 2017, https://www.narcissism.expertscolumn.com/article/mentality-and-personality-narcissist. Accessed 2 Apr. 2017.

[7] Pedersen, Traci. "Millennials Believe They Are the Most Narcissistic Generation." *Psych Central News*, Psych Central, 27 Mar. 2016,

https://www.psychcentral.com/news/2016/03/27/millennials-believe-they-are-the-most-narcissistic-generation/100967.html. Accessed 7 Apr. 2017.

[8] Staff, Mayo Clinic. "Narcissistic Personality Disorder Symptoms." *Mayo Clinic*, Mayo Foundation for Medical Education and Research, 18 Nov. 2014, http://www.mayoclinic.org/diseases-conditions/narcissistic-personality-disorder/basics/symptoms/CON-20025568. Accessed 7 Apr. 2017.

[9] Stein, Joel. "Millennials: The Me Me Me Generation." *Time*, Time, 9 May 2013, https://www.time.com/247/millennials-the-me-me-me-generation/. Accessed 7 Apr. 2017.

[10] Suval, Lauren. "Narcissism and Millennials in the Digital Age." *World of Psychology*, Psych Central, 27 Mar. 2014, https://www.psychcentral.com/blog/archives/2014/03/28/narcissism-and-millennials-in-the-digital-age/. Accessed 7 Apr. 2017.

[11] Kets De Vries, Manfred F.R. "Are You a Victim of the Victim Syndrome?" *Raoul de Vitz d' Avancourt, Fontainebleau, France*, Insead, 2012.

[12] Goudreau, Jenna. "Are Millennials 'Deluded Narcissists'?" *Forbes*, Forbes Magazine, 15 Jan. 2013, http://www.forbes.com/sites/jennagoudreau/2013/01/15/are-millennials-deluded-narcissists/#456e56347dc1. Accessed 7 Apr. 2017.

[13] De Cannonville, Christine Louise. "Narcissistic Victim Syndrome: What the Heck Is That?" *The Roadshow for Therapists Narcissistic Victim Syndrome What the Heck Is That Comments*, The Roadshow for Therapists, 2016, http://www.narcissisticbehavior.net/narcissistic-victim-syndrome-what-the-heck-is-that/. Accessed 7 Apr. 2017.

[14] Kengor, Paul. "The Latter 1940's Frank and the Chicago Crew." *The Communist: Frank Marshall Davis: The Untold Story of Barack Obama's Mentor,* Tantor Media, Inc, 2012, pp. 111-114.

Chapter 6 The Psychological Subversion of the United States of America

[1] "Yuri Bezmenov-Wikipedia." *Wikipedia, the Free Encyclopedia,* Wikimedia Foundation, Inc, 2017, https://en.wikipedia.org/wiki/Yuri_Bezmenov. Accessed 2 May 2017.

[2] IBID.

[3] Kengor, Paul. "Paul Robeson and Progressive Dupes" *The Communist:*

Frank Marshall Davis: The Untold Story of Barack Obama's Mentor, Tantor Media, Inc, 2012, pp. 62-72.

[4] Griffin, G. Edward. "Former KGB Agent Yuri Bezmenov Explains How to Brainwash a Nation (Full Length)." *YouTube,* 29 Dec 2012, youtu.be/5lt1zarINv0. Accessed 2 May 2017.

[5] IBID. Kengor, pp 62-72

[6] IBID. Griffin.

[7] IBID. Griffin.

[8] IBID. Kengor, pp 62-72

[9] IBID. Griffin.

[10] "Yuri Bezmenov: Psychological Warfare Subversion & Control of Western Society (Complete)." *You Tube,* University of California-Los Angeles, 1983, https://youtu.be/5gnpCqsXE8g.
Accessed 2 May 2017.

[11] "Marxism-Leninism." *Merriam-Webster*, Merriam-Webster, 2017, https://www.merriam-webster.com/dictionary/marxism-leninism. Accessed 4 Apr. 2017.

[12] Schuman, Tomas. *Black is Beautiful, but Communism is Not* Almanac, 1985.

[13] IBID.

[14] IBID. Griffin.

[15] IBID. Bezmenov.

[16] Marx, Karl, and Friedrich Engels. *Manifesto of the Communist Party*. https://www.marxists.org/archive/marx/works/download/pdf/Manifesto.pdf. Accessed 4 Apr. 2017.

[17] Guelzo, Allen. "Abraham Lincoln or the Progressives: Who was the Real Father of Big Government?" *The Heritage Foundation*, 10 Feb 2012, http://heritage.org/political-process/report/Abraham-lincoln-or-the-progressives-who-was-the-real-father-big-government. Accessed 3 May 2017.

[18] Loudon, Trevor. *The Enemies Within: Communists, Socialists, and Progressives in the*
U.S. Congress. Las Vegas, NV, Pacific Freedom Foundation, 2013.

[19] Lovell, David W. *Marx's Proletariat: The Making of a Myth*. Routledge Taylor and Francis Group, 2015.

[20] Lovell, David W., et al., editors. "Piercing Together the Past: the Comintern, the CPA, and the Archives." *Our Unswerving Loyalty: A Documentary Survey of Relations between the*

Communist Party of Austraila and Moscow, 1920-1940, ANU Press, 2008, pp. 1-24, www.jstor.org/stable/j.ctt24hcfj.12.

[21] "Defense of Marriage Act - Wikipedia." *Wikipedia, the Free Encyclopedia,* Wikimedia
Foundation, Inc, 24 Mar. 2017,
http://www.en.wikipedia.org/wiki/Defense_of_Marriage_Act. Accessed 11 Apr. 2017.

[22] Brown, Susan Stamper. "Is Progressivism the New Communism." *Western Journalism,*
Liftable Media Inc., 16 Apr. 2012, https://www.westernjournalism.com/is-progressivism-the-new-communism/. Accessed 11 Apr. 2017.

[23] IBID.

Chapter 7 The 45 Goals of Communism: The Creation of the Socialist States of America

[1] Chomsky, Noam. *Who Rules the World?* London, Hamish Hamilton, 2016.
"Communist Goals 1963-How Many Have Been Fulfilled ." *Citizens Review Online,* Citizens Review Online, 28 June 2010,
http://www.citizenreviewonline.org/2010/Jun/communism.html.
Accessed 9 Apr. 2017.

[2] "The Communist Manifesto." *Wikipedia,* Wikimedia Foundation, 4 Apr. 2017,
https://en.wikipedia.org/wiki/The_Communist_Manifesto. Accessed 9 Apr. 2017.

[3] Levin, Mark R. "Five." *Ameritopia: The Unmaking of America,* Threshold Editions, New York, 2012, p. 73.

[4] MARX, KARL. "Chapter Two." *COMMUNIST MANIFESTO,* ARCTURUS PUBLISHING LTD,
S.l., 2017, p. 19.

[5] "Eminent Domain." *Encyclopædia Britannica,* Encyclopædia Britannica, Inc., 4 June 2006, https://www.britannica.com/topic/eminent-domain. Accessed 9 Apr. 2017.

[6] "Eminent Domain." *The Free Dictionary,* Farlex, 2017, https://www.legal-dictionary.thefreedictionary.com/eminent+domain. Accessed 9 Apr. 2017.

[7] "Eminent Domain in the United States." *Wikipedia,* Wikimedia Foundation, 27 Feb. 2017, https://en.wikipedia.org/wiki/Eminent_domain_in_the_United_States. Accessed 9 Apr. 2017.

[8] Larson, Aaron. "ExpertLaw." *Eminent Domain | ExpertLaw,* Expert Law, LLC, 17 Jan. 2015, https://www.expertlaw.com/library/real_estate/eminent_domain.html. Accessed 9 Apr. 2017.

[9] "U.S. DEPARTMENT OF THE INTERIOR." *BUREAU OF LAND MANAGEMENT*, Department of the Interior, 2017, https://www.blm.gov/search?search_api_views_fulltext=Eminent%2BDomian. Accessed 9 Apr. 2017.

[10] "Federal Reserve Act." *Tax Foundation*, Tax Foundation, 2017, http://www.taxfoundation.org/?s=Federal%2BReserve%2BAct%2B. Accessed 9 Apr. 2017.

[11] Staff, Investopedia. "1913 Federal Reserve Act." *Investopedia*, Investopedia LLC, 30 Sept. 2015, https://www.investopedia.com/terms/f/1913-federal-reserve-act.asp. Accessed 9 Apr. 2017.

[12] McKinney, Richard. "Federal-Reserve-Act-Legislative-History-1913." *Law Librarians' Society of Washington DC*, Law Librarian's Society of Washington D.C., 2017, https://www.llsdc.org/FRA-LH. Accessed 9 Apr. 2017.

[13] Kasprak, Nick. "Weekly Map: Inheritance and Estate Tax Rates and Exemptions." *Tax Foundation*, Tax Foundation, 16 Jan. 2017, http://taxfoundation.org/weekly-map-inheritance-and-estate-tax-rates-and-exemptions/. Accessed 9 Apr. 2017.

[14] Walczak, Jared. "Does Your State Have an Estate or Inheritance Tax?" *Tax Foundation*, Tax Foundation, 16 Jan. 2017, http://taxfoundation.org/does-your-state-have-estate-or-inheritance-tax-0/. Accessed 9 Apr. 2017.

[15] "List of United States Federal Executive Orders." *Wikipedia*, Wikimedia Foundation, 1 Apr. 2017, https://en.wikipedia.org/wiki/List_of_United_States_federal_executive_orders#Barack_Obama.282009.E2.80.93present.29. Accessed 9 Apr. 2017.

[16] "Executive Order (United States)." *Wikipedia*, Wikimedia Foundation, 6 Apr. 2017, https://en.wikipedia.org/wiki/Executive_order_(United_States). Accessed 9 Apr. 2017.

[17] "Executive Orders Disposition Tables." *National Archives and Records Administration*, National Archives and Records Administration, 1 Feb. 2017, https://www.archives.gov/federal-register/executive-orders. Accessed 9 Apr. 2017.

[18] "Executive Orders." *Federal Register*, The Office of the Federal Register, 2017, https://www.federalregister.gov/executive-orders. Accessed 9 Apr. 2017.

[19] "Executive Orders." *The White House*, The United States Government, 30 Jan. 2017, https://www.whitehouse.gov/briefing-room/presidential-actions/executive-orders. Accessed 9 Apr. 2017.

[20] "American Community Gardening Association." *Wikipedia*, Wikimedia Foundation, 4 Apr. 2017, https://en.wikipedia.org/wiki/American_Community_Gardening_Association. Accessed 9 Apr. 2017.

[21] "Funding Opportunities." *American Community Garden Association*, American Community Garden Association, 26 Oct. 2016, http://www.communitygarden.org/resources/funding-opportunities/. Accessed 9 Apr. 2017.

[22] "Garden Lease Program." *Stlouis-Mo.gov*, The City of St Louis, 1 Mar. 2017, https://www.stlouis-mo.gov/government/departments/sldc/real-estate/garden-lease.cfm. Accessed 9 Apr. 2017.

[23] "Grants Opportunities for School Gardens." *Grants Opportunities for School Gardens | Community GroundWorks*, Community Shares of Wisconsin, 2017, https://www.communitygroundworks.org/content/grants-opportunities-school-gardens. Accessed 9 Apr. 2017.

[24] "Home." *National Youth Rights Association*, National Youth Rights Association, 2016, https://www.youthrights.org/. Accessed 9 Apr. 2017.

[25] "National Youth Rights Association." *Wikipedia*, Wikimedia Foundation, 5 Mar. 2017, https://en.wikipedia.org/wiki/National_Youth_Rights_Association. Accessed 9 Apr. 2017.

[26] "Our Sponsors." *American Community Garden Association*, American Community Garden Association, 2017, https://www.communitygarden.org/mission/our-sponsors/. Accessed 9 Apr. 2017.

[27] IBID.

[28] Walters, Joanna. "Bernie Sanders: Free Public College Tuition Is the 'Right Thing to Do'." *The Guardian*, Guardian News, and Media, 22 Oct. 2015, https://www.theguardian.com/us-news/2015/oct/22/bernie-sanders-free-public-college-tuition-higher-education. Accessed 9 Apr. 2017.

[29] Hill, Brent Budowsky columnist The. "Bernie Sanders's Great Idea: Free Public College Education." *TheHill*, Capitol Hill Publishing Corporation, 9 June 2015, https://www.thehill.com/blogs/pundits-blog/presidential-campaign/244462-bernie-sanderss-great-idea-free-public-college. Accessed 9 Apr. 2017.

[30] Zornick, George. "Bernie Sanders Just Introduced His Free College Tuition Plan." *The Nation*, Media Matters, 4 Apr. 2017, https://www.thenation.com/article/bernie-sanders-just-introduced-his-free-college-tuition-plan/. Accessed 9 Apr. 2017.

[31] "The Naked Communist, by W. Cleon Skousen." *Izzard Ink Book Publishing*, https://www.izzardink.com/product/the-naked-communist/. Accessed 9 Apr. 2017.

[32] Starr, Penny. "1963 Congressional Record: 'Communist Goals' Include Promoting of Homosexuality as 'Natural, Healthy'." *CNS News*, Media Research Center, 29 May 2015, https://www.cnsnews.com/blog/penny-starr/1963-congressional-record-communist-goals-include-promoting-homosexuality-natural. Accessed 9 Apr. 2017.

[33] "Albert S. Herlong Jr." *Wikipedia*, Wikimedia Foundation, 7 Apr. 2017, https://en.wikipedia.org/wiki/Albert_S._Herlong_Jr. Accessed 9 Apr. 2017.

[34] IBID.

[35] IBID.

[36] "Paul Harvey." *Wikipedia*, Wikimedia Foundation, 6 Apr. 2017, https://en.wikipedia.org/wiki/Paul_Harvey. Accessed 9 Apr. 2017.

[37] Skousen, W. Cleon. "The Naked Communist, by W. Cleon Skousen." *Izzard Ink Book Publishing*, Izzard Ink, 2017, http://www.izzardink.com/product/the-naked-communist/. Accessed 9 Apr. 2017.

[38] Morrow, William. *Paul Harvey's The Rest of the Story*. Garden City, NY, Doubleday Publishing, 1977.

Chapter 8 Today's Interpretation of the 45 Goals of Communism

[1] "Plato Quotes." *BrainyQuote*, Xplore, 2017, http://www.brainyquote.com/quotes/quotes/p/plato403285.html. Accessed 9 Apr. 2017.

[2] "North American Free Trade Agreement." *Wikipedia*, Wikimedia Foundation, 8 Apr. 2017, https://en.wikipedia.org/wiki/North_American_Free_Trade_Agreement. Accessed 9 Apr. 2017.

[3] "North American Free Trade Agreement (NAFTA) | United States Trade Representative." *North American Free Trade Agreement (NAFTA) | United States Trade Representative*, The Office of the President of the United States, 11 Apr. 2016, https://www.ustr.gov/trade-agreements/free-trade-agreements/north-american-free-trade-agreement-nafta/. Accessed 9 Apr. 2017.

[4] "Trans-Pacific Partnership." *Wikipedia*, Wikimedia Foundation, 8 Apr. 2017, https://en.wikipedia.org/wiki/Trans-Pacific_Partnership. Accessed 9 Apr. 2017.

[5] "Trans-Pacific Partnership." *Trans-Pacific Partnership (TPP)*, Trans-Pacific Partnership Washington D.C., 2014, https://www.transpacificpartnership.org/. Accessed 9 Apr. 2017.

[6] Palmer, Doug, et al. "Harvard Poll: Americans Say 'TPP Who?'." *POLITICO*, Politico LLC, 23 Sept. 2016, https://www.politico.com/story/2016/09/americans-say-tpp-who-228598.
Accessed 10 Apr. 2017.

[7] "United Nations." *Wikipedia*, Wikimedia Foundation, 8 Apr. 2017, https://en.wikipedia.org/wiki/United_Nations. Accessed 9 Apr. 2017.

[8] "United Nations." *United Nations*, United Nations, 2016, https://www.un.org/en/index.html. Accessed 9 Apr. 2017.

[9] Skousen, W. Cleon. "Chapter 8." *The Naked Communist*, Izzard Ink, LLC, Salt Lake City, UT,
2014, p. 174.

[10] "Funds, Programmes, Specialized Agencies and Others." *United Nations*, United Nations, 2016, https://www.un.org/en/sections/about-un/funds-programmes-specialized-agencies-and-others/index.html. Accessed 10 Apr. 2017.

[11] "UNESCO and Sustainable Development Goals." *UNESCO*, United Nations, 1 Mar. 2017, https://en.unesco.org/sdgs. Accessed 10 Apr. 2017.

[12] "UNESCO." *UNESCO*, United Nations, 2017, https://en.unesco.org/. Accessed 10 Apr. 2017.

[13] Kincaid, Cliff. "Wolf Blitzer Should Apologize to Allen West." *TheBlaze*, TheBlaze, 14 Apr. 2012, https://www.theblaze.com/contributions/wolf-blitzer-should-apologize-to-allen-west/.
Accessed 10 Apr. 2017.

[14] Brown, Susan Stamper. "Is Progressivism the New Communism." *Western Journalism*, Liftable Media Inc., 16 Apr. 2012, https://www.westernjournalism.com/is-progressivism-the-new-communism/. Accessed 11 Apr. 2017.

[15] IBID.

[16] Fund, John H. "Incumbency Shakers." *The American Spectator*, Liftable Media Inc., 4 May 2012, https://www.spectator.org/35643_incumbency-shakers/. Accessed 11 Apr. 2017.

[17] Loudon, Trevor. *The Enemies Within: Communists, Socialists, and Progressives in the*
U.S. Congress. Las Vegas, NV, Pacific Freedom Foundation, 2013.

[18] "Roe V. Wade - Wikipedia." *Wikipedia, the Free Encyclopedia*, Wikimedia Foundation, Inc, 30 Mar. 2017, https://en.wikipedia.org/wiki/Roe_v._Wade. Accessed 11 Apr. 2017.

[19] "Major Decisions Roe V Wade - Constitution Laws.com." *Constitution*, , 2017, https://constitution.laws.com/supreme-court-decisions/major-decisions-roe-v-wade.
Accessed 11 Apr. 2017.

[20] Mohr, James C. *Abortion in America: The Origins and Evolution of National Policy, 1800-1900*. Oxford UP, 1979.

[21] "Defense of Marriage Act - Wikipedia." *Wikipedia, the Free Encyclopedia*, Wikimedia Foundation, Inc, 24 Mar. 2017, https://en.wikipedia.org/wiki/Defense_of_Marriage_Act. Accessed 11 Apr. 2017.

[22] Matthews, Dylan. "The Supreme Court Struck Down Part of DOMA. Here's What You Need to Know - The Washington Post." *Washington Post*, Washington Post LLC, 26 June 2013, https://www.washingtonpost.com/news/wonk/wp/2013/06/26/the-supreme-court-struck-down-doma-heres-what-you-need-to-know/?utm_term=.c6a2b1ddf0a1. Accessed 11 Apr. 2017.

[23] Rinkle, Ralf. "Defense Of Marriage Act" 5/96 H.R. 3396 Summary/Analysis." *Free Legal Forms & Law Dictionary | The 'Lectric Law Library*, Lectric Law Library, 2017, www.lectlaw.com/files/leg23.htm. Accessed 11 Apr. 2017.

[24] IBID.

[25] "Common Core State Standards Initiative - Wikipedia." *Wikipedia, the Free Encyclopedia*, Wikimedia Foundation, Inc, 26 Mar. 2017, http://en.wikipedia.org/wiki/Common_Core_State_Standards_Initiative. Accessed 11 Apr. 2017.

[26] "Jindal Order Would Make Louisiana Latest State to Pull out of Common Core." *Fox News*, Fox News Network Corporation, 18 June 2014, http://www.foxnews.com/us/2014/06/18/jindal-to-announce-action-against-common-core.html?intcmp=latestnews. Accessed 11 Apr. 2017.

[27] Bidwell, Allie. "Tennessee Governor Signs Bill Stripping Common Core." *U.S. News and World Report*, U.S. News and World Report L.P., 12 May 2015, http://www.usnews.com/news/articles/2015/05/12/tennessee-gov-bill-haslam-signs-bill-removing-common-core-standards. Accessed 11 Apr. 2017.

[28] "National School Lunch Program (NSLP)." *Food and Nutrition Service*, United States Department of Agriculture, 18 Aug. 2016, http://www.fns.usda.gov/nslp/national-school-lunch-program-nslp. Accessed 11 Apr. 2017.

[29] Malkin, Michelle. "Michelle Obama's Control-Freak Lunch Program." *National Review*, National Review on Line, 21 May 2014, http://www.nationalreview.com/article/378436/michelle-obamas-control-freak-lunch-program-michelle-malkin. Accessed 11 Apr. 2017.

[30] Doran, Elizabeth. "Student Complaints Prompt Another CNY School District to Quit Federal Lunch Program Syracuse.com." *Syracuse.com*, Advance Media New York, 4 Sept. 2014, http://www.syracuse.com/news/index.ssf/2014/09/another_cny_school_district_opts_out_of_federa_lunch_program.html. Accessed 11 Apr. 2017.

[31] Kelly, Julie, and Jeff Stier. "The School Lunch Program with an Unappetizing Report Card.

" *WSJ*, Dow Jones Company and Incorporated, 17 June 2015, http://www.wsj.com/articles/the-school-lunch-program-with-an-unappetizing-report-card-1434582719. Accessed 11 Apr. 2017.

[32] Watanabe, Teresa. "Solutions Sought to Reduce Food Waste at Schools –

LA Times." *Latimes.com*, Los Angeles Times Corporation, 1 Apr. 2014, https://www.latimes.com/local/la-me-lausd-waste-20140402-story.html. Accessed 11 Apr. 2017.

[33] IBID.

[34] IBID.

[35] Vernon, Wes. "Howard Zinn: Communist Liar." *RenewAmerica*, Renew America.com,

9 Aug. 2010, https://www.renewamerica.com/columns/vernon/100809. Accessed 11 Apr. 2017.

[36] Flynn, Daniel J. "History News Network | Howard Zinn's Biased History." *History News Network*, George Washington University, 9 June 2003, https://historynewsnetwork.org/article/1493. Accessed 11 Apr. 2017.

[37] Kurtz, Stanley. "Obama and Ayers Pushed Radicalism On Schools." *WSJ*, Dow Jones Company and Incorporated, 23 Sept. 2008, http://www.wsj.com/articles/SB122212856075765367. Accessed 11 Apr. 2017.

[38] "Robert Shetterly - Wikipedia." *Wikipedia, the Free Encyclopedia*, Wikimedia Foundation, Inc, 10 Apr. 2017, https://en.wikipedia.org/wiki/Robert_Shetterly. Accessed 11 Apr. 2017.

[39] Klein, Aaron. "Obama's Education Dept. Partners with Soros." *WND*, World Net Daily, 20 Mar. 2012, https://www.wnd.com/2012/03/obamas-education-dept-partners-with-soros/ Accessed 11 Apr. 2017.

[40] Columbian Missourian. "Communist Party Vice Chairman Speaks at University of Missouri." *Communist Party USA*, Communist Party USA, 12 Nov. 2009, https://www.cpusa.org/article/communist-party-vice-chairman-speaks-at-university-of-missouri/.

Accessed 11 Apr. 2017.

[41] "Government-Controlled Left-Wing Media -- MSNBC, NBC, ABC, CBS, Politico, Washington Post, Time, Newsweek, Al Jazeera, CNN." *Communist Obama Marxist Socialist Maoist Progressive - CommieBlaster*, 2014, http://www.commieblaster.com/misinformation/media.html. Accessed 12 Apr. 2017.

[42] "University of Missouri Labor Studies Class Used to Recruit for Communist Party." *Before It's News*, Before It Was News INC, 10 May 2011, http://beforeitsnews.com/tea-party/2011/05/university-of-missouri-labor-studies-class-used-to-recruit-for-communist-party-622215.html. Accessed 11 Apr. 2017.

[43] Starnes, Todd. "American High School Band Marches with Hammer & Sickle." *Todd Starnes on Radio*, Fox News Network, 14 Sept. 2012, http://radio.foxnews.com/toddstarnes/top-stories/high-school-band-celebrates-russian-revolution.html. Accessed 11 Apr. 2017

[44] Ahlert, Arnold. "Marching Orders: A High School Band's Communist Celebration." *Frontpage Mag*, Front Page Magazine LLC, 25 Sept. 2012, http://www.frontpagemag.com/fpm/145690/marching-orders-high-school-bands-communist-arnold-ahlert. Accessed 11 Apr. 2017.

[45] IBID.

[46] Chiaramonte, Perry. "Mizzou May Pay Price for Campus Protests As Enrollment Plunges." *Fox News*, Fox News Network, 14 Mar. 2016, https://www.foxnews.com/us/2016/03/14/mizzou-may-pay-price-for-campus-protests-as-enrollment-plunges.html. Accessed 11 Apr. 2017.

[47] Neff, Blake. "After Caving To Protests, Mizzou Has A Huge Budget Gap." *The Daily Caller*, The Daily Caller, 10 Mar. 2016, https://dailycaller.com/2016/03/10/shocker-after-caving-to-protests-mizzou-has-huge-budget-gap/. Accessed 11 Apr. 2017.

[48] Fox News Editorial Staff. "Second-graders Taught Labor Politics in Core Curriculum-aligned

Lesson Plan." *Fox News*, Fox News Network, 23 Oct. 2014, http://www.foxnews.com/us/2013/10/23/second-graders-taught-labor-politics-in-core-curriculum-aligned-lesson-plan.html?intcmp=latestnews. Accessed 11 Apr. 2017.

[49] Western Journal News Editor. "Common Core Lesson Teaches Abraham Lincoln's Religion Was "Liberal"." *Western Journalism*, Western Journalism, 7 Feb. 2014,

http://www.westernjournalism.com/common-core-lesson-teaches-abraham-lincolns-religion-liberal/ Accessed 11 Apr. 2017.

[50] "NH Teacher Says He Helped Write Common Core Standards To End "White Privilege"... Weasel Zippers." *Weasel Zippers | Scouring the Bowels of the Internet | Weasel Zippers*, 21 May 2014, www.weaselzippers.us/186769-nh-teacher-says-he-helped-write-common-core-standards-to-help-end-white-privilege/. Accessed 11 Apr. 2017.

[51] Kew, Ben. "Black Lives Matter Protesters at UC Irvine Claim 'Blue Lives Don't Matter'." *Breitbart*, 10 Oct. 2016, https://www.breitbart.com/tech/2016/10/10/black-lives-matter-protesters-at-uc-irvine-claim-blue-lives-dont-matter/. Accessed 11 Apr. 2017.

[52] Van Voorhis, Peter. "'Blue Lives Don't Matter,' Pro-BLM UC Irvine Protesters Say." *Campus Reform*, 9 Oct. 2016, https://www.campusreform.org/?ID=8232. Accessed 11 Apr. 2017.

[53] IBID.

[54] IBID.

[55] "School Indoctrination - Arne Duncan, Kevin Jennings - Communist Obama." *Communist Obama Marxist Socialist Maoist Progressive - CommieBlaster*, Commie Blaster, https://www.commieblaster.com/news/school_indoctrination.html. Accessed 11 Apr. 2017.

[56] IBID.

[57] IBID.

[58] IBID.

[59] Mandarino, Grant. "The New Marxist Art History | International Socialist Review." *Issue #104 International Socialist Review*, Center for Economic Research and Change, 2014, http://www.isreview.org/issue/94/new-marxist-art-history. Accessed 12 Apr. 2017.

[60] Willette, Jeanne. "Marxism, Art and the Artist." *Art History Unstuffed – Art/History/Criticism/Theory*, 11 June 2010,

http://www.arthistoryunstuffed.com/marxism-art-artist/. Accessed 12 Apr. 2017.

[61] IBID.

[62] "Hugh Hefner - Wikipedia." *Wikipedia, the Free Encyclopedia*, Wikimedia Foundation, Inc, 9 Apr. 2017, https://en.wikipedia.org/wiki/Hugh_Hefner. Accessed 12 Apr. 2017.

[63] Watts, Steven. *Mr. Playboy: Hugh Hefner and the American Dream*. Wiley, 2009.

[64] Vile, John R, et al. *Encyclopedia of the First Amendment*. CQ P, 2009.

[65] "LGBT Rights in Communism - Wikipedia." *Wikipedia, the Free Encyclopedia*, Wikimedia Foundation, Inc, 8 Apr. 2017, https://en.wikipedia.org/wiki/LGBT_rights_in_communism. Accessed 12 Apr. 2017.

[66] "Lesbian, Bisexual, Gay, Transgender and Queer Movement." *Marxists Internet Archive*, 2017, http://www.marxists.org/subject/lgbtq/index.htm. Accessed 12 Apr. 2017.

[67] "Engels, Homophobia and the Left." *Columbia University in the City of New York*, Columbia University, 17 Aug. 2002, http://www.columbia.edu/~lnp3/mydocs/sex_gender/engels_homophobia.htm. Accessed 12 Apr. 2017.

[68] De Vogue, Ariane. "Ginsburg Likes S. Africa As Model for Egypt." *ABC News*, 3 Feb. 2012, https://abcnews.go.com/blogs/politics/2012/02/ginsburg-likes-s-africa-as-model-for-egypt/. Accessed 12 Apr. 2017.

[69] Fox News Staff. "Ginsburg to Egyptians: I Wouldn't Use U.S. Constitution As a Model."

Fox News, Fox News Network, 6 Feb. 2012, https://www.foxnews.com/politics/2012/02/06/ginsburg-to-egyptians-wouldnt-use-us-constitution-as-model.html. Accessed 12 Apr. 2017.

[70] "Ruth Bader Ginsburg - Wikipedia." *Wikipedia, the Free Encyclopedia*,

Wikimedia Foundation, Inc, 12 Apr. 2017, https://en.wikipedia.org/wiki/Ruth_Bader_Ginsburg. Accessed 12 Apr. 2017.

[71] IBID.

[72] "Read the Affordable Care Act, Health Care Law." *HealthCare.gov*, Department of Health and Human Services, 2017, https://www.healthcare.gov/where-can-i-read-the-affordable-care-act/. Accessed 12 Apr. 2017.

[73] Waldman, Deana. "Articles: The PPACA Is Emptying Your Wallet."

American Thinker, 22 Mar. 2014, https://www.americanthinker.com/articles/2014/03/the_ppaca_is_emptying_your_wallet.html. Accessed 12 Apr. 2017.

[74] Yette, Samuel F. "The Threat and Tactics." *The Choice: The Issue of Black Survival in America*, Cottage Books, 1996, p. 254.

[75] Yette, Samuel F. "The Threat and Tactics." *The Choice: The Issue of Black Survival in America*, Cottage Books, 1996, p. 255.

[76] IBID.

[77] IBID.

[78] "Newborn Screening Fact Sheet." *National Human Genome Research Institute (NHGRI),*

National Institute of Health (NIH), 11 May 2016,
http://www.genome.gov/27556918/newborn-screening-fact-sheet. Accessed
12 Apr. 2017.

[79] "Fact Sheets." *National Human Genome Research Institute (NHGRI),* National Institute of

Health (NIH), 9 Nov. 2015, https://www.genome.gov/10000202/fact-sheets/.
Accessed 12 Apr. 2017.

[80] Marx, Karl, and Friedrich Engels. *Manifesto of the Communist Party.*
Jefferson Publications, 2015.

[81] Nimmo, Kurt. "MSNBC Host: Your Kids Belong to the Collective » Alex Jones' Infowars:

There's a War on for Your Mind!" *Infowars,* 6 Apr. 2013,

http://www.infowars.com/your-kids-belong-to-the-collective/.
Accessed 12 Apr. 2017.

[82] Freedlander, David. "Melissa Harris-Perry and the Firestorm Over 'Collective'
Parenting." *The Daily Beast,* 11 Apr. 2013,
https://www.thedailybeast.com/articles/2013/04/11/melissa-harris-perry-and-the-
firestorm-over-collective-parenting.html. Accessed 12 Apr. 2017.

[83] Harris-Perry, Melissa. "Why Caring for Children is Not Just a Parent's Job."
MSNBC, 9 Apr. 2013,

http://www.msnbc.com/melissa-harris-perry/why-caring-children-not-just-parent.
Accessed 12 Apr. 2017.

[84] "Tom Connally - Wikipedia." *Wikipedia, the Free Encyclopedia,* Wikimedia
Foundation, Inc, 29 Mar. 2017, https://en.wikipedia.org/wiki/Tom_Connally. Accessed
12 Apr. 2017.

[85] Larson, Arthur. *The International Rule of Law.* World Rule of Law Center, School of
Law, Duke U, 1961, pp. 74-119.

Chapter 9 Black Liberation Theology and its Marxist Roots

[1] "David Walker, 1785-1830 Walker's Appeal, in Four Articles; Together with a Preamble, to the Coloured Citizens of the World, but in Particular, and Very Expressly, to Those of the United States of America, Written in Boston, the State of Massachusetts, September 28, 1829." *Documenting the American South Homepage*, the University of North Carolina at Chapel Hill, 12 Apr. 2017, https://www.docsouth.unc.edu/nc/walker/menu.html. Accessed 12 Apr. 2017.

[2] "Black Theology - Wikipedia." *Wikipedia, the Free Encyclopedia*, Wikimedia Foundation, Inc, 16 Dec. 2016, https://en.wikipedia.org/wiki/Black_theology. Accessed 12 Apr. 2017.

[3] Bradley, Anthony B., and D. Phil. "The Marxist Roots of Black Liberation Theology Acton Institute." *Acton Institute*, 2 Apr. 2008, http://acton.org/pub/commentary/2008/04/02/marxist-roots-black-liberation-theology. Accessed 12 Apr. 2017.

[4] Schmidt, Jeffrey. "The Real Agenda of Black Liberation Theology." *American Thinker*, 19 Mar. 2008, https://www.americanthinker.com/articles/2008/03/the_real_agenda_of_black_liber.html. Accessed 14 Apr. 2017.

[5] "Black Liberation Theology." *Conservapedia*, 30 Mar. 2017, https://www.conservapedia.com/Black_liberation_theology. Accessed 12 Apr. 2017.

[6] Asukile, Thabiti. "Walker, David (1785-1830) | The Black Past: Remembered and Reclaimed." *The Black Past: Remembered and Reclaimed*, University of Washington, 2017, http://www.blackpast.org/aah/walker-david-1785-1830. Accessed 12 Apr. 2017.

[7] IBID.

[8] IBID.

[9] IBID.

[10] IBID.

[11] Jones, Jae. "Black Then David Walker: Abolitionist Smuggled "Appeal for a Slave Revolt" to the South in Used Clothing." *Black Then*, 18 June 2016, http://blackthen.com/david-walkers-abolitionist-smuggled-appeal-for-a-slave-revolt-to-the-south-in-garments/. Accessed 13 Apr. 2017.

[12] Powell, William S. "David Walker, 1785-1830." *Documenting the American South Homepage*, the University of North Carolina at Chapel Hill, 18 June 2016, https://www.docsouth.unc.edu/nc/walker/bio.html.

[13] Walker, David. "Appeal to the Coloured Citizens of the World."

National Humanities Center – Advanced Study in Humanities, 28 Aug. 1829, https://nationalhumanitiescenter.org/pds/triumphnationalism/cman/text/walker.pdf Accessed 13 Apr. 2017.

[14] IBID.

[15] Walker, David, and Peter P. Hinks. *David Walker's Appeal to the Coloured Citizens of the World*. Pennsylvania State Univ. P, 2006.

[16] IBID.

[17] IBID.

[18] "Martin Delany - Wikipedia." *Wikipedia, the Free Encyclopedia*, Wikimedia Foundation, Inc, 25 Mar. 2017, https://en.wikipedia.org/wiki/Martin_Delany. Accessed 13 Apr. 2017.

[19] IBID.

[20] Stanford, Eleanor. "Delany, Martin R. (1812–1885)." *Encyclopedia Virginia*, Virginia Foundation for the Humanities, 6 Aug. 2014, https://www.encyclopediavirginia.org/Delany_Martin_R_1812-1885#. Accessed 13 Apr. 2017.

[21] Roth, Mark. "Martin Delany, 'Father of Black Nationalism'." *Pittsburgh Post-Gazette*, 6 Feb. 2011, https://www.post-gazette.com/life/lifestyle/2011/02/06/Martin-Delany-Father-of-Black-Nationalism/stories/201102060355?pgpageversion=pgevoke. Accessed 13 Apr. 2017.

[22] "Delany, Martin Robison (1812-1885) | The Black Past: Remembered and Reclaimed." *The Black Past: Remembered and Reclaimed*, University of Washington, 2017, https://www.blackpast.org/aah/delany-major-martin-robison-1812-1885. Accessed 13 Apr. 2017.

 [23] Britannica Editors. "Martin R. Delany American Physician and Abolitionist Britannica.com." *Encyclopedia Britannica*, 27 June 2007, https://www.britannica.com/biography/Martin-R-Delany. Accessed 13 Apr. 2017.

[24] Asante, Molefi K, and Ama Mazama. *Encyclopedia of Black Studies*. SAGE Publications, 2007.

[25] IBID.

[26] Levine, Robert S. *Martin Delany, Frederick Douglass, and the Politics of Representative Identity*. U of North Carolina P, 1997.

[27] IBID.

[28] IBID.

[29] Adeleke, Tunde. *Without Regard to Race: The Other Martin Robison Delany*. UP of Mississippi, 2003.

[30] IBID.

[31] Lichtenstein, Nelson, et al. "The Great Depression and the First New Deal." *Who Built America? (2) Working People and the Nation's Economy, Politics, Culture, and Society*, Bedford/St. Martin's, 2000, p. 375.

[32] "Great Depression - Wikipedia." *Wikipedia, the Free Encyclopedia*, Wikimedia Foundation, Inc, 8 Apr. 2017, https://en.wikipedia.org/wiki/Great_Depression#United_States. Accessed 13 Apr. 2017

[33] "Black Separatist." *Southern Poverty Law Center*, 2017, https://edit.splcenter.org/fighting-hate/extremist-files/ideology/black-separatist. Accessed 13 Apr. 2017.

[34] "Nation of Islam - Wikipedia." *Wikipedia, the Free Encyclopedia*, Wikimedia Foundation, Inc, 10 Apr. 2017, https://en.wikipedia.org/wiki/Nation_of_Islam. Accessed 13 Apr. 2017.

[35] "Nation of Islam." *Southern Poverty Law Center*, 2017, https://edit.splcenter.org/fighting-hate/extremist-files/group/nation-islam. Accessed 13 Apr. 2017.

[36] "Wallace Fard Muhammad - Wikipedia." *Wikipedia, the Free Encyclopedia*, Wikimedia Foundation, Inc, 31 Mar. 2017, https://en.wikipedia.org/wiki/Wallace_Fard_Muhammad. Accessed 13 Apr. 2017.

[37] "FBI — Wallace Fard Muhammed." *FBI*, Department of Justice (DOJ), 2017, https://vault.fbi.gov/Wallace%20Fard%20Muhammad. Accessed 13 Apr. 2017.

[38] Evanzz, Karl. *The Messenger: The Rise and Fall of Elijah Muhammad*. Vintage Books, 2001.

[39] Muhammad, Dr. Wesley. "Master W. Fard Muhammad and FBI COINTELPRO." *FinalCall.com News - Uncompromised National and World News and Perspectives*, FCN Publishing, 4 Jan. 2010, http://www.finalcall.com/artman/publish/Perspectives_1/article_6699.shtml. Accessed 13 Apr. 2017.

[40]"Wallie Dodd Fred Ford - Public Member Trees - Ancestry.com." *Search Historical Records - Ancestry.com*, 2017, https://search.ancestry.com. Accessed 13 Apr. 2017.

[41] "W Fard - New South Wales, Australia, Unassisted Immigrant Passenger Lists, 1826-1922 - Ancestry.com." *Search Historical Records - Ancestry.com*, 2017, https://search.ancestry.com. Accessed 13 Apr. 2017.

[42] "FBI — Wallace Fard Muhammed." *FBI*, Department of Justice (DOJ), 2017, https://vault.fbi.gov/Wallace%20Fard%20Muhammad. Accessed 13 Apr. 2017.

[43] "U.S. World War I Draft Registration Cards 1917-1918 Wallie Dodd Ford." *Ancestry.com*, 2017, https://search.ancestry.com. Accessed 13 Apr. 2017.

[44] "Wallie Dodd Fred Ford - Public Member Trees - Ancestry.com." *Search Historical Records - Ancestry.com*, 2017, https://search.ancestry.com. Accessed 13 Apr. 2017.

[45] Steven, Even. "Truth Continuum: Nation of Islam's Founder Was Afghani; Suffered from Diabetes." *Truth Continuum*, 17 Apr. 2011, http://mxmission.blogspot.com/2011/04/four-faces-of-wali-d-fard-muhammad.html. Accessed 13 Apr. 2017.

[46] "FBI — Wallace Fard Muhammed." *FBI*, Department of Justice (DOJ), 2017, https://vault.fbi.gov/Wallace%20Fard%20Muhammed. Accessed 13 Apr. 2017.

[47] IBID.

[48] IBID.

[49] "California Marriage Certificates 1850-1965 Carmen Trevino and Wallie Dodd Ford." *Ancestry*, 2017, https://search.ancestry.com. Accessed 13 Apr. 2017.

[50] IBID.

[51] Vassar, Alexander. *Legislators of California*. The State of California, 2011.

[52] "FBI — Wallace Fard Muhammed." *FBI*, Department of Justice (DOJ), 2017, https://vault.fbi.gov/Wallace%20Fard%20Muhammed. Accessed 13 Apr. 2017.

[53] "Wallie Dodd Fred Ford - Public Member Trees - Ancestry.com." *Search Historical Records - Ancestry.com*, 2017, https://search.ancestry.com. Accessed 13 Apr. 2017.

[54] IBID.

[55] "FBI — Wallace Fard Muhammed." *FBI*, Department of Justice (DOJ), 2017, https://vault.fbi.gov/Wallace%20Fard%20Muhammed. Accessed 13 Apr. 2017.

[56] Steven, Even. "Truth Continuum: Nation of Islam's Founder Was Afghani; Suffered from Diabetes." *Truth Continuum*, 17 Apr. 2011, http://mxmission.blogspot.com/2011/04/four-faces-of-wali-d-fard-muhammad.html. Accessed 13 Apr. 2017.

[57] "FBI — Wallace Fard Muhammed." *FBI*, Department of Justice (DOJ), 2017, https://vault.fbi.gov/Wallace%20Fard%20Muhammed. Accessed 13 Apr. 2017.

[58] "William D Fard in the 1930 United States Federal Census." *Ancestry*, 2017, https://search.ancestry.com. Accessed 13 Apr. 2017.

[59] IBID.

[60] Steven, Even. "Truth Continuum: Nation of Islam's Founder Was Afghani; Suffered from Diabetes." *Truth Continuum*, 17 Apr. 2011, http://mxmission.blogspot.com/2011/04/four-faces-of-wali-d-fard-muhammad.html. Accessed 13 Apr. 2017.

[61] Beyonon, Erdmann D. "The Voodoo Cult Among Negro Migrants in Detroit." *American Journal of Sociology*, vol. 43, no. 6, May 1938, pp. 894-907, *JSTOR*. https://www.jstor.org/stable/2768686?seq=1#page_scan_tab_contents. Accessed 13 Apr. 2017.

[62] Evanzz, Karl. *The Messenger: The Rise and Fall of Elijah Muhammad*. Vintage Books, 2001.

[63] IBID.

[64] IBID.

[65] IBID.

[66] IBID.

[67] Beyonon, Erdmann D. "The Voodoo Cult Among Negro Migrants in Detroit." *American Journal of Sociology*, vol. 43, no. 6, May 1938, pp. 894-907, *JSTOR*. https://www.jstor.org/stable/2768686?seq=1#page_scan_tab_contents. Accessed 13 Apr. 2017.

[68] IBID.

[69] "FBI — Wallace Fard Muhammed." *FBI*, Department of Justice (DOJ), 2017, https://vault.fbi.gov/Wallace%20Fard%20Muhammed. Accessed 13 Apr. 2017.

[70] IBID.

[71] Gibson, Dawn-Marie. *A History of the Nation of Islam: Race, Islam, and the Quest for Freedom*. Praeger, 2012.

[72] "FBI — Wallace Fard Muhammed." *FBI*, Department of Justice (DOJ), 2017, https://vault.fbi.gov/Wallace%20Fard%20Muhammed. Accessed 13 Apr. 2017.

[73] IBID.

[74] Gibson, Dawn-Marie. *A History of the Nation of Islam: Race, Islam, and the Quest for Freedom*. Praeger, 2012.

[75] Muhammad, Elijah. *Message to the Blackman in America*. Muhammad's Temple No. 2, 1965.

[76] Gibson, Dawn-Marie. *A History of the Nation of Islam: Race, Islam, and the Quest for Freedom*. Praeger, 2012.

[77] Muhammad, Elijah. *Message to the Blackman in America*. Muhammad's Temple No. 2, 1965.

[78] "FBI — Wallace Fard Muhammed." *FBI*, Department of Justice (DOJ), 2017, https://vault.fbi.gov/Wallace%20Fard%20Muhammed. Accessed 13 Apr. 2017.

[79] "Leader of Cult Admits Slaying at Home Altar." *Detroit Free Press*, 21 Nov. 1932, p. 1, *Newspapers*.
https://www.newspapers.com/image/97673720/?terms=Detroit%2BFree%2BPress. .
Accessed 13 Apr. 2017.

[80] "Intended Voodoo Victims' Number Still Mounting." *Detroit Free Press*, 27 Nov. 1932, p. 1, www.newspapers.com/image/97680425/. Accessed 14 Apr. 2017.

[81] "FBI — Wallace Fard Muhammed." *FBI*, Department of Justice (DOJ), 2017, https://vault.fbi.gov/Wallace%20Fard%20Muhammed. Accessed 13 Apr. 2017.

[82] "Banished Leader of Cult Arrested." *Detroit Free Press*, p. 6, *Newspapers.com*. https://www.newspapers.com/image/97974724. Accessed 14 Apr. 2017.

[83] "FBI — Wallace Fard Muhammed." *FBI*, Department of Justice (DOJ), 2017, HTTPS://vault.fbi.gov/Wallace%20Fard%20Muhammed. Accessed 13 Apr. 2017.

[84] Gibson, Dawn-Marie. *A History of the Nation of Islam: Race, Islam, and the Quest for Freedom*. Praeger, 2012.

[85] IBID.

[86] "FBI — Wallace Fard Muhammed." *FBI*, Department of Justice (DOJ), 2017, Https://vault.fbi.gov/Wallace%20Fard%20Muhammed. Accessed 13 Apr. 2017.

[87] IBID.

[88] IBID.

[89] IBID.

[90] "Black Liberation Theology." *Conservapedia*, 30 Mar. 2017, https://www.conservapedia.com/Black_liberation_theology. Accessed 12 Apr. 2017.

[91] "Black Theology - Wikipedia." *Wikipedia, the Free Encyclopedia*, Wikimedia Foundation, Inc, 16 Dec. 2016, https://en.wikipedia.org/wiki/Black_theology. Accessed 12 Apr. 2017.

[92] "Black Nationalism - Wikipedia." *Wikipedia, the Free Encyclopedia*, Wikimedia Foundation, Inc, 1 Apr. 2017, https://en.wikipedia.org/wiki/Black_nationalism. Accessed 14 Apr. 2017.

[93] IBID.

[94] Schmidt, Jeffrey. "The Real Agenda of Black Liberation Theology." *American Thinker*, 19 Mar. 2008, https://www.americanthinker.com/articles/2008/03/the_real_agenda_of_black_liber.html. Accessed 14 Apr. 2017.

[95] Saslow, Eli. "Congregation Defends Obama's Ex-Pastor."*Washington Post: Breaking News, World, US, DC News & Analysis - The Washington Post*, 18 Mar. 2008,

https://www.washingtonpost.com/wp-dyn/content/article/2008/03/17/AR2008031702796.html. Accessed 14 Apr. 2017.

[96] "Liberate." *Merriam-Webster's Dictionary and Thesaurus*, vol. 1, Merriam-Webster, 2007,
p. 470.

[97] "Liberation." *Merriam-Webster's Dictionary and Thesaurus*, vol. 1, Merriam-Webster, 2007, p. 470. Accessed 14 Apr. 2017.

[98] IBID.

[99] "Liberation Theology - Wikipedia." *Wikipedia, the Free Encyclopedia*, Wikimedia Foundation, Inc, 10 Apr. 2017,
https://en.wikipedia.org/wiki/Liberation_theology. Accessed 14 Apr. 2017.

[100] "James H. Cone - Wikipedia." *Wikipedia, the Free Encyclopedia*, Wikimedia Foundation, Inc, 24 Jan. 2017, https://en.wikipedia.org/wiki/James_H._Cone. Accessed 14 Apr. 2017.

[101] Boyd, Gloria. "James Hal Cone (1938) - Encyclopedia of Arkansas." *The Encyclopedia of Arkansas History & Culture*, Arkansas State University, 23 Apr. 2012, https://www.encyclopediaofarkansas.net/encyclopedia/entry-detail.aspx?entryID=4595.
Accessed 14 Apr. 2017.

[102] "National Committee of Negro Churchmen Collection an Inventory of the Collection at Syracuse University." *Syracuse University Libraries*, Syracuse University, 2017, https://library.syr.edu/digital/guides/n/nat_com_neg_chu.htm. Accessed 14 Apr. 2017.

[103] "The Church Awakens: African Americans and the Struggle for Justice." *Home The Archives of the Episcopal Church*, 2008, https://www.episcopalarchives.org/Afro-Anglican_history/exhibit/transitions/black_power.php. Accessed 14 Apr. 2017.

[104] Shiver, Kyle-Anne. "Articles: Obama, Black Liberation Theology, and Karl Marx." *American Thinker*, 28 May 2008,
http://www.americanthinker.com/articles/2008/05/obama_black_liberation_theolog.html.
Accessed 12 Apr. 2017.

[105] Cone, James H. *Black Theology, and Black Power*. Orbis Books, 1997.

[106] Warner, Bill. "Islam and Black Liberation Theology." *Political Islam*, CSPI, LLC, 31 Mar. 2008, https://www.politicalislam.com/islam-and-black-liberation-theology/. Accessed 14 Apr. 2017.

[107] "Radical Islam and Black Liberation Theology." *Heaven Awaits*, Wordpress, 26 May 2008, https://heavenawaits.wordpress.com/islam-and-black-liberation-theology/.
Accessed 14 Apr. 2017.

[108] Cone, James H. *Black Theology, and Black Power*. Orbis Books, 1997.

[109] Visser, Steve. "Baton Rouge Police Shooting Leaves 3 Officers Dead .com." *CNN*, 18 July 2016, https://www.cnn.com/2016/07/17/us/baton-route-police-shooting/index.html. Accessed 14 Apr. 2017.

[110] "2016 Shooting of Dallas Police Officers - Wikipedia." *Wikipedia, the Free Encyclopedia*, Wikimedia Foundation, Inc, 4 Apr. 2017, https://en.wikipedia.org/wiki/2016_shooting_of_Dallas_police_officers. Accessed 14 Apr. 2017.

[111] McBride, Brian, and Gilliam Mchney. "Among Dallas Officers Killed, One Was a Father,
Another a Newlywed." *ABC News*, 8 July 2016, https://abcnews.go.com/US/officers-killed-dallas-identified/story?id=40426360. Accessed 14 Apr. 2017.

[112] IBID.

[113] IBID.

[114] "2016 Shooting of Baton Rouge Police Officers - Wikipedia." *Wikipedia, the Free Encyclopedia*, Wikimedia Foundation, Inc, 4 Mar. 2017, https://en.wikipedia.org/wiki/2016_shooting_of_Baton_Rouge_police_officers. Accessed 14 Apr. 2017.

[115] IBID.

[116] IBID.

[117] Ross, Chuck. "Baton Rouge Cop Killer Gavin Long Was Nation Of Islam." *The Daily Caller*, 17 July 2016, https://dailycaller.com/2016/07/17/baton-rouge-shooter-gavin-eugene-long-was-nation-of-islam-member-railed-against-crackers-on-youtube-channel-video/.
Accessed 14 Apr. 2017.

[118] Jansen, Bart. "3 Police Officers Fatally Shot in Baton Rouge; Dead Suspect Identified." *USA TODAY*, 17 July 2016, https://www.usatoday.com/story/news/2016/07/17/reports-baton-rouge-police-officers-shot/87218884/. Accessed 14 Apr. 2017.

[119] Karimi, Faith, et al. "Dallas Sniper Attack: 5 Officers Killed, Suspect ID'd .com." *CNN*,
9 July 2016, https://www.cnn.com/2016/07/08/us/philando-castile-alton-sterling-protests/index.html. Accessed 14 Apr. 2017.

[120] IBID.

[121] IBID.

[122] Warner, Bill. "Islam and Black Liberation Theology." *Political Islam*, CSPI, LLC, 31 Mar. 2008, https://www.politicalislam.com/islam-and-black-liberation-theology/. Accessed 14 Apr. 2017.

[1] The Communist Party of the USA. "An Invitation to African Americans from the Communist Party-Communist Party USA" *Communist Party USA*, 7 Feb 2009, https://cpusa.org/article/an-invitation-to-african-americans-from-the-communist-party/.
Accessed 3 May 2017.

[2] 'The Communist Party USA and African Americans-Wikipedia." *Wikipedia, the Free Encyclopedia,* Wikimedia Foundation, Inc, 2017, https://en.wikipedia.org/wiki/The_Communist_Party_USA_and_African_Americans.
Accessed 3 May 2017.

[3] Robinson, Cedric J. *Black Marxism: The Making of the Black Radical Tradition.*
U of North Carolina P, 2000.

[4] Klein, Aaron. "EXCLUSIVE–New Black Panther Leader: Blacks Need to Migrate to Five Southern States, Form 'Country Within a Country'." *Breitbart*, 10 July 2016, https://www.breitbart.com/big-government/2016/07/10/exclusive-new-black-panther-leader-country-within/. Accessed 14 Apr. 2017.

[5] Mitsotakis, Spyridon. "From The Soviet Files: An American 'Negro Republic' - the Communist Secession Plot." *Breitbart*, 27 Oct. 2011, https://www.breitbart.com/national-security/2011/10/27/from-the-soviet-files-an-american-negro-republic-the-communist-secession-plot/. Accessed 18 Apr. 2017.

[6] Kengor, Paul. The Communist: Frank Marshall Davis: The Untold Story of Barack Obama's
Mentor. Tantor Media, Inc, 2012.

[7] Hicks, Jonathan. "Louis Farrakhan Calls for a Separate Black Court System."
BET.com,
24 Feb 2014,
https://bet.com/news/national/2014/02/24/louis-farrakhan-calls-for-a-separate-black-court-system.html. Accessed 3 May 2017.

[8] Woods, Ashley. "Louis Farrakhan Says African-Americans Should Have Their Own Justice System." The Huffington Post, 24 Feb. 2014, https://www.huffingtonpost.com/2014/02/24/louis-farrakhan-courts_n_4846641.html
Accessed 14 Apr. 2017.

[9] "The Communist Party of the USA." An Invitation to African Americans from the Communist Party-Communist Party USA," Communist Party USA,7 Feb 2009, https://cpusa.org/article/an-invitation-to-african-americans-from-the-communist-party/.
Accessed 3 May 2017.

[10] Caruso, Justin. "Keith Ellison Once Proposed Making A Separate Country For Blacks." The Daily Caller, 26 Nov. 2016, https://dailycaller.com/2016/11/26/keith-ellison-once-proposed-making-a-separate-country-for-blacks/. Accessed 14 Apr. 2017.

[11] "Claude McKay - Wikipedia." Wikipedia, the Free Encyclopedia, Wikimedia Foundation, Inc, 27 Mar. 2017, https://en.wikipedia.org/wiki/Claude_McKay. Accessed 14 Apr. 2017.

[12] Claude Mckay." Biography, A&E Television Networks, 2017, https://www.biography.com/people/claude-mckay-9392654. Accessed 14 Apr. 2017.

[13] "Universal Negro Improvement Association and African Communities League - Wikipedia." Wikipedia, the Free Encyclopedia, Wikimedia Foundation, Inc, 30 Mar. 2017, https://en.wikipedia.org/wiki/Universal_Negro_Improvement_Association_and_African_Communities_League. Accessed 14 Apr. 2017.

[14] "Harry Haywood - Wikipedia." Wikipedia, the Free Encyclopedia, Wikimedia Foundation, Inc, 18 Mar. 2017, https://en.wikipedia.org/wiki/Harry_Haywood. Accessed 15 Apr. 2017.

[15] Britannica Editors. "Universal Negro Improvement Association (UNIA) | Britannica.com." Encyclopedia Britannica, 6 May 2008, https://www.britannica.com/topic/Universal-Negro-Improvement-Association. Accessed 14 Apr. 2017.

[16] Kengor, Paul. The Communist: Frank Marshall Davis: The Untold Story of Barack Obama's
Mentor. Tantor Media, Inc, 2012, pp.38.

[17] Hoover, J. E. "Communism and Minorities." Masters of Deceit: The Story of Communism in America and How to Fight It, Henry Holt and Company, 1958, pp. 250-251.

[18] "Lovett Fort-Whiteman - Wikipedia." Wikipedia, the Free Encyclopedia, Wikimedia Foundation, Inc, 2016, https://en.wikipedia.org/wiki/Lovett_Fort-Whiteman. Accessed 18 Apr. 2017.

[19] "Blacks and Reds." Time, 9 Nov. 1925, p. 29. Accessed 15 Apr. 2017.

[20] "John Pepper - Wikipedia." Wikipedia, the Free Encyclopedia, Wikimedia Foundation, Inc, 25 Mar. 2016, https://en.wikipedia.org/wiki/John_Pepper. Accessed 15 Apr. 2017.

[21] Pepper, John, "American Negro Problems." Workers Library Publishers, 1928, Marxist Internet Archives, https://Marxists.org/history/usa/parties/cpusa/1928/nomonth/0000-pepper-negroprobelms.pdf. Accessed 3 May 2017.

[22] "Renaissance." Merriam-Webster's Dictionary and Thesaurus, Merriam-Webster, 2007, p.682.

[23] "Harlem Renaissance - Wikipedia." Wikipedia, the Free Encyclopedia, Wikimedia Foundation, Inc, 16 Apr. 2017, https://en.wikipedia.org/wiki/Harlem_Renaissance#Dancers.2C_choreographers.2C_entertainers. Accessed 17 Apr. 2017.

[24] U.S. History.org. "The Harlem Renaissance [ushistory.org]." US History, 2017, https://www.ushistory.org/us/46e.asp. Accessed 16 Apr. 2017.

[25] "Alain LeRoy Locke - Wikipedia." Wikipedia, the Free Encyclopedia, Wikimedia Foundation, Inc, 14 Apr. 2017, https://en.wikipedia.org/wiki/Alain_LeRoy_Locke. Accessed 15 Apr. 2017.

[26] Biography.com Editors. "Alain Leroy Locke." Bio, A&E Television Networks, 16 Oct. 2014, https://www.biography.com/people/alain-leroy-locke-37962. Accessed 15 Apr. 2017.

[27] "Zora Neale Hurston - Wikipedia." Wikipedia, the Free Encyclopedia, Wikimedia Foundation, Inc, 2017, https://en.wikipedia.org/wiki/Zora_Neale_Hurston. Accessed 17 Apr. 2017.

[28] "Zora Neale Hurston." The Official Website of Zora Neale Hurston, 2015, http://zoranealehurston.com/. Accessed 17 Apr. 2017.

[29] "The Constitution of the United States of America." Constitution for the United States - We the People, 16 Apr. 2017, http://constitutionus.com/. Accessed 16 Apr. 2017.

[30] "Great Migration (African American) - Wikipedia." Wikipedia, the Free Encyclopedia, Wikimedia Foundation, Inc, 16 Apr. 2017, https://en.wikipedia.org/wiki/Great_Migration_(African_American). Accessed 17 Apr. 2017.

[31] "Sterling Allen Brown - Wikipedia." Wikipedia, the Free Encyclopedia, Wikimedia Foundation, Inc, 28 Feb. 2017, https://en.wikipedia.org/wiki/Sterling_Allen_Brown. Accessed 16 Apr. 2017.

[32] "Theodore Ward - Wikipedia." Wikipedia, the Free Encyclopedia, Wikimedia Foundation, Inc, 2 Mar. 2017, https://en.wikipedia.org/wiki/Theodore_Ward. Accessed 16 Apr. 2017.

[33] "Arana Bontemps - Wikipedia." Wikipedia, the Free Encyclopedia, Wikimedia Foundation, Inc, 2 Mar. 2017, https://en.wikipedia.org/wiki/Arana_Bontemps. Accessed 16 Apr. 2017.

[34] "Chester Himes - Wikipedia." Wikipedia, the Free Encyclopedia, Wikimedia Foundation, Inc, 3 Apr. 2017, https://en.wikipedia.org/wiki/Chester_Himes. Accessed 16 Apr. 2017.

[35] "Jean Toomer - Wikipedia." Wikipedia, the Free Encyclopedia, Wikimedia Foundation, Inc, 15 Apr. 2017, https://en.wikipedia.org/wiki/Jean_Toomer. Accessed 16 Apr. 2017.

[36] "W. E. B. Du Bois-Wikipedia." Wikipedia, the Free Encyclopedia, Wikimedia Foundation, Inc, 2017, https://en.wikipedia.org/wiki/W._E._B._Du_Bois. Accessed 3 May 2017.

[37] "W. E. B. Du Bois (1934), A Negro Nation Within a Nation," The Black Past Remembered and Reclaimed, University of Washington, 2017, http://blackpast.org/1934-w-e-b-du-bois-negro-nation-within-nation. Accessed 3 May 2017.

[38] Mack, Dwayne, "DuBois, William Edward Burghardt (1868-1963)." The Black Past Remembered and Reclaimed, Berea College, 2017, http://blackpast.org/aah/dubois-william-edward-burghardt-1868-1963. Accessed 3 May 2017.

[39] "Cyril Briggs - Wikipedia." Wikipedia, the Free Encyclopedia, Wikimedia Foundation, Inc, 9 Feb. 2017, https://en.wikipedia.org/wiki/Cyril_Briggs. Accessed 14 Apr. 2017.

[40] Salter, Daren. "Briggs, Cyril (1888-1966) | The Black Past: Remembered and Reclaimed." The Black Past: Remembered and Reclaimed, University of Washington, 2017, http://www.blackpast.org/aah/briggs-cyril-1888-1966. Accessed 14 Apr. 2017.

[41] "Richard Wright (author) - Wikipedia." Wikipedia, the Free Encyclopedia, Wikimedia Foundation, Inc, 2017, https://en.wikipedia.org/wiki/Richard_Wright_(author). Accessed 17 Apr. 2017.

[42] "Langston Hughes - Wikipedia." Wikipedia, the Free Encyclopedia, Wikimedia Foundation, Inc, 2017, https://en.wikipedia.org/wiki/Langston_Hughes. Accessed 17 Apr. 2017.

[43] Naison, Mark D. Communists in Harlem During the Depression. U of Illinois P, 2005.

[44] Reid, Brian. "I Am at Home"." Marxists Internet Archive, 2009, https://www.marxists.org/archive/robeson/1935/01/15.htm. Accessed 16 Apr. 2017.

[45] Kengor, Paul. "Paul Robeson and Progressive Dupes." The Communist: Frank Marshall Davis:
The Untold Story of Barack Obama's Mentor, Tantor Media, Inc, 2012, pp. 65-72.

[46] Wright, Richard. Uncle Tom's Children. Harper Perennial Modern Classics, 2008.

[47] "Countee Cullen-Wikipedia," Wikipedia, The Free Encyclopedia, Wikimedia Foundation, Inc,
2017, https://en.wikipedia.org/wiki/Countee_Cullen. Accessed 3 May 2017.

[48] "Joe Louis - Black History." HISTORY.com, A&E Television Networks LLC, 2017, https://www.history.com/topics/black-history/joe-louis. Accessed 17 Apr. 2017.

[49] "Joe Louis - Wikipedia." Wikipedia, the Free Encyclopedia, Wikimedia Foundation, Inc, 2017, https://en.wikipedia.org/wiki/Joe_Louis. Accessed 17 Apr. 2017.

[50] "Joe Louis." Bio, A&E Television Networks, 8 Aug. 2016, https://www.biography.com/people/joe-louis-9386989. Accessed 17 Apr. 2017.

[51] "Jesse Owens - Wikipedia." Wikipedia, the Free Encyclopedia, Wikimedia Foundation, Inc,
2017, https://en.wikipedia.org/wiki/Jesse_Owens. Accessed 17 Apr. 2017.

[52] "Jesse Owens." Bio, A&E Television Networks, 14 Feb. 2016, https://www.biography.com/people/jesse-owens-9431142. Accessed 17 Apr. 2017.

[53] "1936 Summer Olympics - Wikipedia." Wikipedia, the Free Encyclopedia, Wikimedia Foundation, Inc, 17 Apr. 2017, https://en.wikipedia.org/wiki/1936_Summer_Olympics. Accessed 17 Apr. 2017.

[54] History.com Staff. "Owens Wins 4th Gold Medal - Aug 09, 1936." HISTORY.com, A&E Television Networks LLC, 2010, https://www.history.com/this-day-in-history/owens-wins-4th-gold-medal. Accessed 17 Apr. 2017.

[55] "Ralph Metcalfe - Wikipedia." Wikipedia, the Free Encyclopedia, Wikimedia Foundation, Inc, 2017, https://en.wikipedia.org/wiki/Ralph_Metcalfe. Accessed 17 Apr. 2017.

[56] "James LuValle - Wikipedia." Wikipedia, the Free Encyclopedia, Wikimedia Foundation, Inc, 2017, https://en.wikipedia.org/wiki/James_LuValle. Accessed 17 Apr. 2017.

[57] "Mack Robinson (athlete) - Wikipedia." Wikipedia, the Free Encyclopedia, Wikimedia Foundation, Inc, 2017, https://en.wikipedia.org/wiki/Mack_Robinson_(athlete). Accessed 17 Apr. 2017.

[58] "Walter Francis White - Wikipedia." Wikipedia, the Free Encyclopedia, Wikimedia Foundation, Inc, 2017, https://en.wikipedia.org/wiki/Walter_Francis_White. Accessed 17 Apr. 2017.

[59] Dyja, Tom. Walter White: The Dilemma of Black Identity in America. Ivan R. Dee, 2008.

[60] "NAACP: A Century in the Fight for Freedom | Exhibitions - Library of Congress." Library of Congress, 2017, https://www.loc.gov/exhibits/naacp/. Accessed 17 Apr. 2017.

[61] "House Un-American Activities Committee - Wikipedia." Wikipedia, the Free Encyclopedia, Wikimedia Foundation, Inc, 2017, https://en.wikipedia.org/wiki/House_Un-American_Activities_Committee#Precursors_to_the_committee. Accessed 17 Apr. 2017.

[62] "Investigation of Un-American Propaganda Activities in the United States." The Online Books Page, 2017, https://onlinebooks.library.upenn.edu/webbin/metabook?id=diescommittee. Accessed 17 Apr. 2017.

[63] "The American Negro in the Communist Party: United States. Congress. House. Committee on Un-American Activities: Free Download & Streaming: Internet Archive." Internet Archive, National Archives and Records Administration, https://archive.org/details/americannegroinc00unit. Accessed 16 Apr. 2017.

[64] "Hamilton Fish III - Wikipedia." Wikipedia, the Free Encyclopedia, Wikimedia Foundation, Inc, 2017, https://en.wikipedia.org/wiki/Hamilton_Fish_III. Accessed 17 Apr. 2017.

[65] The American Negro in the Communist Party. U.S. House of Representatives-Committee
on Un-American Activities, 1954. National Archives and Administration.
https://www.archives.gov/. Accessed 18 Apr. 2017.

[66] "Records of the House Un-American Activities Committee - NARA Finding Aid:
Charles E. Schamel (ed.) : Free Download & Streaming: Internet Archive." Internet
Archive,
National Records and Archives Administration, July 1995,
https://archive.org/details/RecordsOfTheHouseUn-americanActivitiesCommittee-NaraFindingAid. Accessed 17 Apr. 2017.

[67] "James S. Allen - Wikipedia." Wikipedia, the Free Encyclopedia, Wikimedia
Foundation, Inc,
2017, https://en.wikipedia.org/wiki/James_S._Allen. Accessed 17 Apr. 2017.

[68] "Negroes in Soviet America; June 1935: Historical Manuscripts and Photographs."
The University of Southern Mississippi Digital Collections, 2017,
https://digilib.usm.edu/cdm/ref/collection/manu/id/1660. Accessed 20 Apr. 2017.

[69] D'Amato, Paul. "The Communist Party and Black Liberation." International Socialist
Review, vol. 1, Summer 1997,
https://www.isreview.org/issues/01/cp_blacks_1930s.shtml. Accessed 16 Apr. 2017.

[70] "Harry Haywood Internet Archive." Marxists Internet Archive, 2017,
https://www.marxists.org/archive/haywood/. Accessed 15 Apr. 2017.

[71] "Harry Haywood Archive." The Marxist-Leninist, Wordpress, 2017,
https://marxistleninist.wordpress.com/harry-haywood-archive/. Accessed
15 Apr. 2017.

[72] B, Mike. "The Negro Nation." Marxists Internet Archive, 2010,
https://www.marxists.org/archive/haywood/negro-liberation/ch07.htm. Accessed
20 Apr. 2017.

Chapter 11 The Scottsboro Boys and the Communist Intrusion

[1] "Scottsboro Boys - Wikipedia." Wikipedia, the Free Encyclopedia, Wikimedia
Foundation, Inc, 2017, https://en.wikipedia.org/wiki/Scottsboro_Boys. Accessed
20 Apr. 2017.

[2] Kengor, Paul. "Atlanta 1931-32: The Communist Swarm Scottsboro." The
Communist: Frank Marshall Davis: The Untold Story of Barack Obama's Mentor, Tantor
Media, Inc, 2012, pp. 35-51.

[3] "Scottsboro Trials." Encyclopedia of Alabama, 2008,
https://www.encyclopediaofalabama.org/article/h-1456. Accessed 20 Apr. 2017.

[4] Goodman, James. Stories of Scottsboro. Pantheon Books, 1994.

[5] IBID.

[6] Acker, James R. Scottsboro and Its Legacy: The Cases That Challenged American Legal and Social Justice. Praeger, 2008.

[7] Geis, Gilbert, and Leigh B. Bienen. "Scottsboro (1931) Injustice." Crimes of the Century: From Leopold and Loeb to O.j. Simpson, Northwestern UP, 2016, pp. 49-87.

 [8] Kengor, Paul. "Atlanta 1931-32: The Communist Swarm Scottsboro." The Communist: Frank Marshall Davis: The Untold Story of Barack Obama's Mentor, Tantor Media, Inc, 2012, pp. 35-51.

[9] IBID.

[10] Linder Prof., Douglas O. "Appellate Court Decisions." Famous Trials, University of Missouri-Kansas City School of Law, 2017, www.famous-trials.com/scottsboroboys/1599-courtdecision. Accessed 21 Apr. 2017.

[11] "Scottsboro Boys - Wikipedia." Wikipedia, the Free Encyclopedia, Wikimedia Foundation, Inc, 2017, en.wikipedia.org/wiki/Scottsboro_Boys. Accessed 20 Apr. 2017.
[12] Kengor, Paul. "Atlanta 1931-32: The Communist Swarm Scottsboro." The Communist: Frank Marshall Davis: The Untold Story of Barack Obama's Mentor, Tantor Media, Inc, 2012, pp. 35-51.

[13] "The Scottsboro Boys Trials: A Chronology." Famous Trials, University of Missouri-Kansas City School of Law, 2017, https://www.famous-trials.com/scottsboroboys/1601-chronology. Accessed 21 Apr. 2017.

[14] "Scottsboro Trials." Encyclopedia of Alabama, 2008, https://www.encyclopediaofalabama.org/article/h-1456. Accessed 20 Apr. 2017.

Chapter 12 Communists and Socialists Influence on Big Labor Unions

[1] "Booker T. Washington." BrainyQuote, 2017, https://www.brainyquote.com/citation/quotes/quotes/b/bookertwa122789.html?ct=Booker+T.+Washington. Accessed 23 Apr. 2017.

[2] Lichtenstein, Nelson, et al. "The Great Depression and the First New Deal: 1929-1935." Who Built America? Working People and the Nation's Economy, Politics, Culture and Society Volume 2, Worth Publishers, 2002, p. 375.

[3] McElvaine, Robert S. The Great Depression: America, 1928-1941.
Times Books, 1993.

[4] Bernstein, Michael A. A Perilous Progress: Economists and Public Purpose in Twentieth-Century America. Princeton UP, 2014.

[5] "Unemployment Statistics During the Great Depression." United States American History, Online Highways LLC, 2017, https://www.u-s-history.com/pages/h1528.html. Accessed 23 Apr. 2017.

[6] Lichtenstein, Nelson, et al. "The Great Depression and the First New Deal 1929-1935." *Who Built America?: 2*, Worth, 2002, pp. 387-389.

[7] Lichtenstein, Nelson. "A Nation Transformed: The United States in World War II 1939-1946." *Who Built America?: 2*, Worth, 2000, pp. 385-386.

[8] Lichtenstein, Nelson. "A Nation Transformed: The United States in World War II 1939-1946." *Who Built America?: 2*, Worth, 2000, pp. 387.

[9] IBID. Lichenstein, pp. 387-389.

[10] "New Deal - Wikipedia." *Wikipedia, the Free Encyclopedia*, Wikimedia Foundation, Inc, 2017, https://en.wikipedia.org/wiki/New_Deal. Accessed 24 Apr. 2017.

[11] McElvaine, Robert S. *The Great Depression: America, 1928-1941*. Times Books, 1993.

[12] "Angelo Herndon - Wikipedia." *Wikipedia, the Free Encyclopedia*, Wikimedia Foundation, Inc, 2017, https://en.wikipedia.org/wiki/Angelo_Herndon. Accessed 24 Apr. 2017.

[13] Hatfield, Edward A. "Angelo Herndon Case." *New Georgia Encyclopedia*, 2013, https://www.georgiaencyclopedia.org/articles/history-archaeology/angelo-herndon-case. Accessed 24 Apr. 2017.

[14] "Sharecroppers' Union - Wikipedia." *Wikipedia, the Free Encyclopedia*, Wikimedia Foundation, Inc, 2016, https://en.wikipedia.org/wiki/Sharecroppers%27_Union. Accessed 24 Apr. 2017.

[15] "Southern Tenant Farmers Union - Wikipedia." *Wikipedia, the Free Encyclopedia*, Wikimedia Foundation, Inc, 2017, https://en.wikipedia.org/wiki/Southern_Tenant_Farmers_Union. Accessed 24 Apr. 2017.

[16] Lichtenstein, Nelson, et al. "The Great Depression and the First New Deal 1929-1935." *Who Built America? (2)*, Worth, 2002, pp. 387-389.

[17] IBID.

[18] Kindig, Jessie. "Southern Tenant Farmers Union | The Black Past: Remembered and Reclaimed." *The Black Past: Remembered and Reclaimed*, University of Washington, 2017, https://www.blackpast.org/aah.southern-tenant-farmers-union. Accessed 24 Apr. 2017.

[19] IBID.

[20] Cobb, William H. "Southern Tenant Farmers' Union - Encyclopedia of Arkansas."
The Encyclopedia of Arkansas History & Culture, 2017,
https://www.encyclopediaofarkansas.net/encyclopedia/entry-detail.aspx?entryID=35.
Accessed 24 Apr. 2017.

[21] Law, Michael K. "Alabama Sharecroppers Union." *Encyclopedia of Alabama*, 2016,
https://www.encyclopediaofalabama.org/article/h-2477. Accessed 24 Apr. 2017.

[22] Lichtenstein, Nelson. "The Great Depression and the First New Deal 1929-1935."
Who Built America?: 2, Worth, 2002, pp. 392-396.

[23] IBID.

[24] "United States Presidential Election of 1932 | United States Government |
Britannica.com." *Encyclopedia Britannica*, 2017,
https://www.britannica.com/event/United-States-presidential-election-of-1932.
Accessed 24 Apr. 2017.

[25] "United States Presidential Election, 1932 - Wikipedia." *Wikipedia, the Free
Encyclopedia*, Wikimedia Foundation, Inc, 2017,
https://en.wikipedia.org/wiki/United_States_presidential_election,_1932. Accessed
24 Apr. 2017.

[26] Freidel, Frank. *Franklin D Roosevelt: The Triumph*. Little, Brown and
Company, 1956, *Library of Congress*.
https://ia601602.us.archive.org/1/items/in.ernet.dli.2015.156788/2015.156788.Frankli
m-D-Roosevelt-The-Triumph.pdf. Accessed 24 Apr. 2017.

[27] Lichtenstein, Nelson. "The Great Depression and the First New Deal." *Who Built
America?: 2*, Worth, 2002, pp. 389-391.

[28] Lichtenstein, Nelson. "The Great Depression and the First New Deal 1929-
1935." *Who Built America?: 2*, Worth, 2002, pp. 396-398.

[29] Folsom Jr., Burton. *New Deal or Raw Deal? How FDR's Economic Legacy Has
Damaged America*. Threshold Editions, 2008.

[30] Hawley, Ellis W. *The New Deal and the Problem of Monopoly: A Study in Economic
Ambivalence*. UMI Books on Demand, 1996.

[31] Davis, B. J. "Textile Strike of 1934 | NCpedia." *NCpedia Home Page | NCpedia*, Tar Heel Historian, 2010, https://www.ncpedia.org/textiles/strike-1934. Accessed 24 Apr. 2017.

[32] "Textile Workers Strike (1934) - Wikipedia." *Wikipedia, the Free Encyclopedia*, Wikimedia Foundation, Inc, 2016, https://en.wikipedia.org/wiki/Textile_workers_strike_(1934). Accessed 24 Apr. 2017.

[33] Salmond, John. "General Textile Strike of 1934." *Encyclopedia of Alabama*, Alabama Humanities, 2015, https://www.encyclopediaofalabama.org/article/h-1026. Accessed 24 Apr. 2017.

[34] Gerstle, Gary. *Working-Class Americanism: The Politics of Labor in a Textile City, 1914-1960:*
with a New Preface by the Author, Princeton UP, 2002.

[35] Lichtenstein, Nelson. "Labor Democratizes America 1935-1939." *Who Built America?: 2*, Worth, 2002, pp. 425-436.

[36] Lichtenstein, Nelson. "Labor Democratizes America 1935-1939." *Who Built America?: 2*, Worth, 2002, pp. 439-452.

[37] "Black Cabinet-Wikipedia." *Wikipedia, the Free Encyclopedia,* Wikimedia Foundation, Inc, 2017, https://en.wikipedia.org/wiki/Black_Cabinet. Accessed 4 May 2017.

[38] Ruffin II, Herbert G. "Bethune, Mary Jane McLeod (1875-1955) | The Black Past: Remembered and Reclaimed." *The Black Past: Remembered and Reclaimed*, University of Washington, 2017, https://www.blackpast.org/aah/bethune-mary-jane-mcleod-1875-1955. Accessed 24 Apr. 2017.

[39] Proyect, Louis. "FDR and African-Americans." *Louis Proyect: The Unrepentant Marxist,* 28 Sept. 2008, https://louisproyect.org/2008/09/23/fdr-and-african-americans/. Accessed 4 May 2017.

[40] Lichtenstein, Nelson. "A Nation Transformed: The United States in World War II 1939-1946.
"*Who Built America? (2)*, Worth, 2000, pp. 493-503.

[41] Brinkley, Alan. *The End of Reform: New Deal Liberalism in Recession and War.* Vintage Books, 1996.

[42] Lukacs, John, et al. "Adolf Hitler | Dictator of Germany | Britannica.com." *Encyclopedia Britannica*, edited by Wilfrid F. Knapp and Allan Bullock, 2015, https://www.britannica.com/biography/Adolf-Hitler. Accessed 24 Apr. 2017.

[43] "Adolf Hitler - Wikipedia." *Wikipedia, the Free Encyclopedia*,

Wikimedia Foundation, Inc, 2017, https://en.wikipedia.org/wiki/Adolf_Hitler. Accessed 24 Apr. 2017.

[44] "Adolf Hitler - World War II." *HISTORY.com*, A & E Television Network, LLC, 2017, https://www.history.com/topics/world-war-ii/adolf-hitler. Accessed 24 Apr. 2017.

[45] "Joseph Stalin - Wikipedia." *Wikipedia, the Free Encyclopedia*, Wikimedia Foundation, Inc,

2017, https://en.wikipedia.org/wiki/Joseph_Stalin. Accessed 24 Apr. 2017.

[46] "Glossary of People: St." *Marxists Internet Archive*, 2017, https://www.marxists.org/glossary/people/s/t.htm#stalin. Accessed 24 Apr. 2017.

[47] "Hirohito-Wikipedia." *Wikipedia, the Free Encyclopedia,*

Wikimedia Foundation, Inc, 2017, https://en.wikipedia.org/wiki/Hirohito. Accessed 4 May 2017.

[48] Ambrose, Stephen E. *Citizen Soldiers: The U.S. Army from*

Normandy Beaches to the Surrender of Germany, Simon & Schuster, 2016.

[49] Kengor, Paul. "Just a Purge." *The Communist: Frank Marshall Davis: The Untold Story of*

Barack Obama's Mentor, Tantor Media, Inc, 2012, pp. 69-71. Accessed 24 Apr. 2017.

[50] "Benito Mussolini - Wikipedia." *Wikipedia, the Free Encyclopedia*, Wikimedia Foundation, Inc, 2017, https://en.wikipedia.org/wiki/Benito_Mussolini. Accessed 24 Apr. 2017.

[51] Biography.com Editors. "Benito Mussolini." *Bio*, A&E Television Networks, 22 July 2015, https://www.biography.com/people/benito-mussolini-9419443. Accessed 24 Apr. 2017.

[52] "Doris Miller - Wikipedia." *Wikipedia, the Free Encyclopedia*, Wikimedia Foundation, Inc,

2017, https://en.wikipedia.org/wiki/Doris_Miller. Accessed 24 Apr. 2017.

[53] "Miller, Doris." *NHHC*, 2017, https://www.history.navy.mil/our-collections/photography/us-people/m/miller--doris.html. Accessed 24 Apr. 2017.

[54] Dower, John W. *War Without Mercy: Race and Power in the Pacific War*. Pantheon Books,

1993.

[55] Fikes, Robert. "Tuskegee Airmen The Black Past: Remembered and Reclaimed."

The Black Past: Remembered and Reclaimed, San Diego State University, 2017, https://www.blackpast.org/aah/tuskegee-airmen. Accessed 24 Apr. 2017.

[56] Lichtenstein, Nelson "A Nation Transformed: The United States in World War II 1939-1946."

Who Built America?: 2, Worth, 2000, pp. 517-518.

[57] "Elijah Muhammad - Wikipedia." *Wikipedia, the Free Encyclopedia*, Wikimedia Foundation, Inc, 2017, https://en.wikipedia.org/wiki/Elijah_Muhammad. Accessed 24 Apr. 2017.

[58] "FBI — Elijah Muhammed." *FBI*, Department of Justice (DOJ), 2017, https://vault.fbi.gov/elijah-muhammad. Accessed 13 Apr. 2017.

[59] "Second Great Migration (African American) - Wikipedia." *Wikipedia, the Free Encyclopedia*, Wikimedia Foundation, Inc, 2017, https://en.wikipedia.org/wiki/Second_Great_Migration_(African_American). Accessed 25 Apr. 2017.

[60] "The Communist Party USA and African Americans - Wikipedia."

Wikipedia, the Free Encyclopedia, Wikimedia Foundation, Inc, 2016, https://en.wikipedia.org/wiki/The_Communist_Party_USA_and_African_Americans. Accessed 24 Apr. 2017.

[61] Lichtenstein, Nelson "A Nation Transformed: The United States in World War II 1939-1946."

Who Built America?: 2, Worth, 2000, pp. 517-518.

[62] IBID.

[63] "Executive Orders Disposition Tables." *National Archives*, 2017, https://www.archives.gov/federal-register/executive-orders/1941.html. Accessed 25 Apr. 2017.

[64] Adams, Luther. "Randolph, Asa Philip (1889-1979)." *The Black Past Remembered and*

Reclaimed. University of Washington-Tacoma, 2017,

https://www.blackpast.org/aah/Randolph-asa-philip-1889-1979.

Accessed 5 May 2017.

[65] Wada, Kayomi. "President's Committee on Fair Employment Practice (FEPC)."

The Black Past: Remembered and Reclaimed, University of Washington-Tacoma, 2017,
https://www.blackpast.org/aah/presidents-committee-fair-employment-practice-fepc

Accessed 25 Apr. 2017.

[66] Lichtenstein, Nelson "A Nation Transformed: The United States in World War II 1939-1946.

"*Who Built America? (2)*, Worth, 2000, pp. 518-519.

[67] "Second Bill of Rights - Wikipedia." *Wikipedia, the Free Encyclopedia*, Wikimedia Foundation, Inc, 2017, https://en.wikipedia.org/wiki/Second_Bill_of_Rights. Accessed 25 Apr. 2017.

[68] Miller, Galanty. "The Constitution Is Outdated; Let's Change It." *The Huffington Post*,

3 June 2014, https://www.huffingtonpost.com/galanty-miller/the-constitution-is-outdated_b_5439334.html. Accessed 25 Apr. 2017.

[69] Washington, Ellis. "Obama's Second Bill of Rights." *WND*, 16 Jan. 2010, https://www.wnd.com/2010/01/122116/. Accessed 25 Apr. 2017.

[70] Sunstein, Cass R., and Katy Roberts. "Obama, FDR and the Second Bill of Rights."

Bloomberg View, Bloomberg LP, 28 Jan. 2013, https://www.bloomberg.com/view/articles/2013-01-28/obama-fdr-and-the-second-bill-of-rights. Accessed 25 Apr. 2017.

[71] Daniels, Kit. "Sixth Grade Assignment: Destroy the Bill of Rights » Alex Jones' Infowars:

There's a War on for Your Mind!" *Infowars*, Free Speech Systems LLC, Company, 8 Oct. 2013, https://www.infowars.com/sixth-grade-assignment-destroy-the-bill-of-rights/. Accessed 25 Apr. 2017.

[72] Thalen, Mikael. "Common Core: Sixth Graders Asked To Revise 'Outdated' Bill Of Rights." *Storyleak*, Wordpress, 8 Oct. 2013, https://www.storyleak.com/common-core-sixth-graders-asked-revise-outdated-bill-rights/. Accessed 25 Apr. 2017.

[73] De Vouge, Ariane. "Ginsburg Likes S. Africa As Model for Egypt." *ABC News*, 3 Feb. 2012, https://abcnews.go.com/blogs/politics/2012/02/ginsburg-likes-s-africa-as-model-for-egypt/. Accessed 25 Apr. 2017.

[74] Fox News Editors. "Ginsburg to Egyptians: I Wouldn't Use U.S. Constitution As a Model."

Fox News, 6 Feb. 2012,

https://www.foxnews.com/politics/2012/02/06/ginsburg-to-egyptians-wouldnt-use-us-constitution-as-model.html. Accessed 25 Apr. 2017.

[75] Chomsky, Noam. "Masters of Mankind." *Who Rules the World?*, Picador USA, 2017, p. 258.

Chapter 13 Communist Influence: The Civil Rights Movement Part (I)

[1] "Lenin Quotes." *Marxists Internet Archive,* 2017, https://Marxists.org/archive/lenin/quotes.html. Accessed 5 May 2017.

[2] "Executive Order 9981 - Wikipedia." *Wikipedia, the Free Encyclopedia*, Wikimedia Foundation, Inc, 2017, https://en.wikipedia.org/wiki/Executive_Order_9981. Accessed 26 Apr. 2017.

[3] "A Look at the 1940 Census." *Census.gov,* 2016, https://www.census.gov/newsroom/cspan/1940census/CSPAN_1940slides.pdf. Accessed 6 May 2017.

[4] "Tom Mesenbourg, Deputy Director, Appeared on C-SPAN's "Washington Journal" to Discuss the Upcoming Release of 1940 Census Records by the National Archives - Newsroom - U.S. Census Bureau." *Census.gov*, 12 Apr. 2012, https://www.census.gov/newsroom/cspan/1940census. Accessed 26 Apr. 2017.

[5] MacGregor, Morris J. *Integration of the Armed Forces, 1940-1965*. Center of Military History, U.S. Army, 2001.

[6] "The African American Experience in the U.S. Navy." *NHHC*, Navy History and Heritage Command, 6 Apr. 2017, https://www.history.navy.mil/browse-by-topic/diversity/african-americans.html.
Accessed 26 Apr. 2017.

[7] "Harry S. Truman - Wikipedia." *Wikipedia, the Free Encyclopedia*, Wikimedia Foundation, Inc,

2017, https://en.wikipedia.org/wiki/Harry_S._Truman. Accessed 26 Apr. 2017.

[8] "Harry S. Truman." *Whitehouse.gov*, 2017,
https://www.whitehouse.gov/1600/presidents/harrystruman. Accessed 26 Apr. 2017.

[9] Wada, Kayomi. "President's Committee on Fair Employment Practice (FEPC)." *The Black Past: Remembered and Reclaimed*, University of Washington-Tacoma, 2017,
https://www.blackpast.org/aah/presidents-committee-fair-employment-practice-fepc.
Accessed 25 Apr. 2017.

[10] "Truman Library - Records of the President's Committee on Civil Rights."
Harry S. Truman Library and Museum, 2017,
https://www.trumanlibrary.org/hstpaper/pccr.htm. Accessed 26 Apr. 2017.

[11] "Truman Library: "Opinions About Negro Infantry Platoons in White Companies
of 7 Divisions", July 3, 1945. Record Group 220: Records of the President's Committee on Equality of Treatment and Opportunity in the Armed Services, Army. Negro Platoons in White Companies." *Harry S. Truman Library and Museum*, 2017,
https://www.trumanlibrary.org/whistlestop/study_collections/desegregation/large/documents/index.php?documentdate=1945-07-03&documentid=10-11&pagenumber=1.
Accessed 26 Apr. 2017.

[12] "De Facto Legal Definition of De Facto." *The Free Dictionary*, Farlex, 2008,
http://www.legal-dictionary.thefreedictionary.com/De+Facto. Accessed 15 Jan. 2017.

[13] "De Jure Legal Definition of De Jure." *The Free Dictionary*, Farlex, 2008,
https://www.legal-dictionary.thefreedictionary.com/De+jure. Accessed 15 Jan. 2017.

[14] "Dixiecrats - Wikipedia." *Wikipedia, the Free Encyclopedia*, Wikimedia Foundation,
Inc, 2017, https://en.wikipedia.org/wiki/Dixiecrat. Accessed 26 Apr. 2017.

[15] Holden, Charles J. "Dixiecrats | NCpedia." *NCpedia Home Page | NCpedia*,
University of North Carolina P, 2006, https://www.ncpedia.org/dixiecrats. Accessed
26 Apr. 2017.

[16] Frederickson, Karl. "Dixiecrats." *Encyclopedia of Alabama*, Alabama Humanities
Foundation, 2015, https://www.encyclopediaofalabama.org/article/h-1477. Accessed
26 Apr. 2017.

[17] "Strom Thurmond - Wikipedia." *Wikipedia, the Free Encyclopedia*, Wikimedia
Foundation, Inc, 2017, https://en.wikipedia.org/wiki/Strom_Thurmond. Accessed
26 Apr. 2017.

[18] "24 Jul 1948, Page 1 - St. Louis Post-Dispatch at
Newspapers.com." *Newspapers.com*, 2017,
https://www.newspapers.com/image/138826495/. Accessed 26 Apr. 2017.

[19] "25 Jul 1948, Page 1 - The Anniston Star at Newspapers.com." *Newspapers.com*, 2017, https://www.newspapers.com/image/115705736/. Accessed 26 Apr. 2017.

[20] "Henry A. Wallace - Wikipedia." *Wikipedia, the Free Encyclopedia*, Wikimedia Foundation, Inc, 2017, https://en.wikipedia.org/wiki/Henry_A._Wallace. Accessed 26 Apr. 2017.

[21] "Progressive Party (United States, 1948) - Wikipedia." *Wikipedia, the Free Encyclopedia*, Wikimedia Foundation, Inc, 2017, https://en.wikipedia.org/wiki/Progressive_Party_(United_States,_1948). Accessed 26 Apr. 2017.

[22] Markowitz, Norman D. "The Rise and Fall of the People's Century: Henry A. Wallace and

American Liberalism, 1941-1948 - 1973, Page Iii by Norman D. Markowitz. Online Research Library: Questia." *Online Research Library: Questia*, 1973,

https://www.questia.com/read/95265575/the-rise-and-fall-of-the-people-s-century-henry-a. Accessed 26 Apr. 2017.

[23] "Executive Orders Disposition Tables." *National Archives*, 2017, https://www.archives.gov/federal-register/executive-orders/1946.html#9808. Accessed 26 Apr. 2017.

[24] "Executive Order 9980 - Wikisource, the Free Online Library." *Wikisource, the Free Library*, Wikimedia, 2010, https://en.wikisource.org/wiki/Executive_Order_9980. Accessed 26 Apr. 2017.

[25] "Executive Order 9981 - Wikipedia." *Wikipedia, the Free Encyclopedia*, Wikimedia Foundation, Inc, 2017, https://en.wikipedia.org/wiki/Executive_Order_9981. Accessed 26 Apr. 2017.

[26] "Shelley V. Kraemer - Wikipedia." *Wikipedia, the Free Encyclopedia*, Wikimedia Foundation, Inc, 2017, https://en.wikipedia.org/wiki/Shelley_v._Kraemer. Accessed 26 Apr. 2017.

[27] "Shelley V. Kraemer." *Lawbrain.com*, 2011, https://lawbrain.com/wiki/Shelley_v._Kraemer#Summary_of_Case_Facts. Accessed 26 Apr. 2017.

[28] "Purpose of CC&Rs - FindLaw." *Findlaw*, 2017, https://realestate.findlaw.com/owning-a-home/purpose-of-cc-rs.html. Accessed 26 Apr. 2017.

[29] Stewart, W. J. "Restrictive Covenant Legal Definition of Restrictive Covenant." *TheFreeDictionary.com*, Collins Legal Dictionary of Law, 2006, https://www.legal-dictionary.thefreedictionary.com/Restrictive+Covenant. Accessed 26 Apr. 2017.

[30] "Findlaw's United States Supreme Court Case and Opinions." *Find Law,* Thomson Reuters Business, 2017, https://caselaw.findlaw.com/us-supreme-court/334/1.html Accessed 27 Apr. 2017.

[31] "United States Supreme Court." *Shelly v Kraemer [1948] USSC 63; 334 U.S. 1; 68 S.Ct. 836; 92 L.Ed. 1161; Nos. 72,87 (3 May 1948),* World Legal Information Institute, 2017, https://worldlii.org/us/cases/federal/USSC/1948/63.html.

Accessed 27 Apr. 2017

[32] "Red Scare - Wikipedia." *Wikipedia, the Free Encyclopedia*, Wikimedia Foundation, Inc, 2017, https://en.wikipedia.org/wiki/Red_Scare. Accessed 27 Apr. 2017.

[33] "The Red Scare." *US History.org*, 2017, https://ushistory.org/us/47a.asp. Accessed 27 Apr. 2017.

[34] "Smith Act - Wikipedia." *Wikipedia, the Free Encyclopedia*, Wikimedia Foundation, Inc, 2017, https://en.wikipedia.org/wiki/Smith_Act. Accessed 27 Apr. 2017.

[35] Encyclopedia Britannica Editors. "Smith Act | United States [1940] | Britannica.com." *Encyclopedia Britannica*, 2015, https://www.britannica.com/event/Smith-Act. Accessed 27 Apr. 2017.

[36] Tabler, Dave. "George W. Christians, American Fascist." *Appalachian History*, 2 Mar. 2015, https://www.appalachianhistory.net/2015/03/george-w-christians-american-fascist.html. Accessed 27 Apr. 2017.

[37] Scott, Jason. *Ernie Lazar FOIA Collection Communist Party of the USA*. Department of Justice, 2013. *National Archives and Records Administration*. https://archive.org/details/foia_FBI_MONOGRAPH-CPUSA_Whos_Who.PDF. Accessed 28 Apr. 2017.

[38] "Measuring Worth - Results." *Measuring Worth - Relative Worth Comparators and Data Sets*, 2017, https://www.measuringworth.com/uscompare/relativevalue.php. Accessed 27 Apr. 2017.

[39] "Benjamin J. Davis Jr." *Wikipedia*, Wikimedia, 2017, https://en.wikipedia.org/wiki/Benjamin_J._Davis_Jr. Accessed 27 Apr. 2017.

[40] "Carl Winter." *KeyWiki*, Wikimedia, 2016, https://keywiki.org/Carl_Winter. Accessed 28 Apr. 2017.

[41] "Claudia Jones - Wikipedia." *Wikipedia, the Free Encyclopedia*, Wikimedia Foundation, Inc, 2017, https://en.wikipedia.org/wiki/Claudia_Jones#.22An_End_to_the_Neglect_of_the_Probl ems_of_the_Negro_Woman.21.22. Accessed 29 Apr. 2017.

[42] "Eugene Dennis - Wikipedia." *Wikipedia, the Free Encyclopedia*, Wikimedia Foundation, Inc,

2017, https://en.wikipedia.org/wiki/Eugene_Dennis. Accessed 27 Apr. 2017.

[43] "Gil Green (politician) - Wikipedia." *Wikipedia, the Free Encyclopedia*, Wikimedia Foundation, Inc, 2017, https://en.wikipedia.org/wiki/Gil_Green_(politician). Accessed 28 Apr. 2017.

[44] "Gus Hall - Wikipedia." *Wikipedia, the Free Encyclopedia*, Wikimedia Foundation, Inc, 2017, https://en.wikipedia.org/wiki/Gus_Hall. Accessed 28 Apr. 2017.

[45] "Harold Medina - Wikipedia." *Wikipedia, the Free Encyclopedia*, Wikimedia Foundation, Inc, 2017, https://en.wikipedia.org/wiki/Harold_Medina. Accessed 28 Apr. 2017.

[46] "Henry Winston - Wikipedia." *Wikipedia, the Free Encyclopedia*, Wikimedia Foundation, Inc,

2017, https://en.wikipedia.org/wiki/Henry_Winston. Accessed 28 Apr. 2017.

[47] "Irving POTASH: American. A Member of the US Communist Party from Its Early Years, Potash... The National Archives." *Discovery The National Archives*, National Archives of the United Kingdom, 21 Aug. 2015, https://www.discovery.nationalarchives.gov.uk/details/r/C14895001. Accessed 28 Apr. 2017.

[48] "Jack Stachel - Wikipedia." *Wikipedia, the Free Encyclopedia*, Wikimedia Foundation, Inc, 2017, https://en.wikipedia.org/wiki/Jack_Stachel. Accessed 28 Apr. 2017.

[49] "John Williamson (communist) - Wikipedia." *Wikipedia, the Free Encyclopedia*, Wikimedia Foundation, Inc, 2017, https://en.wikipedia.org/wiki/John_Williamson_(communist). Accessed 28 Apr. 2017.

[50] "Louis F. Budenz - Wikipedia." *Wikipedia, the Free Encyclopedia*, Wikimedia Foundation, Inc, 2017, https://en.wikipedia.org/wiki/Louis_F._Budenz. Accessed 27 Apr. 2017.

[51] "McCarran Internal Security Act - Wikipedia." *Wikipedia, the Free Encyclopedia*, Wikimedia Foundation, Inc, 2017, https://en.wikipedia.org/wiki/McCarran_Internal_Security_Act.

Accessed 28 Apr. 2017.

[52] Hinds, Donald. *Journey to an Illusion: The West Indian in Britain*. Bogle-L'Ouverture, 2001.

[53] Jack, Red. "An End to the Neglect of the Problems of the Negro Woman!" *Libcom*, 8 Jan. 2017, https://libcom.org/library/end-neglect-problems-negro-woman. Accessed 29 Apr. 2017.

[54] McClendon III, John H. "Jones, Claudia (1915-1964) | The Black Past: Remembered and Reclaimed." | *The Black Past: Remembered and Reclaimed*, University of Michigan, 2017, http://www.blackpast.org/aah/jones-claudia-1915-1964. Accessed 29 Apr. 2017.

Chapter 14 Brown vs. Board of Education: The American Civil Rights Movement (II)

[1] "Brown v. Board of Education of Topeka." *Brown v. Board of Education of Topeka - Kansapedia - Kansas Historical Society*, Kansas Historical Society, June 2003, https://www.kshs.org/kansapedia/brown-v-board-of-education-of-topeka/11994.

Accessed 14 Jan. 2017.

[2] Davis, Damani. "Exodus to Kansas." *National Archives and Records Administration*, National Archives and Records Administration, 15 Aug. 2016, https://www.archives.gov/publications/prologue/2008/summer/exodus.html. Accessed 16 Jan. 2017.

[3] Davidson, James W., Lytle, Mark H. "The Madness of John Brown." *After the Fact: The Art of Historical Detection,* McGraw-Hill, 2010, pp. 150-173.

[4] "Plessy V. Ferguson." *LII/Legal Information Institute,* 2017, https://law.cornell.edu/supremecourt/text/163/537. Accessed 6 May 2017.

[5] "Charles E. Bledsoe to the NAACP Legal Department." *Kansas Historical Society*, 1950, https://www.kshs.org/km/items/view/213409. Accessed 6 May 2017.

[6] "McKinley Burnett." *McKinley Burnett - Kansapedia - Kansas Historical Society*, Kansas Historical Society, June 2012, https://www.kshs.org/kansapedia/mckinley-burnett/17784. Accessed 14 Jan. 2017.

[7] "Oliver Brown." *Kansas Historical Society,* 2017, https://www.kshs.org/p/oliver-brown/19363. Assessed 6 May 2017.

[8] "Brown V. Board of Education." *PBS Newshour,* Newshour Productions LLC, 12 May 2004, https://pbs.org/newshour/bb/law-jan-june04-brown_05-12/. Accessed 6 May 2017.

[9] "The Doll Test for Racial Self-Hate: Did It Even Make Sense?" *The Root,* Univision Communications Inc, 17 May 2014, http://www.theroot.com/articles/culture/2014/05/the_brown_decision_s_doll_test_11_facts/3/.
Accessed 10 Jan. 2017.

[10] "Kenneth and Mamie Clark-Wikipedia." *Wikipedia-the Free Encyclopedia,* Wikimedia Foundation, Inc, 2017, https://en.wikipedia.org/wiki/Kenneth_and_Mamie_Clark. Accessed 6 May 2017.

[11] "Kenneth and Mamie Clark Doll-Brown V. Board of Education National Historic Site."
NPS.gov Homepage (U.S. National Park Service), 2017, https://nps.gov/brvb/learn/historyculture/clarkdoll.htm. Accessed 6 May 2017.

[12] Rothstein, Richard. "Brown V. Board at 60: Why Have We Been So Disappointed? What Have We Learned?" *Economic Policy Institute,* 17 April 2014, https://epi.org/publication/brown-at-60-why-have-we-been-so-disappointed-what-have-we-learned/. Accessed 6 May 2017.

[13] Dunn, Adrienne. "Pearsall Plan." *North Carolina History Project*, John Locke Foundation,
2016, https://www.northcarolinahistory.org/encyclopedia/pearsall-plan/.
Accessed 14 Jan. 2017.

[14] Daughtery, Brian J. "Desegregation in Public Schools." *Encyclopedia Virginia*, Virginia Foundation for the Humanities, 2008, https://encyclopediavirginia.org/Desegregation_In_Public_Schools#start_entry.
Accessed 6 May 2017.

[15] "Brown v. Board of Education of Topeka." *Brown v. Board of Education of Topeka – Kansapedia - Kansas Historical Society*, Kansas Historical Society, June 2003, https://www.kshs.org/kansapedia/brown-v-board-of-education-of-topeka/11994.
Accessed 14 Jan. 2017.

[16] "African-American Civil Rights Movement (1954–1968)." *Wikipedia*, Wikimedia Foundation,
4 Jan. 2017, https://en.wikipedia.org/wiki/African-American_Civil_Rights_Movement_(1954%E2%80%931968). Accessed 14 Jan 2017.

[17] "G. Edward Griffin: Communism and the Civil Rights Movement." *YouTube*, 18 Jan. 2014, https://youtu.be/3CHk_iJ8hWK. Accessed 6 May 2017.

Chapter 15 Two Factional Groups: The American Civil Rights Movement (III)

[1] Yette, Samuel F. "5 The Threat and Tactics." *The Choice: The Issue of Black Survival in America*, Putnam, New York, 1971, pp. 185–186.

[2] "Anarchy." *Merriam-Webster's Dictionary and Thesaurus,* Merriam-Webster, 2007, p. 28.

[3] "De Jure Legal Definition of De Jure." *The Free Dictionary*, Farlex, 2008, https://legal-dictionary.thefreedictionary.com/De+jure. Accessed 15 Jan. 2017.

[4] Garrow, David J. *The Walking City. the Montgomery Bus Boycott, 1955-1956.* Brooklyn, NY,
Carlson Pub., 1989.

[5] "Montgomery Bus Boycott." *Wikipedia*, Wikimedia Foundation, 18 Sept. 2016, https://en.wikipedia.org/wiki/Montgomery_bus_boycott. Accessed 25 Jan. 2017.

[6] Olson, Lynne. *Freedom's Daughters: The Unsung Heroines of the Civil Rights Movement
from 1830 to 1970*. New York, Scribner, 2001.

[7] Hendrickson, Paul. "MONTGOMERY." *The Washington Post*, WP Company, 24 July 1989,
https://www.washingtonpost.com/archive/lifestyle/1989/07/24/montgomery/72b9733d-81fc-4367-9f84-b4471f507d74/?utm_term=.3f2c61042ace. Accessed 25 Jan. 2017.

[8] Parks, Rosa, and James Haskins. *Rosa Parks: My Story*. New York, Dial Books, 1992.

[9] "James Blake, 89; Driver Had Rosa Parks Arrested." *Los Angeles Times*, Los Angeles Times,
26 Mar. 2002, https://articles.latimes.com/2002/mar/26/local/me-blake26. Accessed 25 Jan. 2017.

[10] "Women's Political Council." *Wikipedia*, Wikimedia Foundation, 28 Dec. 2016, https://en.wikipedia.org/wiki/Women%27s_Political_Council. Accessed 25 Jan. 2017.

[11] "Montgomery Improvement Association." *Wikipedia*, Wikimedia Foundation, 28 Sept. 2016, https://en.wikipedia.org/wiki/Montgomery_Improvement_Association. Accessed 25 Jan. 2017.

[12] "Southern Regional Council." *Southern Regional Council,* 2017, https://southerncouncil.org/about.html. Accessed 6 May 2017.

[13] "SRC History Timeline." *Southern Regional Council*, 2017, https://southerncouncil.org/history/html. Accessed 6 May 2017.

[14] "Mary Fair Burks." *Wikipedia*, Wikimedia Foundation, 11 Dec. 2016, https://en.wikipedia.org/wiki/Mary_Fair_Burks. Accessed 25 Jan. 2017.

[15] "Jo Ann Robinson." *Wikipedia*, Wikimedia Foundation, 4 Dec. 2016, https://en.wikipedia.org/wiki/Jo_Ann_Robinson. Accessed 25 Jan. 2017.

[16] McKee, Don. *Martin Luther King, Jr.* New York, Putnam, 1969.

[17] "Claudette Colvin." *Wikipedia*, Wikimedia Foundation, 19 Jan. 2017, https://en.wikipedia.org/wiki/Claudette_Colvin. Accessed 25 Jan. 2017.

[18] "Clifford Durr." *Wikipedia*, Wikimedia Foundation, 14 Nov. 2016, https://en.wikipedia.org/wiki/Clifford_Durr. Accessed 25 Jan. 2017.

[19] "Aurelia Browder." *Wikipedia*, Wikimedia Foundation, 28 Dec. 2016, https://en.wikipedia.org/wiki/Aurelia_Browder. Accessed 25 Jan. 2017.

[20] "Mary Louise Smith (Civil Rights Activist)." *Wikipedia*, Wikimedia Foundation, 22 Jan. 2016, https://en.wikipedia.org/wiki/Mary_Louise_Smith_(civil_rights_activist). Accessed 25 Jan. 2017.

[21] "An Act of Courage, The Arrest Records of Rosa Parks." *National Archives and Records Administration*, National Archives and Records Administration, 21 Dec. 2016, www.archives.gov/education/lessons/rosa-parks. Accessed 25 Jan. 2017.

[22] "Weekend: Civil Rights Heroine Claudette Colvin." *The Guardian*, Guardian News and Media, 15 Dec. 2000, https://www.theguardian.com/theguardian/2000/dec/16/weekend7.weekend12. Accessed 25 Jan. 2017.

[23] "Montgomery Bus Boycott." *Wikipedia*, Wikimedia Foundation, 23 Jan. 2017, https://en.wikipedia.org/wiki/Montgomery_bus_boycott. Accessed 25 Jan. 2017.

[24] "The Dark Side of Martin Luther King, Jr." *The Right Perspective*, WordPress and Dynamic News, 3 Apr. 2016, https://www.therightperspective.org/2011/01/11/the-dark-side-of-martin-luther-king-jr/. Accessed 27 Jan. 2017.

[25] Thornton, J. Mills. *Dividing Lines: Municipal Politics and the Struggle for Civil Rights in Montgomery, Birmingham, and Selma*. Tuscaloosa, University of Alabama Press, 2002.

[26] Galla, B. "Civil Rights of the 1950s and 1960s Timeline." *Time toast*, 2007, www.timetoast.com/timelines/civil-rights-of-the-1950s-and-1960s.

[27] "Freedom Riders-Wikipedia." *Wikipedia, the Free Encyclopedia*, Wikimedia Foundation, Inc, 2017 https://en.wikipedia.org/wiki/Freedom_Riders. Accessed 6 May 2017.

[28] Arsenault, Raymond. *Freedom Riders: 1961 and the Struggle for Racial Justice*, Oxford UP, 2011.

[29] History.com Staff. "Freedom Rides-Black History." *History.com*, A&E Networks, 2010, http://history.com/topics/black-history/freedom-rides. Accessed 7 May 2017.

[30] Mack, Dwayne. "Freedom Rides (1961)." *The Black Past: Remembered and Reclaimed*, Berea College, 2017, http://www.blackpast.org/aah/freedom-rides-1961. Accessed 7 May 2017.

[31] Baggett, James L. "Eugene "Bull" Connor." *Encyclopedia of Alabama,* Alabama Humanities Foundation, 2012, https://www.encyclopediaofalabama.org/article/h-1091. Accessed 7 May 2017.

[32] Roberts, Charles K. "James G. "Jim" Clark Jr." *Encyclopedia of Alabama*, University of Alabama, 2015, https://www.encyclopediaofalabama.org/article/h-2147. Accessed 7 May 2017.

[33] "Robert F. Williams-Wikipedia." *Wikipedia, the Free Encyclopedia,* Wikimedia Foundation Inc, 2017, https://en.wikipedia.org/wiki/Robert_F_Williams. Accessed 7 May 2017.

[34] McAdam, Doug. *Political Process and the Development of Black Insurgency, 1930-1970.*
Chicago, University of Chicago Press, 1982.

[35] "Independent Lens. Negroes with Guns: Rob Williams and Black Power, Rob Williams PBS."
PBS: Public Broadcasting Service, 2017, https://pbs.org/independentlens/negroeswithguns/rob.html. Accessed 7 May 2017.

[36] Encyclopedia Britannica Editors. "Robert Williams: American Civil Rights Leader." *Encyclopedia Britannica,* Encyclopedia Britannica Inc, 2016. https://Britannica.com/biography/Robert-Williams. Accessed 7 May 2017.

[37] "Letter from Malcolm X to King." *King Institute Resources,* Stanford University, 1963, https://www.kingencyclopedia.stanford.edu/encyclopedia/documentsentry/letter_from_king_to_malcolm_x.1.html. Accessed 7 May 2017.

[38] "G. Edward Griffin: Communism and the Civil Rights Movement." *YouTube*, 18 Jan. 2014, https://youtu.be/3CHk_iJ8hWK. Accessed 6 May 2017.

[39] Moses, Wilson Jeremiah. *Creative Conflict in African American Thought: Frederick Douglass, Alexander Crummell, Booker T. Washington, W.E.B. Du Bois, and Marcus Garvey.* New York, Cambridge University Press, 2004.

[40] "Black Nationalism." *Wikipedia, the Free Encyclopedia*, Wikimedia Foundation, 2017, https://en.wikipedia.org/wiki/Black_Nationalism. Accessed 9 Feb. 2017.

[41] "Black Separatism." *Wikipedia, the Free Encyclopedia,* Wikimedia Foundation, Inc, 2017, https://en.wikipedia.org/wiki/Black_Separatism. Accessed 7 May 2017.

[42] "Black Supremacy." *Wikipedia, the Free Encyclopedia,* Wikimedia Foundation, 2017, https://en.wikipedia.org/wiki/Black_Supremacy. Accessed 9 Feb. 2017.

[43] "Black Power." Wikipedia, *the Free Encyclopedia*, Wikimedia Foundation, 2017, https://en.wikipedia.org/wiki/Black_Power. Accessed 7 May 2017.

[44] "Afrocentrism." *Wikipedia, the Free Encyclopedia*, Wikimedia Foundation, 2017, https://en.wikipedia.org/wiki/Afrocentrism. Accessed 9 Feb. 2017

[45] "Black Anarchism." *Wikipedia, the Free Encyclopedia*, Wikimedia Foundation, 2016, https://en.wikipedia.org/wiki/Black_Anarchism. Accessed 9 Feb. 2017.

[46] Howe, Stephen. *Afrocentrism: Mythical Pasts and Imagined Homes*. London, Verso, 1998.

[47] Bush, Roderick D. *We Are Not What We Seem: Black Nationalism and Class Struggle in the American Century*. New York, New York University Press, 1999.

[48] Omi, Michael, and Howard Winant. *Racial Formation in the United States: from the 1960s to the 1990s*. New York, Routledge, 1994.

[49] "Racial Formation Theory." *Wikipedia*, Wikimedia Foundation, 1 Dec. 2016, https://en.wikipedia.org/wiki/Racial_formation_theory. Accessed 9 Feb. 2017.

[50] Robinson, Dean E. *Black Nationalism in American Politics and Thought*. Cambridge, U.K., Cambridge University Press, 2001.

[51] Rothenberg, Paula S. *Race, Class, and Gender in the United States: An Integrated Study*. New York, St. Martin's Press, 1998.

[52] "Gloria Richardson." *Wikipedia*, Wikimedia Foundation, 11 Dec. 2016, https://en.wikipedia.org/wiki/Gloria_Richardson. Accessed 9 Feb. 2017.

[53] "Gloria Richardson-SNCC Digital Gateway." *SNCC Digital Gateway,* 2017, https://snccdigital.org/people/gloria-richardson/. Accessed 7 May 2017.

[54] Anderson, Erica L. "Richardson, Gloria (1922-)." *The Black Past: Remembered and Reclaimed,* University of Washington, 2017, https://www.blackpast.org/aah/Richardson-gloria-1922. Accessed 7 May 2017.

[55] "Cambridge, Maryland." *Wikipedia*, Wikimedia Foundation, 6 Feb. 2017, https://en.wikipedia.org/wiki/Cambridge,_Maryland. Accessed 9 Feb. 2017.

[56] "Cambridge Riot of 1963." *Wikipedia*, Wikimedia Foundation, 29 Nov. 2015, https://en.wikipedia.org/wiki/Cambridge_riot_of_1963. Accessed 9 Feb. 2017.

[57] "The Cambridge Riots of 1963 and 1967." *Teaching American History in Maryland - Documents for the Classroom - Maryland State Archives*, The State of Maryland, 2005, https://teaching.msa.maryland.gov/000001/000000/000033/html/t33.html. Accessed 9 Feb. 2017.

[58] "MARYLAND AT A GLANCE." *Maryland Historical Chronology, 1900-1999*, State of Maryland 28 Dec. 2016, https://msa.maryland.gov/msa/mdmanual/01glance/chron/html/chron19.html#1900. Accessed 9 Feb. 2017.

[59] "J. Millard Tawes-Wikipedia." *Wikipedia, the Free Encyclopedia,* Wikimedia Foundation, Inc, 2017 https://en.wikipedia.org/wiki/J_Millard_Tawes. Accessed 7 May 2017.

[60] Maraniss, David A. "J. Millard Tawes Dies, Was Maryland Governor for 8 Years." *The Washington Post*, WP Company, 26 June 1979, https://www.washingtonpost.com/archive/local/1979/06/26/j-millard-tawes-dies-was-maryland-governor-for-8-years/bb81e499-d469-49f4-b0b3-5107a325d22a/?utm_term=.140b51bbd2eb. Accessed 9 Feb. 2017.

[61] Brugger, Robert J. *Maryland, a Middle Temperament, 1634-1980*. Baltimore, MD, Johns Hopkins University Press in Association with the Maryland Historical Society, 1988.

[62] "Harlem Riot of 1964-Wikipedia." *Wikipedia, the Free Encyclopedia,* Wikimedia Foundation, Inc, 2017, https://en.wikipedia.org/wiki/Harlem_riot_of_1964. Accessed 7 May 2017.

[63] "Measuring Worth Results." *Measuring Worth*, Measuring Worth, 2017, http://www.measuringworth.com/uscompare/relativevalue.php. Accessed 16 Jan. 2017.

[64] "1964 Rochester Race Riot-Wikipedia." *Wikipedia, the Free Encyclopedia,* Wikipedia Foundation, Inc, 2017, https://en.wikipedia.org/wiki/1964_Rochester_race_riot. Accessed 7 May 2017.

[65] "List of Incidents of Civil Unrest in the United States." *Wikipedia*, Wikimedia Foundation, 2 Feb. 2017, https://en.wikipedia.org/wiki/List_of_incidents_of_civil_unrest_in_the_United_States. Accessed 9 Feb. 2017.

[66] "The Philadelphia Race Riot of August 1964." *Philly.com.* 2017, https://www.philly.com/philly/blogs/TODAY-IN-PHILADELPHIA-HISTORY/The-Philadelphia-race-riot-of-August-1964.html. Accessed 7 May 2017.

[67] "The North: Doing No Good." *Time*, Time Inc., 4 Sept. 1964, https://content.time.com/time/magazine/article/0,9171,830558-1,00.html. Accessed 9 Feb. 2017.

[68] Eison, Carvin, director. *July '64*. WXXI Radio, 15 July 2014, https://wxxi.org/july64/. Accessed 9 Feb. 2017.

[69] "Watts, California." *Wikipedia*, Wikimedia Foundation, 20 Jan. 2017, https://en.wikipedia.org/wiki/Watts,_California. Accessed 9 Feb. 2017.

[70] History.com Staff, editor. "Watts Riot Begins." *History.com*, A&E Television Networks, 2010, https://www.history.com/this-day-in-history/watts-riot-begins. Accessed 9 Feb. 2017.

[71] Dawsey, Darrell. "To CHP Officer Who Sparked Riots, It Was Just Another Arrest." *Los Angeles Times*, Los Angeles Times, 19 Aug. 1990, https://www.articles.latimes.com/1990-08-19/local/me-2790_1_chp-officer. Accessed 9 Feb. 2017.

[72] Rustin, Bayard. "The Watts." *Commentary Magazine*, Commentary Magazine, 5 Feb. 2017, https://www.commentarymagazine.com/articles/the-watts/. Accessed 9 Feb. 2017.

[73] Woo, Elaine. "Rena Prices Dies at 97; Her and Son's Arrests Sparked Watts Riots." *Los Angeles Times*, Los Angeles Times, 22 June 2013, https://www.latimes.com/local/obituaries/la-me-rena-price-20130623-story.html. Accessed 9 Feb. 2017.

[74] "Los Angeles." *Wikipedia*, Wikimedia Foundation, 9 Feb. 2017, https://en.wikipedia.org/wiki/Los_Angeles. Accessed 9 Feb. 2017.

[75] Nichols, Casey. "Watts Rebellion (August 1965) ." *Watts Rebellion (August 1965) The Black Past: Remembered and Reclaimed*, University of Washington, 2017, https://www.blackpast.org/aaw/watts-rebellion-august-1965. Accessed 9 Feb. 2017.

[76] "Chief Parker Molded LAPD Image--Then Came the '60s: Police: Press Treated Officers as Heroes until Social Upheaval Prompted Skepticism and Confrontation." *Los Angeles Times*, Los Angeles Times 25 May 1992, https://www.articles.latimes.com/1992-05-25/news/mn-236_1_police-brutality. Accessed 9 Feb. 2017.

Chapter 16 Riots, Assassinations, Mayhem-The American Civil Rights Movement (IV)

[1] "G. Edward Griffin: Communism and the Civil Rights Movement." *YouTube*, 18 Jan. 2014, https://youtu.be/3CHk_iJ8hWK. Accessed 6 May 2017.

[2] "July '64." *PBS*, PBS, 2017, https://www.pbs.org/independentlens/july64/timeline.html. Accessed 9 Feb. 2017.

[3] "Muhammad Ali-Wikipedia." *Wikipedia, the Free Encyclopedia,* Wikimedia Foundation, Inc, 2017, https://en.wikipedia.org/wiki/Muhammad_Ali. Accessed 7 May 2017.

[4] History.com Editors. "Muhammad Ali-Black History." *HISTORY.com,* A&E Networks, 2009, https://www.history.com/topics/black-history/Muhammad-ali. Accessed 7 May 2017

[5] "Revolution '67." *PBS*, PBS, 10 July 2007, https://www.pbs.org/pov/revolution67/. Accessed 11 Feb. 2017.

[6] Baggins, Brian. "Black Panther Party." *Marxists Internet Archive,* 2002, https://Marxists.org/history/usa/workers/back-panthers/. Accessed 7 May 2017.
[7] IBID.

[8] "Black Panther Party-Wikipedia." *Wikipedia, the Free Encyclopedia*, Wikimedia Foundation, Inc, 2017, https://en.wikipedia.org/Black_Panther_Party. Accessed 7 May 2017.

[9] "List of Incidents of Civil Unrest in the United States." *Wikipedia*, Wikimedia Foundation,

2 Feb. 2017,
https://en.wikipedia.org/wiki/List_of_incidents_of_civil_unrest_in_the_United_States.
Accessed 9 Feb. 2017.

[10] "Cairo Riot-Wikipedia." *Wikipedia, the Free Encyclopedia,* Wikimedia Foundation.
2017.
https://en.wikipedia.org/wiki/Cairo_riot. Accessed 7 May 2017.

[11] "Race Riot in Cairo, Illinois." *African-American Registry,* Southern Illinois University.
2013, https://www.aaregistry.org/historic_events/view/race-riot-cairo-illinois.
Accessed 7 May 2017.

[12] "1967 Detroit Riot." *Wikipedia*, Wikimedia Foundation, 11 Feb. 2017,
https://en.wikipedia.org/wiki/1967_Detroit_riot. Accessed 11 Feb. 2017.

[13] Fine, Sidney. *Violence in the Model City: The Cavanagh Administration, Race
Relations, and the Detroit Riot of 1967*. East Lansing, Michigan State University Press,
2007.

[14] "Gloria Richardson." *Wikipedia*, Wikimedia Foundation, 11 Dec. 2016,
https://en.wikipedia.org/wiki/Gloria_Richardson. Accessed 9 Feb. 2017.

[15] "Gloria Richardson-SNCC Digital Gateway." *SNCC Digital Gateway,* 2017,
https://www.snccdigital.org/people/gloria-richardson/. Accessed 7 May 2017.

[16] Anderson, Erica L. "Richardson, Gloria (1922-)." *The Black Past: Remembered and
Reclaimed,* University of Washington, 2017, http://www.blackpast.org/aah/Richardson-
gloria-1922. Accessed 7 May 2017.

[17] "Cambridge, Maryland." *Wikipedia*, Wikimedia Foundation, 6 Feb. 2017,
https://en.wikipedia.org/wiki/Cambridge,_Maryland. Accessed 9 Feb. 2017.

[18] "H. Rap Brown." *Wikipedia*, Wikimedia Foundation, 1 Jan. 2017,
https://en.wikipedia.org/wiki/H._Rap_Brown. Accessed 11 Feb. 2017.

[19] Salter, Daren. "Brown, Hubert (H.Rap)/Jamil Abdullah Al-Amin (1943-)." *The Black
Past Remembered and Reclaimed*, University of Washington, 2017,
https://www.blackpast.org/aah/brown-hubert-h-rap-jamil-abdullah-al-amin-1943.
Accessed 7 May 2017.

[20] "Spiro Agnew." *Wikipedia*, Wikimedia Foundation, 11 Feb. 2017,
https://en.wikipedia.org/wiki/Spiro_Agnew. Accessed 11 Feb. 2017.

[21] Carson, Clayborne, and Tom Hamburger. "The Cambridge: How a Night in
Maryland 30 Years Ago Changed the Nation's Course of Racial Politics." *The Cambridge:
How a Night in Maryland 30 Years Ago Changed the Nation's Course of Racial Politics*,
Stanford University, 28 July 1997,
https://web.stanford.edu/~ccarson/articles/cambridge_convergence.htm. Accessed 11
Feb. 2017.

[22] "Where Are You From? - Credo Reference." *Where Are You From? - Credo
Reference*, The Columbia Encyclopedia, 2017,
https://search.credoreference.com/content/topic/los_angeles. Accessed 9 Feb. 2017.

Chapter 17 The Communist Plan to Keep the Black Community Enslaved to the "Almighty State"

[1] "Martin Luther King Jr." *Wikipedia, the Free Encyclopedia,* Wikimedia Foundation, Inc, 2017, https://en.wikipedia.org/wiki/Martin_Luther_King_jr. Accessed 7 May 2017.

[2] History.com Staff. "Kerner Commission Report Released-Feb 29, 1968." *History.com,* A&E Networks, 2010, https://www.history.com/this-day-in-history/kerner-commission-report-released. Accessed 7 May 2017.

[3] "Kerner Commission-Wikipedia." *Wikipedia, the Free Encyclopedia,* Wikimedia Foundation, Inc, 2017, https://en.wikipedia.org/wiki/Kerner_Commission. Accessed 7 May 2017.

[4] "National Advisory Committee on Civil Disorders (The Kerner Report), 1967." *The Black Past: Remembered and Reclaimed.* University of Washington, 2017, http://www.blackpast.org/primary/nationa-advisory-commission-civil-disorders-kerner-report-1967. Accessed 7 May 2017.

[5] Siegal, Fred, et al. "The Kerner Commission Report." *The Heritage Foundation,* 24 June 1998, https://heritage.org/poverty-and-inequality/report/the-kerner-commission-report. Accessed 7 May 2017.

[6] Yette, Samuel F. "5 The Threat and Tactics." *The Choice: The Issue of Black Survival in America*, Putnam, New York, 1971, pp. 255–256.

[7] "Martin Luther King Jr." *Wikipedia, the Free Encyclopedia,* Wikimedia Foundation, Inc, 2017, https://en.wikipedia.org/wiki/Martin_Luther_King_jr. Accessed 7 May 2017.

[8] McKee, Don. *Martin Luther King, Jr.* New York, Putnam, 1969.

[9] "U.S. National Commission on the Causes and Prevention of Violence-Wikipedia." *Wikipedia, the Free Encyclopedia,* Wikimedia Foundation, Inc, 2017, https://en.wikipedia.org/wiki/U.S._National_Commission_on_the_Causes_and_Prevention_of_Violence. Accessed 7 May 2017.

[10] IBID.

[11] IBID.

[12] IBID.

[13] IBID.

Chapter 18 Lyndon Johnson's "War on Poverty" and "Great Society": The 200-Year Plan

[1] "G. Edward Griffin: Communism and the Civil Rights Movement." *YouTube*, 18 Jan. 2014, https://youtu.be/3CHk_iJ8hWK. Accessed 6 May 2017.

[2] "Lyndon B. Johnson-Wikipedia." *Wikipedia, the Free Encyclopedia,* Wikimedia Foundation, Inc, 2017, https://en.wikipedia.org/wiki/Lyndon_b_Johnson. Accessed 7 May 2017.

[3] "Lyndon B. Johnson." *Whitehouse.gov.* 2017, https://whitehouse.gov/1600/presidents/lyndonbjohnson. Accessed 7 May 2017.

[4] Yette, Samuel F. "The Great Society Pacification Programs." *The Choice: The Issue of Black Survival in America,* Cottage Books, 1996, pp. 59-60.

[5] "Americorps VISTA." *Corporation for National and Community Service*, 2017, https://nationalservice.gov/AboutJobCorps/americorpsvista. Accessed 7 May 2017.

[6] "About Job Corps: Statutory Authority." *Welcome to Job Corps,*

Department of Labor, 2017, https://jobcorps.gov/AboutJobCorps/authority.aspx. Accessed 7 May 2017

[7] Yette, Samuel F. "The Great Society Pacification Programs." *The Choice: The Issue of Black Survival in America,* Cottage Books, 1996, pp. 35-56.

[8] "National Head Start Program." *National Head Start Association,* Department of Education, 2017, https://nhsa.org/. Accessed 7 May 2017.

[9] *Temporary Assistance for Needy Families (TANF).* Department of Health and Human Services, 2017, https://acf.hhs.gov/ofa/programs/tanf. Accessed 7 May 2017.

[10] *A Brief History of the AFDC Program.* Department of Health and Human Services, 1997, https://aspe.hhs.gov/hudportal/HUD. Accessed 7 May 2017.

[11] Page, Stephen B., and Larner, Mary B. "Introduction to the AFDC Program." *The Future of Children Welfare to Work*, vol. 7, no. 1, Spring 1997, pp. 20-27. Accessed 7 May 2017.

[12] *Medicare Home Page.* Department of Health and Human Services, 2017, https://medicare.gov/. Accessed 7 May 2017.

[13] *Medicaid: Keeping America Healthy.* Department of Health and Human Services, 2017, https://medicaid.gov/. Accessed 7 May 2017.

[14] "Latest Federal Priorities Data: Unemployment, Labor Force, Medicare, Medicaid." *National Priorities Project,* 2017, https://nationalpriorities.org/blog/2013/12/17/latest-federal-priorities-data-unemployment-labor-force-medicare-mediciad/. Accessed 7 May 2017.

[15] Riedl, Brian. "50 Examples of Government Waste." *The Heritage Foundation,* 6 Oct 2009, https://heritage.org/budget-and-spending/report/50-examples-government-waste. Accessed 7 May 2017.

[16] "National Debt." *U.S. National Debt Clock: Real Times,* 2017, https://usdebtclock.org/. Accessed 7 May 2017.

Chapter 19 Conclusion: What's the Point?

[1] "G. Edward Griffin: Communism and the Civil Rights Movement." *YouTube*, 18 Jan. 2014, https://youtu.be/3CHk_iJ8hWK. Accessed 6 May 2017.

[2] IBID.

[3] *The Black Population 2010.* U.S. Census Bureau, 2011, https://www.census.gov/prod/cen2010/briefs/c2010br-06.pdf. Accessed 7 May 2017

[4] "Latest Hate Crime Statistics Report Released-FBI."

Federal Bureau of Investigation, 9 Dec 2014, https://www.fbi.gov/news/stories/latest-hate-crime-statistics-report-released.

Accessed 7 May 2017.

[5] "We Should Measure Welfare's Success by How Many People Leave Welfare, Not by How Many Are Added.-Ronald Reagan." *BrainyQuote,* 2017, http://www.brianyquote.com/quotes/quotes/r/ronaldreag183978.html. Accessed 7 May 2017.

[6] Unruh, Bob. "Obama's 'national Civilian Security Force' Endorsed." *WND*, 1 May 2015, https://www.wnd.com/2015/05/obamas-national-civilian-security-force-endorsed/. Accessed 10 May 2017.

[7] "Homepage." *Communist Party USA*, 2017, https://www.cpusa.org/. Accessed 10 May 2017.

[8] "Homepage." *DART*, 2017, https://thedartcenter.org/. Accessed 10 May 2017.

Front Cover: Protesters take pictures in front of the burning Juanita's Fashion R Boutique on West Florissant Avenue, during the November 24, 2014, Ferguson,

Missouri Riots. Protesters created civil disobedience and major property damage/destruction totaling in the millions of dollars. Photo courtesy of St. Louis Post-Dispatch/Robert Cohen

CONTACT THE AUTHOR

WEBSITE
HTTPS://WWW.CBRIANMADDENAUTHOR.COM/

FACEBOOK
HTTPS://WWW.FACEBOOK.COM/CBRIANMADDEN44/

TWITTER
CBRIANMADDENAU1

EMAIL
CBRIANMADDENAUTHOR@GMAIL.COM

ABOUT THE AUTHOR

C. Brian Madden is a military veteran, who has served his country honorably for over 20 years, as a United States Navy Hospital Corpsman. While serving in that capacity, he was an active participant during Operations Desert Shield, Desert Storm, Iraqi Freedom and Enduring Freedom, Afghanistan.

He has earned both a Bachelor's Degree in Health Administration and Undergraduate Certification in Healthcare Management from the University of Phoenix. Mr. Madden also earned a Journeyman Instructor/Facilitator Certification from San Diego City College.

C. Brian Madden is the author of several books, to include *"The Way It Should Be Taught"* and *"A Gateway into History"* series of Non-Fiction books.